To outsiders ancient South America is synonymous with the Incas. Originally a small unremarkable group, the Incas, under their leader Pachacuti, conquered most of their known world within a single lifetime. But before the Incas there were some ten millennia of prehistory, centuries in which great civilizations rose, flourished and, inevitably, fell. Chavín, with its fanged gods and hallucinogenic drugs; Huari, a massive militaristic state; the Manteño, who held the most valued substance of the Andes in their power; the Quimbaya, who developed the most beautiful gold work the world has ever seen – all were part of the unique history of the continent. *Ancient South America* provides an incisive view of this exotic continent and its remarkable past. The origins of agriculture, ceramics, and metallurgy, and the complexities of Andean mythology are covered clearly and non-dogmatically, as are developments in the tropical regions of the continent. The contributions of these cultures to modern civilizations are enormous yet still little appreciated.

Cirencester College, GL7 1XA
Telephone: 01285 640994

ANCIENT SOUTH AMERICA

CAMBRIDGE WORLD ARCHAEOLOGY

CAMBRIDGE WORLD ARCHAEOLOGY

ANCIENT SOUTH AMERICA

KAREN OLSEN BRUHNS

San Francisco State University

CAMBRIDGE
UNIVERSITY PRESS

Published by the Press Syndicate of the University of Cambridge
The Pitt Building, Trumpington Street, Cambridge CB2 1RP
40 West 20th Street, New York, NY 10011-4211, USA
10 Stamford Road, Oakleigh, Melbourne 3166, Australia

First published 1994
Reprinted 1996

Printed in the United States of America

Library of Congress Cataloging-in-Publication Data is available.

A catalogue record for this book is available from the British Library.

ISBN 0-521-25920-7 hardback
ISBN 0-521-27761-2 paperback

To T.W.

CONTENTS

ILLUSTRATIONS

All maps and tables were drawn by Tom Weller. All unattributed photographs are by the author.

TABLES

ACKNOWLEDGMENTS

It is only when you begin a massive project like this that you find out how many good friends, including colleagues you have never met, that you really have. A great many people contributed materially to this work, sending me unpublished manuscripts, papers they had published in hard-to-find places, new field information, drawings and, above all, photographs of sites I had never been to (or had been to in a driving rain or sand storm), artifacts that were not part of the sort of great traveling show of artifacts that appear in every publication on the Andes or wherever, and just plain nicer or more appropriate pictures of things I felt should be illustrated. To each and every one of the people listed below (and probably some I have unjustly omitted) I owe a great debt of thanks.

I would especially like to thank Tom Weller, who did all the maps and charts and a great many of the drawings, took care of all the computer set up and print out (and the inevitable computer crises), and who, in general, guided me through the wonderful world of book publication, doing most of the actual technical work himself. A man who will index is truly a pearl of great price. Jane Becker did a lot of the other drawings; David Lance Goines kindly lent the use of his computer equipment for copying and modifying maps and plans. John Rowe and Patricia Lyon very generously let me have the run of their library, even though they had a good idea of just how many years I would be underfoot. The staff of the Phoebe Apperson Hearst (formerly the Robert H. Lowie) Museum of Anthropology at the University of California, Berkeley, especially Frank Norick, Madeleine Fang, Eugene Prince, and Lawrence Dawson, let me photograph pieces from the South American collections, provided other photographs, and put up with my needing to get into lots of locked cabinets to check accession numbers. Many thanks are also due to Hernán Crespo Toral, Olaf Holm, Ernesto Salazar, Myriam Ochoa, René Cardoso, Jaime Idrovo, Dominique Gomis, and José Luis Espinosa of the Museo del Banco Central del Ecuador for nearly a decade of aid and encouragement in Ecuador, to Cornelio Vintimilla, Alicia de Vintimilla, and Berta Vintimilla de Ordoñez for their enthusiastic encouragement of the Pirincay project, to Lynn Hirschkind and Stuart White of Cuenca for alpaca lore and a very damp visit to the pajonal, to Lynn Meisch for textile instruction, to Costanza di Capua and Presley Norton of Quito and Patricia Netherly for their unending hospitality and help with coastal archaeology, to Jim Burton for all the geological insights, to Clemencia Plazas, Oscar Osorio, Warwick Bray, Gerardo Reichel-Dolmatoff, and Augusto Oyuela for new publications and new data from Colombia, to Charles Cecil and the California Academy of Sciences for photographs, space to work, and coffee (well, maybe not for the coffee), to Cristina Bubba, Pio Cruz Flores, and the people of Coroma for letting me help with retrieving their kidnapped ancestors and thereby not only getting to know a group of wonderful people, both in Coroma and in the US, but for the learning situation of getting a really close look at the sleaze of the looting/collecting world and the US judiciary, to Thomas Lynch and Karen Stothert, who read drafts of the earliest ever chapters, to the Deans and the PRDC committees at SFSU who have blessedly kept giving me bits of money for research and, finally, to the Document Delivery Services (formerly the Interlibrary Loan Services, but now with a handsome new sign) for unfailing courtesy and efficiency in obtaining a lot of really strange stuff so that I could follow references, arguments, and the progress of projects around the South American continent.

An archaeology book really stands or falls on the merit of its illustrations. Facts change; pictures are always useful. I tried to use as illustrations sites or parts of sites and artifacts that haven't been published and republished, if only to give this book a little more interest to my colleagues who know all about South America already. I would like to express my deepest gratitude for photographs and drawings (and a lot of accompanying data) to the following people: J. S. Athens, Elizabeth Boone and Dumbarton Oaks, Margaret Bird and the late Junius Bird, Henning Bischoff, Arthur and Daniel Blystone, Elisabeth Bonnier, Jean-François Bouchard, Richard Burger, James Burton, Holly Carver and the University of Iowa Press, Karen Mohr Chávez and Sergio Chávez, Donald Collier, Charles Stanish and the Field Museum of Natural History, Chicago, Claude Chauchat, Thomas Cummins, Warren DeBoer, William Deneven, Thomas Dillehay, Christopher B. Donnan, Leon Doyon, Edward Dwyer, Jane Dwyer†, Sylvia Forman†, Donna Garaventa, Terence Greider, David Hatch, Olaf Holm, Margaret Hoyt, Wesley Hurt, William Isbell, Lucy Lewis Johnson, Gregory Jones and Patricia Moore, Río Abiseo National Parks Project, University of Colorado, Boulder, Yae Koda, James Kus, Alan Lapiner†, Thomas Lennon, Lyn Lowry, Earl Lubensky, Thomas Lynch, Donna McClelland, Carol Mackey, Ann Mester, The Metropolitan Museum of Art, New York, Lynn Meisch, Albert Meyers, George Miller, Anne Paul, The Peabody Museum, Harvard University, The University of Pennsylvania Museum, Donald Proulx, Jeffrey Quilter, Gerardo Reichel-Dolmatoff, Raphael X. Reichert, John W. Rick, Michael Rodman and Amy Oakland Rodman, John H. Rowe, Izumi Shimada, Nigel Smith, Karen Stothert, Donald Thompson, Teresa and John Topic, Dwight Wallace. To all of you much thanks for the photos, permissions to use drawings, and the information you all sent along with your pictures.

STILL A NEW WORLD

South America is probably the least known continent in our over-explored, over-publicized world. Africa has become as familiar to schoolchildren and television viewers as their own backyard; even the most remote parts of Asia are much the same, but South America is seldom seen or discussed except when there is a particularly large-scale disaster or a particularly nasty change of government. Why this should be is an enigma. The rest of the world has considerable economic and political ties – both open and illicit – with the various South American countries, but nevertheless they remain apart from our consciousness. We are largely ignorant of their cultures, their geography, their resources, and, especially, of their past. Most people have heard of the Incas, of course. Some may even have heard of El Dorado, the gilded man, but few have heard of anything more. Even with the passion for tourism characteristic of our times, South America remains relatively little visited and much of its past is inaccessible to anyone but a determined specialist with access to large libraries and abundant travel funds.

The following is an attempt towards rectifying this situation by presenting an indication of how tremendously varied, unique, and even exotic, the prehistory of South America was. This is an extremely general and very incomplete treatment; it is frankly impossible to do justice to 10,000 years' history of an entire continent in a single volume of manageable length. So I have had to pick and choose and indulge in favoritism; many notable cultures, interesting peoples, and significant developments have been left out. Moreover, there is not equal coverage of all the continent; the Andes, particularly the central Andes, have been heavily emphasized and all else oriented towards events in this relatively small area. There are some good reasons for this. First, it was within the Andean mountain chain that the first complex cultures, civilizations if you will, developed and where civilization reached its most elaborate form in terms of complex social and political organizations, advanced technologies, international religions, major art styles, and the other things that we tend (if rather vaguely) to associate with civilization.

For a number of reasons, including good preservation, accessibility of the countries, the monumentality of the remains, and the association of some of these remains with one of the relatively few well documented prehispanic states, more archaeological field work has been carried out in the central Andes, especially in Peru, than anywhere else. In addition, more of this work has been published and, just as important, there is a much better control of time, something which is essential when one is trying to write the history of prehistoric peoples, than there is elsewhere upon the continent. Thus the arrangement of this book has been pegged to events in the central Andes. This is not to

1.1 Modern political divisions, capitals, and other important cities of the South American continent.

say that important events did not take place outside of the Andes; they most certainly did and there is no more reason to peg events in, say, Venezuela to those in Peru or Bolivia than there is to peg events in Southeast Asia to those in western Europe (or in any event, there was not before the coming of the modern era). However, the archaeology of France is much better known than that of Laos, and a synthesizer might be forgiven for arranging a Eurasian prehistory book with major reference to Europe, if only because there is more information, culturally and chronologically, from Europe. Because of the necessity to select for those cultures which were really major in terms of their influence on others or which present especially interesting historical or technological problems, hundreds of others have been skipped over or ignored. I have attempted to compensate for this in selecting as references (given at the end chapter by chapter) works which will lead the reader to what she or he wishes to find out. The bibliography is not a comprehensive one by any means, nor is it designed for the scholar who wishes to find out all there is on a particular subject; it is, however, a useful one for the non-professional, in that on any given subject I have tried to include sources which will both inform and lead the interested to the names and the already published works of those who have something to say on the subject the reader may be interested in. I have selected for references in English, although I have certainly included important works in other languages, mainly Spanish, when these are the appropriate source and if they might be available to the interested reader. Since so many libraries are going on-line and since the wonders of fax machines, photocopying, and interlibrary loan services are generally available, this bibliography does include some things it most certainly did not when I began to put it together. I have, however, and reluctantly it must be confessed, left out very important references when these can be found only in really exceptional research libraries. The real problem with the kind of bibliography this book has is that all material dealing with a specific culture or area of interest is not located under the same subheading. This means that a certain amount of perseverance is called for to find a reference to whatever topic, since some references have had to be heuristically placed. For this I apologize.

Because this is not meant to be a technical treatise, I have used conventional spellings throughout: Inca instead of "Inka," Tiahuanaco in place of "Tiwanaku" and so on. Although there is a tendency in South American archaeology to use the Quechua (Inca language) spelling, there is little standardization and all too many people attempt to write what they fondly believe to be Quechua without having much idea of what they are doing. Therefore, I have used the hispanicized forms, if only because these are much easier for a non-Spanish, non-Quechua speaker to comprehend.

The South American continent, when first contacted by Europeans in the sixteenth century, presented a tremendous variety of cultures ranging from hunting and gathering nomads, living in small social groups with minimal material cultures, up to a huge multinational conquest state, that of the Incas. These societies were the contemporary exemplars of a process of historical differentiation and cultural development which had begun some 10,000–12,000 years previously, when the first inhabitants, the Paleoindians, moved south via Panama and into the late ice age grasslands of the high Andes. Within some thousands of years these peoples had settled down, invented agriculture, pottery, weaving, and metallurgy, domesticated animals and were doing all of the things which in the Old World we regard as being preparatory to the development of that much maligned thing "civilization." Our view of civilization is, inevitably, Eurasian centered and has been, through the process of standardized education, much codified into an ethnocentric mold. Most of us more or less subscribe to the canons put forth by the great British archaeologist V. Gordon Childe, whose criteria for being civilized included not only such obvious core elements as full-time specialization of labor, dense populations concentrated into urban centers, a class structured society with a well-defined ruling class who held control over a concentration of surplus goods and labor which they deployed towards their own ends, monumental "public" works such as palaces, temples, irrigation systems, etc., but also such secondary characteristics as the knowledge of metalworking, wheeled vehicles, and writing. These latter characteristics either were not present or were very unimportant in many American cultures and, indeed, many European scholars somewhat capriciously excluded the American continents from consideration as centers of early civilizations because of the differences between them and what was thought to have happened in the Near East and Europe. However, any concept of civilization must explain what happened on a world-wide scene, not simply in a part of it which happens to be ancestral to much of our own culture. The Americas, and South America in particular, from a theoretical viewpoint are extraordinarily important towards testing our ideas of the human dynamics of civilization, because this area saw the development of pristine civilizations totally separate from those of Eurasia. Thus those characteristics which the American civilizations share with Eurasian ones, in terms of social structures, technologies, and developmental processes, must be part and parcel of the process of civilization in general. With this in mind a careful look at the American cultures shows us that a number of items and technologies once commonly held to be characteristic of civilizations are really not all that necessary. For example there are numbers of ways to deal with such things as transport and record keeping besides wheeled vehicles and writing. Wheels are not much good in vertical (or heavily forested and riverine) landscapes nor are they useful when there are no draft animals (unless you have the wheelbarrow, a Chinese invention). The problem of building roads for wheeled vehicles has not really been solved in much of the South American continent, despite their having had access to Eurasian modes of transport for half a millennium. Verticality, heavy rainfall, seismic instability, and similar factors lead to tremendous expense in building and maintaining the wide, hard-surfaced tracks needed for wheeled vehicles. It is notable that South America was the scene of the first large-scale peacetime use of airplanes. Even today one walks (or occasionally takes a horse or canoe) to many of those places one cannot fly.

We think of writing as being inextricably intertwined with civilization, mainly because it has been with ours – even though near-universal literacy is a quite recent ideal. Yet writing was very late in Eurasia and, like large-scale irrigation systems, may well be a result of civilization, not a contributive factor to its development. Eurasian

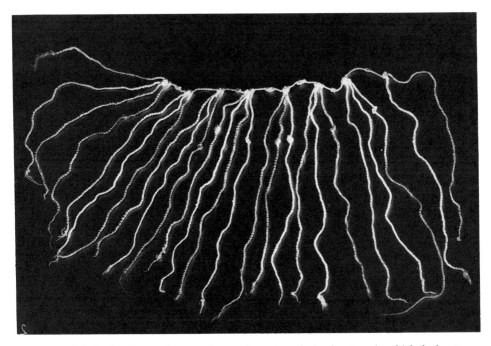

1.2 Quipu. Inca quipus work on an ingenious decimal system, in which the knots are arranged in a place system and the number of turns in each overhand knot is the number itself. This example is from the Ica Valley of Peru and is pre-Inca.

writing arose from geometric tokens used for bookkeeping. In South America mnemonic devices were also used for records, but went in a different direction: the quipu, a system of knotted cords (Figure 1.2). Quipus are known in a fully developed form from the first major conquest state that we know of, that of the Huari. They probably have a considerably greater antiquity. The existence of the quipu (and of similarly complex systems of mnemonic devices in some of the ancient Mexican civilizations) suggests that we should seriously review the role of writing in our own.

The working hypothesis of this volume is that, of course the South Americans had civilizations, in the sense of having complex societies with elaborate social and political organizations, institutionalized religions, international art styles, and developed technologies. That all these characteristics were somewhat different from those of Eurasia in form and order of appearance, and that ideological organizations were equally different, is also taken as a given. We cannot define the world by us; the human experience is somewhat greater than that. The organizational approach taken in this volume is geographical and chronological. This has proven inconvenient in many cases, if only because a whole continent does not move in concert, but it is a useful way to give a general overview and to enable a general comparison of cultures at any given time. This given time is necessarily somewhat loose. We have no written calendars for South America prior to the European invasions. Some native histories were recorded after the conquest but these extend history back only a century or so and are notoriously difficult to use, especially since some of the Peruvian peoples had the same idea as Eurasian potentates, which was that history needed to be rewritten to their own order. Thus we are thrown back on archaeological chronologies and upon such archaeological dating methods as cross-dating and radiocarbon dating. These methods have their limitations, but do give us a general idea of when something happened. I have taken the liberty of continuing some narratives for longer than the space of time the chapter is supposed to cover, again largely because all the world was not pegged to the Andes. It seems unnecessarily confusing to break some traditions, such as, for example, those of the Barrancoid and Saladero peoples of the Orinoco, into bits which do not correspond to their own development, so these have been treated in one lot, regardless of chapter heading.

The theoretical approach taken in this volume is loosely that of culture history. That is, it is descriptive and takes as a given that the artifacts we find and their associations, how they relate to one another in the archaeological context, are the representatives of a past cultural system and that by carefully recovering and studying these artifacts and their associations we can come to some understanding of that system. This is incomplete; all archaeological reconstructions are incomplete unless they owe more to the imagination of the writer than to the facts of the archaeological record, but it gives a certain freedom from the fallacies of misplaced ethnocentricity in interpretation, an ethnocentrism usually drawn from exclusively western social theory. Marxist and other eurocentered stage theories of interpretation of the past are quite prevalent in South American archaeological reporting and are implicit in some of the chronological schemes used, such as those proposed for Ecuador and loosely adapted to other areas. However, there are tremendous difficulties in implementing such schemes, mainly because the data are, as usual, unruly and seldom fit *a priori* decisions of what ought to have happened. Culture history is, or tries to be, a factual statement of what did happen as best we know, laying a basis for further discussion of meaning and pattern from the archaeological record. Some of the theoretical and methodological problems in dealing with these data, problems related both to the nature of archaeology and to the theoretical stance of specific archaeologists, are brought up when necessary to a clarification of the presentation. In general what a valued colleague refers to as "greater conceptions" have been avoided as unnecessary in a general treatment such as this book tries to be. As to whether the story of South America's past really shows the existence of a utopia now ruined by degenerate man, progress towards a truly egalitarian state of being (similarly now ruined by degenerate man), or even just the variety of the human response to life, I leave to the reader to decide.

CHAPTER 2

A MATTER OF TIME

The prehispanic cultures of South America did not develop writing systems of their own. Alternative systems of notation, such as the Inca quipu (a system of knotted strings which served as standardized mnemonic devices for a trained class of administrators, the quipucamayoc, people trained to remember what these quipus recorded) seem to have been developed in a number of places, but the horrors of the conquest and forced christianization of much of South America caused the loss of these traditional systems and of the people who could remember what was encoded. Thus, although the surviving quipus can now be read as to numbers, the items whose numbers were recorded and what was to be done with them are gone forever. Unfortunately this seems to have included historical and calendrical information. Some of the Spanish priests and administrators were interested in the cultures they were destroying and recorded bits and pieces of native history, but this material is very incomplete and, in any event, seldom refers to events much more than a century or so before the European invasions. Since there is archaeological evidence of human occupation of the continent since the end of the last glaciation, this has meant that most dating of ancient cultures has had to be done through archaeological means.

Until the mid-1900s archaeological dating systems were quite rudimentary, consisting of stratigraphic sequences, where these could be obtained through excavation, and seriation. Connections between sites or cultures were established by means of cross-dating. With cross-dating one looks for objects from a site or culture of known age in a site of unknown age or for evidence of significant stylistic or technological influence from one culture on another. This kind of dating usually depends upon complex decoration of artifacts or on the specifics of complex technologies, such as certain kinds of metallurgy, which we can be relatively certain were not developed over and over again independently. If the dated culture or site and the undated one are relatively close together spatially or along a well-traveled route, it is quite likely that the appearance of these objects is not heirloom collecting or that the identical technology is not a fortuitous parallelism and hence that the two sites/cultures are, on one level at least, contemporary.

The first archaeological cultures of South America to be dated were, of course, those of the time of the Spanish invasions. In western South America materials from the Incas could be given absolute dates since there is enough historical information on the Incas that it was known that their spread through the Andes was a rapid (and short-lived) phenomenon. In the early twentieth century, Max Uhle, who was a very influential figure in early Andean archaeology, postulated a similar rapid spread for the Tiahuanaco culture in Bolivia and Peru, establishing an earlier horizon line in those areas. A horizon line, in archaeological usage, is when a culture spreads very rapidly over a wide area in a short period of time, leaving characteristic artifacts which can be used to link sites within a large geographic area together at one point in time. In the central Andes the Inca, the Tiahuanaco-Huari and, perhaps, the Chavín spread are true horizon lines. It seems likely that the Chorrera phenomenon in Ecuador is a similar horizon line, although we as yet know very little about it.

In some other regions it was also possible to identify the material culture of the inhabitants of the time of the conquest, so that this could be dated. Most materials could, however, only be assigned relative dates and there were (and are) considerable problems of looking at the prehistory of the continent in other than local terms.

With the discovery of radiocarbon dating in the late 1940s and, just as important, with the discovery of the bristlecone pine calibration of radiocarbon dates (calibration of dates is essential since the radioactive carbon content of the earth's atmosphere has not remained the same through time) it became possible to put dates in calendar years, absolute dates, to many of the prehispanic cultures of South America. There have been, however, considerable practical and theoretical problems in dating ancient South America, many of these being inescapable in archaeology in general. In some areas it has proved difficult to obtain suitable samples for radiocarbon dating owing to poor organic preservation. This is especially the case in the tropical lowlands, but is a significant problem in some of the wetter regions of the Andes as well. Even where there is good preservation of organic materials it is often difficult to obtain samples whose associations are appropriate, that is, samples whose context is such that it is certain that the sample really does date the pottery style or building phase. In sites which were occupied for many centuries and in which there has been considerable architectural activity there are always problems of context owing to leveling, filling, and reuse of wood in a land where trees are scarce and/or wood-working tools are of stone. Renewal of offerings with burials and reuse of burial goods with later burials, both attested to archaeologically and ethnographically, complicate the problem of obtaining suitable samples. There is also the problem of the considerable expense that radiocarbon dating entails and this, combined with other problems, has led often to a culture being dated by means of a very few samples much separated in time, a situation which does not lead to confidence in its temporal placement. Related to this is the simple fact that even with numerous samples and the best possible laboratory, one cannot arrive closer to an event than about 150 years. The nature of radiocarbon dating is such that it gives you a time span within which an event occurred, not the actual date of the event. As radiocarbon dates have been traditionally expressed by using the midpoint of this range and expressing the standard deviation in plus/minus so many years, it has proved easy for the unwary to assume that the midpoint has more reality than any other year within the range. This is not the case (and some current calibration charts give a range, not a midpoint, because of abuses in this direction).

Other methods of absolute dating, such as thermoluminescence and archaeomagnetic dating are only now beginning to be widely used in South American archaeology. Mainly these are used to clarify calibrated radiocarbon dates. The development of accelerator (AMS) methods of radiocarbon dating, which use very small samples, are also helping with the clarification of problems of time, since it is now sometimes possible to date the thing itself, the actual corn grain or bone or pottery residue; but there remain numbers of extremely gray areas in our understanding of the temporal succession of ancient cultures.

Because one can so seldom get as precise as exact years, archaeological time tends to be expressed in terms of relative chronologies with absolute dates put in where these can be obtained. In some areas these relative chronologies, worked out on the basis of stratigraphic evidence and careful stylistic analysis of artifacts, are extremely detailed and lead to units of contemporaneity, that is pieces of time in which all events are assumed to be contemporary, of as little as twenty-five years. This is comparable to the chronologies worked out for Greek ceramics and, indeed, the same methodologies were used to develop chronologies in both areas. Unfortunately, such detailed chronologies are available only for a few areas, mainly the south coast of Peru; in other regions lack of appropriate material, lack of stratigraphic excavation, or lack of appropriate analysis of excavated materials has led to much larger units of contemporaneity.

Units of contemporaneity are generally called phases (which may be named or numbered, according to the whim of the excavator), and are often grouped together into larger cultural or temporal units. Here another problem emerges: the confusion of time and culture. Much archaeological interpretation of time has been done on the basis of the idea of stages, the idea that on the world scene cultures pass through the same sequence of development in terms of economy, social and political organization, etc. This is an idea which has been lurking in western thought since the first preserved writings of the presocratic philosophers, although often expressed in more allegorical forms, such as the ideas of "ages" of gold, silver, or bronze. Stage theory, in the nineteenth century, came to be called cultural evolution and the idea was added that cultures which currently (or in the past) had not passed through all the stages and become "modern" were somehow stuck at a lower stage of development. Although such ideas have never been proved anywhere in the world, they remain popular and are very prevalent in expositions of prehistory. They are especially popular in South America because of the Marxist orientation of numbers of scholars and their students, Karl Marx having been working and writing during the heyday of social/cultural evolution theories. Thus many studies present schemes of Preclassic, Classic, and Postclassic, popular in earlier studies, or Early Farmers, Experimenters, Cultists, Master Craftsmen, City Builders, etc. (Table 2.1). Usually these named stages were proposed early in the research and most can be shown to have little connection with reality as expressed in the archaeological record. For example, the so-called City Builders stage in Peruvian prehistory ignores the fact that the great development of urbanism in native cultures was centuries previous to this stage. The Formative stage in northern Andean studies encompasses both simple foragers and major civilizations with far-flung trade networks, international art styles, and obviously fairly complex social and political systems. In no case have these *a priori* schemes of how prehistory ought to have happened been vindicated by actual excavation, a sad commentary on one of western culture's most long-lived ideas.

Table 2.1 *Comparison of proposed chronological schemes for South American prehistory.*

PERU

Year	Rowe (Ica Valley)	Bennett and Bird	Uhle	Mason, Kidder et al.
1600				
1500	Late Horizon	Imperialists	Inca	
1400				
1300	Late Intermediate Period	City builders	Late	New Kingdoms and Empire
1200				
1100				
1000				
900	Middle Horizon	Expansionists	Tiahuanaco/Epigonal	City Builders
800				
700				
600				
500		Master Craftsmen		Regional States Florescent
400	Early Intermediate Period			
300				
200				
100 AD		Experimenters		
BC 100				Regional States Formative
200				
300				
400	Early Horizon	Cultists	Early	Cultist Temple Centers
500				
600				
700				
800				
900				
1000				
2000	Initial Period	Early Farmers		Horticultural Villages
3000	Preceramic			
4000		Hunters		
5000				
6000	Paleoindian			Paleoindian
7000				
8000				

	N. W. ARGENTINA	COLOMBIA	VENEZUELA	ECUADOR
	Gonzales	Reichel-Dolmatoff	Rouse and Cruxent	Meggers
1600			Indohispanic	
1500	Imperial			Inca
1400		Caciques	IV	
1300	Regional Development			Integration
1200				
1100				
1000				
900	Formative		III	
800				
700				
600		Regional Development		
500				Regional Development
400			Neoindian	
300			II	
200				
100 AD				
BC 100				
200	Archaic			
300			I	
400		Formative		
500				Formative
600	Pre-Agricultural			
700				
800				
900			Mesoindian	
1000				
2000				
3000				Archaic
4000				
5000	Paleoindian	Paleoindian	Paleoindian	
6000				
7000				Paleoindian
8000				

One attempt to overcome this situation in Peru has been to propose a master sequence based upon the detailed archaeological sequences from the Ica Valley. Here three named horizons (early, middle, and late) correspond to the appearance of influence from three major expansionist movements, those of Chavín, Huari/Tiahuanaco, and the Incas, alternating with eras of local development, the intermediate periods (Table 2.1). The preceramic eras prior to this are, like stages, characterized by a technology or in this case, a technological lack, but are not treated as unitary (there having been considerable regional and temporal diversity in Peru in the Preceramic). This system, although widely used in Peru, has not been extended or adapted to other areas, most of which tend to depend upon some version of archaeological stages for the presentation and interpretation of archaeological remains.

In the following chapters, because of the non-comparability of the interpreted chronologies of different countries, cultures are presented in terms of absolute time as determined through radiocarbon dating. There have been enough radiocarbon samples analyzed to give general dates to most cultural traditions of the continent. The dates presented are fairly conservative as it is evident that there are areas of serious dissension in dating many cultural traditions. Further research will doubtless modify these chronologies and will certainly refine them. Table 2.2 represents a current consensus, not an immutable one.

Table 2.2 *Radiocarbon based chronologies for South American prehistory.*

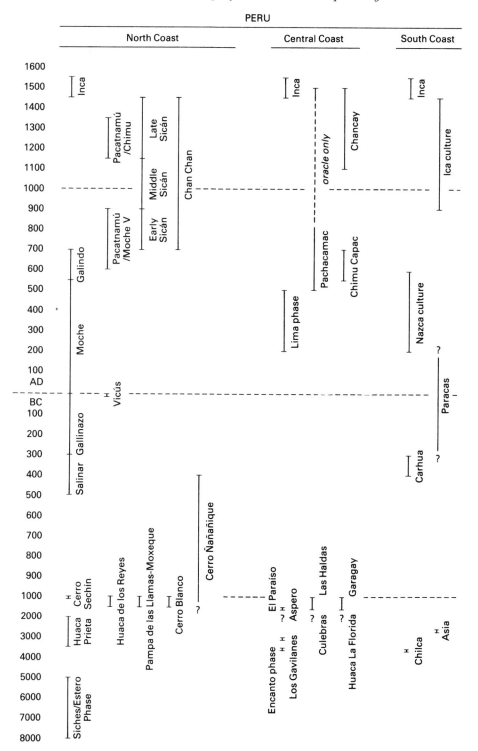

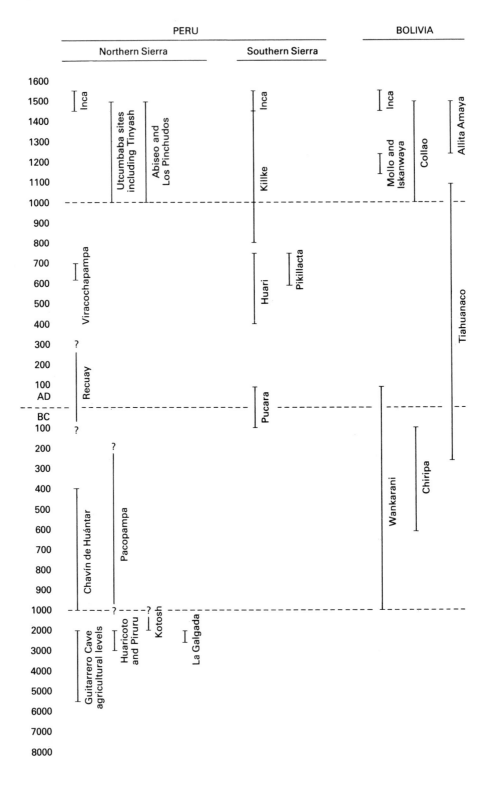

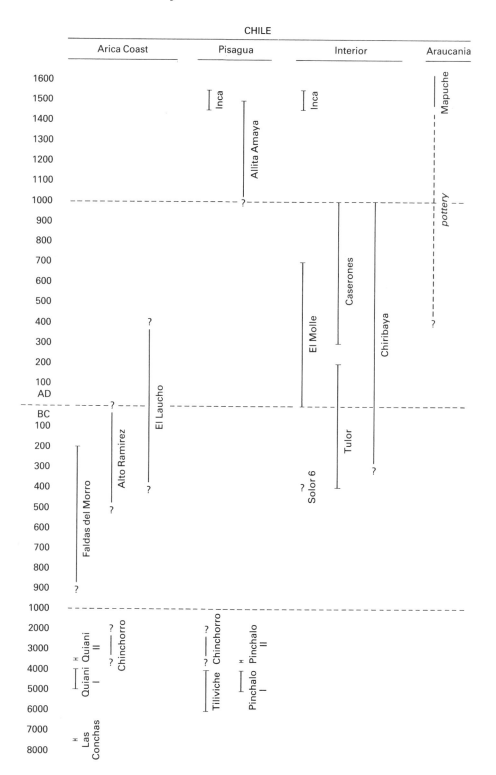

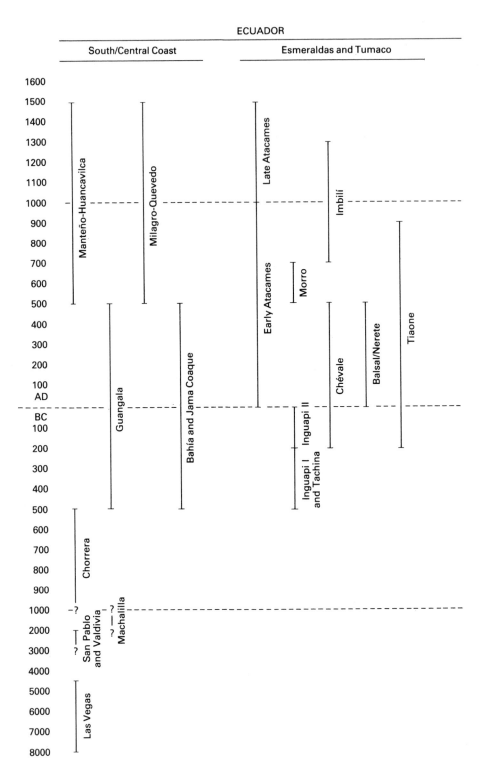

ECUADOR

South/Central Coast | Esmeraldas and Tumaco

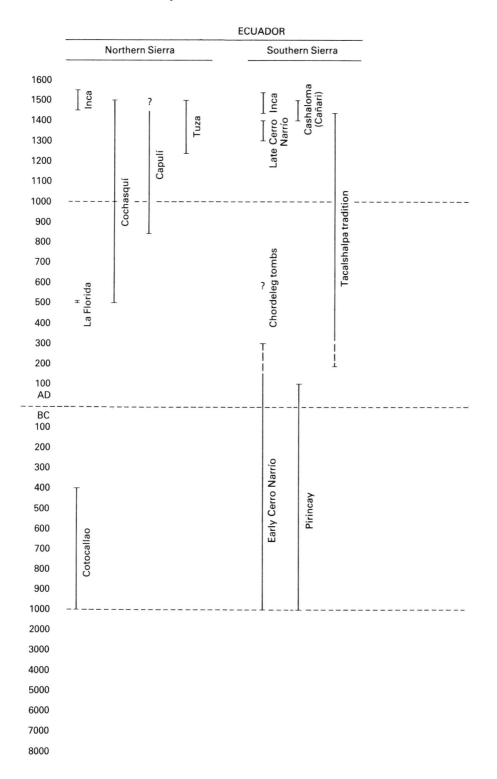

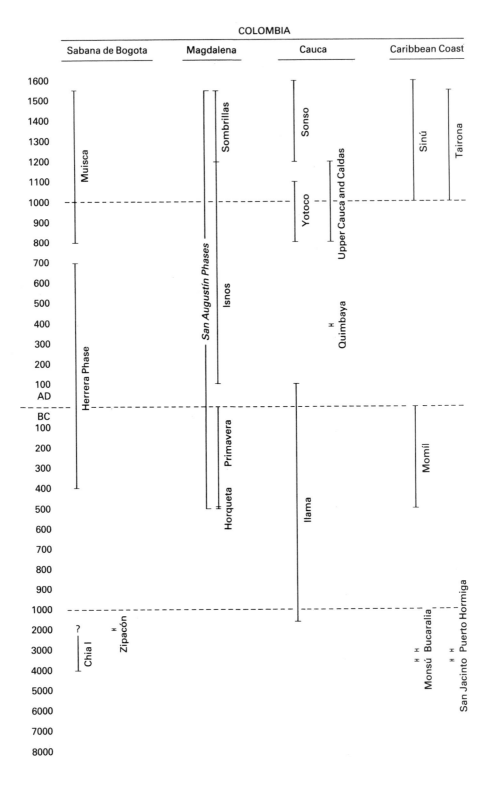

COLOMBIA

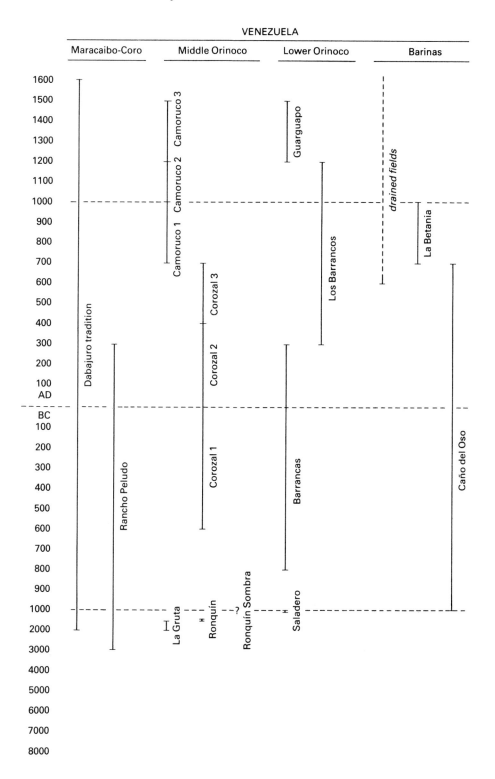

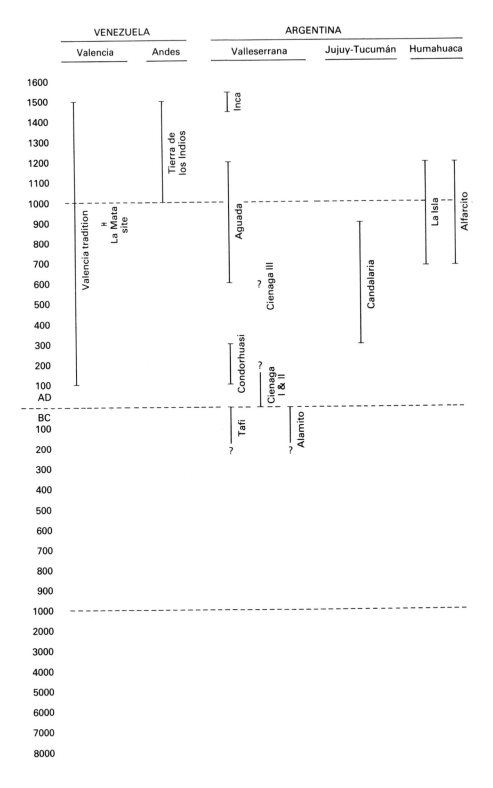

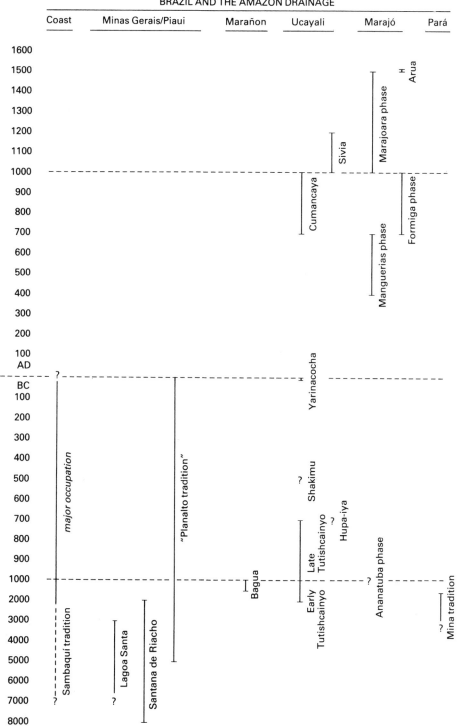

BRAZIL AND THE AMAZON DRAINAGE

BRAZIL AND THE AMAZON DRAINAGE

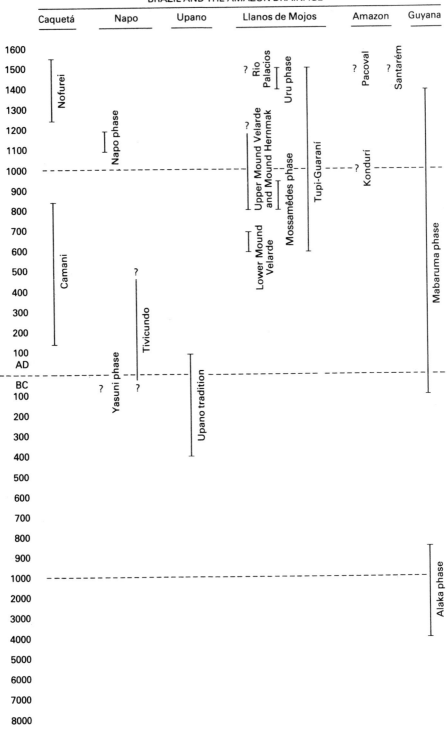

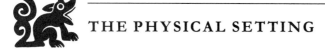

CHAPTER 3

THE PHYSICAL SETTING

The South American continent is extraordinarily diverse in the range of environments it offers. Most of the continental land mass lies within the tropics so that climate and seasonal variation are largely determined by altitude and by the local regime of rains. The types of temperature variations which dwellers in the temperate climates tend to think of as seasonal are not particularly marked except in the southern, temperate, reaches of the continent and in some specialized microenvironments.

The most outstanding features of South America are the mass of the Andes mountains and the huge tropical river systems of the Orinoco, Amazon and La Plata (Figures 3.1 and 3.2). The Andes dominate the western continent, stretching from the Caribbean coast to Tierra del Fuego, rising abruptly from a coastal plain and falling away to the east in a wider band of progressively lowering hills. The mountain band itself is variable in both altitudes and width. In Colombia three major ranges are separated by the valleys of the Cauca and Magdalena rivers; these narrow in Ecuador to a narrower band of two ranges with a series of intermontane basins separated by transverse ranges (nudos or "knots") and a significantly wider (though occasionally hilly) coastal plain. The northern Andes are well watered and originally supported heavy forest ranging from cloud forest, through the tropical deciduous forests to true rainforest. Much of this cover has disappeared through agriculture and lumbering, resulting in low secondary brush forest, cane breaks of giant bamboo ("caña brava," *Gyneum sagitatum*) and open savanna in the river valleys, intermontane valleys and the highland plains; the largest of these is the Sabana de Bogotá (Figure 3.3). To the south in Peru and Bolivia the Andes reach their widest extent with a larger concentration of very high peaks. Permanent snow line is at approximately 5700 m. Below Siches the coastal plain narrows and is broken by numbers of short transverse ranges which reach or nearly reach the sea. Generally there are three major ranges of mountains separated by rivers, although in the region of the Callejón de Huaylas there are only two ranges. The eastern of these is the Cordillera Blanca, the "White Range," so called because many of the peaks are eternally topped with snow; the western and lower range is the Cordillera Negra. The Andes are seismically active and feature a large number of active volcanoes (Figure 3.4). Rampant volcanism has substantially affected both the growth of civilizations in this region and what we know about them. This is particularly marked in the north where a series of ashy volcanoes were very active until *c*. AD 800, limiting human use of much of southern Colombia and obscuring earlier cultures in areas within the ash falls. The position of western South America along the edges of the Nazca plate also leads to seismic instability. This is a trembling land where strong earthquakes are

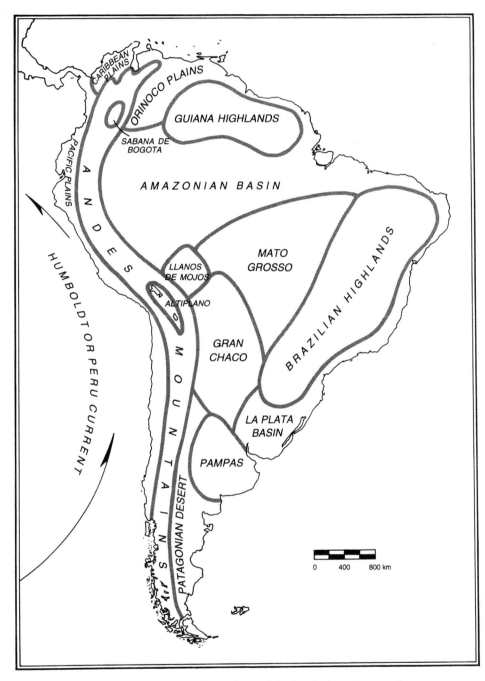

3.1 Major physiographic regions of the South American continent.

3.2 Major geographic features of the South American continent.

3.3 Typical scene in the northern highlands. Cleared forest and caña brava near San Agustín, Colombia (see also Chapter 12).

frequent enough to have had and to have considerable economic and cultural effects (Figure 3.5). In the highlands earthquakes add a new danger, the huayco or mud slide, caused by landslides breaking the natural dams of glacial lakes and causing massive movement of mud, water and rock down the narrow valleys.

The highland valleys and basins, with their good soils and seasonal rains, are and were a major focus of human activity in the Andean region. Furthermore, the rivers which drain these valleys facilitated contact with the tropical regions to the east and the coastal plains. The large rivers of the central Andes, with the exception of the Santa, all flow east or northeast into the Amazon lowlands. The Bolivian altiplano, the basin of Lake Titicaca, at an altitude of over 4000 m, is the largest of these valleys and one of the few that is a true basin: Lake Titicaca drains into Lake Poopó and then through a series of progressively saline lakes into salt pans (Figure 3.6). The rich resources of the lakes with their reeds, fish, and birds, along with the fertile soils and the proximity of both high puna for grazing and the semitropical yungas with their abundant plant resources (wood, drug plants, tobacco, fruits, etc.) were perhaps one reason for the early development of urban civilization in this region of the highlands, with the existence of deposits of various metallic ores being another important resource. In the north the temperate high savannas, such as the Sabana de Bogotá, with their rivers, lakes, generous rains and deep alluvial soils were favored areas of occupation, first for hunting in the forests which originally covered them and then, later, for agriculture. The same

3.4 Sangay Volcano, Ecuador, during a minor eruption in July 1990. The ash plume of this volcano is blown to the west and major eruptions have resulted in ash fall as far away as Guayaquil.

was true of the series of highland valleys in Ecuador. Today the altitudinal limit for agriculture in the Andes is slightly below 5000 m, with specialized highland crops such as potatoes (*Solanum tuberosum*), other tubers, and grains such as quinoa (*Chenopodium quinoa*) forming the major crops at the higher elevations.

The very high grasslands – humid páramo in the north, desert-like puna in the south – were somewhat less utilized. Páramo tends to be very cold and wet, often with near continual fog and rain, and was generally avoided except by travelers over the mountains and by visiting hunters (Figure 3.7). Today, the most visible ancient remains in these foggy heights are the ancient roads and occasional resting place of the Incas and their predecessors. The puna, cold dry grasslands above the altitude at which agriculture is practicable, were important because of the herds of camelids which grazed there and which were first hunted and then herded by humans (Figure 3.8). An early

3.5 The Plaza de Armas in Huáraz, Peru, after the 1970 earthquake.

development of pastoralism characterizes the Peruvian and Bolivian highlands, although the southern puna regions of Bolivia and Chile are too dry and cold to support any intensive exploitation by humans (they were, however, important hunting regions, especially in the vicinity of the high salt lakes and salt pans and later were extremely important mining regions owing to their wealth of copper ores). To the southeast the Argentine Andes are likewise dry, with barren slopes in much of the region and cactus and semi-deciduous scrub forest in the rest. Mixed forests covered some of the Chilean Andes in the temperate latitudes, giving way to dense conifer and temperate rainforest which, coupled with the very broken topography and cold, extremely humid climate, made these areas inhospitable to human occupation south of the island of Chiloe (the southernmost limit of agriculture). In historic times the coasts were utilized by canoe nomads, the Alacaluf, who exploited the shore and water resources. Archaeological evidence indicates that their economic pattern is one which had developed as early as 4000–3000 BC.

The coastal plains of the Andes form a second focal point of human occupation. The narrow Pacific coast of Colombia is rainforest, giving way to an unstable coastline of mangrove in southern Colombia and much of Ecuador. Behind the tidal mangrove swamps there tends to be interior humid savanna and forested hills. Although the Santa Elena Peninsula of Ecuador is an occasionally humid desert, with some seasonal precipitation, most of the central coast of Ecuador is seasonal deciduous forest and seaside manglares. The coast around the Gulf of Guayaquil is drowned and the very

3.6 Uru man poling a reed boat on Lake Titicaca. The Urus have been pushed off the mainland and onto the reed islands of the lake by other indigenous peoples and mestizos.

wide coastal plain is a tangle of estuaries, swamps, and overflow lands (Figure 3.9). This gives way to semi-arid desert with scrub and high desert cover and then to the completely arid conditions of the Peruvian and northern Chilean coast. Here, outside of the oasis river valleys, formed by a series of short rivers which originate in the Andes and flow into the Pacific Ocean, there is virtually no life (Figure 3.10). Rain falls but rarely and the amount of rain decreases as one goes south, culminating in the extraordinarily arid Atacama desert of northern Chile, where even the Andes get no precipitation. The cause of this aridity is the warming of the moisture-bearing clouds which the winds move off the Pacific Ocean and onto the land. The resultant temperature inversion keeps rain from falling, but leaves the coast cool and overcast for much of the year. In some areas the fog is trapped by the winds against the coastal hills

3.7 Puna grassland in Junín province, Peru. This high-altitude (here 4300 m above sea level) dry grassland was important to the earliest hunters as well as to later pastoralists. Pachamachay Cave (see Chapter 4) is located in the rock outcrop in the center.

where it supports a seasonal xerophytic forest, the lomas. The lomas supported seasonal populations of deer, camelids, etc. and were an important resource to coastal dwellers. Today over-exploitation and local drying trends have decimated the once extensive coastal cloud forests. Moving upwards, the clouds do not cool enough to drop their rain until about 2500 m in elevation. Although the coastal desert is habitable in the oasis valleys, the steep and arid western escarpment of the Andes was and is little utilized, owing to lack of water, relatively infertile soils, and the prevalence of several insect-vectored diseases such as leshmaniasis (a disease which, like leprosy, causes ulceration of the soft tissues of the body) and verruga, which causes sores to appear over the body, leading to the afflicted person dying of blood poisoning.

The winds which cause the aridity of the coast are responsible, in part, for its major resource: the incredible richness of marine life. The winds, aided by the coriolis force, move the ocean waters northwest and, as the surface waters are skimmed off, they are replaced by upwelling from the lower, colder counter-current. These waters are particularly rich in nutrients and as they move into the sunlight of the shallower sea levels an enormous growth of phytoplankton is encouraged, a verdant pasture for copepods and other herbivorous creatures which in turn are fed upon by fishes,

3.8 Alpacas in the high grasslands (pajonal) of Cañar Province, Ecuador. Camelids were reintroduced to this region in 1984 after reckless killing and disease had caused them to become extinct in the early colonial period.

3.9 Coastal manglar near Anllulla in coastal Ecuador. The mangrove swamps and estuaries are a rich source of mollusks, fish, animals, and birds and were early exploited by humans wherever they occurred.

3.10 Most of the Peruvian desert is utterly without life, but every 20 miles or so a short river, whose origin is in the Andean rains, cuts the desolate landscape and provides oases for plants, animals, and humans. The Nepeña Valley of northern Peru, looking upriver towards Jimbe.

including vast schools of anchovies. These are then prey for larger organisms: fish, sea mammals, and birds. The result of this Humboldt Current is that the coast of Peru and northern Chile supports one of the world's richest marine avifauna. This in turn supported human endeavors from the earliest inhabitants to the present. This is a very stable ecosystem save for the phenomenon of El Niño, so-named because it often arrives around Christmas. The causes of Niño are very complex and rest in ocean currents and wind patterns in the south Pacific, but what happens along the South American coast is a sudden change in the direction of the winds. This causes rain upon the coast, coupled with a cessation of the upwelling and a movement southwards of the tropical counter-current. The sudden lack of food causes cataclysmic disruption of the entire food chain: the surviving small fish leave, the birds and sea mammals die by the millions, dead organisms generate volumes of hydrogen sulfide which makes the coast smell foul and discolors ships and buildings (hence its grim name El Pintor) and red dinoflagellates similar to the toxic red tides of North America appear in sheltered waters, causing the surviving mollusks to become poisonous to higher life forms. Coupled with the rains, which usually cause catastrophic flooding, the Niño, if severe, can severely disrupt the ecosystem, and the local cultural systems, for decades to come. Rain on the coast is usually accompanied by drought in the highlands, so that there is little respite. Although the Niño phenomenon is felt to a minor extent most years in southern Ecuador and northernmost Peru where the Humboldt Current veers oceanwards and currents and

3.11 The Andes and Licancabur Volcano from Quitor, San Pedro de Atacama.

winds are in more of a flux, it is much less frequent farther south (Figure 3.1). Folklore claims a Niño every seven years although in this century there was one in 1925 (very severe), others in 1953, 1957, and 1965 (lesser in magnitude), a stronger one in 1972 (whose effect was amplified by heavy overfishing of the current) and then the catastrophic, long-lasting Niño of 1981–3, whose effects were felt on the fisheries of the entire Pacific Coast as far north as Alaska and which seems to have modified weather patterns in much of the world.

The southern coast is beyond the effects of most Niños, but also has much less water. Many of the rivers do not reach the coast and northern Chile is almost entirely arid, save for several oases and the Loa River Valley. The oasis of San Pedro de Atacama and the coastal fringes were most used in prehistory, except in wetter cycles, which can be traced by the existence of ancient settlements along dry washes in areas which are now totally dry (Figure 3.11). This desert gives way to a temperate climate inland in the central part of that country. The Mediterranean-like climate of central Chile today supports an important wine industry, the heritage of Italian and German immigrants. In the past, however, it was the home of sedentary farmers such as the Araucanians, or Mapuche, who survive today in spite of considerable oppression from the dominant governments.

The eastern slopes of the Andes are precipitous and heavily forested, with cloud forest in the upper altitudes (Figure 3.12). This pattern of vegetation extends south into Bolivia, being replaced by more temperate deciduous forest above the Gran Chaco. The Chaco is covered with scrub forest and grassy plains, responses to seasonal flooding and to the extension of the bitter frosts of the Patagonian desert into this area. Patagonia itself experiences severe winter cold and low precipitation and is covered with bunch grass and scrub (Figure 3.13). This changes to mesquite brush land on the Argentine plains and basins. The basin margins of northwest Argentina were the main areas of more intensive human use in the "southern cone," owing to the availability of water from the mountain streams.

Apart from the Andes there are two other large upland areas in South America: the Guinea and the Brazilian highlands. These are both formed of highly weathered base poor rocks. The southeastern Brazilian highlands start with a continuation of the grassy prairies and mimosa gallery forest of the pampas giving way to deciduous forest in the valleys. Thickets of Araucaria palm and maté (*Ilex paraguariensis*) on the upland prairies alternate with open grasslands. In much of the area, including the Matto Grosso, the soils are thin and relatively poor. There is a marked rainy–dry season alternation in these uplands with frosts, and even snow, at the higher altitudes. This region was an early focus of human activity, although seminomadic hunting and gathering cultures characterized much of its prehistory.

The Guinea highlands, located roughly between the Amazon-Yapuré and the Orinoco rivers, occupy all but a narrow coastal strip of the Guineas and most of northern Brazil. Much of the area is sedimentary rock, supporting forest but with very little in the way of fertile soil. The rivers originating in the Guinea highlands are poor in nutrients; coastal areas are mangrove swamps which yield to fresh-water swamp inland, with clusters of palms on the drier elevations. Rainforest begins along the Brazilian coast, though the mangrove swamps still fringe the actual coastline. Much of the interior of northeastern Brazil is arid steppe with cactus and low woody plants. The rest of the Caribbean coast of South America is generally arid, with thorn scrub, cactus, and grass and with very little rainfall. The Caribbean coast of northern Colombia is likewise arid but extensive swamps and flood plains characterize the lower drainage of the Magdalena River (Figure 3.14).

The tropical lowlands of the three great river systems are the other outstanding ecosystems of South America. These huge rivers (the Amazon may be shorter than the Congo or the Mississippi, but the annual discharge into the Atlantic Ocean is many times that of either of these two rivers, resulting in fresh water some hundreds of kilometers out to sea from the mouth) form in one sense an interconnected system: the Amazon system is connected to the Orinoco by the Casiquiare Canal which drains into

3.12 At Machu Picchu, Pachacuti Inca's country estate, deforestation shows the pronounced relief and human attempts to tame it through terracing of both Machu Picchu and the peak of Huayna Picchu in the background. The montaña tends towards a vertical, heavily forested landscape.

3.13 Southernmost Patagonia is a cold desert with some scrub vegetation and grass which supports herds of guanacos, an important resource for hunters in this region from the Paleoindian period to the nineteenth century. Cañadon Condor, Magallones, Chile.

both the upper Orinoco and the upper Negro River (Figure 3.15). During the rainy season the flood waters of the Essequibo River of Guyana meet those of a tributary of the Negro (so called because its waters are dark). To the south the annual flooding of the Llanos de Mojos and the Gran Chaco merge the waters of the Paraguay and Madeira rivers into an immense lake and a net of waterways reaching to the estuary of the La Plata is formed. It is small wonder that the major means of communication and migration in the tropical lowlands (and some of the more temperate ones) was by water. Much of the land around all of these river systems is characterized by extensive seasonal flooding which, depending upon the origins of the flood waters, either enriches the land or leaches it.

The Orinoco River, for much of its length, is surrounded by savanna (llanos). On the upper Orinoco these are drier and less extensively flooded, with gallery forest along the streams and broad grassy expanses (Figure 3.16). Farther downstream, however, yearly flooding is extensive and only the levées formed by alluvial deposits, augmented by sand blown from the river bed in the dry season, are above water (Figure 3.17). Gallery forest exists along the levées, although it is generally a two-story forest and the upper story may contain deciduous species. Behind the river channel are tributary streams, some few permanent lakes, and many seasonal lagoons. Swamp forest exists in the wet savanna

3.14 The Caribbean coastal plain near Cartagena, Colombia. This swampy region was the scene of some of the earliest sedentary, pottery-making peoples in South America. This photograph is of the very early Canapote site.

with stands of palm trees, which were economically of extreme importance to the ancient inhabitants, occupying bits of higher ground. Much of the wet savanna was of little use to the ancients, although late in prehistory attempts were made to extend the land available for cultivation by the construction of drained field systems, with the farmers living on artificially raised mounds, often connected by causeways. These systems extend along much of the Orinoco and into Guyana and Surinam. A similar development is seen to the south in the likewise seasonally inundated Llanos de Mojos of Bolivia (Figure 3.18) as well as in the San Jorge floodplain of the río Magdalena of northern Colombia and in the floodplain of the Guayas and Daule rivers in southern Ecuador. The function of all of these systems seems to have been to provide drier land with better drainage for agriculture and, in some instances, the canals between the raised lines may have served as refugia and traps for fish.

The southern lowlands consist of a very smooth plain in the northern part of the Gran Chaco and the huge alluvial lowlands of the Paraguay-Paraná rivers. The Chaco plain is first flooded and then baked solid with the changing seasons. The Paraguay-Paraná region forms one of the world's largest regions of swamp and swamp forest; palms are the major economic plant.

The Amazon proper has, of course, made its way into popular imagination as one of the world's greatest tropical rainforests, the "Green Hell" celebrated in so many stories and films. The Upper Amazon, west of the Madeira River (the major southern tributary

3.15 The meeting of the Negro and Amazon rivers in Brazil. The brown, turbid waters of the Amazon are rich in animal life while the clear, black waters of the Negro, coming off the ancient Guinea shield, are extremely poor in nutrients.

of the Amazon) is an area of relatively restricted recent alluvial soils and active meandering rivers whose upper reaches (in the Andes) tend to have narrow canyons with small flood plains. The region is marked with ox-bow lakes, some new, some destroyed by later loops, some completely filled in. The levées along the active river channel always are the highest land and were (and are) the areas chosen for use by humans although investigation of the interfluvial areas is now beginning to show that these too were heavily utilized (Figure 9.21). This has led to some problems in trying to reconstruct the prehistory of the region since the actively moving rivers often have washed away old levées. The dry river beds are also good for agriculture if the crops have a short growing season and form some of the best (if seasonal) farming land in the region. The lower Amazon is a trough with the old formations of the Guiana and Brazilian highlands coming close to the river bed and a rather restricted flood plain, characterized once more by a maze of river arms, ox-bows and back swamps. The major tributary mouths and the mouths of the Amazon itself are deeply drowned. The dominant vegetation type throughout is rainforest, although there is a certain variation in amount and seasonality of rainfall as one traverses the length of the river. Vegetation types correspond to drainage, with swamp forms and wet prairie formations characterizing the active flood plain and hardwoods, softwoods, palms, vines, etc. ("typical jungle") being found on the less often flooded and better drained surfaces. As

3.16 The upper reaches of the Orinoco plain near Guamal, Colombia. Gallery forest along rivers and creeks and savanna in between water courses is a common vegetation pattern throughout lowland South America.

is usual in tropical ecosystems, there tends to be a great diversity of species but a low frequency of individuals of any given species in an area. Most of the soils are poor, with nutrients concentrated in the vegetation and litter on the forest floor; once clearing is accomplished they leach at an alarming rate and become barren laterite in a matter of years. Animal resources within these tropical systems echo the distribution of plants. Most species are small or solitary, with relatively large ranges. Hunting can be best accomplished during the rainy season, when animals as well as humans concentrate on high ground. This is a situation which invites over-hunting, a situation which may have encouraged the development of cannibalism by later groups in the region. Birds and monkeys form the major species hunted by tropical forest groups in modern times, with peccary, tapir, rodents, etc. playing a minor role. Monkeys roasted whole bear an uncanny resemblance to barbecued children and it has been suggested that numbers of the so-called cannibals were wrongly accused of anthropophagous tendencies by Europeans who saw them eating cooked monkeys. The great wealth of protein throughout the riverine tropics comes from the waters themselves: fish, crocodilians, turtles, etc., and tends to be restricted in availability to a given season. During the rainy season fish spread out and seek the turbulent waters of the streams where most nutrients are to be found. Thus they are difficult to harvest, given any of the technologies

3.17 Near the mouth of the Orinoco River in Venezuela.

available (spears, hook and line, nets, poison, weirs). Most fishing is done in the dry season, when the flood waters are retreating and the fish have fewer options for escape. This is again a situation liable to human abuse, even with relatively low population densities.

The faunal situation of the tropical lowlands is mirrored throughout the continent. With the exception of the immeasurably rich waters off the coast of Peru and northern Chile, with their concentrations of mollusks, fish, marine mammals, and marine birds (important more perhaps for their guano, early used as fertilizer, than as foodstuffs themselves), and the puna and some of the southern temperate savannas, with their herds of camelids, the faunal situation is one of small to medium-sized animals which are either solitary or live in small groups. The camelids were early domesticated in the Andes (the llama is probably descended from the wild guanaco), along with one rodent, the guinea pig (*Cavia* sp.), but other species were labor intensive to hunt unless carefully managed and controlled (as the Incas and, perhaps, some earlier peoples did with vicuñas and deer). Forest hunting, especially, seems to have become more of a high-status sport than a serious economic activity; the majority of protein came from fish, birds, and monkeys, depending upon the season and the specific environment of a given culture. Contrary to much casual propaganda, the tropical lowland soils are not particularly fertile, except for some very special – and limited – areas; the major regions of intensive agricultural activity were in the Andean highlands and adjacent coasts, where the combination of domesticable camelids (plus guinea pigs, dogs, and ducks),

3.18 The Llanos de Mojos in Bolivia are, like much of the Orinoco and parts of the Ecuadorian coast, flooded annually. Here an artificial causeway connects villages (seen as the "islands" of trees in the distance), cutting through a vast expanse of raised fields.

rich marine resources, and fertile alluvium early led to dense, sedentary populations and the development of complex societies.

It is very evident that the natural environment delimited the regions in which dense populations could develop, and hence the changes in social structure, economic practices, and ideologies that population growth seems to give rise to. The regions of major cultural development in South America remained along the western margins of the continent, from northern Chile through Colombia and inland to the eastern margins of the Andes, until the introduction of foreign domestic animals, cultigens, and technologies (coupled with both deliberate and involuntary genocide of the native inhabitants) led to the modern agro/industrial states of South America. Problems of deforestation, pollution, and outright destruction of the environment are increasing rapidly as people attempt to impose crops and technologies of a very different origin on the essentially tropical and often vertical topography of a fragile continent.

CHAPTER 4

THE FIRST PEOPLES: 12,000–6000 BC

There is little doubt that the peopling of South America was a part of the great migrations of *Homo sapiens sapiens* during the last glaciation. Despite some suggestions to the contrary, all evidence indicates that the South American peoples came from North America via the Central American isthmus. It seems likely that they moved down the mountain chains for, despite the inconveniences of topography, these were the areas which were open terrain and supported the larger herbivores in which the earliest hunters apparently had a strong interest. It is possible that there were also movements down the coast but these have proved harder to investigate, since a fair amount of the continent's coastline was drowned by rising sea levels at the end of the Pleistocene. Sites in those areas of western South America that have experienced uplift or, at least, have not subsided, are not among the earliest known and it seems quite possible that in South America, as in much of the rest of the world, adaptations to water's edge or coastal environments were one part of a series of economic realignments resulting from growing populations and from environmental changes at the end of the ice ages (Figure 4.1).

A much-discussed problem is that of when did these peoples begin to arrive? Dating sites of the Paleoindians has traditionally been difficult and rather imprecise, as well as being clouded by unfounded allegations of very early dates of arrival made on the basis of inner conviction rather than hard fact. The development of radiocarbon dating and, especially, of accelerator techniques for processing small samples, has clarified some problems, but has created others because of unclear cultural or geological associations of many dated materials. Moreover, at present the dendrochronological calibration of radiocarbon, the conversion of radiocarbon years into calendar years, does not extend back into the period of the last glacial. This means that any radiocarbon dates must be regarded as speculative. It has also become clear that geological dating and dating by associated fauna are not as precise as might be wished. Indeed, there is a certain amount of circularity to most arguments about the arrival and evolution of the Paleoindians. Currently, despite claims of great age for several sites, the earliest epoch for which there is any reliable evidence for a human presence on the continent is *c*. 10,000 BC. There are very few sites so early, but they are found in a number of regions, a distribution consistent with Martin's hypothesis that hunters encountering a naive prey population would rapidly advance across the land masses, occupying, however briefly, all appropriate ecozones, until naive populations had been exhausted and new adaptations, including greater sedentism, had to be made. From *c*. 10,000 BC onwards sites are increasingly common and by the end of the Paleoindian period (conventionally dated

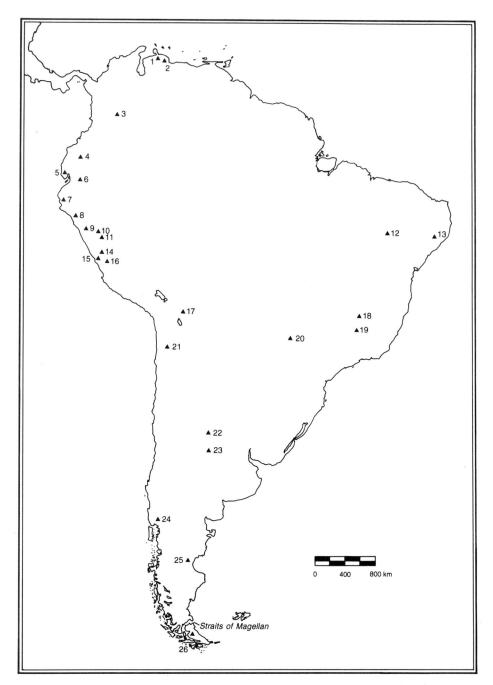

4.1 Early sites mentioned in the text. 1. Muaco, Taima Taima, Río Pedregal, 2. Coro Plain, 3. Sabana de Bogotá, Facatativá, 4. El Inga, Ilaló, 5. Vegas, 6. Chobshi Cave, 7. Talará tar pits, 8. Moche and Chicama Valleys, 9. Guitarrero Cave, 10. Huargo Cave, 11. Lauricocha Cave, 12. Pedra Furada, 13. Bom Jardin, 14. Pampa de Junín, 15. Chivateros, 16. Ayacucho, 17. Viscachani, 18. Santana de Riacho, 19. Lagoa Santa, 20. Alice Boër, 21. Salar de Talabre, 22. Ayampitín, 23. Intihuasi Cave, 24. Monte Verde, 25. Los Toldos, 26. Tierra del Fuego: Palli Aike, Fell's Caves, Englefield, Bahia Buena, Punta Santa Ana.

somewhere between 8000 and 6000 BC) all available environmental niches seem to have been occupied and there was considerable cultural variation both in economic adaptation and in material culture.

The climate of terminal Pleistocene and early Holocene South America is best described as variable and unstable. In most cases where there is sufficient evidence to reconstruct the past environment, a fair amount of local fluctuation is evident. Glaciation was largely confined to the Andes at all times, but there were localized advances and retreats which affected human habitation in the mountains. Schobinger's hypothesis that the Amazon was cool and arid during most of the Pleistocene is now generally accepted and this chilliness and aridity seem to have affected much of the southeastern continent. Along the northern part of the west coast, however, there are indications of a warmer and more humid climate during the latter part of the Paleoindian epoch. It has been suggested that the Humboldt Current had moved farther south so that more of the coast was affected regularly by periodic Niños. Mangroves are known to have extended much further south than they do today and at Talará on the northern Peruvian coast there is ample evidence for utilization of this niche by early populations. A more humid, or at least foggier, regime is also suggested by the evident dependence of central coast Peruvian hunters upon what appear to be large areas of lomas vegetation (much more extensive than today). In central to southern Peru and Chile there may have been little climatic change. However, we must not forget the possibility of extremely rapid environmental change, especially in situations like this where precise temporal control is lacking. For example, in 1971 a two-week rain on the Santa Elena Peninsula of Ecuador changed, literally overnight, economic adaptations and settlement patterns, as people swarmed from the interior onto the peninsula, bringing their cattle with them, and as farmers began to plant in regions which had not been agricultural for nearly a century. This would surely leave a mark in the archaeological record, but interpreting this mark would be extraordinarily difficult and might well lead to unwarranted conclusions concerning a longer humid period. Western South American environments were also strongly affected by volcanism and, perhaps, by localized subsidence along the shore. These could and did very rapidly change local environments and almost certainly had an influence upon the occupants of the areas, but again, these influences are almost impossible to pinpoint archaeologically. The role of the episodic El Niño current and of tsunamis is also hotly debated, especially in dealing with later cultures, but may have been a crucial element in the late dependence upon agriculture along much of the central Andean coast.

The terminal Pleistocene cultures had somewhat different animal resources to utilize than did the later peoples. Horse, mastodon, glyptodon (a giant armadillo), megatherium (a very large ground sloth), and a series of other large herbivores supplemented the still extant guanaco, llama, and vicuña. Associations between extinct fauna and artifacts remain one of the rarer, but best, indications of human presence at this time, although, as mentioned, we cannot be certain to within several millennia of the dates of extinction of creatures like megatherium or the mastodon. There also is some reason to think that several of these species did survive in very limited numbers in isolated refugia until considerably later, although this has been difficult to pinpoint

4.2 Monte Verde, southern Chile: living surface of work zone with stone and bone
artifacts associated.

exactly owing to the impreciseness of dating techniques available and the widespread
assumption that all associations between now extinct animals and artifacts must be
evidence of Pleistocene occupations.

Examination of the earliest South American sites reveals that even at the beginning of
human occupation of the continent there was considerable cultural diversity, a diversity
doubtless related to the local environments and the local species exploited. Few of these
sites have yielded projectile points, giving fuel to the long-lasting argument concerning
a "pre-projectile point horizon," an hypothesized initial period of occupation in which
projectile points were missing from the cultural inventory. As has been pointed out in
great detail by numbers of Paleoindian specialists, the "pre-projectile point horizon"
seems to take in every dubiously dated and culturally mixed site on the continent.
Projectile points had been part of many human tool kits for millennia before the
occupation of the American continents. It is quite possible that the lack of projectile
points in some of these early sites is due to the nature of the site, to archaeological
sampling, or to the use of non-lithic projectiles, such as bone, bamboo, or fire-hardened
wood. These latter are found in slightly later sites and were typical of many of the later
peoples of both lowland and coastal South America. It is also possible that bolas or
slings, instruments widely used in hunting up to the present, were in use by some of the
early hunters. Support for this comes from the Monte Verde site in south-central Chile
where sling stones and what seem to be bolas were found in close association with the

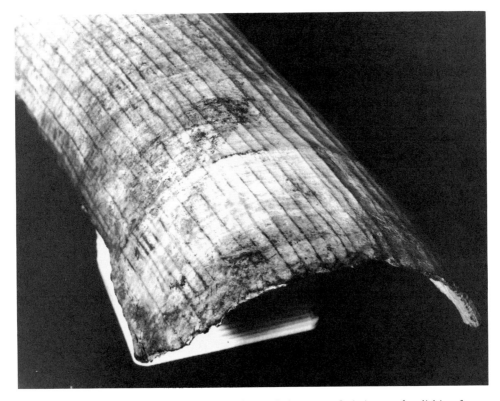

4.3 Monte Verde: worked mastodon tusk fragment. Striations and polishing from use are clearly visible along the surface.

remains of mastodon. The Monte Verde site is dated to between 12,000 and 10,000 BC and includes, besides the sling stones and mastodons, remains of bone and wooden tools, hafted stone tools, rather crude chopping and scraping tools and the remains of twelve rectangular wooden and skin huts with shallow clay-lined brazier pits inside (Figure 4.2). The excavators suggest that cooking may have been done communally as large hearths were found centrally located outside the huts. It should be noted that the associations between the supposed hearths and the samples taken for dating are not universally accepted. Many people doubt the earlier dates for this site and there are some who doubt the associations between the animal remains and human activity.

Tools from Monte Verde do not include any stone projectile points although both flaked and ground stone tools were found in close association (Monte Verde is a single period of occupation site). These tools are similar to those reported from other early sites on the continent. Only a few bifacially worked tools (hand axes and choppers) were found. Wooden tools, including a lance-like object, hafts for stone tools and digging sticks, were common, the first time such suspected implements have been found in Paleoindian contexts. Some tools of mastodon bone and tusk were also found (Figure 4.3).

The Monte Verde site is also important in that it shows a varied resource base, not simply big game hunting. Wooden mortars and grinding stones attest to the importance of plant food. A wide range of tubers, including potatoes, rhizomes, seeds, nuts, berries, and leafy vegetables have been recovered from the hearths, storage pits, and living surfaces of the site. The presence of a wide range of seasonally available plants indicates that Monte Verde was a fairly permanently occupied hamlet, not a seasonal camp of nomadic hunters. The presence of a building of substantially different layout from the huts may be evidence of some sort of communal structure for ceremonial or recreational activities. The exceptional organic preservation at Monte Verde gives us some idea of how much of the cultural inventory is missing from most other Paleoindian sites and thus how skewed many of our interpretations of early lifestyles must be. The Alice Boër site in Saõ Paulo state, Brazil, is dated (level 14 of Bed III) to approximately the same time span as Monte Verde. This site is clearly stratified (although Bed II was badly disturbed by ants). A stemmed projectile point and the stems of two more were found in this early level, following several layers with unifacial artifacts only. The Alice Boër points are very early and it has been suggested that they may have been redeposited. Contracting stemmed points similar to the level 14 ones are more common in the upper levels of the site. However, there are other indications of a very early human presence in central and northeast Brazil during what was a generally much colder and damper period than today. A series of sites have been located, all characterized by a unifacial flake stone industry lacking stone projectile points. Several of these sites, such as Arroyo dos Fôsseis, show associations between these tools and extinct fauna.

Extravagant claims for other extremely early sites in Brazil, especially the Pedra Furada rock shelter, seem unfounded, resting as they do upon carbon dates from dubious contexts and upon tools which may well be "ecofacts." Although many have hailed Pedra Furada as a major find regarding the early history of humans upon the continent, the general nature of the tool assemblage and, especially, the remains of paintings, fallen and mixed with the cultural levels, suggest a significantly later date than the very early one that has been claimed. In terms of artifacts and pictograms, Pedra Furada is part of a widespread cultural tradition in the area which dates to c. 5000 BC, not c. 30,000 BC.

Very early sites have also appeared in Patagonia. The first clearly stratified Paleoindian sites to be excavated in South America were Fell's Cave and Palli Aike Cave on the Straits of Magellan in southernmost Patagonia. Here Junius Bird, despite the lack of absolute dating techniques and of comparative materials in the 1930s, recognized the great age of the deposits, noting that the earliest levels were associated with bones of extinct giant ground sloth and horse. Later work in Patagonia and re-excavation at Fell's Cave suggest a date of c. 8000 BC for the Magellan 1 industry, whose most typical artifact is the fish tail point (Figure 4.4). This particular point type has a very wide distribution, having been found as far north as Guatemala. Where dating of its occurrence is possible, it always seems to fall in the 9000–7000 BC range.

Earlier remains have been found at the site of Los Toldos, where excavations in a series of caves have uncovered large, thick flake tools and unifacial points in association

4.4 Artifact sequence from Palli Aike Cave, Tierra del Fuego, Chile. The fish tail points are found in the second register. In the top register are historic Ona tools.

4.5 Site M 18, Sono Otway, Magallones, Chile. A beach-side camp of early fishers and hunters.

with guanaco and extinct horse and camelid. This is followed by the Toldense culture which includes bifacial core tools, pressure flaked and fish tail points, and bone awls and spatulas. This occupation also seems to be accompanied by the earliest clearly datable rock art in the Americas, some fragments of rock wall with red-painted silhouette hands collapsed into the artifact-bearing strata. The Toldense culture of Los Toldos disappears *c*. 9000 BC and there is a substantial gap in the occupation of the cave.

Beginning *c*. 9000–8000 BC the number of sites known increases tremendously and there are many sites which have good organic preservation, which are stratified or which indicate the various adaptations of human society to the still fluctuating environment (Figures 4.5 and 4.6).

From the northern Andes a series of rock shelters on the Sabana de Bogotá (El Abra, Nemocón, Sueva, Tequendama) show an occupation of that ecozone by small groups of specialized hunters who had stone projectile points and who exploited an essentially modern fauna of deer, peccary, agouti, guinea pigs, and various other small animals. The rock shelters seem to have been foci of sporadic, perhaps seasonal, occupation (Figure 4.7). They continued to be used both as temporary shelters and as burial places through a series of climatic changes which brought the forest into these higher altitudes until the region was largely abandoned in an era of extreme aridity *c*. 4000 BC. Faunal and other evidence indicates that the early hunters probably did not move down into the lowlands, but rather confined their yearly round to the high plains and páramo regions. The lucky preservation of human remains shows that the physical type associated with

4.6 Straits of Magellan from the beach north of Cabo San Isidro, Magallones, Chile. Although this landscape is bleak, the wealth of sea and land life made it attractive to indigenous South Americans from the Paleoindian period until they were exterminated by Europeans in this century.

4.7 The Rocas de Sevilla on the Sabana de Bogotá, Colombia. The El Abra rock shelters are located within this formation.

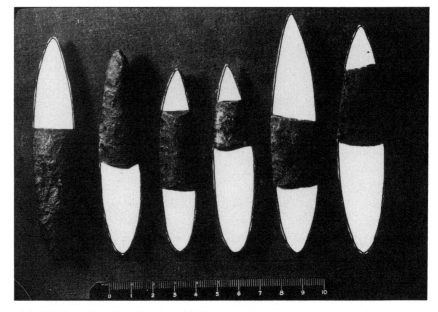

4.8 El Jobo points from Venezuela. The paper reconstructions show how big these leaf-shaped points were. Some may have served as knives rather than lance points.

these early sites was somewhat different from that of the historic Chibcha (Muisca) and shows some affinities with (although it is clearly not identical to) early human remains from Lagoa Santa and related sites in southeastern Brazil.

In adjacent Venezuela a series of sites on the now arid Coro plain show a similar adaptation. The former water hole of Muaco contains a great variety of animals, including many now extinct forms, along with flakes, scrapers, broken and burned bones, and some modern material in a very jumbled deposit. Very close to Muaco (1750 m east) another water hole, Taima-Taima, is less disturbed and a series of tools, including stones of non-local origin that the excavators suggest may have been for smashing glyptodon shells and remains of numbers of El Jobo type lanceolate points, were found in association with a fauna similar to that of Muaco (Figure 4.8). Less than 100 km away a series of terraces on the río Pedregal have yielded a sequence of tools all made of the local quartzite. The upper (and hence earliest) terrace has unifacial flake tools and crude chopping tools, followed by smaller but still crude bifacial tools with El Jobo points appearing on the lower middle terrace and a style of triangular stemmed points, the Las Casitas points, on the current flood plain. The western Venezuelan sites all seem to represent populations of hunters on the open, perhaps more humid, plain. Taima-Taima and Muaco are water hole kill sites and show that a large variety of animals was taken although it is probably a safe assumption that the early Venezuelans, like other hunters, preferred the larger herbivores when these were available. The río Pedregal terraces show a change in tools which probably reflects changes in fauna and plant foods exploited. These tool assemblages tend to be cumulative, that is new types are added, but old ones retained, so that one may assume that new tasks or new prey were being added while old ones remained.

Owing to an unstable coastline, heavy vegetation, and lack of investigation, other coastal or lowland sites have not been identified in northern South America. The Vegas complex of the Santa Elena Peninsula of Ecuador appears at the very end of the Paleoindian period, and marks a general move towards maritime exploitation, broad spectrum foraging and incipient agriculture. From northern Peru south to Chile numbers of sites have been located in the coastal desert. At the Talará tar seeps a number of camp sites and artifact scatters have been studied. The Amotepe assemblage, dated to approximately 9500–6000 BC, is found at a series of locations, each overlooking the tar seeps, suggesting that the users of these tools were waiting for animals to get mired and thus be easier prey. The following Siches-Estero assemblages are post-Paleoindian and show a change towards extensive exploitation of *Anadera tuberculosa*, a mangrove mollusk, just as has been noted in coastal Ecuador. The Talará region today is in the zone of transition between the arid Peruvian coast and the wet tropics of the northern Andean littoral and is climatically unstable. There is good reason to think that the region was wetter in this early period, since mangroves were obviously present along the coast until about 3000 BC.

Further to the south in the Moche and Chicama valleys a series of sites pertaining to the Paiján complex have been identified. Most are open air sites and associations between the tools and extinct megafauna are unclear. The diagnostic tool of this complex is the Paiján point, a long, thin, stemmed point (Figure 4.9). This point seems to have been made on an intermediate form, a blank, which the investigator, Claude Chauchat, has identified as identical to Chivateros bifaces. These large, pointed, axe-like tools were first discovered at the Chivateros workshop site near Ancón on the central coast. Chivateros and some related sites are near the remnants of extinct lomas. The sites are large workshops in the steep hills along the coast where there are outcrops of a fine-grained quartzite (Figure 4.10). This was apparently a favored material for tool making and tools in all stages of manufacture have been found in these workshops. All are percussion flaked and there seems to be a preponderance of wood-working tools. Some Paiján-like points have been found in these sites, but the relationship between the large bifaces and these points was not recognized in the initial explorations. There is also some evidence of successive humid and arid periods from the central coast. Apparently much of the Peruvian coast shared a common culture of hunters exploiting the fauna of the wooded river valleys and then abundant lomas using these long-stemmed points on jabbing or throwing spears. Probably plant food resources were being exploited and there is some indication that fishing had started to be important in local economies, although not as important as it was later to become.

Highland sites are abundant throughout the Andes in this time frame. Aside from the Sabana de Bogotá sites discussed above, evidences of early hunting and foraging peoples have been found throughout the Andes.

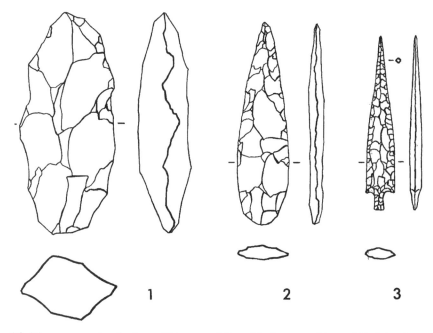

4.9 The process of reducing a Chivateros biface (1), first to a thinner bifacial point (2), and then to the long, thin Paiján point (3).

4.10 The Chivateros site near Ancón, Peru; Edward Lanning and Thomas Patterson, the excavators of the site, are the two front figures.

4.11 Chobshi Cave in the southern highlands of Ecuador. Rock shelters such as this were popular with the early hunters and, indeed, continue in use until the present as temporary shelters or camps. Charles Cecil, standing as scale at the highest point of the rock shelter roof, is 1.8 m in height.

In northern Ecuador a series of sites have been investigated in the vicinity of Quito. The El Inga site, one of the first to be extensively studied, has produced fish tail points in a disturbed context (the site is partly on a modern soccer field). El Inga is also less than 300 m from an obsidian source. The Ilaló sites investigated by Ernesto Salazar show that obsidian exploitation was an important part of the early hunters' utilization of the high wet grasslands. A series of "mines" and workshops in the area and to the north at Mullamica show extensive utilization of the obsidian perhaps both for immediate use and for caching or trade. The faunal resources of the páramo were relatively poor but included mastodon in the lower parts of the grasslands. Deer, both the white-tailed deer (*Odocoileus virginianus*) and brocket deer (*Mazama* spp.), as well as the diminutive pudu (*Pudu* spp.), the spectacled bear (*Tremarctos ornatus*), the mountain tapir (*Tapiris pinchaque*), and various small rodents were still known in the vicinity in this century. The location of the Ilaló sites and other highland sites shows the importance of high-altitude ecosystems to the nomadic hunters, even those north of the range of the wild camelids. The large obsidian outcrops of the Pinchincha cluster were also doubtless as important to early hunters as they were to the later peoples of northern Ecuador.

The unfortunately very disturbed site of Chobshi Cave in the southern highlands of Ecuador shows a similar range of species exploited (Figure 4.11). No fish tail points were found at Chobshi, although willow leaf points of the Ayampitín type, a type consistently associated with the later Andean hunting and gathering cultures, were discovered, along with rhomboidal points and stemmed and barbed points of various

4.12 The mouth of Guitarrero Cave, near Yungay, Peru, showing work in progress.

types made of a large variety of locally available stones. Obsidian artifacts were rare at Chobshi, perhaps traded in from the north. The excavator, Thomas Lynch, concludes that Chobshi Cave represents the end of the Paleoindian tradition and a diversification of the resource base by local peoples, a situation which seems to mirror that of many of the Ilaló sites.

To the south, Guitarrero Cave in the Cordillera Negra of northern Peru shows links in its earliest levels with Chobshi Cave, although its closest artifactual ties are with Peruvian highland sites of similar age (Figure 4.12). Guitarrero Cave is important because of its stratification and organic preservation, which have allowed a much fuller study of economic adaptations and general culture than is true for so many early sites (Figure 4.13). Guitarrero was also excavated by Thomas Lynch, who sees the yearly round of the ancient inhabitants of Guitarrero Cave as involving movement around the large and environmentally diverse Callejón de Huaylas. The cave itself was probably used at the end of the rainy season when vegetal sources were most abundant and deer were plentiful. Guitarrero Cave has also yielded evidence of very early cultivation of plants and of the change from an extractive economy to one which featured agriculture and camelid pastoralism.

Lauricocha Cave, just to the south near the source of the Marañon river, shows a

4.13 Anthony Ranere troweling the Complex II levels of Guitarrero Cave. These levels yielded beans, cordage, and other perishable artifacts and have provided evidence of extremely early domestication of plants in the high Andes. In the background are the remains of later tombs built over and into the Complex II deposits.

seasonal exploitation of the puna environment. During the early periods of occupation of this cave (beginning *c.* 7500 BC) the glacier margins were somewhat lower and the puna was correspondingly larger. Lauricocha, too, is stratified and was, for many years, the only Paleoindian site known in Peru which preserved clear evidence of the sequence of cultural changes at the end of the Pleistocene and during the early Holocene. The inhabitants of Lauricocha hunted deer and camelids with a series of different points. The essential orientation of the Lauricocha inhabitants does not seem to have changed very much through the millennia until the introduction of domesticated camelids and the beginnings of pastoralism and the use of ceramics. Lauricocha is one of the few early sites which contains human remains in clear cultural contexts. Seven burials in the Lauricocha I deposits show a population with long heads and relatively broad faces, somewhat different from the later coastal populations. A tendency towards dolicho-cephaly, however, typifies highland populations to the present so that it is not particularly surprising to find this physical trait in the earliest inhabitants of the region.

Huargo Cave in Huánuco at an altitude of 4050 m above sea level (Lauricocha is at an equivalent altitude) is another stratified site which yielded remains of horse and llama, the worked rib of a scelotherium and a bone point. Paleobotanical evidence indicates that the environment at this time was colder and more humid than it is today.

Work on sites around the Pampa de Junín has produced evidence of a somewhat

4.14 Panaulauca Cave on the Pampa de Junín, Peru, a high-altitude (4150 m above sea level) base camp used from 8000 BC to AD 1000.

different economic pattern. The earliest occupants of the region seem to have been small nomadic bands who briefly utilized the small Pachamachay and other caves (Figure 4.14). By about 7000 BC however, they seem to have changed their subsistence strategy to specialized exploitation of camelids, almost certainly vicuña. The excavator, John Rick, suggests that the Pachamachay hunters were utilizing the cave as a base camp, living in it for much or most of the year, and harvesting the highly territorial and predictable (both in general habits and in reproductive ones) vicuña (Figure 4.15). Smaller, less intensely utilized rock shelters in the puna probably, according to this scenario, represent temporary hunting camps for harvesting vicuña in territories more than a day's walk from the base camp.

The Pachamachay materials present us with an extreme case of economic specialization, perhaps, but one which makes good sense given the species available for exploitation. Puna resources are very limited, much more so than those of the wetter páramo regions to the north. Aside from camelids the only important resources for humans are those found along the lake shores where some water plants, birds, and fish are available. However these are smaller and give less return for energy spent in obtaining them. Moreover, heat retention is a problem in the puna and getting wet is dangerous. Today people who fall in water go to bed for the rest of the day to replace the heat lost. A society which had simpler shelters and, presumably, simpler heating and other household arrangements might well avoid water's edge areas except in the warmest weather.

4.15 Floor of Pachamachay Cave on the Pampa de Junín. This late preceramic level shows an extremely high density of tools, including both projectile points and unifacial tools of various types.

Given the specific circumstances of the high puna, a highly specialized and rather sedentary group exhibiting little change through time might be expected. With the introduction of domesticated camelids, of course, patterns of exploitation of the puna changed and increased contact with outside societies commenced.

It is notable that just to the south of the Pampa de Junín the site of Ucumachay shows a much more diversified subsistence base. The inhabitants of this site, which is very near lower altitude valleys, depended heavily upon deer and had a more generalized hunting adaptation very similar to that found in other central Andean sites.

The excavations of Richard MacNeish near Ayacucho have been claimed to show the earliest occupation of the Andes yet known. While these claims have not been substantiated, later occupations of the series of caves he excavated are well established. The tool inventory from these caves is quite similar to that from Guitarrero and other early sites in the central Andes and includes tanged projectile points, gravers or burins, presumably for wood, bone or leather working, and a number of unifacial and bifacial tools. MacNeish sees the projectile points of the Huanta and following complexes (in which more types of projectile points appear) as representing a specialization to big game hunting, although shortly thereafter grinding tools and other indications of a heavy dependence upon plant foods appear in the archaeological record.

Numbers of sites have been discovered in the southern highlands of Peru and along the high ridge of the Andes which separates Chile and Bolivia. Most of these seem to be

4.16 The tool assemblage from Viscachani, Bolivia. This huge workshop site has yielded thousands of non-diagnostic tools such as these.

slightly later although, given the somewhat greater humidity of this area during the terminal Pleistocene and early Holocene, it seems likely that early occupations did exist. Numbers of sites have been found around the salares in the Atacama desert, apparently the remains of temporary campsites. Tools include blanks for large ovate tools and obsidian cores and debris found on the shores of the Salar de Talabre where a quarry was located. Over the border into Bolivia a number of lakeside campsites have yielded artifacts which seem to correspond to the Puripica complex as it was in the Atacama desert. Puripica tools include Ayampitín-like points and percussion flaked knives and show certain similarities to materials excavated at Lauricocha (II) as well. The presence of mortars indicates the exploitation of plant resources, but cannot be used as an indication of a later date.

In highland Bolivia the most famous site is that of Viscachani, a huge workshop by the side of a now dry glacial lake on the road from La Paz to Oruro. Numerous collections have been made from Viscachani and several "chronologies" have been suggested, on the basis of very little evidence (Figure 4.16). Viscachani seems to have been used for a very long time and implements typical of several industries have been found, including large bifacial knives, various flake tools, Sandia-like points, Ayampitín-like points, and so on.

The Ayampitín industry itself was first defined on the basis of discoveries in northwestern Argentina. The type site is an open air camp in the Department of Córdoba, exposed when a gully cut through the archaeological deposits. The industry includes the famous willow leaf points, many flake tools, and abundant grinding tools.

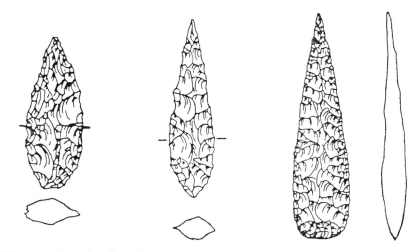

4.17 Ayampitín points from Guitarrero Cave. Ayampitín points, like fish tail points, are found widely across Andean South America, indicating, perhaps, their usefulness.

Ayampitín points have now been found at numerous other sites, of which the best known, because of its stratified deposits, is Intihuasi Cave. Here Ayampitín points were found to be more common in the lower levels although associated with other point styles as well (Figure 4.17). A second early northwest Argentinean industry is that of Ampajango, first identified in the Department of Catamarca. This industry is characterized by crude percussion flaking and a lack of projectile points. Because of its crudity it is often been considered to be early, although the poor workmanship may well be due to the refractory nature of the tough igneous rock used to form the characteristic flake tools and not to any earlier, more inept, population.

Sporadic finds of Paleoindian-type artifacts have been made in most of southeastern South America. A continuing occupation of Patagonia and Tierra del Fuego has been well documented. Apparently in the later Paleoindian period the division between inland guanaco hunters and maritime oriented hunter-fisher-gatherers began. Excavations at the Englefield site, Bahia Buena, and Punta Santa Ana on the Straits of Magellan show bone harpoons of various sorts to have been common. Other tools include bone awls, hammerstones, and obsidian scrapers and points. Obsidian tools are rare in interior sites and in eastern Patagonia, as well as in the more recent sites on the Straits of Magellan. This was a period of warmer, damper climate with a concomitant increase in forest. Apparently a fair amount of hunting on land typified these later Fuegians and their neighbors. In northern Patagonia numbers of sites along the shore have been found which date to the very end of the Paleoindian period or slightly later. These are shell mound sites along bays. These sites were occupied for thousands of years on a seasonal basis and dating is not very precise. Most show a maritime oriented people who used shell as a basic material for the fabrication of tools, containers, and other implements. Stone tools were relatively coarse and made on flakes from black basalt pebbles found along the shore. This Sanmatiense industry is typified by cutting tools and crude choppers. There is some indication that later peoples hunted inland for part of the year, since projectile points appear in the cultural inventory. North of Patagonia these basic industries were replaced (in the Buenos Aires region) by somewhat more sophisticated tool making techniques.

Sporadic finds of Paleoindian materials have been made in northeastern Argentina, Uruguay, and Paraguay; all show that by the early Holocene this entire region was occupied, sparsely perhaps, but occupied, by hunters and gatherers. These occupations are best known from southeastern Brazil, where energetic programs of investigation, especially in the caves and rock shelters which are abundant in much of the region, have provided a clear picture of the most ancient cultures. The Lagoa Santa Cave is famous for its human remains, which were originally claimed to be extremely early and to represent a somewhat different physical type from that of the modern Indians. These claims have long been shown to be erroneous, although the proponents of early glacial humans in the area remain vociferous. Re-excavation of Lagoa Santa and investigations in the many other caves which dot the region show that there was a Paleoindian occupation. Hunters exploited some of the large and now extinct Pleistocene fauna, but rather shortly switched to a more varied diet of mollusks, birds, and the medium-sized, mainly solitary, animals such as deer, paca (*Cuniculus paca*), agouti (*Dasyprocta aguti*), armadillo (*Dasypus* spp.), etc. which today typify this ecozone. Excavations in the Santana de Riacho rock shelter, where organic preservation is excellent, showed the use of wooden points and other wooden tools, as well as abundant bone and stone implements. Polished stone tools appear in the latest preceramic burials in this rock shelter. Work in the planalto has revealed remains of a similar set of cultures, characterized by an industry of unifacial flake tools. Stone projectile points are lacking in many sites until about 7000 BC, when fancy bifacially worked quartzite points appear (Bom Jardim and Pernambuco sites). All of these groups appear to have been seminomadic, utilizing the rock shelters on a seasonal basis, although some sites which were located near mineral sources and exceptionally rich food resources were more permanent. The dead were buried in the rock shelters, usually flexed and occasionally covered with ocher. At the Lapa Vermelha site, however, the dead seem to have been simply left in the site, which was then abandoned for a period. This practice is still found among some tropical forest groups, who leave the corpse in the house and move.

In Southwestern Goiâs a lithic tradition called Paranaiba has been delineated. Paranaiba tools are unifacial, thick flake implements and include some fruit processing equipment. The subsistence base is said to have been mainly hunting during the colder period of *c.* 8000–6000 BC.

The southeastern Brazilian sites are most noted for their abundant petroglyphs, some of which may date to this early epoch (Figure 4.18). It is notoriously difficult to date rock art, however, and even though pigments and pigment processing equipment have been found in some early contexts, the same pigments were used for cosmetics as well as for wall paintings. Most studies of the rock art have been classificatory, setting up stylistic groups and then attempting to seriate these into some sort of chronology. These

4.18 Petroglyphs from the planalto of Brazil. This scene of people gathering honey (?) or perhaps painting petroglyphs on a cave ceiling probably dates to considerably after the earliest occupation of Brazil. Dating petroglyphs is notoriously difficult.

attempts have not been notoriously successful. None of the rock paintings appears to show now-extinct fauna. Besides geometric patterns, various modern animals are common, especially deer. Humans, including scenes of various activities, also appear, as do representations of plants. Although the rock art is definitely prehistoric, most of the shelters in which it occurs were occupied for many centuries and, even after their abandonment as residences, they continued to be used ritually until very nearly the present era. It is possible that some of the petroglyphs do date to the earliest inhabitants of the region, but this is virtually impossible to prove.

The Paleoindian period came to an end between approximately 8000 and 6000 BC, depending upon specific sites and cultural definitions. Although the traditional picture of these first inhabitants of the South American continent is that of nomadic hunters of big game, this picture is becoming increasingly modified as research into these cultures continues. It is evident that the earliest arrivals were hunters, probably specializing in the larger herbivores such as the elephant, horse, and camelids which occupied the open savannas of the upper altitudes of Central and South America. It is also evident that some now extinct species were important to some of these groups. But associations between Pleistocene fauna and human remains are still relatively rare and it does not appear as if these larger species long survived human predation and the forces of climatic change. Most of the Paleoindian cultures seem to have changed their prime orientation to one of more generalized hunting and gathering. The site of Monte Verde, with its abundant vegetal remains, shows that even the very early hunters, who were killing large animals, did not disdain vegetable food. Better recovery techniques for small bone (including fish) and plant remains suggest, in fact, that fish, birds, and small animals, along with seeds and fruits, were extremely important in the diet of the

Paleoindian hunters. Even though specialized hunting has been said to have been characteristic of Upper Paleolithic peoples in much of the world, it has perhaps been over-stressed, to the under-appreciation of other sources of food. The Pampa de Junín sites do show a heavy emphasis upon hunting and, indeed, upon hunting a single species, the vicuña, but this is a unique, rather limited ecosystem. Other groups seem, from the very beginning, to have had a broader subsistence base. This is only reasonable, since the climate was unstable and humans were having to adjust their material culture and tastes to changing habitats. That they were successful is shown by the evidence of growing populations throughout the Paleoindian period and into the succeeding epochs. By 6000 BC most of the available ecosystems of South America were inhabited and being exploited by humans who were hunting a wide variety of animals, gathering plant and animal foods and, in some areas, beginning to experiment with plant and animal domestication.

CHAPTER 5

SETTLING DOWN: 6000–3500 BC

The hunting and gathering cultures of the terminal Pleistocene and early Holocene did not disappear overnight. Over much of the continent the broader based foraging strategies typical of most later hunters continued to be dominant for some thousands of years. However, *c.* 6000 BC, or perhaps a little earlier on the western margins of the continent, there was a notable population increase along the seashore. The earlier hunters had, of course, been active in the coastal valleys for a long time. Their activities along the coastal plain are much less well known, although it has been suggested that the slim, long points typical of some of these later hunting peoples were, in fact, being used as fish spears. Beginning in the seventh millennium coastal sites, many with attendant shell mounds, started to become common. The best known of these cultures are along the Pacific coast from the Santa Elena Peninsula of Ecuador to near Antofagosta, in northern Chile (Figure 5.1). The Caribbean region witnessed a similar phenomenon, but this is less well known. The land hunting cultures survived in the Venezuelan savannas where the site of Canaima in the state of Bolivar dates to this period, or slightly later. Canaima is a workshop/camp site with abundant tools, including triangular, barbed projectile points and scrapers, out of a local jasper. All tools suggest a purely land hunting economy.

However, in central and western Venezuela and in Colombia several sites show that there was a littoral tradition developing, albeit at a somewhat later date than on the Pacific coastline. Most of the Venezuelan shell mound sites date to *c.* 2500 BC or later. Both preceramic and ceramic-bearing sites are known and the better known sites show that some agriculture was being practiced. No precursors of these sites have yet been identified. In adjacent Colombia ceramics-yielding shell mound sites are earlier than elsewhere on the continent. The alluvial plains of the Caribbean lowlands of Colombia are very hot; extensive estuaries lined with mangrove swamps bisect the arid littoral savanna and the flood plains of the rivers are characterized by numerous ox-bow lakes and lagoons. Agriculture is not possible in this environment without fairly sophisticated water control (drainage, irrigation), but the estuaries, rivers, and coast offer an abundance of fish, shellfish, crocodiles, iguanas, turtles, and waterfowl, and small mammals are plentiful. The forests which existed in the region up to perhaps 150 years ago were sources of palms, whose fruit was an important food, honey, other fruits, mammals, and birds. The type site of this region is Puerto Hormiga, a group of shell mounds on a now silted outlet of the Magdalena River (Figure 5.2). The principal mound is a ring of clam shells, the remains of what was once a small village of small flimsy houses arranged in a bracket-shaped pattern, with entrances into the central plaza

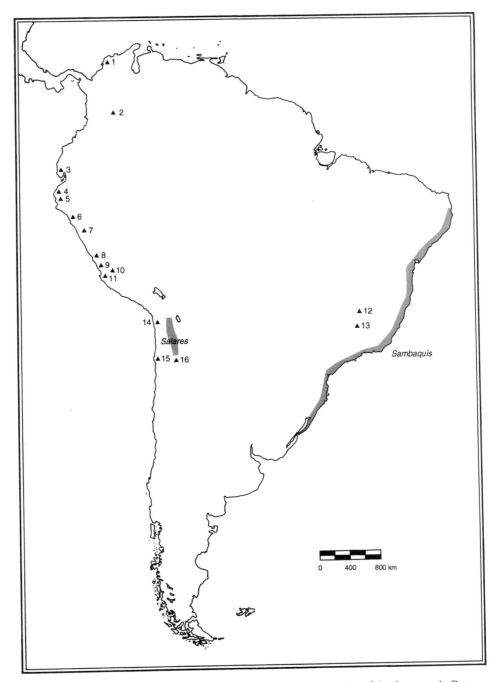

5.1 Principal preceramic and early ceramic sites mentioned in the text. 1. Puerto Hormiga, Monsú, San Jacinto, Bucarelia, 2. Sabana de Bogotá, Tequendama, Zipacón, Chia, 3. Vegas, Valdivia, Loma Alta, Real Alto, 4. La Emerenciana, 5. Talará, 6. Huaca Prieta, 7. Guitarrero Cave, 8. Ancón, 9. Paloma, Chilca Valley, 10. Ayacucho, 11. Cabezas Largas, 12. Santana de Riacho, 13. Lagoa Santa (Minas Gerais), 14. Quiani, Taltal, Tiliviche, 15. Las Conchas, 16. Atacama.

5.2 Excavations at the Puerto Hormiga shell mound on the Caribbean coast of Colombia. The slight rise caused by the accumulation of garbage and the high shell content of this garbage are clearly visible.

diagonally across from each other on either end of the communal space. Puerto Hormiga is dated to about 3100 BC and all levels contain ceramics, including two decorated wares (see Figure 8.1). None of the vessel fragments shows signs of having been used in the fire but the shellfish (mainly clams and oysters) were apparently cooked. What appear to be boiling stones are abundant in the midden, suggesting that stone boiling was the prevalent culinary practice, at least for shellfish. The ceramic vessels themselves were probably used for the preparation and serving of liquids (beer? soup?). Grinding stones and hammerstones for the preparation of plant foods are abundant, as are a variety of scraping tools and large choppers made of a local chert. A number of sites similar to Puerto Hormiga, perhaps even earlier, and with different ceramics have been located as well, showing that this lifestyle was widespread along the Caribbean coastal plain.

The site of Bucarelia, about 150 km inland on the Magdalena River, reveals another version of this coastal culture. Here the economic base was not shellfish gathering and small-game hunting but river fishing; the dominant tools are large bone harpoons. At Bucarelia only the more compact of the fiber tempered wares of Puerto Hormiga are in evidence, along with a similar sand tempered decorated ware.

In the highlands, the sites on the Sabana de Bogotá continued in use for a time, their tool inventories showing a continued adaptation to forest conditions. Prismatic blades and spokeshaves (probably for straightening spear shafts) are common implements. Deer were an important part of the diet, as were rodents, especially the guinea pig.

There is a notable increase in the size of the bones of the guinea pigs in Zone III of the Tequendama rock shelters, a fact that the excavators suggest is an indication of incipient domestication. Shells of land gastropods are also common in the midden, showing an increasing importance of gathering. *C.* 4000 BC there was a significant decrease in the number of sites in the Sabana and surrounding highland regions, although these areas were not completely abandoned as sites such as Chia I were occupied for some thousands of years more. Chia I, however, contains numbers of hammerstones (along with its standard Abriense tool inventory) and the excavator, Gerardo Ardila, suggests these indicate a new importance of tuber and root foods in the diet. The decline in population corresponds very closely to an interval of extreme aridity in the Colombian highlands and it has been suggested that the long dry spell, with the shrinking of the forests and drastic decrease in their resources, was one factor which led to the development of the shoreline communities dependent upon water resources, gathered plant food and, ultimately then, led to new forms of food acquisition. Chia I overlaps in time the Zipacón rock shelter with its remains of ceramics and agricultural products (maize, sweet potato, avocado, *Prunus*). The site dates to the second millennium BC and is the only evidence for early agriculturalists on the Sabana. The Sabana sites were not reoccupied until *c.* 500 BC when agricultural peoples of the Herrera Phase colonized the region, bringing with them incised and punctate decorated ceramics. The Herrera Phase peoples then occupied the Sabana until *c.* AD 800 when peoples recognizable as the historic Muisca appear in the area.

The Pacific coast of Colombia and northern Ecuador is unstable owing to ocean storms, tsunamis, and active river/estuary systems. This region has yielded few indications of early populations; presumably these sites are under water or have been washed away as the sea continually modifies the coastline. Our best view of events in this area comes from the Santa Elena Peninsula where the Vegas culture has been extensively studied by Karen Stothert. The Vegas people are the earliest known inhabitants of this now arid region. The contents of their sites show a fairly intensive use of all the available ecosystems of the region. The Vegas sites tend to be in locations where a number of different resource zones were readily available for exploitation. Most are near water and mangrove-bearing areas since the mangrove mollusk *Anadera tuberculosa* was important in their diet. However, unlike some of the truly maritime oriented peoples further south, although fishing was very important to the Vegas people, land hunting seems to have been important as well. Deer, peccary, fox, lizard, rabbit, birds, and snakes were hunted and eaten. Vegetable food, both gathered and perhaps grown, included maize, squash, and gourds. Sites were apparently semi-permanent and occupied throughout the year. The tool inventory was rather simple, including many flakes of local chert, some heavy choppers, hammerstones, grinding stones and ocher, the latter presumably used for body decoration. Burials show both dolichocephalic and brachycephalic individuals and burial practices were quite varied. Both shallow and deep burials of flexed individuals were found associated with hammerstones rubbed with ocher. Secondary burials, both single or of multiple individuals were also found in shallow and deep pits; occasionally single flexed and secondary burials were associated (Figure 5.3).

5.3 Double burial of the Vegas culture, Santa Elena Peninsula, Ecuador. The flexed, articulated skeleton of a woman was buried with the disarticulated bones of an adolescent of about 14 years old. The way the bones of the child are placed indicates that they were wrapped in a packet of some sort.

5.4 Excavation of a small circular house located within the deep aceramic shell mound deposits at Ancón, Peru. Circular houses of various sizes, usually with perishable walls and thatched roofs, were typical of many preceramic coastal cultures.

The Vegas complex is dated to 8000–4700 BC and was apparently terminated by a long dry period during which the peninsula was abandoned.

To the south near the Talará tar pits the Siches-Estero phase (8000–5000 BC) shows sites similarly located on dry ground overlooking estuaries. The Siches-Estero peoples were gathering quantities of *Anadera* but were also fishing for sharks, catfish, etc. in the estuaries. There is no evidence of deep sea fishing. The stone industry is one of direct percussion on local quartzite and includes many pointed tools, denticulates, and spokeshaves. Cup-shaped mortars, stone bowls, net weights, and ground T-shaped stone axes also occur. A similar axe was found in a Vegas burial. The tool inventory shows a major emphasis on wood working and upon gathered plant and shell foods. A second site, El Estero, is located on a pass through the hills to the coast, on the edge of a now dry pond. This site seems to have been a manufacturing station for ground stone axes, as these are found in all stages of manufacture.

Most of the other early preceramic sites investigated in coastal Peru are somewhat later. The Encanto phase at Ancón, for example, has an initial date of *c.* 3600 BC. Encanto sites are inland from the Bay of Ancón, in an area with no potable water (Figure 5.4). Several of the sites are located near now dead lomas areas. The type site, Encanto, is 5 km inland and covers an area somewhat larger than 100 × 200 m (an unknown portion of the site is covered with sand dunes). The Encanto tool inventory includes sea-shell artifacts, some flaked stone tools, projectile points, and manos and metates. Extensive use of the rocky shore is evidenced by the numerous rock-perching molluskan remains found in the midden, along with many small fish vertebrae and deer bones. The bulk of animal food is maritime in origin. Plant remains, including domesticated bottle gourd, squash, and sedge seeds show a growing importance of plant foods. It is presumed that the squash and gourd, plants which need little care, were grown on the river flood plain where they could simply be sown and then ignored until they bore. Shortly after the Encanto phase most of the Peruvian coast underwent considerable population growth and cultural development.

However, by 3500 BC there were still only scattered villages of semi-sedentary hunters and fishers along most of the strand. From the south coast at Chilca a house dating to this time period has been excavated. It is circular and semi-subterranean with a superstructure of grass and cane tied with grass ropes to braces of cane and whalebone. The house is very similar to structures which were until recently being constructed by fishermen in the area and much like early houses located not just along the coast at Ancón and on the Santa Elena Peninsula, but to the houses excavated by Jean Guffroy in Loja in the southern Ecuadorian Andes. The Chilca house was abandoned after some sort of tragedy (the excavator suggests disease or food-poisoning) in which seven individuals of varying ages and sexes died and were placed in the house, wrapped in junco grass mats. The house was then deliberately collapsed and covered with sand. The Chilca site was occupied long before this house (and many others like it) were built and continued to be occupied for some time after the multiple burial. The Chilca midden shows a preponderance of shell and fish bone with some marine mammals. The whalebone used in the house construction probably came from a beached whale since no water craft suitable for whaling were ever possessed by the ancient Peruvians. Wild plant foods are represented in the midden as is the bottle gourd, the major source of containers for food and liquid in all these preceramic cultures.

Excavations by Jeffrey Quilter at Paloma, on the northern edge of the Chilca Valley on the edge of a loma, have revealed a fishing village like Chilca I, with similar houses and quite similar burial practices. Paloma is of great interest because of the carefully excavated and analyzed burials found at the site. These give us considerable information not only on mortuary practices, but on health and mortality in this ancient fishing population. The Palomans buried their dead in their houses, starting with burials along the walls and usually finishing the occupation history of the house when a burial, always of an adult male, was made in the center of the house. Sometimes, however, the dead were simply left on the floor and the house destroyed around them. The locations of the burials *vis-à-vis* the houses Quilter thinks indicate the importance of the family in life and death, an importance perhaps greater than that of the village or group as a whole. The largest number of burials are of infants and young children, reflecting an infant mortality of over 30%. The large number of women who died in their thirties rather than younger, as is common in simple societies, suggests that deferred child bearing was one means of limiting the population. The preponderance of dead female infants suggests another means of population limitation. The Paloma people suffered from a number of infirmities including carcinomas, tuberculosis, broken bones, and osteoarthritis. One young man had obviously died of shark bite, probably a common danger for fishermen in this region. Finally the discovery of a double burial of two men (one in his late 40s the other 21 years of age), laid to rest in an embrace, accompanied with an unusual number of offerings, is eerily like that of the "lovers" excavated by Karen Stothert at the Las Vegas site in Ecuador. Quilter suggests that one of the men of Burial 142 may have been a shaman because a calcite crystal was associated with the burial, as was a staff. These are artifacts often associated with shamans in South America.

Cultures of this era of gradual transformation from hunting and gathering to more sedentary gatherers, fishers, and farmers are better represented in the highlands where a number of the major cave sites mentioned in the previous chapter have occupations dating to this era. At Guitarrero Cave the earliest remains of cultivated beans, *Phaseolus vulgaris* and *Phaseolus lunatus* (the common bean and lima bean, respectively) in South America have appeared in levels dating to *c.* 8500–5500 BC. There is no doubt that these beans were fully domesticated, since they are as large as modern specimens and have none of the features of wild beans. Ulluco (*Ullucus tuberosus*) and oca (*Oxalis* spp.) were also exploited, although they may not have been truly domesticated. Lúcuma (*Pouteria lucuma*), pacay (*Inga* spp.) fruits and cactus fruits also appear in this early diet and were, perhaps, semi-domesticated. During the same time span there was a change in emphasis from deer to camelids which suggests that, as in the slightly later levels 5 and 4 of Ucumachay Cave on the southern Pampa de Junín, a process of intensification of camelid exploitation was taking place through increasing control over camelid territories and the breeding of the semi-domesticated camelids. This ultimately led to herding the camelids and further breeding control as well as the emergence of the modern domestic species. Similar evidence is reported from the Ayacucho caves. Ucumachay has also yielded the first evidence of domesticated dog in Peru, in level 5 (*c.* 5500–4200 BC), somewhat earlier than such remains appear at Pachamachay (where the inhabitants were still engaging in highly specialized vicuña predation) and at Lauricocha. Evidence of guinea pig domestication is less abundant, although domesticated guinea pigs appear on the coast by about 2500 BC; this argues for an earlier domestication in the highlands, where they are found wild, although little evidence is yet forthcoming.

Virtually nothing is known of the preceramic eras in the southern highlands, including the altiplano, although the hunting sites around the salares on the Bolivian-Chilean border also continued in use. Numbers of workshops have been identified along the salares and on the middle terraces of the río Loa. These show a varied tool assemblage in which small projectile points and some microlithic tools are notable. The Patapane site in the salt puna, along with a number of other highland open campsites, shows a gradual change from the exploitation of the relatively stable wildlife of the puna (an exuberant avifauna, especially around the still extant shallow saline lakes, small animals such as the guinea pig, viscacha, and chinchilla, camelids, and deer, here *Hippocamelus anticencis*), to permanent sites which the excavators think indicate that camelid domestication was accomplished and that camelid pastoralism had become a dominant mode of subsistence. Plant remains at Patapane include ulluco, oca, and isañu (*Tropallum tuberculum*), showing that as in Peru the modern highland diet of camelid flesh and tubers was being established.

5.5 Excavation of a stratified midden at Caleta Abtao near Antofagosta, Chile. The extreme dryness of the desert preserves shell, bone, and plant remains so well that the relative importance of these elements in the ancient diet is readily discernible.

Chilean sites on the coast and the coastal plain have been much better explored (Figure 5.5). The Las Conchas culture, just to the north of Antofagosta, dates to *c.* 7500 BC and is the first indicator of a move towards coastal exploitation. It is hypothesized that the settlers of this shell midden came from the inland valleys and oases where there is some evidence of contact with the coast. Las Conchas tools include choppers and flake tools, pressure flaked core tools, mortars, plummets, and a series of bone tools apparently used for digging shellfish. Geometric sandstone objects whose use is unknown also characterize the Las Conchas cultural inventory (Figure 5.6). A large percentage of the Las Conchas diet was made up of shellfish, especially a local abalone (*Concholepas concholepas*), several species of keyhole limpet (*Fisurella*), fish, and sea lions. Land animals are represented by the guanaco and some unidentified birds. Las Conchas is remarkable in that it has preserved very early evidence for the use of hallucinogens in South America. The mortars found at Las Conchas are unexpected since there was apparently little or no plant food available for grinding. Their small size also suggests that they must have been used for some purpose other than food production (i.e. for pigments, seasonings, tobacco, or other drugs). Analysis of some small seeds found in the midden showed, even though the exact species could not be identified, that the seeds contained harmine, an alkaloid which is one of the psychotropic elements in ayahuasca (or yaagi, *Banisteriopsis* spp.), a hallucinogenic plant used by modern lowland groups. Presumably the seeds were ground to make snuff, one of the standard ways of ingesting

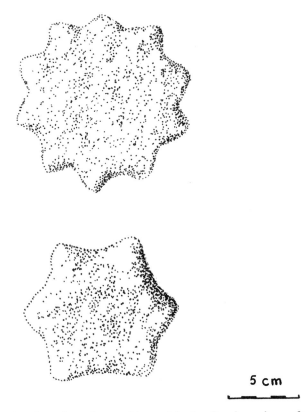

5 cm

5.6 Enigmatic sandstone objects of the Las Conchas culture of the Chilean coast, also near Antofagosta.

hallucinogenic substances in South America. Chemical analyses of snuffs from later contexts (the Solcor 2 cemetery) show that the snuffing material contained a number of alkaloids which are found in trees of the *Anadenanthera* (formerly *Piptadenia*) genus. The samples were taken from bags buried with the dead which contained tubes, trays, and the material to be used on them. Evidence of snuff taking in the form of tablets and bone or wooden snuffing tubes is common from slightly later contexts throughout the Andean region and coastal Brazil and the use of hallucinogenic substances in curing and divination continues to this day in much of South America.

Along the coast the "Shell Fishhook Culture" of Junius Bird (now generally called Quiani I) has been found at a large number of sites. The culture was originally named from its distinctive fishhooks cut out of mussel shells (which distinguished it from the slightly later cactus fishhook makers) and is now known to have occurred from Quiani to south of Taltal (Figure 5.7). Quiani I appears *c.* 5000 BC and represents a specialized littoral adaptation. Fish, shellfish, sea lions, turtles, and birds made up the majority of the Quiani diet; guanaco bone artifacts show that the Quiani people did some inland hunting as well. The appearance of mortars may indicate some use of plant foods, including a continuing use of hallucinogens. Quiani I sites are large shell mounds,

5.7 Shell and cactus spine fishhooks of the Las Conchas culture. Similar fishhooks were used by many peoples along the coasts of South America.

reflecting their most abundant source of protein. Tools include both the shell fishhooks and composite hooks made of a bone point tied to an elongated weight, harpoons, barbed bone points, stone knives and projectile points, and other specialized fishing and marine hunting gear. The presence of deep sea fish in the midden indicates that fishermen had some means of getting out to deep water, perhaps either the inflated sea lion skins used in southern Peru from ancient times until quite recently or reed floats similar to the *caballitos del mar* still used in northern Peru (Figure 5.8). A reed boat of this type was found at the much later (third century AD) site of Caleta Huelén. Beginning *c.* 4000 BC, domesticated plants begin to appear in the Quiani I sites indicating a general experimentation with domesticating plants, including maize (which is very early in this complex, perhaps as early as *c.* 6000 BC), although the role of agriculture remained negligible.

Quiani II, the "Cactus Fishhook Culture" of Bird appears *c.* 3500 BC. Fishhooks and the barbs on harpoons began to be made of cactus spines (in Peru cactus spine fishhooks are earlier than shell ones, in Chile it is the reverse). The economy was essentially unchanged: shore gathering and fishing supplemented by some land hunting remained the major economic activities. A cemetery at Quiani contained extended burials. The bodies had few offerings other than clothing of woolen cords and vegetable fiber loincloths. Both Quiani I and II had access to domesticated corn. Cotton appears at the very end of Quiani II. Otherwise the role of agriculture, at least for the production of food, was minimal. Domesticated plants apparently came from the interior. Work at the site of Tiliviche 1b, located by a dry quebrada of that name some 32 km inland, has produced evidence of early maize agriculture and this is probably the source of the

5.8 Fisherman with his reed boat/float (*caballito del mar*) near Huanchaco, Peru. Note the bamboo lath paddle. There are no trees in this arid land to provide long enough pieces of wood for paddles.

coastal corn. Tiliviche 1b is located about 1000 m above sea level and is an oval of rubbish and house remains some 80 × 55 m in size. The approximately ninety houses are similar to the Chilca house in form and materials. This region, although a saline pampa with only seasonal watercourses today, appears to have had more water in the 6000–4000 BC time frame of Tiliviche 1b. The tool inventory includes, besides abundant mortars and pestles, stone projectiles, scrapers, etc., bone tools, including engraved spatulas, and shell fishhooks. Shellfish remains are common in the midden, as are those of other fish and marine mammals. Abundant remains of wild plants used both for food and for fiber and construction materials were found. However, the most interesting aspect of Tiliviche 1b is that there are remains of maize of the race *Piricinco coroico*. The site seems to have been a seasonal one and the excavators suggest that it is the campsite of transhumant fishers-hunters, pausing on their round from coast to mountains to grow a little corn. Interestingly enough the contemporary site of Aragón (level 5), 5 km south of Tiliviche, shows little evidence of use of marine resources and no corn, although later occupations do indicate significantly more interchange with the coast.

The northern Chilean sites indicate a precocious development of agriculture in one sense, although any reliance upon domesticated crops for subsistence lay far in the future. The climate during this period seems to have been more humid with warmer sea temperatures, as evidenced by the presence in Las Conchas middens of species which are no longer to be found in the waters off northern Chile. A cooling trend (with a short regression to warmer conditions) seems to have begun by *c.* 3000–2000 BC with the rapid development of modern cold-water conditions. The more amiable climate of these preceramic cultures may have fostered the evidently growing population through more abundant resources in many ecozones. However, claims of true transhumance for these communities may be premature, since there are other factors which could account for the interchange of foodstuffs and tool types between them (intermarriage, kin ties of long standing, gift exchanges, trade, etc.). The interior communities in particular may have been seasonal settlements.

A similar move to the coast took place in eastern South America along the coasts of Argentina and Brazil. The Patagonian situation has been mentioned previously. Shell mound sites continue through this period (and, indeed, for centuries beyond), showing a seasonal use of the littoral resources. In the planalto of Brazil the centuries between 7000–4000 BC saw a climatic optimum, a hot and humid period in which vegetation was considerably more abundant. During this period many of the rock shelters were abandoned and shellfish gatherers appear along the beaches and estuaries. The phenomena of the abandonment of the interior and the population of the water's edge may be related. This is the time when the sambaquís, the huge shell mounds which formerly lined the coast of southeastern Brazil, first appear (Figure 5.9). The major occupation of the sambaquís was somewhat later, beginning *c.* 2000 BC, but the move towards exploiting the coastal resources seems to have begun much earlier (Figure 5.10). To the south and west of the planalto the rock shelters of Minas Gerais were not abandoned as speedily. Lagoa Santa has some burials of a gracile folk dating to this time period and Santana de Riacho shows a continuing occupation. The preservation conditions in this latter rock shelter are particularly good and show the extensive use of wood and bone for tools as well as the importance of vegetable foods and vegetable fibers. Some ground stone tools appear in these levels, including manos, axes, fragmentary receptacles, and a schist labret. Palettes, shells, and brushes for painting are found in the burials along with remains of palm nuts and roasted pequi fruits. This site was apparently a rainy season camp, to judge from the mollusk and fruit remains. Although no other remains of other cultivated plants have been found, maize does appear in the third-millennium BC levels. This is a rather aberrant appearance of corn and no other sites have, as yet, yielded similar remains. Protein sources include a giant snail of the Strophocheilidae, which yields about 100 gm of meat per mollusk, and deer, the latter increasing in numbers significantly through time. Other, smaller, forest animals were hunted as well. Most of the food remains are from fireplaces, a good indication that these are actually remains of meals. Burials were commonly made in the rock shelter, many of them of people lacking some body part. The flexed bodies had the arms raised by the head, a common feature of burials in this region. Some heaps of cordage suggest that the bodies were wrapped in their hammocks or in large pieces of netting. Grave goods include flaked stone tools, wooden objects, and similar utilitarian offerings. There was a sexual and age division of offerings; males were buried with stone tools and females and juveniles with wooden artifacts and vegetable offerings. The

5.9 Sambaquí de Carniça, near Laguna, Santa Caterina State, Brazil. Although both mined and excavated, the immense size of this Brazilian shell mound is immediately visible.

Santana rock shelter is one of the few sites in which there is some indication of the age of the petroglyphs which are so abundant in this region. Fallen blocks in the lowest level, dated at *c.* 7000 BC have some red and yellow X-like figures on them and representations of deer and fish in red and black. At the neighboring rock shelter of Sucupia similar figures are covered with calcite, indicating a certain antiquity here as well.

The Santana de Riacho rock shelter and others in the region give an interesting picture of a lifestyle of seasonal movements to harvest plant and animal species. Although open air sites are said to abound in the little valleys that edge the Sierra do Cipó, few have been investigated. Some of these sites have semi-subterranean houses typical of the later preceramic and early ceramic cultures of the region. Future investigations of these sites should yield more specific information concerning the development of maize agriculture and its role in population growth and social change in this region.

By *c.* 3000 BC much of the Caribbean coast and the Andean coastal region was dotted with small semi-permanent settlements dependent upon a combination of fishing,

5.10 The sambaquí peoples exploited the forested land adjacent to the shore. Remnant forest on Santa Caterina Island near Florianopolis, Brazil.

shellfish gathering, hunting, and some amount of agriculture. Less is known of the inland groups, although it is suspected that they were agricultural at a somewhat earlier date (at least in Peru, where evidence from Guitarrero Cave in the Callejón de Huaylas has yielded very early dates for domesticated beans and, just slightly later, cultivated rhizomes, peppers, and, by *c.* 5500–2000 BC, maize). However, open air villages remain less known so that our best understanding of this period perforce comes from coastal sites. A good example of these small coastal villages, albeit a slightly later one, is Huaca Prieta in the Chicama Valley of northern Peru (Figure 5.11), excavated by Junius Bird. Huaca Prieta was the first preceramic village in Peru to be systematically investigated. This sedentary population at the mouth of the Chicama River first lived in flimsy cane and adobe houses above ground, but soon changed to semi-subterranean houses lined with cobbles (Figure 5.12). Subsequently investigated preceramic sites in the north show much the same pattern, except that the houses are sometimes lined with adobe bricks. Presumably they had perishable superstructures of cane and grass. The inhabitants of Huaca Prieta were completely without ceramics, depending upon gourds for dishes and containers. The economic base was shoreline and river valley gathering, with surprisingly little terrestrial hunting being practiced. Sedge tubers, cattail bulbs, and fruits were gathered, but the increased role of agriculture is evident from the first occupation. In the damp soils of the valley flood plain a number of crops were grown, including achira, lima beans, canavalia beans, chile pepper, and, occasionally, cotton. It is the widespread growing of cotton that sets off the later Peruvian preceramic. Even in

5.11 Huaca Prieta, Chicama Valley, Peru. This immense mound is formed entirely of superimposed levels of trash and architectural remains. The name "Dark Site" comes from the high organic content of the mound, which makes it darker than the surrounding non-cultural dirt.

sites where dependence upon agriculture was apparently minimal, cotton is present. All cotton seems to be *Gossypium barbadense L.*, of which numbers of domesticated, feral, and wild forms are known in South America. Variations in fiber color (brown, reddish brown, "near-white," etc.) seem, from archaeological specimens, to have been selected for very early in the domestication process. The earliest examples of cotton still have a small boll and the fuzzy seed characteristic of wild cottons, indicating a very early stage in the domestication process. Boll size increased rapidly through time, showing clearly the interests of these early plant breeders.

At Huaca Prieta, where organic preservation was very good, numbers of twined textiles have survived. These show the textile arts to have been highly developed and a number of themes and patterns which were to remain favorites throughout prehistory ornament these early textiles. Designs were achieved both by changes in direction of the twining, creating a textural difference, and by dyeing with indigo. This latter may have still been wild, although it is easy to grow. However, the process of converting the indigo plant into a dye is fairly complicated and again indicates the sophistication of these seemingly simple farmers and gatherers. Fish nets, bags, baskets, and other textile implements were also made by twining and looping (Figure 5.13). The tool inventory of Huaca Prieta is relatively simple: flaked stone knives, choppers, net weights, scrapers, rare stone bowls, bone awls, thorn needles, and so on. Apparently water craft were lacking.

5.12 Cut through Huaca Prieta showing the superimposed levels of construction. Until power equipment became common, people throughout the world found it simpler to level their old buildings and rebuild on top.

5.13 Fragmentary sling from Huaca Prieta. Slings are still used for hunting birds and small animals and herding camelids.

Sites similar to Huaca Prieta have been found all along the coast of Peru and southern Ecuador. The Ecuadorian sites, however, are much more highly developed than the Peruvian ones. Pottery, full reliance upon agriculture, economic specialization and, perhaps, functionally differentiated architecture all appear very early, anticipating the appearance of these features in the rest of the Andes by some centuries.

The best known of these early Ecuadorian cultures is that of Valdivia, whose type site is a small fishing village just to the north of the Santa Elena Peninsula (Figure 5.14). Excavations at Valdivia in the 1950s, conducted by Emilio Estrada, Betty J. Meggers, and Clifford Evans, showed that ceramics were present by about 3000 BC. This early ceramic tradition is largely one of bowls and semi-closed cooking vessels; small, solid figurines, mainly of females, are also common (see Figure 8.2). The ceramics are competently made and fired and the decorations on some forms are esthetically sophisticated. Curiously enough, a geometric face motif on bowls of Valdivia Phase III–IV (Betsy Hill's seriation) is nearly identical to similar face motifs on engraved gourds from Huaca Prieta, suggesting some contact between the cultures of Ecuador and Peru even at this early date, perhaps some sort of down-the-line trade between the Valdivia villages and those of northern Peru. Since Valdivia sites have now been found as far south as the Peru-Ecuador border (and very likely occur in Peru as far south as Tumbes), ideas of contact which once seemed far-fetched become more plausible. The discovery of spondylus shell ornaments in Preceramic sites in Peru is another indication of some trade between these coastal cultures.

Valdivia itself was a village of flimsy cane houses, probably very similar to those still being built (Figure 5.15). People depended heavily upon the sea for food; fish both from estuaries and from the rocky shoals and reefs are found in Valdivia middens. Apparently

5.14 The archaeological village of Valdivia in coastal Ecuador, is largely coterminous with the modern village but also extends out of the way of floods onto the higher dune region. The high shell content of the site is visible in this photograph as are the holes made by looters.

water craft, either dugout canoes or balsa rafts, were used, to get several kilometers offshore to where the fish were. A Valdivia shrine on the island of La Plata, 23 km off shore and a site which retained its ritual importance until the coming of the Spanish, testifies to the sea-going abilities of these early fishermen.

Valdivia sites are found inland as well; sites such as Loma Alta, 15 km from the sea, show the diversification of Valdivia economy and the dependence of the shore and inland villages upon each other's produce. This is a common practice today and even villages which are literally contiguous, such as Valdivia and San Pedro, are occupationally specialized, forming bonds through the exchange of foodstuffs.

Valdivia domesticated crops included cotton, gourds, achira, canavalia beans, and maize. The distribution of settlements and the pattern of their founding suggest an agricultural people practicing floodplain agriculture and moving, as populations grew, to occupy and farm all the available land of the river valleys of the Guayas coast. Some swidden agriculture may have been practiced on the forested hill slopes, especially in wet years. Certainly this is strongly indicated by the succeeding Machalilla period. Hunting deer, peccary, and birds was important at all Valdivia sites. Domestic dogs were present, both as food and as offerings. From Loma Alta there is also some evidence of cannibalism. Fish were traded inland, presumably in exchange for agricultural produce, as both coast and inland had the same wild species available for hunting.

5.15 Traditional house at Salango, north of Valdivia. Houses such as these, which differ only slightly from those built in ancient times, are now being replaced by cement block and acrylic sheet roof construction. The houses are constructed upon stilts not only for ventilation, but because these coastal regions often flood in storms or in El Niño years.

One of the most thoroughly investigated Valdivia sites is Real Alto, located on an old strand in the Chanduy Valley to the south of the Santa Elena Peninsula. Real Alto is a large village of about 300 × 400 m in size, although debris is not distributed equally over the area. The major occupation was in Valdivia III when the inhabitants of Real Alto lived in large houses with mud plastered walls and thatched gabled roofs. The size of these suggests that they housed extended families rather than nuclear ones. The houses were arranged around a long rectangular plaza which was divided into two segments by two larger, special purpose buildings. One of these, placed on a natural rise modified with stairs cut into the clay, has been named the "Fiesta House" by the excavators, as it contained a number of refuse pits, filled with the remains of drinking bowls, larger pots apparently used for liquid containers, and serving dishes. The animal remains represented in these refuse pits – razor clams, crab claws, lobster, scallop, and turtle remains and deer bone – are different from ordinary midden contents and may represent the remains of meals made up of delicacies. The excavators, Donald Lathrap and Jorge Marcos, suggest that this building was used for ceremonials involving beer drinking and special meals and that the vessels used in the ceremonies and the garbage from the meals were ritually disposed of within the building itself. Across from the "Fiesta

House" was the "Charnel House," a largish, non-domestic structure associated with a large number of burials. The most important burial was of a woman found in a tomb under the threshold. A series of stacked secondary burials and the dismembered, apparently defleshed, body of a young man with seven chert knives were buried next to the woman. The excavators suggest that the secondary burials represent periodic offerings to the woman under the threshold, with the dismembered male being the last (and hence not removed and replaced) of a series of sacrifices (some later publications on Real Alto suggest that the secondary burials may not have been offerings, however, but simply interments of family members or other designated people in this special house). Other burials at Real Alto are less well known except that there seem to be dedicatory or guardian burials at every structure.

Real Alto later turned from a large village with a ceremonial focus on these two structures to a simple ceremonial center as people moved out to occupy more and more of the river floodplains and formed first satellite communities and then important centers away from Real Alto. Donald Lathrap has suggested that this process may have been accompanied by intensified activity in the Fiesta and Charnel Houses with Real Alto becoming a true ceremonial center for the dispersed population, beginning as early as Valdivia III. By Valdivia VI the Charnel House was abandoned and the Fiesta House suffered a similar fate in Valdivia VII. Other centers had taken over the functions of Real Alto.

By 2500 BC agriculture was firmly established both in the highlands and along the coasts of Andean South America. Shortly thereafter evidence for agricultural communities began to appear in the less well-known regions of Amazonia and the eastern tropical highlands. In Ecuador, northern Chile, and in some of the Peruvian sites there seems to have been economic interchange between the inhabitants of the major environmental zones; an exploitation of verticality which was to remain typical of Andean societies until modern times. Just how this interchange was organized and how long the chains of exchange were is a matter of some discussion. Vicuña skins in the burials of Cabezas Largas in southern Peru certainly show some continuing contact with the adjacent highlands. The presence of harmine-containing seeds at Las Conchas may well indicate similar exchanges. The prevalence of snuff trays and snuffing tubes at many of the only slightly later sites along the coast (including Huaca Prieta) could be evidence of interaction between the highland and even the tropical forested zones and the coast. Unfortunately there are a great many substances which can be utilized as hallucinogens in the form of snuff. These include tobacco (*Nicotiana* spp.) (native to the Bolivian yungas, but capable of growing in a wide variety of ecosystems), *Anadenanthera peregrina*, a leguminous tree (the distribution of *Anadenanthera* snuffs today includes the Orinoco and Amazon basins, the Andes south to Chile, and the Pacific coast), the bark of several species of *Viriola*, and a number of other less well-known trees and plants. Given the abundance of sources for hallucinogenic snuffs it is hard to pinpoint any particular line of exchange of these without detailed analyses of snuff remains from individual sites.

The appearance of various domesticates underlines the importance of this interregional contact and exchange. Potatoes (*Solanum tuberosum*), surely the Andean crop *par excellence*, appear as a gathered crop at Monte Verde, Chile by 10,000 BC. At 8000 BC they appear at Tres Ventanas in southern Peru (although the deposits are mixed) in a still wild form. The earliest known highland potatoes (which are of highland origin) are *c.* 3800 BC at Ayacucho, where they may be domesticated. Definitely domesticated potatoes appear at large numbers of coastal sites in the later preceramic, along with sweet potatoes (*Ipomoea batatas*), jicama (*Polymnia* spp.), and achira (*Canna edulis*).

Manioc (*Manihot escuelenta* Krantz), a tuberous plant whose wild forms are spread throughout the American tropics from Brazil to southern Mexico, *may* appear on the Peruvian coast as early as 5000 BC and remains of it are reported from Chilca *c.* 3500 BC (Figure 5.16). Manioc also appears in Level IV of Guitarrero Cave in the highlands and is definitely present by *c.* 2000 BC at the preceramic Los Gavilanes in the Huarmey Valley. Squashes too appear in a large number of later preceramic coastal Peruvian sites and may be present in the Ayacucho caves during the Piki phase (*c.* 4000 BC, although these remains may be gourds). Squash is definitely present in the Guitarrero II and IV levels. Numbers of different species seem to be represented and the pattern of distribution is consistent with multiple domestications as well as diffusions of this important plant. Beans, both *Phaseolus* and *Canavalia*, have a respectable antiquity although it is the canavalia bean which has the wider early distribution, being found in numbers of sites along the coast of Peru and in Valdivia sites in Ecuador. Cotton, the signifier of the late preceramic in Peru, actually was found sporadically in earlier epochs. The Valdivia culture seems to have had cultivated cotton. Edward Lanning claimed there was cotton in the Encanto phase of the central Peruvian coast and it is possible that even earlier cotton is present at Chilca. Work on the distribution of wild cottons is continuing but the abundance of feral forms is a confusing factor. Wild cottons were apparently available to both Peruvians and Ecuadorians although the appearance of cotton in the colder highlands must be an indication of trade with warmer valley or coastal areas. No cotton has been found at Guitarrero Cave, although its presence is claimed for the Piki and Chihua phases of Ayacucho. This cotton has not been classified botanically and may be wild (Figure 5.17).

The other major domesticate of the Andes is corn (*Zea mays*). There are numbers of problems in the study of the origins and spread of corn, and, although the presence of corn has been claimed as prima facie evidence of early contact between South America and Mexico, this is not certain. The evidence for early corn is discussed in Chapter 6.

The distributions of domesticated plants and animals in these early sites and the order of their appearance then suggest both diverse centers of domestication and considerable, although perhaps short-distance and not highly organized, exchange between groups occupying different ecozones. The exploitation of verticality in the central and southern Andes began at this time and it is quite possible that contact between groups and a rising desire among peoples for products not available in their own region led shortly to the appearance of considerably more complex societies.

5.16 A field in southern Colombia shows some of the staple crops, both indigenous and imported. A manioc plant (*center*) grows in a field with maize and bananas (imported from Asia). Ulluco plants, also grown for their tubers, twine along the ground. Fields like this, although messy by Euroamerican standards, are ecologically much sounder in the tropics than clean, straight-plowed gardens.

5.17 Wild cotton on the Santa Elena Peninsula, Ecuador. This useful plant seems to have been first used wild, but was shortly domesticated by coastal dwellers in Ecuador and, perhaps, Peru.

CHAPTER 6

THE PROBLEM OF MAIZE

Of the many plants domesticated by the native peoples of the Americas, none has caught the interest of scholars as much as corn (*Zea mays*). Even though root and tuber crops such as potatoes (*Solanum* spp.) and manioc (*Manihot escuelenta*) were perhaps more important to native economies, corn, because it is a grain and because western agriculture is largely grain based, has been seen as being the key to all advanced cultural development in the Americas. The priority of intensive investigations into the prehistory and ancient economies of Mesoamerica, an area in which maize agriculture was extremely important, has likewise influenced studies in South America, as investigators have tried to impose Mesoamerican-based models of agricultural development upon an entirely different continent (Figure 6.1).

Theories regarding the origin of *Zea mays* have been around for a very long time. Presently there are three separate, somewhat competing, schemes concerning the origin(s) of this useful plant. All of them take as an *a priori* stand that the sole origin of domesticated corn was somewhere within the modern states of Mexico or Guatemala. Paul Mangelsdorf of Harvard has held, throughout his long career of seeking the ancestors of corn, that the domesticated corns descended from a wild tripsicum grass, now extinct. Mangelsdorf saw both the domesticated maizes and the favored ancestral species of other seekers for corn origins (teocinte, *Zea mexicana* and other species) as being descended from these grasses. The strength of Mangelsdorf's theory is that it accounts for a number of separate origins of domesticated maize in various environmental zones, not excluding those of South America. George Beadle and Walton Galinat, two other botanists who have spent their lives working on the origins of corn, see teocinte, especially perennial teocinte (a species of which has recently been discovered) as *the* ancestor. Teocinte, which is today found in the wild state only in Mexico and northwestern Central America, is morphologically very similar to maize, being separated from it by a very few traits, such as two kernels in each cupule and two rows of kernels – as opposed to the many rowed domestic maize with its single kernel per cupule – and a shattering rachis so that the seed may be naturally dispersed, a feature that domestic corn has not had for millennia. Both Mangelsdorf and Beadle/Galinat have done extensive back-breeding to try to recreate the original domesticated form. Working from the teocinte theory, Hugh Iltis in 1983 proposed a more radical origin of corn. He suggests that corn did not evolve in the manner of the Old World grains, that is by a series of genetic traits being selected for individually until the desired form was reached, but rather came about through an almost instantaneous change in the male tassel of teocinte which then became the cob of the resulting corn. This sexual reversal

6.1 Woman vendor in the Cuzco market in the southern Peruvian highlands. Aside from a variety of different colors of maize she is selling several kinds of potatoes, ocas, and ullucos, all of which are more important than maize in the local diet.

of the tassels can occur through human intervention but also through infection with corn smut, viral attacks, or environmental changes. The role of humans in this was, according to Iltis, probably through recognizing the larger cobbed form with its easier-to-harvest seeds and then perpetuating them through selective planting. Iltis's theory, although compelling in some ways, conflicts with ethnographic evidence of corn breeding and changes in race distribution among the modern Kekchi Maya of Guatemala, a people who continue a non-modern way of life, including agricultural practices essentially unchanged since the prehispanic epochs.

Since all of these theories (with the exception of some of the earlier publications of Mangelsdorf) postulate an origin in Mexico somewhere between 10,000 and 5000 BC, they also must involve some means of transmission of maize to South America. It is in this area that both botanical and archaeological theories of maize origins are the weakest.

The South American corns tend to be quite different from those of Mexico/Central America in shape of cob and kernels, and in the characteristics of the seeds. The flour corns are apparently all South American in origin, and there is a series of soft corns in southeastern South America which are much different from anything grown in Mexico (these appear to be special races developed for making native beer, chicha, a drink which was a staple of many native diets, not just a recreational beverage). Dent corns are found in the temperate latitudes of South America, Mexico, and North America, although it has been suggested that the dent corns represent late adaptations to colder temperate environments. There is some overlap in racial groups between Mexico and South America. The antiquity of these groups in either place is not really known.

Until rather recently most archaeological evidence regarding the growing of corn was indirect. Manos and metates were claimed to be prima facie evidence that people were growing corn and grinding it and the appearance of these implements in the archaeological record was thus assumed to show maize agriculture. However, many South American peoples do not grind corn for use, but eat it roasted on the cob or boiled in soups or stews. Indeed, the distribution of treatment of corn kernels with lime to make hominy (which is then generally eaten whole as mote, although occasionally ground to make tamales or corn cakes) is very limited. This technique could well be a postcolumbian introduction. In the central and part of the southern Andes corn is ground using rocker mills, bataanes, on a stone, wooden or other hard, flat surface. Manos and metates and bataanes are commonly used to grind other materials, both foodstuffs and industrial materials such as ceramic clays, ores for smelting, and pigments for painting and for dyeing textiles. Other evidence of corn use comes from representations in sculptures or ceramics, but representational art styles are unfortunately limited to a few cultures and all are rather late for considering questions of the origin or origins of cultivated corn (Figure 6.2).

In the past decade or so the number of projects which have set out to recover botanical materials through screening, flotation, taking of pollen and phytolith samples, and the analysis of these recovered materials by specialists has escalated. The result has been a very large increase in the amount of evidence concerning early agriculture and diet. Current evidence indicates that *Zea mays* was widely, although sporadically, known in South America from *c*. 6000 BC onwards.

The earliest evidence of corn in this region is actually from Panama, culturally part of South America, although a separate political entity since the last century. Here *Zea* pollen has been found in deposits dating to *c*. 6000 BC. This may well indicate, since there is no evidence of agriculture in Panama at this early date, that the wild relatives of corn were found considerably to the south of where they exist today.

Most other evidence comes from western South America. In Ecuador it has been postulated that the Vegas and Valdivia peoples of southwest coastal Ecuador grew corn from *c*. 6000 BC onwards. The evidence rests upon phytolith identification in the Vegas deposits and upon rare Valdivia phytoliths and the dubious identification of a corn kernel cast in a Valdivia vessel of indefinite date. Despite the vagueness of such evidence it is quite likely that the Vegas and Valdivia peoples grew maize. Certainly by the

6.2 A late Moche "maize god" from Peru. Maize does not seem to have become a true staple in many coastal Peruvian cultures until perhaps AD 500–600. This "maize god" – identified as a supernatural by his huge fangs – has maize cobs as rays emanating from his back but he holds a bunch of manioc tubers.

succeeding Machalilla and Chorrera-Engeroy cultures (1200–800 BC and 800–200 BC respectively) maize agriculture was well established along the coast of Ecuador. This is, of course, somewhat late to have any bearing on the problem of ultimate origins, although it is worth noting that the earliest, well-attested maize agriculture involved races similar to those grown in Ecuador today. Despite some extravagant claims of antiquity, corn agriculture in the highlands cannot really be well documented until the end of this period, when small-kernel corns appear nearly simultaneously throughout the Ecuadorian Andes, suggesting a swift introduction from elsewhere. However, there is some evidence from the southeastern Amazonian region of Ecuador that maize was present from *c.* 4000 BC. Both pollen and phytoliths have been identified from lake sediments at Lake Ayauch. This is contemporary with the coastal Vegas occurrence and lends credence to the early cultivation of maize on the coast.

Maize cultivation is well documented for north central Colombia, where investigations of the first millennium BC Ilama ("Early Calima") culture have indicated that corn was a common cultigen. Here the earliest corn (identified first from phytoliths and later from charred remains) seems to be a precursor of the Chapalote/Na Tel/Pollo race. Slightly later and considerably more abundant Yotoco remains (beginning *c.* 100 BC) show that both this race and a larger-kernel one, perhaps ancestral to a modern Colombian race of maize called Cabuya, were being grown (Figure 6.3).

In Peru maize agriculture dating to the terminal preceramic eras is well documented and there is some evidence of earlier maize. A whole series of sites (e.g. Los Gavilanes, Aspero, Río Seco de León, Ancón) along the central coast show maize agriculture to have been quite common in this region by 2500–2300 BC. A similar date for maize comes from the central highlands from the Ayacucho Cave sites. Where races can be identified all seem to be precursors of later popular Peruvian races, especially Confite Morocho, Confite Chavinense and Kculli (Figure 6.4).

Evidence of even earlier maize agriculture (or maize utilization) comes from northern Chile where a number of sites have now yielded remains of maize in the 5000–2000 BC range. The earliest of these is the site of Tiliviche, in the interior Pisagua drainage, where remains of the species *Piricinco coroico* have been found; the 5000 BC date for this site is apparently conservative. Maize remains, as well as maize pollen, have come from the Tarapacá site, dated *c.* 4500–4400 BC, and San Pedro Viejo shows growing of maize, cranberry beans, and squash in a slightly later period, seemingly as adjuncts to a mainly hunting and gathering economy. A number of other sites have early maize, although the precise chronological placement of these is still somewhat uncertain.

To date then the evidence seems to indicate that maize agriculture was making a certain impact on the economies of the coastal and inland coastal valley peoples of the Andean region by about 4000–3000 BC, with some earlier loci to the north and south. At this time the main emphasis of many local economies was largely upon hunting and gathering and, indeed, maize did not become a staple crop of much of the Andes until a great many centuries later. All of these early sites in which races of maize can be identified show precursors of modern local races being grown.

A final find shows that maize was being grown not only in the Andes but in

6.3 A maize field at Tierradentro in the Colombian highlands. One of the most unusual sights to outsiders is the utter verticality of many Andean fields.

6.4 Inca terraces at Pisac, near Cuzco, Peru. The elaborate Inca terraces were designed by government engineers and were an attempt to extend maize-growing land in all regions for the beer without which no government or ritual occasion was complete.

southeastern South America at a similar date. The rock shelter of Santana de Riacho in the state of Minas Gerais has yielded maize kernels, seeds of wild plants, and the remains of palm fruits in a stratum dating to *c*. 3000 BC. This is a region in which dependence upon agriculture is not attested to until very much later. However, it is also a region in which almost all archaeological attention has been focussed on the abundant rock shelters, despite good evidence that these were used only at certain seasons or for ceremonial activities. Although the existence of open encampments is mentioned, none has been published. Some of the modern era peoples of the southeast were mainly hunters and gatherers (either by choice or because they had been forced out of their former territories), but are known to have grown some maize for beer, along with a few industrial plants such as cotton (for bowstrings and hammocks). Thus the existence of cultivated maize in these early foraging societies is not unreasonable.

The age and distribution of maize in South America suggest that all of the evidence concerning the origin of this most useful plant is not in and that theories which postulate Mexico as the sole region of dispersal may well be considered reductionist and inadequate. Current theories also tend to ignore the historical framework. There is no evidence that the distribution of teocinte, if teocinte is the ultimate ancestor, was the same in the twentieth century AD and the sixth millennium BC. Indeed, the phytoliths from the Vegas site in Ecuador are reputed to be rather teocinte-like. The distribution of species of maize may be assumed to have changed through the millennia with the movements of peoples, the expansion of states (such as the Incas) which encouraged corn raising, changes in climate, etc. Moreover, the radical changes in distributions of cultivated plants, domesticated animals, and cultural traits brought about by the events of the early Colonial period (which included widespread slaving and movements of peoples) have hardly been documented at all, as people have been more interested in the impact of European plants upon America and vice versa than in the effects of long-distance contact between American peoples. Numbers of plant and animal species are almost certainly early colonial introductions in both areas, not evidence of precolumbian interchange. Archaeological evidence suggests how weak the theories of a single origin and deliberate introduction of maize into other regions are. The peoples of Mexico and of South America who were the earliest maize farmers were semi-nomadic, or newly sedentary, foragers who practiced a little agriculture on the side and who had a rather simple material culture. There is no evidence of water craft capable of making long voyages on the open sea in either place until much later periods (if indeed these ever existed). To suggest that the very early incipient farmers were in the habit of making regular long-distance sea voyages in whatever direction is patently absurd. Yet, for maize agriculture to have had a single point of origin in Mesoamerica and then to have appeared virtually simultaneously at a number of widely separated sites in South America, the corn-bringers would have had to indulge in direct contact, bypassing the large numbers of non-agricultural societies in between Mesoamerica, the northern, central and southern Andes, and southeastern Brazil.

A final consideration is that the evidence currently available concerning plant domestication and the spread of agriculture from Eurasia (and from Mexico and South America as well) suggests that virtually no plant or animal had a single locus of domestication. People were experimenting with the growing and modification of a number of plants; the same plants were being experimented with in numbers of sites and regions. Simplistic theorizing, coupled with the widespread desire for there to have been multiple prehistoric migrations, has flawed a great deal of archaeological reconstruction in the Americas. Maize has often been a major pillar of such reconstructions; it may also prove to be a weak one.

CHAPTER 7

CULTURAL INTENSIFICATION IN THE ANDES: 3500–2000 BC

At approximately the same time as Real Alto and other sites in the northern Andes were flourishing, cultural intensification began to appear in Peru (Figure 7.1). Both on the coast and in the highlands, towns and ceremonial centers with permanent architecture and special purpose buildings appeared, suggesting that the local societies had begun to develop specialists (other than farmers) who were channeling their excess energies and supplies into large-scale projects. The earlier of these societies still completely lacked ceramics.

In the highlands several sites of this period have been studied. The first to be intensively investigated was Kotosh, near modern Huánuco. Here several preceramic ceremonial structures were encountered, rectangular enclosures of stone and clay, one of which was preserved to a sufficient height to preserve small niches in the walls which contained bones and other offerings. Below two of these niches were crossed human forearms modeled in clay, the earliest relief sculpture from Peru. The enclosures also contained small set-off "patios" each with a central hearth which had a ventilator tunnel dug through the floor to the exterior of the main enclosure. These hearths had been extensively used and repaired. Similar remains come from the site of Huarikoto, a site which may have been a true ceremonial center, visited only for rituals. Here a series of ceremonial hearths have been excavated, of different shapes, but all carefully slipped with fine clay and used for burning offerings. Once used they were carefully sealed and a new floor constructed. The Huarikoto hearths were apparently in the open or enclosed only with a perishable structure of some sort, but were renovated and used over many hundreds of years. Similar remains at other (more important?) sites are surrounded by permanent buildings and have ventilators, presumably to ensure a draft and the near total consumption of the offerings of meat, shell, and special stones such as quartz crystals. This particular set of structures and the rituals carried on in them are called the Kotosh Religious Tradition (Figure 7.2). At Kotosh only the ceremonial structures were excavated, and Huarikoto either had its main occupation at some distance from the ceremonial hearths or was a vacant center (a tradition which continues to this day in parts of the Peruvian highlands), but at La Galgada, on a tributary of the Santa River, survey has revealed that there was a town surrounding the two main civic or ceremonial structures (Figure 7.3). About fifty houses survive of the town; an unknown number were destroyed by modern road building through the site area. Two temple structures were found at La Galgada; the north one, in its lowest levels, contained a ceremonial fire-pit chamber like those of Kotosh and Huarikoto (Figure 7.4). The structure was already some 13 m high at this point and there must be substantial earlier remains

7.1 Principal late preceramic/early ceramic sites discussed in the text. 1. Machalilla, 2. La Galgada, 3. Huarikoto, 4. Kotosh, 5. Culebras, 6. Cerro Sechín, Las Haldas, 7. Aspero, 8. El Paraíso, 9. Huaca la Florida, Cardal, Tablada de Lurín, Los Gavilanes, 10. Waywaka, 11. Chinchorro, Tarapacá, and Guatacondo Valleys, 12. Caserones site.

7.2 Two small preceramic temples at Pimapiru, Peru. These temples, dating to *c.* 3000–2500 BC, predate the better known Kotosh Religious Tradition temples at Kotosh, La Galgada, and Huarikoto. The circular structure in front has a hearth with subterranean ventilator.

7.3 Excavations of the ceremonial area of La Galgada, Peru, showing the sequence of superimposed buildings within the mound.

underneath the fire pit chamber. This dates to about 3000 BC. A complete rebuilding of the temple was done about 200 years later with new ceremonial chambers being constructed, finally, about 2000 BC (contemporary with the first appearance of pottery at the site). Another rebuilding and enlargement transformed the temple into a U-shaped arrangement of rectangular rooms around a patio, a layout characteristic of the later religious structures of Peru. The north temple of La Galgada is a massive structure with huge stone walls topped with an ornamental dado. It was covered with polished pearly white plaster. The south temple (begun *c.* 2500 BC), though smaller, is similar and also has a ceremonial fire pit. Numbers of colored feathers were found on the floor and the hearths were surrounded by a bench, suggesting some sort of small, sedentary, ceremony. The south temple shows clearly the reuse of these ceremonial chambers as tombs. In rebuilding, which involved filling previous chambers to make a higher platform, the old chambers were blocked off with large stone slabs and an entrance through a small shaft in the fill of the upper levels to the floor of the new structure would

7.4 South Mound excavations at La Galgada, Chamber C-11:1–3. This square chamber covers an earlier room which was converted to a tomb. There is a fire pit with ventilator in the center of the room, located right in front of the door.

7.5 Looped bag with design of black winged, spotted serpents on yellow, La Galgada.

be constructed. In the tombs were placed three to five bodies accompanied by elaborate twined textiles, jewelry, baskets, and other personal belongings. Textiles seem to have been a major art form of the ancient inhabitants, and looped bags, especially, were elaborately decorated with designs of birds, snakes, and geometric patterns (Figure 7.5). Use of the heddle loom appeared along with the first ceramics; plain (although occasionally decorated with painting) narrow belts seem to have been the major product of the true loom.

Ceremonial pits similar to those of the highlands are also found at a number of contemporary sites on the coast along with other types of ceremonial constructions and evidence of quite different offertory practices. Small, presumably independent, villages such as Huaca Prieta continued to be occupied and, indeed, became more common. There is considerable variation in house type, from simple grass huts like those of Chilca and Paloma to fairly complex, multiroom stone and adobe structures like those of Asia in the Omas Valley. Some larger towns also began to appear; Asia may be such, Culebras definitely is one. Culebras may cover much of the north flank of the bay of the same name, perhaps 300 sq m *in toto*. The structures at Culebras are varied: the hillside upon which the site is constructed is cut into large stone terraces and there are reportedly some interior passages or galleries. Most construction is of natural stone blocks from the surrounding hills, but details such as rounded corners and the construction of niches into the walls of some of the larger buildings show a knowledge of stone cutting. The lower terraces are covered with small, rectangular agglutinated houses, semi-subterranean and consisting of several rooms, one of which is a kitchen, with a guinea pig enclosure. Burials were made in the houses and in the rubbish fill of some of the larger buildings. There is also a separate cemetery which may indicate some social or occupational differences between the inhabitants of Culebras.

Los Gavilanes in the Huarmey Valley likewise gives evidence of a developing complexity of social order. The first occupation of Los Gavilanes was simply domestic, a number of houses along the desert strip. These, however, were associated with some larger stone structures of unknown use. Some time later the site was abandoned, the previous structures destroyed, and a series of some forty-seven stone-lined pits dug. These pits were used to store corn, covered with sand to keep the grain dry and safe from insects, a method used until very recently in the area. The excavator, Duccio Bonavia, calculates that this site alone (there is another similar one nearby) could have held something over 450,000 kg, indicating that it was the storage facility for a community or group of communities, presumably located on the flood plain and now destroyed.

The most outstanding feature of the late preceramic in Peru, however, is the appearance of sites with large-scale ceremonial architecture. The best known of these are Aspero, above the port of Supe, Huaca la Florida in the Lurín Valley, and El Paraíso (also known as Chuquitanta) in the Chillón Valley, as well as the huge early ceramic period site of Las Haldas just south of the Casma Valley. Aspero was the first of these preceramic sites with monumental architecture to be so identified. Here some six fieldstone and clay platforms, some with stairs, were built by filling rooms with rubble. The platforms are rectangular and were painted white, red, and yellow. One has niches and faces on a rectangular plaza. There is evidence of burning on the platforms and there are some associated pits which may indicate that a version of the Kotosh Religious Tradition was being practiced at Aspero. Aspero is also claimed to be one of the earliest Peruvian ceremonial sites to show a U-shaped formation, although not all of the mounds are so arranged and, indeed, not all have a frontal pit. Aspero is not a vacant ceremonial site; there are some 13 ha of midden surrounding the platforms, indicating a resident population of considerable size. The amount of labor involved in building the various platforms shows that some form of corporate labor must have been involved in their construction, as is evident at many of these large preceramic/early ceramic sites. The Huaca La Florida site does seem to have a U-shaped layout, with a central pyramid with an atrium surviving to 17 m above land surface and two wings some 3–4 m high and 500 m long. The pyramid was built before about 2100 BC, with the north wing and the south wing being of slightly later construction. It was built rather rapidly, probably within a century or so, its construction, use, and abandonment spanning the period of the introduction of pottery to this part of Peru.

Although there are a large number of similar sites from this time period, the most impressive is that of El Paraíso, which covers over 58 ha along the Chillón River (Figure

7.6 General view of El Paraíso, Peru, showing one major construction and its wings. The site is far too large to show on a single photograph.

7.6). This site is very late, having been in full use somewhat after 1600 BC and is completely aceramic. Eleven architectural units have been discovered, all but one on the south side of the river. The two largest (II and VI) are parallel structures 400 m long. However, there is no neat disposition of structures into U-shaped plans, even though there is a definite control of space and access within the site. It is possible that the various buildings were connected by free-standing walls, but there has been considerable tractor damage to the site. Unit I, whose central structure has been reconstructed, was built of roughly trimmed stone blocks, laid in clay mortar and plastered with the same material (Figure 7.7). The platform was constructed by filling old rooms with bags of stones. The bags are all the same size in any given construction phase (some five to six have been isolated) and were made by piling rock onto a group of cords and constructing the bag at the quarry site. Jeffrey Quilter, who has most recently been working at El Paraíso, thinks that the uniform nature of the bag fill may indicate some form of labor tax involving identical modular units (similar practices have been noted at Aspero, where Robert Feldman has similarly suggested corporate labor payments as the key to the organization of construction). Little evidence of habitation has been found at El Paraíso and it seems probable that the multiroomed structures of the site served as storerooms and, perhaps, workrooms, as well as sites for rituals. The oldest and largest room of Unit I contains a sunken rectangular pit with remains of many superimposed floors, all burned. Tiny circular pits filled with charcoal were located in each corner of the main pit. Also from Unit I came an "idol": a large unworked stone painted red and wrapped in cotton cloth, associated with a miniature fiber bag like those used for rock fill, but filled with cakes of lime wrapped in coca leaves. These and other enigmatic remains at El

7.7 El Paraíso, Unit I, the reconstructed platform and room group at the center of two wings. Like later Peruvian "pyramids" those of El Paraíso were actually platforms for building and courtyard constructions.

Paraíso show yet another version of the Kotosh Religious Tradition, here with a single large hearth rather than the smaller ones seen in the highlands. The cyclical reuse of this hearth is similar, but other remains such as the dedicatory cache of the idol, and the identification of some rooms in Unit II as aviaries, as well as the sheer size and non-residential nature of the site are rather different from practices evidenced at other coastal sites of similar date.

El Paraíso is contemporary with another huge architectural complex, that of Las Haldas, located on the rocky desert shore some 30 km south of the Casma Valley. The initial occupation of this site was preceramic, but the first standing architecture dates from *c.* 1650 BC and is associated with the introduction of ceramics to this part of the coast. The major constructions are somewhat later. These consist of eighteen (or more) platform-courtyard groups constructed of fieldstone set in mud mortar, plus two sunken circular structures of the same materials (Figure 7.8). Platform and terrace fill was first of earth, but soon changed to stone-filled reed bags as at El Paraíso. Floors were sometimes made of colored (red or yellow) clay. The largest constructions are lined up on a series of five terraces overlooking the ocean. None of the buildings, with the possible exception of a building on top of Structure 1, is oriented to the sea. The orientation of other platforms seems to be towards the sunken circles. One of these, the Main Circle, shows evidence of having had a large fire built inside it, although the other

7.8 Structure 1, Las Haldas, Peru. The construction of large upright slabs with smaller blocks filling between them is one common on early monumental constructions, including those of Cerro Sechín and Chavín de Huántar. The surrounding midden, as can be seen in the foreground, contains immense quantities of shell.

has no such evidence (Figure 7.9). All of these buildings seem to have been roofless except for the building on Structure 1, which might have been roofed. Las Haldas provides some of the earliest information we have on architectural design methods. During the late occupation of the site concrete was in use and buildings were laid out using a stick and string. The most elaborate structures, 1, 2, and 3 at the north end of the terrace system, were never finished and the stick and string being used to even out the rebuilding of the façade were simply left in place. This and some other evidence indicates that Las Haldas was abandoned very suddenly. When it was reoccupied a short time later, the new occupants built themselves small, flimsy houses within the large precincts.

The midden of Las Haldas shows, as might be expected, a preponderance of marine remains, including many different types of mollusks, sea bird and sea mammal bones, and both shallow and deep water fish. Cultivated plants are represented by corn (kernels only), cotton, avocado, beans, squash, and gourd. Tillandsia "grass" seems to have been the main fuel source. Tillandsia may have been available close to the site, but all other plants, as well as water, would have had to have been hauled a considerable distance. The source of these products may be indicated by a 60 m wide avenue which issues north from the site towards Casma and survives to a distance of 2 km.

7.9 The Main Circle at Las Haldas. Although much larger than the highland examples, the "ceremonial circles" at Las Haldas are evidently part of the Kotosh Religious Tradition.

Within the Casma Valley there are a number of sites contemporary with Las Haldas and it is tempting to see some sort of linkage between the inland sites associated with agricultural land and the maritime-oriented Las Haldas, as remains of sea foods and shells have been found in some abundance at these inland sites. The most famous of these sites is Cerro Sechín, first excavated by Julio C. Tello, the founder of modern Peruvian archaeology. Cerro Sechín is one of the very few coastal sites decorated with stone carvings. The site occupies a spectacular location between two high rocky spurs dominating the lower part of the Sechín arm of the Casma Valley. The central building, which has been the focus of most attention at the site, is a huge platform almost exactly 52.70 m on a side, built of clay and rubble and with the rounded corners characteristic of much coastal architecture. The most outstanding characteristics of the building are the more than 300 low-relief stone slabs which adorned the lower retaining wall of the platform. Two of these, representing upright banners laced to staves, flanked the main stairway (which was rebuilt at least once). The other reliefs show a procession of fully dressed persons carrying ceremonial staffs or clubs, each occupying a single large stone (Figure 7.10). Between these personages are numbers of smaller slabs carved with disarticulated human remains: heads, bodies – both whole and halved – limbs, intestines, spines, eyes and so on (Figure 7.11). All figures are in low relief, set off by wide, deeply incised grooves. The technique of representation and a slight resemblance

7.10 Cerro Sechín, Casma Valley, Peru. The uprights of the lower platform of Sechín have figures carved upon them. This warrior with his decorated and plumed hat, face paint, and elaborate loincloth is typical of the full figure sculptures at this site.

7.11 A trophy head sculpture from Cerro Sechín. The freshness of this head is indicated by the stylized blood falling from the neck and eye.

in subjects (trophy heads and mutilated humans) have led some people to suggest that these carvings are related to the famous Danzante sculptures of Monte Albán in southern Mexico. This supposed relationship forms part of an elaborate argument which purports to show that the Chavín culture of Peru and the Olmec of Mexico were one and the same. Unfortunately, the non-Olmec affiliation of the Danzantes has now been demonstrated beyond a doubt and the pre-Chavín construction of the Cerro Sechín temple has been likewise established. The dating of these two sculptural manifestations alone (200–150 BC for the Danzantes, many centuries later than the 1200 BC of the Cerro Sechín sculptures) should banish such fantasies from sentient consideration.

The making of fired ceramic vessels, long considered to be a hallmark of the neolithic, was very late in Peru and followed upon other, more substantial, evidence of increasingly complex cultures with a variety of religious practices, and the development of some fairly large permanent settlements and of permanent, sophisticated and truly monumental architecture. This in itself suggests that there were some kinds of social and political groupings larger than a single site. How these groups were held together is another matter. Thomas Patterson has suggested that the small egalitarian villages were allied through marriage and other exchanges, pointing out that female burials are rare at many of these sites and when they exist are often secondary, suggesting the body may have been brought in from a distance, i.e. the village of (married) residence. The large structures, he claims, were built for ritual purposes by the larger cooperating group, perhaps under the authority of village elders or priests. Unfortunately, we have very little data on the specifics of social organization save that from the late preceramic onwards there is evidence of a growing complexity of undertakings, including the huge architectural complexes, and these must have been linked with increasing social and political complexity as well. Evidence of burials such as one at Aspero where, on the midline of a platform, an infant and an adult were buried, the infant with a large number of grave goods, showing either the dedication of the building with these burials (as sacrifices?) or a retainer buried with a child too young to have achieved high status in its lifetime, indicates that hereditary statuses must have been becoming established. At El Paraíso Jeffrey Quilter and his colleagues have suggested that these very large centers were founded to develop and then to control large-scale cotton production. The cotton was essential in the largely maritime economies of many of these sites (nets, lines) as well as being used both for utilitarian clothing and for the elaborate textiles which were a source of wealth and a manifestation of prestige in Peru. Numbers of these sites show little evidence for established hierarchies such as richly furnished burials or large-scale religious art work, indicating that, although ruling elites were probably coming into existence, indeed seem to have been in existence at some sites such as Aspero, they had not yet assumed the central place they were to occupy in later cultures. This early development of monumental sites is confined to the central Andes. In Ecuador the Valdivia culture continued onwards and the precocious developments of the Ecuadorian cultures did not immediately lead to major changes in social structure or political complexity. The Valdivia farmers yielded (in ceramic style, at least) to those of Machalilla. People were still living in small to largish villages of wattle and daub structures, often with one or more larger, presumably ceremonial, structures located on platforms in the center of the village. Efforts to define larger polities on the basis of distribution studies of settlements have not yet proved very fruitful and it seems likely that the largest political units were those of a single river drainage or, in the highlands, of a single valley, at best. Machalilla ceramics are characterized by shallow carinated bowls and occasional bottles and vases, decorated with red paint or, more commonly, with incision (Figure 7.12). The Machalilla farmers and fishers, had begun some inter-area trade and also appear to have been ancestral to the first really major artistic florescence in Ecuador, that of Chorrera.

A lack of cultural intensification is also seen in the southern Andes, although in the later preceramic, beginning somewhat prior to 2000 BC, a curious culture or subculture called Chinchorro is widely spread throughout the northern maritime region of Chile. The Chinchorro culture, Max Uhle's "Aborigines de Arica," is characterized by an unusual development of funerary practices, including artificial mummification. In the most elaborate Chinchorro burials the brain and interior organs of the body were removed and all sorts of materials, wool, unspun vegetable fibers, basketry fragments, twigs, etc. were stuffed into the body cavity and inside the skull; these were then glued together with a plant resin. Sticks were inserted along the limbs so that they would stay

7.12 Machalilla-style stirrup bottle found at El Descanso, near Cuenca, Ecuador. Bottles such as these indicate the important role Ecuadorian cultures played in the stylistic development of coastal Chavín ceramics.

in place, muscles were plumped out with grass, thread, and other materials, a mask covered the face, and a wig of human hair was placed on the head. The body was then covered with a thin layer of clay (Figure 7.13). A simpler version of body preparation only involved covering the body with clay. The bodies were buried in a stiff, extended position (much different from the more common flexed burials of contemporary Chilean and southern Peruvian cultures), wrapped in mats or sea mammal skins, with marine shell necklaces, seal and bird bone flutes and rattles, feather capes, and similar personal belongings. Among these appear some bits of copper. Not everyone seems to have merited such treatment, although apparently males, females, and small children were mummified in roughly equal numbers (with a slight preponderance of infants). Other than this rather unusual treatment of some of the dead, the culture was basically unchanged from the littoral-oriented hunters and gatherers of the previous millennia and no explanation for this flowering of an unusual mortuary cult exists.

The succeeding Faldas del Morro and El Laucho phases witnessed the beginnings of ceramics in the south. Increasing interaction with the altiplano and, perhaps, the tropical yungas is seen as more elaboration appears in the textiles, wood artifacts reflect highland themes, and the appearance of metallurgy also suggests ties with highland cultures. However, in many senses El Laucho is the heir to the more ancient maritime cultures and the new introductions elaborate, but do not change, the basic cultural adaptations.

In the east–west inland valleys, especially Tarapacá and Guatacondo, burials in bundles with coverings of the skins of sea birds and clothing made of both cotton and wool show the importance of interregional exchange in northern Chile. These burials also contain offerings of textile manufacturing tools, gourds, algorrobo pods, quinoa, and cotton, along with tools for both sea and land hunting. At much the same time, at the site of Caserones in Tarapacá, Lautaro Núñez has identified a culture which depended upon gathering algorrobo and cultivating maize. Ties with the highlands are shown in the ceramics, which are stylistically like those of Wankarani.

Explanations as to why there should have been a rather sudden and dramatic series of cultural changes in the central Andes, as opposed to a fairly continuous and slow cultural development in the north and south, have been varied. It is evident that the foundations of the Peruvian preceramic florescence were laid in the earlier epochs, but opinions as to the origins of all of these traits differ. On the one hand there are those who, like Edward Lanning and Michael Edward Moseley, have argued for the earliest Peruvian civilizations being founded on a maritime economy in which agriculture and other domesticates were not particularly important. These theories are a direct challenge to conservative archaeological thought which holds that the basis of all civilizations must be grain agriculture. Scholars who hold that agriculture must have been present and important to allow for the evident surpluses which would have been needed to finance large structures are divided between those who hold for an as yet undemonstrated importance of corn and those who champion one of the tuber or root crops which were demonstrably important in the ancient economies, more important, in fact, than any grains until *c*. AD 500. Richard Burger has added some fuel to this

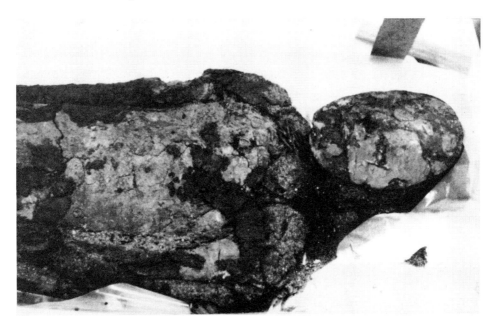

7.13 Chinchorro mummy. The limbs have been straightened with inserted sticks and the face covered with clay which was then painted bright blue. From the site of Morro-1, Burial 1, Body 3, Chile.

argument by his demonstration that corn, even when present, was not really a staple, but rather a ceremonial food (probably in the form of chicha). There has been an inclination on the part of archaeologists to overlook the exceedingly complex system of purely local cultigens in the Andes, as most of these did not become entrenched in the better-known Eurasian food systems (except, of course, for the potato). To simplify the picture considerably, there are also those who champion the role of the tropical lowlands in the development of Andean civilizations, pointing to a possible lowland origin of many important crops and suggesting that in South America, as perhaps in southern Mesoamerica, a combination of grain crops with tuberous crops made it possible to achieve large surpluses and the wherewithal to support an emerging elite and their supporting craftsmen.

Lanning and Moseley note the fundamental changes undergone by coastal Peruvian society beginning *c*. 3500 BC. They postulate that hunting and gathering were replaced by fishing and collecting and then were replaced by irrigation agriculture. The Encanto phase represents the earliest of these fisher folk. The Cotton Preceramic sites described above were, in this scheme, founded on an intensive exploitation of localized, abundant, and perennial shore and shallow water resources. The biomass carried by the sea off the coast of Peru and northern Chile is one of the world's richest and the sheer amount of food available from the sea, they argue, would have meant a delayed and irregular reliance upon agriculture. Those areas in which, however, there was the juxtaposition of several resource zones, such as particularly rich shellfish beds and a river valley with its riparian zones of wild plants and damp soil for whatever agricultural products were wanted by the local peoples, may have produced larger sites with a resident population simply because of the ease of exploiting different resources from a single base. On the other hand, sites of considerable size grew where there was only the sea to depend upon, and these do not fit this model. Moseley sees the development and spread of irrigation agriculture as coming from the highlands, with the first irrigated regions being up valley where water flow is stronger and irrigation takes less labor and a less developed knowledge of water flow and waterlogging and salinization processes. However, as has been noted often in studies of cultural development in Asia, irrigation agriculture brings its own set of constraints; the greater productivity of irrigation agriculture is linked with greater and more lengthy labor investments and with considerably more cooperative and synchronized labor than is involved in shoreline exploitation.

The maritime scenario tends to downplay the effects of El Niño or other fluctuations in ocean resources. Critics of the maritime exploitation theory have suggested that perhaps too little has been made of El Niño and that the nutritional value of mollusks has been grossly overrated. If one calculates the protein actually available in mollusks and calculates the quantity consumed by controlled samples of midden one sees that, although mollusk shells are the major component of midden, the much smaller sea mammal component would have provided more calories. Moreover, from calculations of protein consumed and estimated midden size versus site size, either a laughably small number of people were actually involved in the construction and maintenance of the large Cotton Preceramic sites, or some other major sources of foodstuffs were available (although Richard Burger's recent work at Cardal in the Lurín Valley of Peru indicates that the immense structures were the result of small increments over the years and thus smaller populations may well have been involved in their construction). This leads back to the whole problem of archaeological preservation and the need for specialist analysis of plant remains. Plant materials, even in the extremely arid conditions of the central and southern Peruvian coast, are less likely than bones and shells to survive in the midden. They are especially less likely to survive in any immediately recognizable form, so that it is essential to have expert analysis of these materials, something which has not been done often enough. Another factor in preservation is that of the location of sites. Those sites on the desert strand are more likely to survive because of aridity and lack of intensive reuse of the shore. One can presume that the early farmers of the coast were utilizing the floodplains of the rivers, living near their fields. Fields in the beginning may not have been too permanent nor, probably, were the residences of the farmers. Surviving ancient housing in Peru is almost entirely from the desert strips where it has not been in the way of the later irrigated farmlands. Thus it is entirely possible that any traces of these early floodplain farmers are gone, leaving us with only the larger ceremonial structures and the buildings and middens which have not been destroyed in later activities, that is to say, mainly those structures along the desert coast. Analysis of plant and animal remains such as has been done at Los Gavilanes and Las Haldas, to name only two sites, shows a wide variety of foodstuffs were available. Las Haldas must have imported these materials, since there is no water within a several hours' walk of the site. This may indicate, as numbers of critics of the maritime hypothesis have suggested and as seems quite evident from the contemporary Valdivia culture, that there was some sort of symbiotic relationship between the peoples of the river valleys and of the coastal sites. However, more site-oriented excavation coupled with expert analysis of midden materials is necessary before either the maritime or the agrarian hypothesis can be seriously evaluated.

The counter-hypothesis, that the eastern slopes and tropical lowlands were of consummate importance in the development of complex societies in Peru, has been most forcefully stated by Donald Lathrap, at first in the context of the religious iconography of the Chavín culture. Lathrap noted the appearance of non-highland species on a piece of sculpture called the Tello Obelisk, which depicts two caymans with supernatural attributes and appended plant materials. The cayman is not found in the highlands and species such as manioc, achira, cotton, and capsicum pepper are likewise not highland cultigens, although they do grow in the warmer highland valleys and on the coast. Caymans were found in some coastal rivers as well, weakening this hypothesis still further. Also, from non-iconographic studies there is growing evidence of the importance of interchange between the various ecological zones of the Andes from the early preceramic period onwards. It is quite possible that this interchange involved not only desired luxury goods such as skins and feathers and, perhaps, hallucinogenic substances, but also some cultigens and supernatural concepts. On the debit side there is very little evidence as yet for any developments on the eastern side of the Andes which are comparable to those of the coast and highlands and continuing archaeological research in this region shows only simple farming communities whose closest ties are with other lowland communities (to judge from similarities in ceramic styles). At this point, although there has been considerable discussion of the dynamics of a situation which manifestly led to the development of complex societies in one area and not in others, there is little consensus concerning causes of this development. What is evident, however, is that the historical sequence of subsistence and craft technologies in South America was considerably different from that observed in the archaeological record of Eurasia and that definitions of civilization and the way it develops based solely upon Eurasian models are clearly inadequate.

CERAMICS: THEIR ORIGINS AND TECHNOLOGY

The art of making pottery came relatively late in South America and its origin(s) and diffusion followed a somewhat different trajectory than that observed in Eurasia. The earliest ceramic traditions known are from northern Colombia, from Monsú, Puerto Hormiga, San Jacinto, and other sites in the same region. Even at this early time (Monsú ceramics date to approximately 3500 BC; those of Puerto Hormiga are about 500 years later; San Jacinto may be earlier than either site) there were several very different traditions present. Puerto Hormiga cannot be derived from the earlier Monsú; they are very different, even though the two sites are quite close to one another. Monsú vessels are mainly globular or rounded in shape and a tecomate-like form is most common. There are also some plates and remains of large griddles, which suggest that manioc was being grown and consumed as a toasted cake of the kind eaten by lowland peoples up to the present. The earliest periods, Turbana (3800[?]–3400 BC) and Monsú (3400–3000 BC), are characterized by ceramics decorated with incision and punctation in curvilinear patterns. Both wide, shallow incisions and narrower, deeper ones are present. The earlier Turbana period ceramics seem to have more elaborate decoration than the succeeding Monsú ones. Following the Monsú period, the site was abandoned for over a thousand years and finally reoccupied by people belonging to the late prehistoric Sinú chiefdoms.

Puerto Hormiga demonstrates a somewhat different culture and the excavator, Gerardo Reichel-Dolmatoff (who also excavated Monsú), has suggested that the shell mound represents a semi-sedentary, non-agricultural people. The ceramics found at Puerto Hormiga are quite sophisticated and at least three wares are present: the first two are fiber-tempered, one with some type of long string-like fibers which left tubular hollows in the ceramic when it was fired, giving the paste a sponge-like consistency. A second ware has an organic temper: short grass blades were crushed before they were added to the clay. A third ware has a sand temper. The long-fiber tempered pottery is the most common and was made into undecorated containers; the leaf tempered paste was made into thick-walled bowls, occasionally with plastic decoration. The sand tempered ware, on the other hand, was always carefully finished and decorated. Decorative techniques include incision, impressions, dentate rocker stamping, and small modeled zoomorphic adornos (Figure 8.1). The decorated wares show a certain affinity to later wares of northern Colombia and Venezuela, especially those of the Barrancoid tradition. Puerto Hormiga does not have any preceramic occupation at all; the beginning occupation date is approximately 3100 BC. The area around this site has remains of numerous preceramic and early ceramic shell mounds similar to Puerto

8.1 Sherds of various wares from Puerto Hormiga, Colombia. The variability in this early ceramic assemblage is evident. The incised and modeled head at the bottom is clearly ancestral to the important and long-lived Barrancoid ceramic tradition of northern Colombia and Venezuela.

Hormiga and Monsú, suggesting that ceramics in this instance, as in Danish Ertebölle, developed in a situation of sedentary fishers and shore/estuary gatherers.

In Ecuador a nearly contemporary ceramic tradition has been identified, first at the fishing village of Valdivia (which gave this culture its name) and then at numbers of other sites along the coast from the province of Manabí south to the Ecuador-Peru border near modern Arenillas. The Valdivia tradition may have been preceded by a slightly earlier ceramic style, called San Pablo, although so few remains of San Pablo pottery have been found in stratigraphic context that it has yet to be adequately described. The earliest Valdivia ceramics appear *c.* 3100 BC and, like those of Colombia, are technically and esthetically sophisticated. The common vessel forms are bowls and

8.2 Two Valdivia figurines. Most Valdivia figurines show nude women at various stages of life: adolescence, full maturity, pregnancy, etc. The meaning of the two-headed figurines is not known. These particular examples also demonstrate a growing problem in prehispanic art history: fakery. These little ladies were made by modern Valdivians, using ancient models, ancient clay sources, and ancient firing technologies. The results decorate museums and private collections the world around.

ollas, with the shapes and decorations of bowls, in particular, being good temporal indicators. A large variety of decorative techniques were practiced, including various kinds of incision, excision, punctation, ripple burnishing, cord impression, and red slip painting. Decorative techniques also change through the thousand or so years of the Valdivia tradition. Other clay artifacts include hollow and solid figurines in a number of styles; most represent nude females (Figure 8.2).

These precocious ceramic traditions, as far as is known, were unique in South America for nearly a thousand years, although claims are now being made for an equal, or greater, antiquity for the Taperinha site in Brazil. Given the ever mounting evidence that sedentary gatherer-farmers are quite prone to invent ceramics, wherever they may be, an early date for ceramics in the Amazon is perfectly reasonable. However, the first short reports and press releases have not contained enough information to evaluate this site as yet.

Somewhat before 2000 BC ceramics began to appear in a number of other regions of South America. In eastern Venezuela along the Orinoco the La Gruta style dates to perhaps as early as 2100 BC. La Gruta pottery is an early representative of the Saladoid series, a tradition in which technology, shape, and decoration of ceramics were remarkably conservative through time. These are sand tempered ceramics fired in an oxidizing atmosphere and decorated with shallow incision, red and/or white paint applied after firing, and carved zoomorphic adornos. Forms include large pottery griddles, large bowls and basins, jars, and some animal effigy vessels. A second, minor ware has vegetable temper and only simple incised decoration.

In western Venezuela the Rancho Peludo style, the first representative of the Dabajuaroid tradition, first appears at the type site *c.* 1900 BC. Rancho Peludo pottery is sand tempered and relatively coarse. Shapes include ollas with out-curved rims, and in-curved bowls, some with round bottoms and others with tall annular bases. Decoration is simple and plastic: appliqué fillets, textile or mat impression, or punctations. Some modeled human heads are also found. Rancho Peludo pottery also includes clay griddles, suggesting that bitter manioc cultivation and preparation was very widely spread by the time of these early ceramic styles.

In the rest of extra-Andean South America the appearance of ceramics tended to be much later. Most of these later traditions can be stylistically related to contemporary ceramics of areas with which they were in contact or may, as in the case of much of Amazonia, be the result of actual migration of ceramics-making peoples into the region. For example, along the coast of Brazil, in the state of Pará, numerous sites of the early Mina tradition have been investigated. These are shell mound sites which were occupied for a very long time. They exhibit a water's edge orientation, with the gathering of local mollusks, especially *Anomalocardia brasiliana*, and fishing being the main economic activities. Bone points, polished stone axes, and hammerstones show foraging for other foodstuffs. The ceramics of the Mina phase, dated from 3000–1600 BC, are mainly utilitarian rounded vessels with crushed shell temper and red wash decoration. Stylistic links can be seen between these ceramics and later (beginning) traditions of Bahia to the south (Periperi Tradition) and the Alaka phase of Guyana.

In the central Andes ceramics began to appear *c.* 2300–1800 BC. On the far north coast of Peru the San Juan, Negritos, and Paita styles of the Piura region are obviously derived in form and technology from Ecuadorian counterparts. At Huaca Prieta ceramics appear all at once somewhat after 1800 BC. The Early Guañape style, featuring pointed-base jugs and ollas and a number of bowl forms, plus some suspiciously Ecuadorian-like figurines, also dates to this time frame. The Tolón style of Jequetepeque shows a very definite ancestry to later north coast styles in its incised and modeled decoration. One Tolón piece depicts a male with a tump line carrying a huge load; the earliest known representation of what was to be a favored theme in many later styles. It seems quite likely that the interest both in incised and in modeled decoration characteristic of north coast Peruvian traditions owes its inspiration to the earlier and contemporary traditions of Ecuador, those of Machalilla and Chorrera. On the central coast, ceramics appear at the large ceremonial site of Las Haldas *c.* 1800 BC and to the south early ceramics appear at Erizo in Ica and at Hacha in Acarí, somewhat before those of Las Haldas. These various traditions are not stylistically connected with the northern ones and are probably the result of several independent inventions or, perhaps, stimulus diffusion, as are many of the highland styles.

In the highlands the early Toril style of the Callejón de Huaylas may date as early as 1800 BC and is clearly related to the earliest ceramics of Las Haldas. The Kotosh Huaira-Jirca phase ceramics probably date to *c*. 1500 BC and, far to the south around Cuzco, the Chanapata and Qaluyu styles are roughly contemporary. The only early ceramic complex yet defined for the altiplano is that of Chiripa, beginning somewhat before 1300 BC.

Finally, by *c*. 1500 BC the first ceramic style identified in the montaña region, Early Tutishcainyo, appeared in the area just north of the modern city of Pucallpa. What is remarkable about the early ceramic traditions of Peru is their diversity and their evident ancestry, in many cases, to later local or regional ceramic traditions. Early Tutishcainyo ceramics, for example, show most of the characteristics of later Amazonian styles, including carinated and/or flanged open vessels, carinated bowls, and large urns, all with incised (or incised and painted) geometric patterns. The shapes and the size distribution of these shapes suggest that some of the vessels were intended for brewing and drinking manioc beer, whereas others fall into (modern) standard ranges for food serving. The Peruvian north coast styles from the beginning (excluding those of the far north) show an interest in modeling which was to continue until well after the Spanish conquest. The Chiripa style is very obviously an early example of the very closely related Titicaca basin styles of later epochs and so on.

Theories of the origins of South American ceramics are as diverse as the ceramic styles themselves. Aside from those who see native ceramic traditions being at least partly *sui generis*, diffusionist theories have had considerable play. Most of those theories which call for the introduction of ceramics from the Old World are patently absurd. However, in 1956 Estrada, Meggers, and Evans began to publish their ideas concerning the Valdivia culture, then the earliest known ceramics-making culture on the west coast of the continent. They claimed that Valdivia ceramics were introduced by fishermen of the Jomon culture of Japan: fishermen who had been blown off course and, upon ultimately landing in Ecuador, had introduced the art of pottery making to the local peoples. Evidence presented for this scenario includes rocker-stamped decoration, bone-shaped impressions and similar simple geometric, plastic decorative motifs. Some decades of further research into early Ecuadorian ceramics (of which Valdivia is not the earliest representative), the Jomon culture, and the nature of the ocean currents, have dismissed this hypothesis. It has, for example, been pointed out that the ocean currents alone make such a voyage improbable, discounting the unsuitability of the available sea craft, the sheer distance involved, and similar caveats.

Other speculators looking for a distant point of origin have turned to Mesoamerica. Unfortunately the earliest Mesoamerican traditions are too late to be ancestral to those of South America and are themselves both diverse and, in most cases, quite obviously ancestral to their own local traditions, having nothing in common in terms of form or decoration with the ceramics of either Caribbean Colombia or Valdivia. Claims of later ceramic interchange, whether looking to Asia or north to Mesoamerica, ring just as false, as they too rest upon mistaken temporal equations or on such widely spread decorative techniques as dentate rocker stamping, red on natural tan clay slip decoration, simple incised or painted geometric designs, etc. It is possible that ongoing research in Central America will both reveal earlier ceramics than are now known and suggest ties between Central and South America. At the moment, however, the very diversity of the earliest ceramics on the continent and the obvious continuity of some ceramic traditions from these earliest examples, is most parsimoniously explained as the result of multiple inventions of ceramic technology, coupled with stimulus diffusion and outright borrowing and/or migration of ceramics-using peoples into regions without their own ceramic tradition.

The technology exhibited in the various ceramic traditions of South America is relatively simple. It does, however, show that extreme sophistication of design and high esthetic ideals can be achieved with uncomplicated tools. The potter's wheel was not present in the Americas and all ceramics were hand built. A version of the *tournette*, mistakenly called a slow wheel, was widely known. The *tournette* can be a fired ceramic base onto which the damp clay is molded forming a base, coils of clay being added to build up the vessel while it is turned on the fired clay mold. Some *tournettes* are simply a wooden board, often placed on a round-based bowl, which is used as a turntable base upon which the vessel is constructed. These implements can be turned relatively fast and southern Mexican Mayan potters can actually achieve enough speed to have a slight assist from centrifugal force in forming the vessel. More commonly, however, *tournettes* are used to turn large vessels as they are being made, to turn a finished vessel as it is being scraped and wiped, and to aid in painting designs such as horizontal stripes on a rounded vessel. Because the vessel is turned during these processes, the surface results can be uncannily like those achieved on a true wheel and unwary scholars have thought that a wheel must have been employed in vessel formation.

Most vessels were formed by coiling or by slab construction (or some combination thereof) with pinching and hand modeling being common secondary decorative techniques (Figure 8.3). The paddle and anvil method of building vessels was known and survived until recently on the north coast of Peru. It is still used in those parts of Ecuador where northern Peruvian ceramic practices were introduced by the Incas. Techniques for making numbers of identical vessels were highly developed, especially in northern Peru. Shortly before the beginning of the Christian era, fired clay potters' molds were invented. The earliest known of these are in coastal Ecuador, where the Chorrera potters used a single-piece mold to form the front half of hollow figurines. Molds were considerably later to the south, but they became very popular along the north coast of Peru, where first the coastal Chavín-related cultures and then the Moche switched to molds to form vessels and ceramic artifacts such as whistles, figurines, and similar small objects. Many Moche vessels were formed using multiple-piece molds. Plain vessels, mainly those with low relief decoration, were often made in large multiples from the same mold. These vessels could then be painted differently to make them appear singular artifacts. An interesting experiment with the only collection of Moche grave lots in the United States, at the Hearst (formerly the Lowie) Museum of

8.3 Eduardo Calderón of Huanchaco, Peru, molding a replica of a prehispanic bottle. Simple two-part molds such as this were in common use in Ecuador and northern coastal Peru from *c.* 2000 BC.

the University of California, Berkeley, showed that the more elaborate vessels showed signs of pre-burial use on their bases, whereas the mass produced, simpler jars and bottles had evidently been acquired specially as grave goods, as they showed no wear marks. In later Moche times the tendency towards mass production accelerated; fine line painted vessels from the northern Moche sphere show scenes in which great quantities of small jars are depicted. This is matched by Moche 4 grave lots from Moche, which show a sudden increase in simple, crudely finished jars. These mass production techniques carried over into later cultures in the north, although along the south and central coast, and in the adjacent highlands, vessels were formed by pinch, coil, and pulling techniques until the colonial period.

Slip casting, which is the means by which most modern dishes are produced, was known on the south coast for a brief period of time at the end of the Early Horizon, when it was used for casting pan pipes and spouts; some other peoples may have known of the technique, but it was never really common.

Decorative techniques included all of those known to the modern potter, with the exception of vitreous glazes. In the montaña regions of Peru and Ecuador, the appearance of a glaze was, and is, mimicked by rubbing the still-warm vessel with plant resin. This gives a slick, shiny finish, although it is, of course, easily damaged by exposure to heat. With the arrival of the Spanish, western glazing techniques found an appreciative audience in some native traditions, although slip painted or unpainted ceramics continued to be made over much of the continent and are still commonly made and used for both domestic and decorative purposes.

An unusual form of acquiring a red and black vessel without double firing was known in South America from almost the earliest ceramic traditions. This was organic resist or "negative" painting. In this decorative technique a vessel was fired so that it had an oxidized red or light colored surface. The cooled, fired vessel was then coated with an organic material, probably of vegetable origin, which was liquid enough to seep into the porous fabric of the vessel. Next those areas which the potter wished to remain the base red or buff color were painted out with slip, leaving the design areas uncovered. Finally the vessel was heated until the exposed organic-material-coated areas charred. When cool the now dry slip was brushed off, leaving a vessel with black decoration. This organic black paint is quite sturdy, although it disappears if the vessel is heated too hot or if it is fired once again. Although some have suggested that wax was used, in a batik-like technique, experiments have shown that the wax does not char, but merely runs and burns, leaving a mess. Wax was also not available to many of the peoples who favored organic resist decoration, which was most of the cultures of western South America, at least from time to time.

Iridescent painting, another technique unique to the Americas, involves making a superfine slip by suspension of the ground clay particles in water. The fine particles remaining after the grosser ones have sunk to the bottom are dispersed by adding an electrolytic agent such as tannic acid, so that the microscopic platelets of clay float in a parallel alignment. When a vessel which has been painted with such a solution is fired the painted areas acquire a hard glossy finish which will not absorb carbon as easily as the unpainted (or painted with an ordinary slip) parts of the vessel. If the vessel is then subjected to post-fire smudging, the fused microslipped areas will acquire an iridescent quality, particularly notable when the vessel is wet. Iridescent painting is a very subtle effect and it was not widely used. It is mainly found in ceramics of the Late Formative period in southern Ecuador, although the appearance of this unusual technique in Guatemala has been considered by some to be evidence of direct contact.

Many peoples appear to have fired their pottery by the open pit method (Figure 8.4). Although an experienced potter can control the flow of oxygen quite well and produce both oxidized and reduced (as well as smoked) wares, it can be difficult to get a high temperature with a purely open method. There is evidence of more sophisticated versions of this type of firing, utilizing walled enclosures (either walled patios or specially built firing fields with high walls), which more closely approximate temporary kilns. Remains of these have been found in northern Peru, where they were used (as they still are today) to fire large storage vessels and other forms which would not fit easily into small kilns. Although it has often been said that the potter's kiln was absent in the Americas, when archaeologists began to look for kilns they found them. In the Lambayeque Valley, a project directed by Izumi Shimada has been directed at recovering workshops as well as studying ceremonial and mortuary aspects of the Sicán and earlier cultures. Here, along the Poma Canal, a series of more than fifty-seven kilns,

8.4 Open firing of ceramics in Mr. Calderón's workshop patio. The pit on the right shows the ceramics covered with sherds and animal dung. It will then be covered with earth to produce black ceramics, while the upper firing, which is open, will produce oxidized red ceramics.

in four distinct strata, was uncovered. These kilns are associated with abundant remains of Cupisnique (a north coast Chavín-related style) and must date to mid-first millennium BC. The size of the workshop (not all of which was uncovered) suggests to Shimada and his colleagues that ceramics production was already in the hands of full-time specialists. This is very much the case with the later Moche traditions; several Moche ceramics production sites have been found, each producing different types of pottery. To the north a large workshop with lines of kilns has been discovered near Puerto López, Ecuador. Manteño style black-ware ceramics were being produced here and traded over a considerable area of coastal Ecuador.

It seems more than likely that the other major styles of western South America, or at least those which were either technically complex (as in Nazca) or being produced on an immense scale like Moche, Chimu, and Manteño pottery, were likewise produced in specialist workshops using kilns or other methods of heat and oxygen control.

There is considerable variety in the South American ceramic traditions, a variety which continues into the present, although many traditions are becoming moribund with the influx of metal and plastic containers. The time depth of many styles is likewise considerable, with many traditions being traceable back to the first ones known in a region. The continuities in Amazonian and northern Peruvian ceramics have been mentioned. In the southern highlands of Ecuador open firing under reducing conditions coupled with a terminal oxidation to redden the iron oxide painted decoration on vessels is found in the first Formative traditions and continues to the present in the ceramics of Jatunpamba even though the actual formation process in Jatunpamba was influenced by the Incas. Today, ancient ceramic traditions are being saved from extinction or are being revived for the tourist trade and for sale as "antiquities" on the illegal art market. Many techniques, such as resin painting, organic resist painting and even, perhaps, iridescent painting, have been resuscitated or reinvented for these new customers, who might be viewed as the spiritual heirs of those ancient South Americans who picked up a Recuay vase or a Chorrera pot to take home as a souvenir.

THE FIRST CIVILIZATIONS: 2000–200 BC

By the time of the introduction of ceramics into Peru large ceremonial centers which were the religious and administrative foci of regional populations were common throughout the highlands and the coast (Figure 9.1). Changing political and economic situations are mirrored in the history of these; many of the large preceramic centers such as El Paraíso and Huaca La Florida were abandoned, other sites such as Kotosh continued in use, and a series of new and imposing centers was being founded. One of these was Chavín de Huántar, located in the small highland valley of the Mosna River. This river flows eastwards and is part of the huge drainage system of the Marañon River, a major tributary of the Amazon. The valley also has good farm land and is within easy reach of the puna pastures.

Chavín was founded as a ceremonial center during the period of the introduction of ceramics to Peru, probably both as a religious center and as a strategic site for the control of traffic and trade between the Callejón de Huaylas (the Santa River is a major arterial to the coast) and the tropical forest to the east. The main religious constructions are associated with a cut-stone-faced temple, which survives to over 12 m in height (Figure 9.2). It is decorated with low relief carvings of birds and felines in a very distinctive style. Stone heads, representing various mythical animals and humans, were tenoned into the walls of the platform. The earliest temple was a modified U in plan with a circular sunken plaza between the two wings, a plan obviously related both to the large preceramic temple complexes on the coast and to those of the Kotosh Religious Tradition (Figure 9.3). The apparently solid temple platform is riddled with interior galleries filled with offerings: elaborate pottery, stone cups and mortars, marine fish and shells, and even a female skull, laid with a ring of infants' milk teeth around it. Deep in the center of the platform is one of the few remaining cult objects of precolumbian times, a shaft of white granite nearly 5 m high carved in low relief with the depiction of a smiling male (Figure 9.4). This figure has a number of supernatural attributes, including the fanged mouth that became a signifer of supernatural status throughout ancient South America. This deity, called the Smiling God, is associated with figures of birds, butterflies, and similar creatures which indicate that he was probably a sky deity of some sort. Later additions to the temple were associated with other major deities: a supernatural pair of caymans and then, finally, a frontally depicted male holding a staff in each hand. This Staff God was to become popular in other parts of Peru and formed a model for the depiction of later deities. Although there are no examples from Chavín itself, painted textiles in purest Chavín style from the south coast site of Carhua show that the Staff God had a female counterpart who was associated with domesticated

9.1 Principal sites and traditions of the first millennium BC. 1. Rancho Peludo, 2. Coro, 3. Los Barrancos, 4. Parmana, Ronquín, Corazal, 5. La Gruta, 6. Esmeraldas, La Tolita, Tumaco, Atacames, 7. Salango, 8. Chorrera, 9. Cerro Narrío, Pirincay, 10. Cerro Ñañañique, 11. Huaca de los Reyes, 12. Pakopampa, Moxeque, Cerro Blanco, 13. Chavín de Huántar, Kotosh, 14. Garagay, 15. Paracas Peninsula, 16. Pucara, 17. Tiahuanaco, Wankarani, Chiripa, 18. San Pedro de Atacama.

9.2 The main temple ("El Castillo") at Chavín de Huántar, Peru. The Black and White Portal, its pillars finely carved with supernatural raptorial birds, provided access to the last temple.

9.3 The sunken circular plaza of Chavín de Huántar. Part of the most ancient construction, the "Old Temple," this plaza has obvious stylistic resemblances to constructions of the Kotosh Religious Tradition. The plaza is faced with cut stone and is decorated with reliefs of pumas, spotted felines, and other figures associated with the cult of the Smiling God.

9.4 The Lanzón, a shaft of white granite with the figure of the Smiling God carved upon it. The peculiar shape, which is the natural form of the shaft, became associated with cult objects and is seen in stone reliefs of later cultures in Peru.

9.5 Highly kenned reliefs of a jaguar and a hawk from the underside of a cornice on El Castillo. On the jaguar guard hairs and whiskers have become snakes, the spots guilloches with eyes, and parts of the body emerge from mouths. The lower mouth on the tail is located at that point at which a cat twitches its tail. The hawk sports snake kennings on some of the long feathers and a fanged mouth behind his identifying beak.

plants and animals. Paired male–female deities were important in many later Andean religions. There is little other direct evidence concerning Chavín religious beliefs or practices, although a figure from the sunken plaza carries a San Pedro cactus, a plant known for its hallucinogenic properties and still used in traditional curing ceremonies.

The temple of Chavín is clearly related to earlier religious structures in the central Andes, but it is much more elaborate and the sculpture, pottery, and other artifacts associated with it are highly original in their elaborate representational style. This art style and the religion it was associated with were extremely influential in much of the rest of Peru. Chavín art is basically naturalistic and the major subjects are human beings, bird, snakes, felines, and other animals. Most of these figures, and the shells, plants and so on associated with them, are apparently attendants to the main deities. Deities and supernatural figures are indicated by "kennings," a type of figurative expression in which body parts are visually compared to such elements as mouths, snakes, and eyes (Figure 9.5). Generally speaking, the more important a figure is, the more kennings it will have; although sheer numbers of kennings on a single figure increase through time, producing a final art style that is truly baroque in its ornamentation. However, the basic figures of Chavín art always were the major deities and their human, bird, and animal attendants.

Chavín art is expressed in a number of media, including small stone carvings and vessels, sculptured ceramics, pyro-engraved gourds, carved shell, hammered and cut-out gold ornaments, and textiles. The carved and sculptured bottles and open dishes of the Chavín style are heavy, generally dark in color, and bear distinctive geometric designs such as circles and guilloches as well as images of the supernaturals, their attendants, or their signifers (Figure 9.6). The ceramics depict a wider range of subjects than the stone sculptures, especially the ceramics from coastal Chavín-related sites (Figure 9.7). Here can be seen the origin of the long-lived north coast traditions of sculptured ceramics. Stirrup bottles and other closed forms depict both religious and genre themes: aside from the supernaturals there are people making offerings, wild and domestic animals and plants of the region (sometimes in combination, such as the association between small spotted cats, *Felis colacola*, and columnar San Pedro cactuses), architectural complexes, and various artifacts. Metal working spread over the central Andes and was beginning to move north, although most known Chavín metal is simple gold jewelry and clothing decorations. Metal objects also show supernatural figures and the secondary figures associated with them. Textiles exhibit a number of new decorative techniques: all are made on the heddle loom and woven cloth replaced the elaborate twined fabrics of the preceramic eras. Painted textiles are thought to have been one medium through which the elaborate iconography of Chavín religion was spread great distances from its source, as numbers of these recovered (unfortunately by huaqueros) in southern Peru show the full panoply of Chavín religious motifs painted in purest Chavín style (Figure 9.8). Wrapped weft fabrics and tapestries also became popular and, on the south coast of Peru, embroidery was developed into a major art form. Chavín de Huántar was an urban center, one of the earliest in the Andes. Beginning as a ceremonial center with a small resident population and supported by people living in hamlets scattered through the several local ecosystems, by *c.* 1450 BC (Chakinani phase), the population began to concentrate around the temple. Within about a century this settlement grew to a densely occupied town covering some 40 ha. A planned settlement of small houses, carefully constructed drainage systems, and massive government storage facilities within and without the temple precincts, Chavín possessed the elements which were to become standard in later Andean cities.

The religion of Chavín and the art style which celebrated it were extremely influential in Peru for nearly a thousand years. Some political influence may also have been

9.6 Carved coastal Chavín stirrup bottle. The cat faces on this piece have become stylized almost past the point of recognition.

9.7 Modeled coastal Chavín stirrup bottle with a theme which continued through north coast ceramic traditions until after the European invasions: a man carrying a deer on his back, perhaps as an offering or as part of a deer hunt ceremony.

9.8 Spotted cat done in tie dye and painting on a cotton textile, from Carhua, Peru. Owing to the small size (about 15 cm in length) and the medium, this cat has only the guard hairs and the tail twitch kenned.

involved, although the extent of any Chavín polity is difficult to gauge. At its height it seems probable that Chavín had administrative and economic control over a number of highland valleys, including part of the Callejón de Huaylas, and the neighboring puna regions. They may also have had some control over the nearer montaña and they certainly controlled a major trading route to the montaña and the tropical lowlands from the very beginning. The presence of ceramics from many different coastal and highland sites in temple offerings and domestic refuse argues strongly for consistent interchange with those areas as well, something which is reinforced by the appearance of Chavín-style artifacts and Chavín-influenced motifs in other media in a large number of sites from central Peru into Ecuador.

These sites show considerable architectural evidence for massive cultural influence from Chavín. At Pacopampa, a three weeks' llama caravan trek to the north of Chavín,

9.9 Adobe giant head on the temple of Huaca de los Reyes, Moche Valley, Peru. Although definitely influenced by Chavín, the development of a distinctive coastal style is clearly visible in this and related sites.

the main temple was remodeled into an approximation of the main temple of Chavín. At the same time stone sculpture was introduced and there is evidence of the influence of the monochromatic Chavín ceramic tradition on the painted local tradition. On the coast at the important site of Caballo Muerto, some 20 km inland in the Moche Valley, the most important temple (Huaca de los Reyes) was remodeled and decorated with large adobe sculptures in Chavín style (Figure 9.9). These are similar to those seen on the 30 m high pyramid at Moxeque, in the Casma Valley, here associated with an earlier large ceremonial and storage center, Pampa de las Llamas. Both sites have large images brightly painted in many colors; at Moxeque these were ranged in niches across the front of the pyramid, though the Huaca de los Reyes ones are to the interior facing the main courtyard. The architectural statuary at these sites, and at the central coast site of Garagay, represents local variants of the Chavín artistic tradition, not slavish copying of motifs from Chavín itself. Many of the coastal sites have U-shaped structures like the New Temple of Chavín, although these are often combined with local architectural features. The murals and painted adobe reliefs at Garagay clearly show Chavín derivation and include a head with mucus pouring from its nose (a reference to the flow of mucus which inhaling hallucinogenic snuffs induces), felines, and strange insect-like creatures. Other sites, such as Cerro Blanco in the Nepeña Valley, have carved and painted adobe relief decoration derived from Chavín ceramics. Not all sites show architectural influence. Huarikoto, for example, continued the Kotosh Religious Tradition, with its sunken hearths for burned offerings, and Chavín influence is mainly visible in some trade goods. At Kotosh itself, however, there are many imported vessels from Chavín and the local ceramic tradition changed from one which was quite close to tropical forest styles to an imitation of Chavín ceramics. Stone architecture here is comparable to the rougher domestic architecture at Chavín and the virtual lack of obsidian, coupled with the abandonment of several formerly imposing sites in the immediate vicinity of Kotosh, suggests that Chavín may have been prospering at the expense of Kotosh and its allies. Many of the northern and central highland and coastal sites indicate a situation in which Chavín was heavily influencing local art and architecture. Outright copies of Chavín artifacts were produced and imports from Chavín have been found in many of these sites. Products from the same sites have also been found at Chavín indicating fairly close ties of exchange as well as clear prestige relationships.

A very different situation arose on the south coast of Peru. Here the Paracas culture, although early influenced by the cult of the Smiling God and, much later, subject to renewed influences from the cult of the Staff God (and Goddess), reworked Chavín motifs into their own highly independent religion and art style. Most information on the Paracas culture comes from ceramics and textiles, although a number of U-shaped structures have been located in the Ica Valley. One of these, Animas Altas, has murals of supernatural figures in the same style as Paracas pottery. This local ceramic tradition shows some Chavín influence in technology. However, instead of featuring highly sculptural, monochrome vessels, designs were outlined by incision; after firing the vessels were covered with brilliantly colored mineral pigments in a resin base. Although Chavín influence is evident in early ceramic motifs, such as birds, feline faces, and some geometric designs, a series of indigenous cults characterized south coast religion. In the earlier of these the major deity is a figure called the Oculate Being, a creature with a human or feline body, large round eyes and a semi-circular smile (see Figure 13.6). The Oculate Being is associated with knives and trophy heads; along with his cult, caches of trophy heads begin to appear in archaeological contexts. This is the first evidence of the widespread warfare and head taking which characterized the centuries to come.

The famous mummy bundles of the Paracas Peninsula, with their multitudes of elaborately embroidered textiles, come from the very end of the Paracas culture (Figure 9.10). Many of these are associated with a very different, fine orange and white monochrome pottery, modeled into delicate fluted and globular bottles. Along with this experimentation in modeled, unpainted ceramics, the polychrome deity representations found on the resin painted pottery were transferred, briefly, onto textiles: clothing, hangings and the like, many of which were then buried with the dead. The Paracas burials are found in two types of tombs. The Cavernas burials are in bottle-shaped tombs dug through the sand into the bed rock where masses of mummy bundles were deposited. The Necropolis tombs are deposits of burials in the remains of abandoned buildings, and often consist of a single very large and elaborate burial near the multiple burials. Both types of burials seem to have been nearly contemporary. All ages and, presumably, both sexes are represented in the Paracas burials and there is a considerable amount of variation in the elaboration of the individual mummy bundles, suggesting that entire families or some similar group may have been buried in a given tomb. The

9.10 Cerro Colorado on the Paracas Peninsula, southern Peru. The remains of looted tombs are clearly visible around the hill and in the foreground.

mummies were not specially prepared; the dry heat of the desert accomplished the mummification. The bodies were placed seated in a basket with various pieces of clothing and other items around them and then sewn into a plain cotton shroud. More textiles, clothing, mantles, bags, headdresses, slings, etc. were piled on, accompanied by plant materials, animals, trophy heads, combs, pots, jewelry, tools, and other items, and then another shroud was sewn on. The more elaborate the burial, the more layers of textiles, artifacts, and shrouds (Figure 9.11). The textiles have images of deities and ritual actors embroidered on them in several distinct styles which, however, are definitely contemporary as they are found on sets of clothing in the same bundles. The embroidered motifs include the Oculate Being, in human, bird, and feline form, human figures wearing costumes of a host of different supernaturals (see Figures 13.6 and 13.7), as well as more naturalistic birds, animals, fish, plants, and geometric designs, some of which may refer to types of weaving techniques.

By the late centuries of the first millennium BC international art styles and religions, large political units, urban centers, and sophisticated economic systems involving interchange between far-flung regions were established and continued to characterize the central Andean region throughout prehistory. The regions contiguous to the central Andes were involved in trade with the various Peruvian cultures on a regular basis and numbers of their products, such as spondylus, were essential to the Peruvians, but there is no evidence of the kind of pervasive influence in all aspects of culture that is seen in the sites of the Peruvian highlands or coast. There is some indication that interchange with the montaña cultures played an important role in the development of Chavín religion and economy, but there is no evidence that Chavín influenced the montaña cultures to any development past that of small villages practicing shifting agriculture. The closest

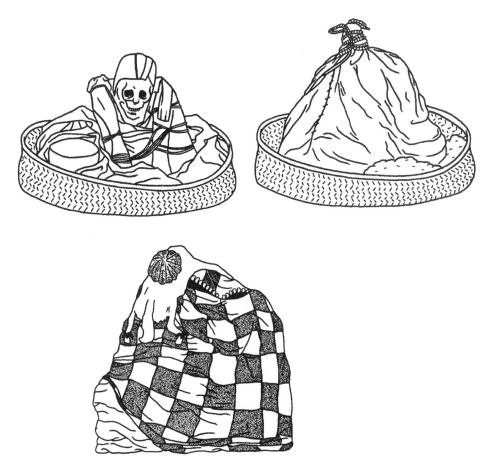

9.11 Paracas mummy bundle. These drawings show how the body was placed in a basket, covered with belongings, clothes and offerings, enshrouded, and the process repeated numerous times until the penultimate covering, in this case an animal skin headdress over an elaborately embroidered mantle. The final stage, when the bundle was once more shrouded in plain cloth, is not shown.

ties of these cultures, at least from later phases, were always with the eastern Amazon lowlands and they were inimical to the idea of being drawn into the Peruvian political sphere. However, the importance of trade in the development of the Peruvian civilizations is evident. The major advantage of the site of Chavín is that it controls a major access between the highland valleys (and their routes to the coast) and the montaña. Many of the highland and coastal sites which were drawn into the orbit of Chavín share locations which control movement of people and goods between the major environmental zones. It is at this time that the first known roads appear on the coast. Pre-Inca roads have been intensively studied only in the Moche Valley where a number of roads of this time period have been found. These connect sites (or parts of sites such as at sprawling Caballo Muerto) and also show that intervalley and coastal–highlands exchange was an important aspect of the local cultures. Trading links between major environmental regions seem to have been important in those areas of the

Andes which were outside of the direct Chavín sphere of influence, even in those situations in which such trade did not lead to any early development of large urban cultures.

Although the southern highlands, especially the altiplano of Bolivia, were outside the range of direct Chavín influence, they seem to have borrowed some ultimately Chavín ideas from the south coast cultures as somewhat later, in Pucara and Tiahuanaco, supernatural figures which appear to have been derived from the angels and the Staff God of Chavín achieve paramount importance in a new state religion and religious expansion.

During the last millennium before the modern era agricultural and pastoral villages were expanding on the altiplano and the beginnings of large settlements and of ceremonial architecture and stone sculpture appear. The Wankarani culture, centered to the north and northeast of Lake Poopó, is the first exemplar of a way of life which remains little changed to the present. The earliest Wankarani remains date to around 1200 BC; the culture was enveloped by the expanding Tiahuanaco polity in the early centuries AD. Wankarani towns were walled accumulations of round adobe houses which were painted yellow on the interior and red on the outside. The adult dead were buried under the clay house floors. These settlements were very permanent and, over the centuries, sites became small hills from the superimposed remains of houses and middens. The Wankarani grew potatoes and quinoa and herded camelids. These latter seem to have been a focus of ceremonial beliefs, since the only evidence of ceremonial architecture surviving from Wankarani sites are stone tenon heads of llamas or alpacas. It has been suggested that these were stuck in the ground in clusters at the site center (Figure 9.12), although the remains of some green quartzite slabs at the site of Uspa Uspa suggest that ceremonial buildings may have once been present.

A similar economic orientation to that of Wankarani is seen in the Chiripa culture, found around the southern end of Lake Titicaca. The Chiripa type site has two major occupations, of which the later, dating to *c*. 600–100 BC, is the most important. Chiripa was a temple complex formed of a series of rectangular buildings around a central patio which contains a sunken rectangular temple. The walls of the structures are double and have interior bins which were used to store foodstuffs such as chuño and quinoa, and other materials. The ceramics of Chiripa are tricolored; one of the most characteristic forms is a trumpet, used apparently in religious rituals. Chiripa was part of the Yaya-Mama Religious Tradition, a tradition whose complex iconography, centering around a male-female pair of deities, was expressed on stone low relief carved stelae found throughout the northern altiplano (Figure 9.13). Chiripa itself apparently was the model for later temple structures, most notably the Kidder Temple at Pucara.

Further to the south the Alto Ramirez culture of northern Chile shows close contacts with the cultures of the altiplano. Although Alan Kolata and others have suggested that the florescence of this and the slightly later cultures of San Pedro de Atacama was due to their being on the receiving end of llama caravans managed by altiplano peoples, the situation is by no means clear. Interregional exchange, however, was apparently very important in the development and growing prosperity of these southern cultures and many of their artifacts show a certain correspondence with contemporary styles of the

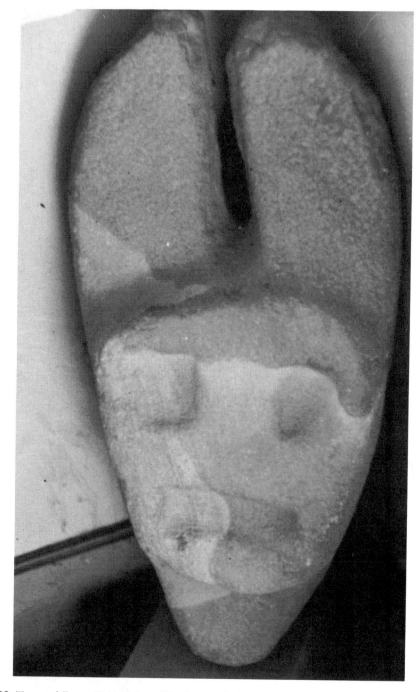

9.12 Tenoned llama (?) head from Wankarani, Bolivia.

9.13 Stele I from Taraco, Peru. The roll-out drawing shows the dual female and male deities.

altiplano. Alto Ramirez villages, however, are groups of semicircular houses in adobe, with associated artificial burial mounds. Ceramics are monochrome, polished and often modeled. Highland traits are mainly seen in the textiles, which show a clear affiliation with the contemporary altiplano styles and, slightly later, full altiplano religious iconography becomes common in these southern sites.

Far northern Peru and the southern highlands of Ecuador show some reflection of the Chavín expansion. Chavín-influenced ceramics have been found at a number of sites in the Piura Valley, although local traditions remained strong and it is surmised that much of the Chavín-related material is, in fact, imported from Zaña to the south. Excavations at Cerro Ñañañique have shown, however, that large U-shaped structures dominate the early phases of occupation at this important site and that local ceramics do show some continuities both with provincial Chavín styles and with contemporary styles of southern highland Ecuador. In Ecuador, however, although the expansion of inter-area trade may have been influenced by Chavín owing to the beginnings of the use of spondylus and strombus shells as sacred symbols by Peruvian cultures, local developments are much more in evidence. Specialized trade centers had apparently been

9.14 The Paute River Valley near Pirincay, Azuay Province, Ecuador, looking upstream. This little valley, even though the river is not navigable, has formed a major route of contact between the montaña and the highlands of southern Ecuador since the second millennium BC.

established some time in the late second millennium BC in the highlands, although only one of these, Pirincay to the northeast of Cuenca in the Paute Valley, has been thoroughly investigated. Pirincay was located to control traffic between the lowlands and the important highland valleys of Cuenca and Cañar (Figure 9.14). A secondary (?) function of the site was as a rock crystal bead manufacturer; such beads were highly valued on the coast. At about 400–200 BC increased contact with both the northern coast and the tropical lowlands of Peru is evinced by the appearance of trade ceramics and then by the rapid introduction of maize agriculture, llama pastoralism with its concomitant feasting and sacrifices, and complex metallurgy.

Along the coast of Ecuador a series of closely related cultures are found in this same *c.* 1300–300 BC time range. Although local names have been given to regional manifestations, many Ecuadorian archaeologists prefer to refer to them all as *chorreroid* after the Chorrera tradition of the south coast. The Engeroy culture, for example, is a chorreroid culture of the Santa Elena Peninsula. The chorreroid traditions feature extremely fine ceramics, with a large percentage of modeled vessels, especially various bottle forms, some of which have whistles incorporated. In the Chorrera tradition proper there is an extensive use of iridescent and organic resist painting. Hollow figurines are common (Figure 9.15). Chorreroid traditions are found along the coast up into southern Colombia, and in the highlands Chorrera imports have been found at a

9.15 Chorrera figurine of a male from coastal Ecuador. The elaborate painting and incision on the body represent body paint and, perhaps, tattoos, not clothing. The small double earrings and helmet-like hair are typical of Chorrera figures.

number of sites, including both Pirincay and Cerro Narrío, on main routes from the highlands to the Guayas Basin and the southern coast of Ecuador. Chorrera in many ways represents a continuation of cultural patterns which had been long established in Ecuador. Chorrera sites are small to medium-sized villages. Burials show some status differentiation, and it is at this time that long-distance trade networks to assure regular supplies of luxury goods seem to have become firmly established. A late Chorrera burial from Salango had a gold nose ornament, the earliest excavated metal from the northern Andes.

There is evidence for population growth, and the multiplicity of chorreroid ceramic styles may be explained both as influence of one tradition on others and as migration into previously unoccupied regions. One of these was the northern coast of Ecuador and southern coast of Colombia where the series of cultures which are variously called Esmeraldas, La Tolita, Tumaco, or Atacames are found. The tropical coastline here is open to the sea and has active shifting sand bars and beaches. Rivers and estuaries cut the

9.16 The Inguapi estuary near the site of the same name, in southern Colombia. The mangroves and estuaries form an especially rich ecosystem for fishing and farming peoples.

narrow coastal plain and there is a strong development of mangrove reaching several kilometers inland (Figure 9.16). This area is seismically very unstable and subject to tidal waves. The prehispanic cultures of the region have been known mainly for their elaborate modeled ceramics and the small gold objects which have washed out of the tolas, the earthen house platforms of the middle phase of this series of closely related cultures (Figures 9.17 and 9.18). The modeled vessels, figurines, and relief plaques show humans with artificially shaped heads (a common cosmetic device in much of the ancient world) and elaborate jewelry, erotic and ritual scenes, monstrous figures, and animals (Figure 9.19). Metallurgy, in the form of small tools and ornaments of gold and copper, was known and many of the sites have been destroyed in mining operations aimed at recovering the gold. Recent work in both Colombia and Ecuador has given a much better picture of this culture, which has previously been known mainly through materials from clandestine excavations. The first occupation of this region is ceramically related to the chorreroid traditions farther to the south. The early sites (Inguapi phase in Tumaco, Tachina phase in Esmeraldas) are on estuaries some distance inland, and contemporary occupations with related ceramic styles are seen in the Santiago–Cayapas River basin even further inland (Mafa and early Selva Alegre phases). Sites directly on

9.17 Mound (tola) 5 at Inguapi before excavation. These platforms kept buildings above the often flooded and usually damp ground.

9.18 Excavation of Mound 5 shows the broken pottery of earlier phases incorporated into the platform. Most Tolita figurines and vessels come from fill and are hence eroded and broken.

9.19 Tolita-style monstrous figure, perhaps a supernatural impersonator. This particular figure also appears in the stone sculpture of San Agustín. The feathered or scaled all-in-one garment is found mainly on figures which seem to be ritual performers.

the coast may have existed, but have almost certainly been destroyed by natural forces. The economy of the Tolita peoples varied from area to area. The earliest levels of the Inguapi site show a great many line weights, indicating the importance of fishing, and crustacean remains, but very little evidence of collecting the abundant mangrove mollusks, whereas the La Propicia site in Esmeraldas reveals that mollusks were a major food source in that region. Organic preservation is poor to non-existent in this very hot and rainy land. The lack of stone projectile points may show that inland hunting was not important, although it is very possible that spears of chonta palm wood were being used instead, something that was very common in much of Colombia (where stone projectile points are extremely rare).

Figurines provide no clues to mammals of economic importance as the major species shown are felines, saurians, owls, and kinkajous. It seems probable that agriculture was practiced and a characteristic artifact of the region is a ceramic plate with pieces of stone set in it, a grater which may have been used for manioc, although it has been suggested that the smaller ones were fish scalers. Many of these are, quite appropriately, in the form of a fish. Trade was apparently important and in later phases an active trade with the highlands is attested to by the presence of coral, pearls, chonta palm, marine shells, and other coastal products in the tombs of many highland sites and by obsidian on the coast (the nearest obsidian sources are near Quito). Transportation on the coast was and is almost entirely by boat, and canoe models are common in the art of the region (Figure 9.20). That long-distance contact was sufficiently intense to allow for the spread of religious ideas is shown by the appearance of several supernatural figures which appear both in the stone sculpture of San Agustín and in the ceramic art of Tumaco (Figure 9.19).

The succeeding phases lack chorreroid characteristics although contact with other coastal and highland cultures is very evident in the subjects and modes of representation of modeled ceramics. There is some evidence, in the form of metates, for the introduction of maize or other seed processing although, as mentioned previously, metates are used for a great many things that have nothing to do with maize or maize grinding. Cotton may have been grown, since ceramic spindle whorls are present, although they are not abundant. Figures are shown in elaborate costumes which suggest that the textile arts were highly developed. From about 500 BC–AD 500 (Tiaone, Tolita, Early Atacames phases) there was a fairly homogeneous culture in the region. Settlements were apparently rather small and strung out along the estuaries. In Ecuador the practice of building artificial mounds as bases for houses began some time during this period. Ceramic house models show a variety of rectangular houses with gabled, presumably thatched, roofs. The relatively small sizes of the artificial mounds suggest that nuclear or small extended families occupied these houses. Some sites, such as Inguapi, have some larger mounds which may have had larger buildings on them; refuse on the mounds shows their essentially domestic character. Burials were made within the mounds, under or near the houses. Both primary burials and cremations are known and found in the same sites, perhaps indicating differential treatment of the dead. Most burials have offerings of ceramics, tools, and personal adornments.

9.20 Tolita-style model of two people paddling a dugout canoe. Canoes seem to have been the major means of transport in northern Ecuador, whereas the river rafts appear to have been much used in the huge, meandering rivers of the Guayas Basin, later being converted to coast-wise transport as well.

A major interruption in the occupation of the region seems to have taken place sometime after AD 800–900 and the late prehistoric culture is completely different in terms of its ceramics. These late peoples were traders as well as farmers and fishermen and economically must have been continuing the cultural patterns established so many centuries before.

In the eastern and northern tropics a different cultural trajectory is seen. Agriculture and ceramics making slowly spread along the major river systems and, perhaps, along the coast. There are some nearly unsurmountable problems in dealing with the culture history of the riverine lowlands. The first of these is preservation. Hot, humid regions have poor organic preservation, yet we know from history and ethnology that the major part of the material culture of the tropical forest and savanna dwellers was (and is) of perishable materials such as feathers, baskets, woven textiles, and wood. Because of the scarcity of stone in these alluvial areas, most tools and weapons were made of wood as well. Even pottery is often in poor condition from centuries of waterlogging and is eroded and fractured to the point that all one can say is that there once was pottery. The tropical river systems of lowland South America are active and meandering. Since we know from history and ethnography that the preferred sites for settlements were on the high ground of river banks and levées along ox-bow lakes we know that many have been destroyed as the rivers have moved, often quite rapidly, back and forth across the floodplains, destroying old channels, their banks, and the sites which were on them. A very large percentage of the sites discovered in the tropical lowlands have been found as redeposited cultural materials or as artifacts eroding out of river banks. Recently, however, evidences of a substantial interfluvial occupation, both in the Ecuadorian *oriente* and in the Brazilian Amazon, have been found. Ongoing investigation of these sites, which have better preservation, promises greatly to enlarge our knowledge of these lowland horticultural societies. The topography and vegetation make travel except by water (or air) difficult, since many of the traditional paths are no more; river banks are often the only way to locate sites except in areas where farmers are clearing land (Figure 9.21).

The earliest ceramics making cultures yet identified in the western Amazon drainage come from the upper Marañon and upper Ucayali rivers. In the hot savannas of the region where the lower Utcubamba River joins the Marañon, Ruth Shady and Hermilio Rosas have identified an early phase called Bagua. On the basis of similarities of Bagua ceramics to ceramics from Kotosh and Pacopampa, they date the Bagua Phase to about 1500–1200 BC. Bagua ceramics include open vessels and bottles, some with highland-like incised designs and others with fine line incision and polychrome paint. This is an area which was later an extremely important source of deer, although midden deposits indicate that camelids and riverine resources were also being exploited and that agriculture was being practiced. The Bagua phase is important, even though its dating is a bit insecure, because it does show the contemporaneity of a number of different types of ceramic decoration as well as indicating the early importance of highland–lowland interaction.

On the Ucayali River, on the ox-bow lake of Yarinacocha, Donald Lathrap uncovered a series of sites which show an occupation of that area from a time more or less contemporary with Bagua down to the present. The earliest phase, Early Tutishcainyo, represents the remains of people living in wattle and daub houses built on stilts on the high edge of the alluvium. Early Tutishcainyo ceramics have some post-fire red painting and on this basis Lathrap considers them contemporary with Kotosh-Chavín. Most of the vessels are of forms which are fairly typical of many lowland traditions; these include various cooking vessels, open bowls and what, on the basis of ethnographic analogy, may well be beer cups. Late Tutishcainyo shows a fair amount of stylistic change and the area may have been abandoned for some centuries. Late Tutishcainyo does show some continuities with the putatively earlier phase, including double spout and bridge bottles and fine line incision. It is followed by Early Shakimu, which is found stratified over Late Tutishcainyo at San Francisco de Yarinacocha, and which has a single carbon date of 650 ± 100 BC. This later tradition, with its composite silhouette vessels, double spout and bridge bottles, and simple bowls is evidently a descendant of Late Tutishcainyo, with, perhaps, some evidence of exterior ideas and contacts in the elaborate excised designs covered with a lustrous red slip found on some open bowls. Although the excavator would like to see these as being "inspired" by Chavín and representing a misunderstood Chavín iconography, their similarity with other lowland traditions indicates some rather different ties, as does the very post-Chavín date. It is possible that the Yasuni phase of the Napo River begins as early as the Tutishcainyo traditions. Yasuni materials are found in small, thin refuse deposits on high ground along waterways, indicating, perhaps, smallish villages whose economic adaptation was to farming the alluvium and fishing and collecting in the streams, a viable way of life in this region until the twentieth century. Yasuni pottery has both

9.21 The Amazon basin between the Xingú and Tocantins rivers in Brazil. The circular areas are probably archaeological sites.

carinated and bell-shaped bowls with sand and cariapé temper and with some fine cross-hatched decoration, recalling very slightly materials of the Ananatuba culture of the Amazon proper. First identified on Marajó Island at the mouth of the Amazon and dated to *c.* AD 700, Ananatuba pottery has been being steadily pushed back in time, beginning with a 980 BC carbon date from site J-26 on that island. Ananatuba ceramics have a ground sherd temper and are mainly rounded bowls and jars. No griddles have been found associated and it seems unlikely that manioc was being grown or, at least, grated and processed into cakes. Decoration consists of brushing, red slipping, broad line incision, and some zoned hachure. The Castanheira site shows a small island village surrounded by a side loop of a river. Other sites are quite small as well; apparently the Ananatuba people lived in small villages. They are succeeded on Marajó by a somewhat different ceramic tradition, called Mangueiras, and a considerable population growth is

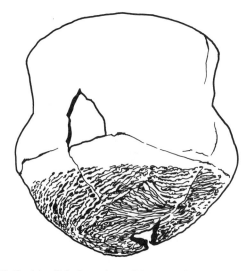

9.22 Rancho Peludo-style cooking vessel with characteristic roughened bottom. This kind of corrugation was widely used for domestic vessels in lowland South America as, indeed, it was in much of the world.

evident. Meggers and Evans suggested invaders and assimilation, although Simões has countered with ideas of either local population growth and invention/diffusion of some new forms and decorative techniques or else abandonment and re-occupation of the high-ground sites by these later Mangueiras peoples. Materials related to Mangueiras have been found farther upriver, at Punta de Jauarí, somewhat upriver from the mouth of the Tapajós. The site is seasonally inundated and the occupants must either have had pile dwellings or have moved to high ground during flood time. The site shows considerable imported stone waste and tools, including polished T-shaped stone axes, manos, and metates. A major activity was shellfish gathering, although hunting forest animals was also important. Ceramics have either shell temper (the earlier, Castalia phase) or cauxí temper (the later Jauarí phase). Jauarí pottery has some zoned hachure decoration like Ananatuba pottery, but differs in modeled adornos and in the presence of tubular ceramic pipes, a characteristic of the Mangueiras people.

The prehistory of the Orinoco is somewhat better known because of decades of work by José Cruxent, Irving Rouse, Mario Sanjoa, and Iraida Vargas, their students and associates. The Rancho Peludo style, first representative of the Dabajuro cultural tradition, has already been mentioned. Rancho Peludo itself is a large, multi-occupation site in the Coro area and was inhabited from *c.* 1800 BC until the 16th century AD. The Dabajuro cultural tradition is one of the longest lived in northern South America, surviving into the present with the continuation of such features as finger roughening of vessel bodies (Figure 9.22). The home of this cultural tradition is the Maracaibo-Coro coast although it spread into the Andes and along the coast to the Dutch Antilles in its final phases. Early representatives of this tradition indicate that agriculture was important, since clay griddles, presumably for toasting manioc, are present, although locations of sites indicate that forest and savanna hunting and river resources were just as important as farming the alluvium. The later Dabajuro sites on the coast and farther down the Orinoco show a simpler version of the largely plastically decorated ceramic style and have manos and metates as well, perhaps evidence of corn agriculture. The Dabajuro peoples along the coast buried their dead in the shell midden, but the more western sites show urn burial. Other than some stone ornaments, often identified as amulets, there is no evidence of religious practices aside from the burials. Although the early sites have clay griddles, it is postulated that the Dabajuro peoples were mainly corn farmers and that their spread was associated with the introduction of corn agriculture to much of Venezuela.

Along the middle and lower Orinoco there were two major ceramic traditions, one, the Barrancoid tradition, featuring incision and modeling, the other, the Saladero or Saladoid tradition, featuring both incision and red and white painted decorations. The Barrancoid tradition is earliest in the east, where it dates to approximately 1000 BC (although some have tried to relate the early Puerto Hormiga style of Colombia to the Barrancoid tradition because of stylistic similarities). Barrancoid pottery is thick and grit tempered, with finely smoothed surfaces. The most typical form is a bowl with a short annular base and a broad flanged rim. Incised geometric decoration is found on all vessel parts and zoomorphic and anthropomorphic modeled lugs and spout figures are common. Some vessels are painted red, black, or yellow, but all retain the incised pattern outlines. Double spout and bridge bottles are quite common as are large vessels which were not used for burial. It is surmised that these were used for brewing beer. Clay griddles and the lack of grinding stones suggest manioc cultivation. Bone points were used for hunting. One localized tradition within the general Barrancoid tradition is that of Los Barrancos, characterized by thinner, finer pottery with more elaborate incised and excised designs (Figure 9.23). The Los Barrancos style, aside from its esthetic importance, is of interest because it seems to have spread east into Guyana, where it is known as the Mabaruma tradition.

The Saladero tradition is known from excavations at a series of sites along the middle Orinoco, especially from the area of Parmana. Here ceramics of the La Gruta tradition were made by a people who lived year round on a high levée with easy access to gallery forest, lagoons, and the river and its islands. Abundant heavy griddle fragments and stone chips (from graters?) are taken to indicate manioc agriculture. Saladero ceramics tend to be fine with a sand temper. The primary shape is a wide bell-shaped bowl with a flat base. True modeling is absent in this tradition which featured red and white painting in curved patterns. Other ceramic remains include fire dogs as well as griddles. Tools were of chert. In the Parmana region Anna Roosevelt's excavations have shown the La Gruta tradition to have been succeeded about 1600 BC first by a style called Ronquín and then (*c.* 1100 BC) by Ronquín Sombra (there are, however, certain objections to these dates and there are those who see the entire middle Orinoco sequence as not beginning until slightly after the beginning of the Christian era). These show steady population growth in the area and, with the identification of more sites, some indication of dry-season fishing camps on the lagoons and rainy-season hunting camps.

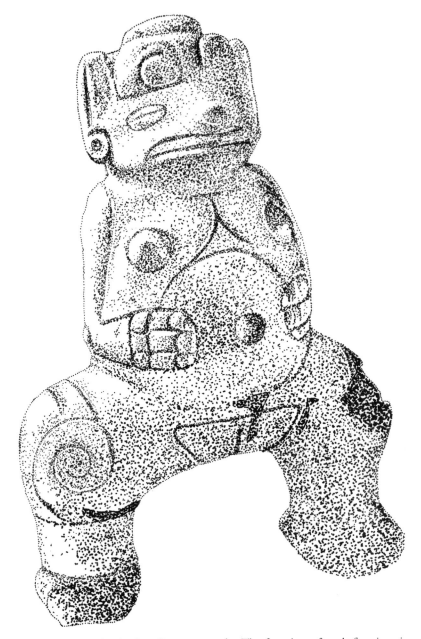

9.23 Female figurine in the Los Barrancos style. The function of such figurines is completely unknown. Many ancient South American cultures made human and animal figurines, presumably for different purposes, whatever these may have been.

The Ronquín and Ronquín Sombra occupations were succeeded by the Corozal phases, beginning *c*. 800 BC (or AD 800 in the short chronology). This very different tradition includes cauxí-tempered gray to buff ceramics decorated with red-filled curvilinear and rectilinear motifs and some plain appliqué designs. The shapes are different than those of the preceding Saladero vessels and from Corozal I onwards there is an abundance of thin griddle fragments in the refuse. Corozal I is the last phase with thick ceramic griddles and a small amount of maize has been identified from sites of this period. The appearance of grinding tools along with maize and canavalia beans has been taken to indicate a major change in crops, although it should be noted that the new thin griddles are essentially the same in shape as the older thick ones. The maize identified from Corozal is similar to the race Pollo, an 8/10 row popcorn. Study of C13–C12 ratios in the bones of Corozal burials shows that the early Corozal people ate little corn, but that by Corozal III corn was the major constituent of the local diet. Corozal settlements have larger quantities of refuse and are the first settlements on mounds in the wet savanna. Roosevelt sees her work at Parmana as showing that the introduction of maize agriculture into an already agricultural area made possible population growth and the development of socially stratified societies ("chiefdoms"). Although there are some legitimate criticisms of this theory, it is evident that by the sixteenth century large, fairly socially and politically complex societies were to be found along the Orinoco. These were obviously the result of a long development in this area.

By the late centuries BC, throughout much of the Andes and the adjacent tropical areas, agriculture, settled life, and the beginnings of fairly complex social structures were well established. Metallurgy had begun and, in the central Andes, the first major civilizations appeared. In many ways this period was a culmination of all that had gone on before: the developments in economy, crafts, and architecture that had started some thousands of years previously. In the ensuing centuries new cultural developments were to be added to those that had gone before and a new element – warfare for territory – was shortly to become common on the cultural scene throughout the Andean region.

CHAPTER 10

TEXTILES: THE HIGH ART OF SOUTH AMERICA

Usually archaeologists, in trying to reconstruct early societies, are restricted to the imperishable bits of the material culture of the past. Such is not the case in parts of South America. In coastal Peru and Chile, because of the extremely dry climate, quantities of perishable materials have survived. Among these are textiles, so that for this area we have direct evidence concerning the religious, political, and esthetic importance of this art. As textiles were the major art form, occupying roughly the same niche that paintings and sculpture do in our system of values, this is very fortunate. Textiles were the main bearers of complex messages; for the most part architecture, painting, and sculpture followed textile forms. In the rest of the continent, unfortunately, survival of textiles is much poorer and we have only isolated examples. These, however, show us that the textile arts were very highly developed in many prehispanic cultures and give us a keen sense of what has been lost.

The textile traditions of most of the New World cultures (including those of Mexico, where only a few shreds remain of what was apparently an equally highly developed art) share similar technologies and materials (except for wool, available only to the Andean peoples). The primary materials of textiles were the various bast fibers, mainly from bromeliads and agaves, cotton, and the wool of the American camelids. The wool of the alpaca was most common; llama wool is coarser and appears to have been mainly used for utilitarian fabrics. Vicuña wool is extremely fine and silky; in Inca times it was used for the very finest and highest-status textiles as, indeed, it is today. The vicuña has never been domesticated and its wool must be gathered from hunted animals. Some of the southern Andean peoples seem occasionally to have used guanaco wool, presumably taken from animals killed in the hunt or taken as babies and tamed. The guanaco was likewise never domesticated. Animal and human hair were also very occasionally used, and feathers, in combination with a woven or netted fiber base, were very important. Metal was used in the form of sequins and other sewn-on sheet-metal ornaments; the art of drawing wire was not known to the ancient Americans and so there was no metal thread. Bark cloth was widely manufactured, especially in preceramic times, although it was seldom elaborately decorated or used for high-status garments or hangings.

Fibers were used both in their original colors and dyed. Wool takes dyes better and more easily than cotton and very early there developed a trade in wool which, in areas in which camelids were not grown in numbers, was largely used for decorative areas or visible areas of textiles. A straightforward manner of identifying textiles made in coastal Peru is to look at the covered elements: these are generally of the cheaper cotton on the coast, as only the lands where wool was grown could afford it for both elements. Cottons come in a range of colors from pure white through tans and yellowish tans to a dark brown; different colored cottons seem to have been grown deliberately for use undyed. Camelid wools come in many of the same colors as well as in black.

A number of vegetable dyes were in common use throughout much of the continent. Among these indigo (*Indigoferia tinctoria*) was the common blue color. By varying the strength of the dye bath indigo will color fiber or textiles palest blue to nearly black. A large series of plants give shades of yellow and orange. Red was obtained from two sources: a madder-like root of the genus *Ralbunium*, and cochineal from the husks of an insect which feeds upon an *Opuntia* cactus. Although madder is much harder to obtain (it is the small root of an inconspicuous plant which grows in rocky soil) it was by far the most common red dye used by the embroiderers and weavers of Paracas. Work by Max Salzman of California Polytechnic University has shown that the majority of Paracas textiles were dyed with madder. Preferences in dyes seem to have changed through time and later coastal textiles were mostly dyed with cochineal. Madder dyeing, however, survived in the highlands through the colonial period. Achiote, the seeds of the shrubby *Bixa orellana*, does not make a permanent textile dye, although it was (and is) widely used both as a cosmetic and as a food coloring/flavoring.

Work on the mordants used in ancient South America is just beginning. Apparently camelid and human urine were important in dyeing as well as in metallurgy (where they were used in depletion gilding). Other acids may also have been used. With this relatively small array of natural colors and dye stuffs the ancient Andean peoples were able to arrive at a phenomenal range of colors and tints and elaborate textiles were quite rightly one of the most highly valued craft productions in the proto-historic cultures.

Fibers were spun by hand rolling and twisting, perhaps the earliest method. Fine camelid threads, used to string tiny beads, have been found at San Pedro de Atacama in a series of sites in the Tulán quebrada; although thread is abundant there are virtually no spindle whorls in the midden deposits, suggesting that hand twisting had been developed to a high art. More commonly fiber was spun with the aid of a hand-held spindle with a small ceramic, stone, or wooden weight (the spindle whorl) on the end. Such spindles can be used hanging free or supported on a piece of ceramic or other hard material while the spinner is seated (Figure 10.1). This simple equipment produces a strong thread of any desired fineness, although the finer threads tend to be spun on a supported spindle. The size of the spindle shaft and the whorl are related to the material being spun and the fineness of the thread to be produced. Several surviving ancient textiles have more than 200 threads to the square inch and are considerably finer than modern percale. Depending on the direction of the spin the thread has an S or a Z twist. The direction of twist is culturally and regionally specific. In precolumbian Peru textiles from the north coast were generally woven with S-spun thread, those of the south coast with Z-spun thread. Those of the central coast started out being Z-spun but later became largely S-spun, apparently reflecting the predominant foreign influences on the central coast societies. Today S-spun fabrics are common, but ponchos and other outer garments usually have a few rows of Z-spun weaving (lloque) on the edges, as this is

10.1 Indigenous women spinning in the Cajamarca market, highland Peru. Although it is common in the Andes for all ages and sexes to spin, in public one mainly sees women spinning, as they wait for family, friends, or the bus.

thought to protect the wearer magically. Plied yarns were produced with the same device, except that plying whorls are generally a bit larger than spinning whorls.

When the whorl is removed, the spindle can be used as a spool or bobbin. Encased bobbins such as those used in western weaving were apparently unknown to the ancient South Americans. The material being spun was supported on a forked wooden distaff. This could be as simple as an unmodified stick, although some finely made examples are known. In Ecuador the distaff was usually a tripod arrangement of sticks which was set up on the ground.

Spinners today prefer to clean their cotton themselves since machine-ginned cotton does not spin well. Small amounts of cotton are picked and formed into little cones which are then used for spinning. Similar cones and little wads of carded wool have been found in ancient work baskets.

Although it is commonly claimed that throughout the Andes women are the spinners and weavers, this is not so and apparently from very early there was considerable variation in the sexual division of labor (Figure 10.2). At both Paloma and Cardal in coastal Peru burials of men with weaving implements have been found. Unfortunately many archaeologists "sex" their burials by the funerary offerings and simply assume that all burials with weaving implements are females. Ethnographic studies have shown that spinning is more age specific than sex specific, although in parts of Peru women spin and men ply. From the earliest records to the present it seems that from northern Peru to northern Ecuador men were the weavers while women were in charge of the farms, a fact that the Spanish, among whom women wove and men did the agricultural work, found unnatural. Men also are weavers in much of Bolivia; Inca histories refer to both male and female master weavers, although among the Incas themselves weaving was mainly a woman's task. We have virtually no archaeological information regarding who did the spinning and weaving in the rest of South America, although again ethnographic and historical records suggest that just who was involved in the textile arts was highly variable by ethnic group and, occasionally, by what was being produced (Figure 10.3).

It is only from the Andean region that we have any significant body of data concerning the history of textile production. The earliest textiles from Peru are all twined, a non-loom technique. Twining involves manipulation of paired wefts around stationary warps; often the latter are attached to a frame to hold them equidistant (a frame is essential for larger or more complex twined pieces). By manipulation of the warps and securing them with the wefts a great many textural and openwork effects can be achieved. Twining may have come into South America with the Paleoindians, as the possession of string for binding, hafting, and carrying is essential even to a technologically minimalist way of life. The earliest textiles surviving in South America are from Guitarrero Cave in the Callejón de Huaylas of Peru. Here, in levels dated to 8600–8000 BC, have been found examples of spiral interlocking and open simple twining, both with a Z weft. Closed simple twining appears about 8000 BC and in Complex III, dated with a single radiocarbon date of 5780 ± 150 BC, is what may

10.2 Man weaving on the backstrap loom, Kolta, Ecuador. The Spanish were horrified to discover that in much of the northern Andes the men wove and the women did the farm work, as this was contrary to European custom.

10.3 Shipibo woman weaving on the backstrap loom, Peru.

possibly be the earliest example of loom weaving on the continent ("possibly" because, although the fabrics were woven on a loom, there is some likelihood of these fabrics being intrusive from a later level). These fabrics are warp face plain weave, as are most later fabrics from the site, and are in natural brown tints. Other materials, such as bags, etc., continued to be twined. The early Guitarrero Cave textiles are all of non-cotton fibers. These are nearly impossible to identify as to species when spun, but apparently an earlier preponderance of *Bromeliaceae* gave way to *Fourcroya* in the later levels. By about 3000 BC evidence for twined textiles using cotton as well as bast fibers is abundant. From the Paracas Peninsula at the site of Cabezas Largas a large cemetery yielded extended bodies wrapped in reed mats (or vicuña skins) with elaborate twined cloaks of bast, cotton, and featherwork. At Huaca Prieta on the north coast, only slightly later, a large variety of elaborate textiles was found, including pattern weaves and openwork fabrics approximating the later gauzes. All were twined. From the roughly contemporary La Galgada in the highlands, a series of burials in tombs in the main ceremonial construction had the naked bodies wrapped in bark cloth and cords. Mantles found with several of the male and female bodies are looped or twined. The heads were covered with stocking caps of patterned single-element looping and associated twined bags were often elaborately decorated (see Figure 7.5). The Cabezas Largas bodies had similar caps.

Twining is significantly slower than weaving and, late in the preceramic period, the heddle loom appeared on the coast. The commonest form of loom used in the Americas is a backstrap loom, in which one end is attached to a post or beam and the other end to a belt worn by the weaver (Figure 10.3). By her or his movements the weaver provides the needed amount of tension. The heddle or heddles are usually provided by a series of strings looped around every other (or some other pattern in multi-shed textiles) thread and a stick. The stick when pulled upwards separates the sheds. This loom is very efficient and adaptable. It has the added advantage of being portable; one can take it down, roll it up and put it out of harm's way when not in use, a fact probably as appreciated by ancient weavers as it is by modern ones. With a backstrap loom the maximum convenient width of a textile is about 35 cm. A master weaver can weave wider cloths, but is limited by arm spread. This problem was solved by the occasional use of gang looms; a number of weavers would work the same wide loom, a feat which is much more difficult than it sounds.

In some cases, as has been suggested for Inca tunics, which are woven with a short warp and a long weft, it seems evident that some sort of frame loom was used. Several small frame looms survive from the coast, all apparently used to weave miniatures; the only ceramic depiction of such a loom dates to the Inca period. Frame looms are also known from southern Peru and the Bolivia highlands where they are used to weave the modern successor of the tunic, the poncho, as well as other garments. The staked loom is in some ways not as easy to use as the backstrap loom and textiles produced on it tend to have less complex figured weaves.

Armed with this simple equipment the ancient Andean weaver was able to produce some of the most complex and sumptuous textiles the world has ever seen. Although preferences for specific weaves varied with time and place, from the second millennium BC onwards there was an elaborate development not simply of plain weaves, but of slit (kilim) tapestry, interlocking tapestry (slightly later), supplemental warp and weft techniques ("brocades"), double cloth, gauzes, and numbers of techniques which are completely unknown among the relatively unsophisticated weavers of the west. Decorative techniques included (besides woven-in patterns of various types) painting, embroidery, plaiting, netting, and a type of plush created by a technique very similar to contemporary rya which was used to create the square hats typical of the Huari culture of the mid first millennium AD. Metal and, perhaps, shell sequins were widely employed as decorative elements as were beads, feathers, and fur. Feather garments and hangings were produced by attaching feathers to a netted foundation or, occasionally, by gluing them to a textile backing.

Andean clothes were relatively simple; the prevailing mode was, as one scholar has put it, "droopy rectangular." Male garments in most of the continent included a loincloth of some sort; a rectangular cloth held by a belt or some form of "diaper" with its own ties (Figure 10.4). A kilt or a sort of apron worn over the buttocks appears in some cultures (see Figures 12.5, 13.2, and 13.3). In the central and southern Andes in cold weather or for formal wear this was supplemented by a rectangular tunic whose length, width, and decoration were apparently regulated by fashion and social position (Figure 10.5, see also Figure 13.5). The tunics could be of a single shed or of two to three sheds sewn together. Some tunics have sleeves, woven in one piece with the shirt or

10.4 Vicús figurine of a warrior. The diaper-like loincloth is clearly visible. Probably the resist painted circles on his torso represent a tie-dyed shirt. This technique was common from the Early Horizon onwards in Peru. North coast Peruvian warriors often tucked their shirts into their loincloths. The figure also wears face paint and a large, decorated turban. He carries a little club and square shield.

10.5 Christina Bubba holds a checked tapestry uncu (tunic) in natural black and white and dyed yellow and red alpaca wool. This uncu dates from the later sixteenth century. Preserved in one of the ceremonial bundles of Coroma, Bolivia, it shows that Inca costumes retained their importance long after the Inca empire was destroyed. This uncu is one of three that were stolen from the Ayllu Pallpa in the 1980s and have disappeared into United States and European collections.

10.6 Human skull from the south coast of Peru. The dry climate has preserved both the hair and the headdress. The latter is a kilim tapestry folded and lightly stuffed band with a single decorated end. The wrapping around the head is original.

separate rectangles sewn in position. In Ecuador the tunic was replaced by a tabard: a heavily decorated rectangular garment open at the sides and often quite short. This garment is related to the historic and contemporary kushma, which again does not have the underarm seams sewn up. The poncho as we know it today is a development of sixteenth century Argentine Indians, who recycled their indigenous tunics into an outer garment, opening up the seams for ease in riding. All of these garments were woven to size, as cutting and tailoring were not practiced in the Americas. Sometimes shaped garments were produced, a technique which first appeared in the preceramic (Cabezas Largas), but continued sporadically until the sixteenth century AD. Shaping involves manipulation of the warps or wefts and a change in the weave to expand or contract the web. A rectangular mantle of some sort, sandals or other foot gear, and a headdress completed the costume. Headdresses, in particular, could be very elaborate (as they are today among surviving lowland tribes). Head cloths, turbans, headbands, and caps, many elaborately decorated, were most common, with elaborate constructions involving feathers, ribbons, bird and animal skins and bodies, and metal and other ornaments appearing on important people or in rituals (Figure 10.6; see also Figures 13.7 and 13.8). Among the Inca, headdresses were regulated by law so that one could tell at a glance a man's social position and ethnic affiliation. This custom may well have earlier antecedents. A bag of some sort generally completed the male costume. These bags are often the most decorated pieces of a man's garments. They are usually called coca bags, but in a culture without pockets a purse of some sort is essential and the bags were obviously multifunctional, not limited to carrying coca paraphernalia (leaves, póporo [container of lime], and spatula).

Women's clothing was simpler and consisted of a large rectangle of cloth which was folded, pinned and tied with a belt to make a dress much like the Classic *peplos* (see Figure 12.6). In the northern Andes and in parts of Amazonia women wore only a wrapped skirt or a small loincloth. Many Colombian and Ecuadorian ceramics and statues show that going naked was customary in the warmer areas; again a practice which is still seen in parts of the tropical lowlands of eastern South America. Women also sometimes wore mantles and usually had a carrying cloth, a smaller rectangle of decorated cloth used as a wrap and also probably (as among Indian women today) to carry everything from the baby to the firewood. Sandals, headgear, and jewelry seem, from representations in the art, generally not to have been as elaborate as those of men. However, any serious study of women's clothing is hampered by the fact that most archaeological textiles known are undocumented, that is they come from looters' operations, not proper excavations. It is very difficult in the face of this and of the general lack of scientific sexing of bodies to assign any given rectangle of cloth to the category of women's clothing.

Aside from garments cloth was, of course, used for domestic purposes, for bedding, towels, diapers, sacks for transporting merchandise, and so on. Cloth was also, in a sense, money, since some communities paid their taxes in cloth or in the raw materials for textiles. Fibers and textiles were also important items in long-distance trade. Camelid fibers and textiles have, for example, been found in early contexts in coastal Ecuador, in the deep shaft tombs of La Florida near Quito and in the eighth century AD tombs of Nariño in southern Colombia. There is little evidence for the keeping of camelids in northern Ecuador until very late and none at all for pastoralism in Colombia. Evidence for very long-distance trade in textiles is seen in the occasional appearance of a Peruvian motif in the art of some far away culture, such as the appearance of the north Peruvian Moon Animal in the headdresses of several San Agustín (southern Colombia) statues.

The importance of cloth in the Andean region is attested to from history, from ethnography, and from archaeological evidence. With the help of early historical documents concerning the Incas it is possible to delineate many of the same patterns in early cultures, suggesting that the situation in the sixteenth century AD was one of long duration. The Incas had sumptuary laws which governed what sorts of cloth a person could have or wear. Many of the surviving Inca garments are, in fact, uniforms pertaining to the civil service. There is some suggestion that many of the tunics surviving from the preceding state, that of Huari, were the same. The Incas basically had two types of cloth, domestic plain weave and warp pattern cloth intended for ordinary people and domestic uses and kompi (cumbi), a finely woven, multicolored tapestry, which was restricted to use by the nobility except where the Inca himself had given some to a person of lesser status. Cloth was an integral part of the social, political, and religious systems. Politically cloth and the raw materials for cloth were extremely important tax stuffs. Local administrators, often members of the pre-Inca ruling class absorbed, with suitable supervision, into the Inca hierarchy, had access to community cloth and to wool for their wives or servants to weave. Since soldiers and servants were often paid in cloth, this was quite useful from the local administrator's point of view. Cloth was important not simply for use as garments or hangings; it had important religious functions. Many of the life crisis ceremonies of the highland peoples involve special or new garments. Thus at the boys' puberty ceremonies complete sets of new clothing were needed for the boys. Likewise cloth was essential in marriage as new garments were used for the rituals and for the gift exchanges which reinforced kin ties. In royal Inca initiations and marriages numerous sets of garments were needed, since clothes were changed at various steps in the rituals; also more and larger gifts of cloth were necessary for these state events. The Sapa Inca on marriage gave gifts of cloth to the courtiers as well as to relatives.

Death also involved cloth, as the body was washed, dressed, and wrapped. Mummy bundles could use hundreds of meters of cloth, especially among peoples, such as those of first millennium BC Paracas, in which the elite dead were turned into huge bales of clothing, artifacts, and wrappings. In the highlands in historic times the wrappings of the dead and offerings, including cloth, were renewed at intervals, a practice which continued well into the colonial period. Other ritual uses of cloth involved offerings of cloth to the temples, the dressing or wrapping of holy images in cloth (some of these may have been made of cloth themselves), and sacrifices of cloth in which the cloth was buried or burned.

From modern Coroma in Bolivia we see another use of cloth: oracles. The garments of the ancestors are preserved in sacred bundles by each kin group (ayllu). These serve as the visible evidence of the kin group's unity and right to its lands; through offerings and rituals to the cloths the ancestors speak to their descendants and guide them through the tribulations of life (Figure 10.5). Without these ancestors to protect them, misfortune will surely destroy their society. It says something about western values that foreign art dealers have stolen numbers of these sacred textiles to sell to collectors and museums as art works, thus committing genocide as surely as if they had slaughtered the Coromans themselves.

In the past another ritual use of cloth was as hangings and decorations of temples and shrines. Several sets of hangings which were probably temple or palace furniture have been found, all, unfortunately, by huaqueros. Two of these sets date to about 1200 AD. One is a series of blue and yellow feather hangings with geometric designs. The other is a series of painted cotton cloths showing naked prisoners, warrior birds, and other religious-martial motifs. By far the most interesting set of painted hangings, however, dates to the first millennium BC and pertain to the Chavín culture. They have been said to have been looted from the site of Carhua just south of the Ica Valley. These cloths,

10.7 A Staff Goddess painted on one of the cotton textiles from Carhua. Her breasts are kenned as guilloches and the double-fanged mouth both forms her belt and shows her toothed vagina. The staves she carries are unusually simple.

which are painted and tie-dyed (plangi), may be the answer to how the elaborate religious imagery, reflections no doubt of a complex theology, spread from Chavín in the northern highlands to much of the rest of Peru. The textiles show in detail deities (especially the Staff God and Staff Goddess), their supernatural companions, and a host of associated plants and animals (Figure 10.7). The hangings suggest that there may have been some differences between the Chavín religion as practiced in southern Peru and that practiced at Chavín itself, as well as providing further evidence that one of the attractions of Chavín religion was its use of hallucinogenic substances, especially the San Pedro cactus.

Numerous other fragments of what may have been ceremonial cloths survive from most time periods and cultures. Moreover, the repetition of religious motifs upon clothing found in elite burials suggests that members of the ruling classes may have identified themselves with the supernaturals, either as descendants or as special devotees.

Outside of the central Andean area our information concerning textiles and their social function is quite scanty. The impression of two textiles on a fired lump of clay from a Valdivia VI–VII (*c.* 2150–1950 BC) site in coastal Ecuador shows a Z-spun single-ply plain weave and another piece of plain weave with paired warps and wefts, perhaps scraps cobbled together into a bag. The site has also yielded perforated sherd disks which were probably used as spindle whorls. A find of dyed camelid fiber in a Machalilla site suggests the spread of wool northwards. This is confirmed by discoveries at the highland site of Pirincay where camelid pastoralism was introduced late in the first millennium BC. Significantly, there is a huge increase in the number of spinning and weaving tools following the appearance of the camelids. Pirincay also gives us our first evidence of the peculiar Ecuadorian warping system in which the two ends of the warp are interspaced on a rod, forming a tube. This rod is pulled out when the textile is finished and the tubular fabric then turns into a rectangle. Camelid wool also appears in a copper-sequined textile from one of the royal tombs at La Florida on Pinchincha volcano above the city of Quito. This and the cotton fabrics found with it as clothing, shrouds, and so on, date to shortly before AD 500.

Excavations in a series of cemeteries in southern Colombia in the state of Nariño have provided some rare textiles from that country. Previously the only ancient Colombian textiles known were a few pieces found in dry caves in the northeast of the country. These date to the terminal prehistoric period and are of natural cream and brown cottons, plain or with simple interlocking patterns and small geometric painted designs. The Nariño textiles show a much more developed textile art dating to the thirteenth or fourteenth century AD. Both cotton and camelid fibers were used and blue, yellow, and red dyes (unanalyzed as yet) were known. The textiles are of twill – a rather uncommon weave in the central Andes – plain weave, and slit tapestry, the latter used for decorative borders on the cloth. Painted ceramic statuettes (Figure 10.8) from the same culture show similar patterned cloths and indicate that there was a fairly elaborate development of the textile arts in the Colombian highlands. Decorated stone and ceramic spindle whorls are common in Colombian cultures where there are no surviving textiles.

The absence of spindle whorls does not mean that there was no textile production as many peoples, especially in the tropical lowlands, hand twist fibers. However, clothing was not as complex in the tropical lowlands of the Orinoco, Amazon, and La Plata rivers and their tributaries. Figurines show that elaborate body decoration was common. This may have been done with cylinder "seals" and stamps, artifacts which are quite commonly found in archaeological sites in the lowlands (Figure 10.9). Similar objects are used today to apply body ornamentation since throughout this vast area nudity or minimal clothing seems largely to have been the rule (Figure 10.10). Some of the eastern Amazonian peoples wear (or wore) a large ankle-length tunic (called a kushma) and other Andean-derived garments. The large tunic, although it may seem inconvenient for hunting and gardening in the forest, serves as a much needed protection against insects. Similar garments are worn by the Lacandon Maya of lowland Mexico, for the same reason. Preservation conditions are so poor in much of the lowlands that we are left with very little to go on save the figurines.

Some textiles have survived in archaeological sites in southeastern Brazil; all are twined, although both cotton and bast fibers appear. The Mucurû phase of Río de Janeiro, which dates to about AD 550, has yielded twined cotton textiles of several

10.8 Two views of a Capulí-style figurine from Nariño in southern Colombia. The woman wears a very elaborately figured skirt. Fragments of cloth from this region indicate that a wide range of decorative weaving techniques was known.

10.9 Roller stamps from central Colombia. Both roller and flat stamps were widely used to decorate the face and other parts of the body in much of South America. The practice survived until recently in some Amazonian regions.

types. This culture did not use spindle whorls. At the Alfredo Wagner site in Río Grande do Sul, which may be earlier, twined bags, nets, ropes, and other textile objects of imbe fiber (*Phylodendron* sp.) have been found in aceramic contexts. Spindle whorls are found in the Mossamêdes culture of the state of Goiás at the beginning of the ninth century AD and by the twelfth century cylinder "seals" also appeared (Urû phase). There have been some other stray finds of bits of fiber or textile; all suggest that twining was the major technique (as indeed it was in historic times) in most of the tropical lowlands and that although cotton was fairly widely grown, bast fibers were equally common. The products of these fibers were mainly bags, nets, belts (perhaps), hammocks, and similar humble utilitarian items with little decoration. The major decorative emphasis of the historic lowland cultures was on elaborate feather ornaments, body painting, and other types of perishable decoration. Virtually none of this has survived from the prehispanic eras.

10.10 Figurine vase of the Caldas Complex of central Colombia. Although a personage of some importance, indicated by his being seated on a bench, this figure wears naught but a headband, face and body paint, and a somewhat drunken smile.

CHAPTER II

METALLURGY

The exploitation of metals as primary materials for objects has often been considered to be one of the hallmarks of civilization. In South America the origins of complex metallurgy (that is, the use of metals as something more than a special, more malleable kind of rock) can be traced to the central Andean republics of Peru and Bolivia. The later metallurgical traditions of Ecuador and Colombia are almost certainly derived from the Peruvian one; Central American and southern Mexican metallurgy is clearly borrowed from Colombia.

In the central Andes there were at least two major metallurgical traditions. These were not completely separate and seem to have cross-fertilized one another, although there is little firm evidence for this until the Inca expansion, when one alloy, tin-copper bronze, was elevated to the status of official state metal. One of the two centers appears to be the northern highlands and adjacent coast with their abundant copper ores of various types (including copper arsenides), gold, and silver. The other was the altiplano with, again, abundant oxide and sulfide copper ores, deposits of cassiterite (tin oxide), silver ores, and gold.

Studying the history of metallurgy in the Andes has been extremely difficult because the vast majority of metal pieces known have been looted and are without any reliable geographical or cultural context. To complicate the issue, objects in ancient styles have been fabricated and sold to dealers and collectors as genuine antiquities since the colonial era, resulting in both stylistic and technological studies which are very general and riddled with problems of the cultural affiliation of the pieces studied.

The earliest metal known to be worked in the Andes was gold, probably from placer deposits (later, gold veins in quartz were also exploited). From the site of Waywaka in the south central highlands of Peru a gold-worker's tool kit was excavated in contexts dating it to the period of the first ceramics in this region, *c.* 1800 BC. Hammers and an anvil show that specialized tools for working metal were already present and that considerable care was being taken in fabricating hammered gold objects. Small bits of gold foil flakes were found at Waywaka, along with cylindrical beads of lapis lazuli and, although no finished metal objects were excavated, it seems evident that the metal-worker here was also the jeweler. Hammered gold ornaments continued to be the hallmark of Andean metallurgy into the Early Horizon. Elaborate golden ornaments in the Chavín style have been found by huaqueros at numbers of sites along the coast and in the highlands. In 1989 at the site of Kuntur Wasi in Cajamarca province, three evidently elite tombs were excavated by the University of Tokyo Archaeological Mission. Two of the tombs contained, among other offerings, hammered gold crowns and pectorals with chavinoid decoration in the Cupisnique substyle, a substyle which is also seen in Monolith 1 at the site and in the ceramic offerings in the tombs. To date nothing as elaborate has been found at Chavín itself, although some gold foil was found there, albeit in fairly late contexts (*c*. 600 BC). Similar materials have been found at Kotosh in earlier contexts, approximately 1000 BC. These finds and numbers of undocumented pieces show that the fabrication of ornaments such as clothing decorations, crowns, earrings, necklaces, etc. of sheet gold was widespread in the central Andes by the late centuries BC. Technological innovations included welding and soldering, the fabrication of three-dimensional objects by joining preshaped metal sheets, and the making of gold alloys. Finds at Pirincay, in southern Ecuador, show that gilding was also known by this time.

Copper smelting may have been established in the altiplano by this time, as copper slags have been reported from the sites of Wankarani, Pukara de Belén, La Joya, and Chiripa in the highlands, and from Santa Lucia and Chullpapata in the Cochabamba Valley. All these sites were occupied at much the same time as those which produced the Peruvian gold work. The ores which have been analyzed are all copper sulfates, which may indicate that ores were being traded in from the drier areas to the west on the Chilean-Bolivian border. Smelting sulfide ores is considerably more complex than smelting oxides and involves a number of steps, yet in the southern highlands it seems to appear along with the much simpler reduction smelting methodologies. Copper alloys are rarer in Peru at this early date. A small bead of a silver-copper alloy found at Malpaso on the central coast is the earliest piece known (*c*. 2100 BC). This is an alloy which became very popular later in coastal metallurgy because, when hammered, a silvery surface results. Such pale coloration was evidently highly valued by the ancient Peruvians; even some of the so-called agricultural implements from after AD 1000 seem to have been treated to get a silver-colored surface (in this case from metallic arsenic). From just slightly later, on the Tablada de Lurín, large numbers of gilt copper ornaments and metaled, partly forged copper mace heads appear, indicating that considerable experimentation with copper metallurgy and/or fairly intimate contact with the southern highlands was involved.

Really intensive work with metals followed these beginnings in short order. Our best information is from the Moche culture of the north coast (*c*. 200 BC–AD 600), where, although production levels may not have been high, metal was common. Metal-workers appear to have been using oxide ores, but experimenting with the sulfide ones, and had invented a method for winning silver from lead sulfide ores. A unique modeled vessel shows the method of smelting in a temporary furnace made of adobe bricks with the draft furnished by blow tubes (Figure 11.1). The resultant ingots were then processed into sheet metal and cut and hammered into various implements.

Most Moche and contemporary metalwork was for the production of ornaments. The variety of these had increased and included hollow figures made of sheet metal held together by tab and slot closures, rattles, cups and bowls, large animal and human masks, ear spools, necklaces, etc. Metal was, by this time, commonly combined with stone and shell inlay and some bimetallic pieces were being fabricated. More utilitarian

11.1 Moche modeled vessel showing a smelter with three men using blow tubes to increase the heat. A fourth man, perhaps an overseer, is handling one of the sheets of metal produced. Also visible on top of the smelter are T-shaped headdress ornaments of the type worn by runners.

items such as chisels and mace heads were manufactured, but many of these show elaborate mythic decoration, indicating their special purpose. The high value and symbolic importance of metal among the Moche are shown by the practice of burying the dead with a piece of metal in their mouths (and in their hands in wealthy burials). The metal objects so utilized were always broken or damaged by folding. The "royal" burials of Sipán, La Mina, San José de Moro, and Loma Negra show that Moche rulers or high priests were routinely buried with an incredible wealth of metal objects, another testimony to the high value, and to the abundance, of metal in this society.

Copper and copper alloy objects were routinely gilded or silvered, the original color apparently not being much valued. The gilded copper objects were often made of an alloy which came to be very important in all of South and Central American metallurgy: tumbaga. This is a gold-copper alloy (often with some silver as well) which is significantly harder than copper, but which retains its flexibility when hammered. It is thus ideally suited to the formation of elaborate objects made of hammered sheet metal. In addition, it casts well and melts at a lower temperature than copper, always a

consideration when fuel sources were limited and the sole sources of a draft were the wind and men's lungs. This alloy can be made to look like pure gold by treatment of the finished face with an acid solution to dissolve the copper, and then by hammering or polishing to join the gold, giving a uniformly gold surface (depletion gilding or *mise en couleur* gilding). Gilt copper objects were also produced by electrochemical deposition of a tremendously thin gold surface onto the finished face of the object. The huge numbers of gilded copper ornaments from the tombs at Loma Negra in the Piura Valley show this technique to have been fully developed in the northern Moche provinces, although dating of these finds is not at all secure.

Many of these objects are of arsenic bronze, smelted from sulfide ores. It is not known whether the techniques of sulfide smelting were learned from the metallurgists of the altiplano, who may have been doing sulfide smelting for a century or more, or if the process was independently invented in the north. Arsenic bronze became increasingly common in later centuries, spreading with the Huari state, and so what westerners might recognize as the beginnings of a true "metal age" were firmly established by AD 700–800. Excavations by Izumi Shimada at a series of sites around Bataan Grande in the Lambayeque Valley show clearly the organization of smelting and stock metal production. Other sites show that the metal ingots or blanks were imported for the

11.2 One of a five-furnace set of smelting furnaces at Cerro de los Cementerios in the Lambayeque Valley, Peru.

large-scale production of finished artifacts. The ore was mined at Cerro Blanco, where the mines continued to be used into the colonial period and beyond, then carried by people or llamas (the presence of algorrobo seeds in llama dung shows that llamas were being kept in some numbers on the coast) down a straight 4 km road to the site of Cerro de los Cementerios, a site in use from *c*. AD 700 to 1532. This site has furnished the first evidence of industrial-scale smelting from South America and strongly indicates the importance of metal in later prehistory in that country. Rows of small pear-shaped furnaces with the end built up to form a primitive chimney were found (Figure 11.2). These furnaces were loaded with fuel and ore, covered with large sherds and fired, the draft coming from one or more people using blow tubes with ceramic tuyères on the ends. The end result of this smelting was a mass of slag with small droplets of copper (prills) in it. This was then crushed using rocker mills, the prills manually extracted, and sent off to other areas of the site or other sites (such as Pampa Grande) to be formed into ingots, blanks, or into the copper "axe-money" that was so important a production of this area (Figure 11.3). The size and arrangement of the furnaces suggest strongly that smelting was done by families, with the elderly and/or children doing the tedious but not physically demanding prill extraction. Organization of the labor force by family was a salient characteristic of the Inca state and seems to have been characteristic of earlier states as well.

The Peruvian metallurgical tradition was largely one of hammered and joined pieces, mainly ornaments for people, objects, or buildings. A small amount of casting in open

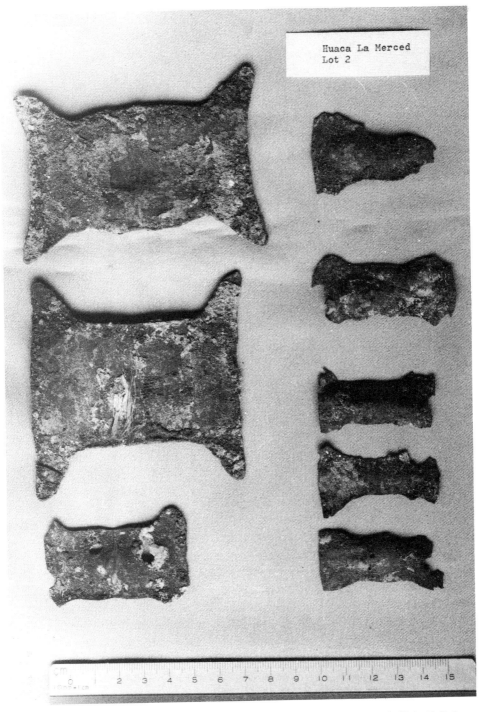

11.3 Axe-monies from a partially looted tomb at Huaca la Merced, Sicán Religious
Precinct, Lambayeque Valley. These were originally bound together in standard
number lots. Some of the string that once held the larger axe monies together is
still visible.

molds may have been practiced, but, in general, casting was not part of Peruvian metallurgy, probably because wax-producing bees are not found in the area. Less is known about the southern highlands development of metallurgy, except that in contrast to the arsenic bronze tradition of the rest of Peru, tin bronze was the common alloy. It has always been presumed that it was the southern tradition which diffused into Chile and northwestern Argentina as there is very strong evidence of Tiahuanaco influence, if not actual control, of much of this area. However, metallurgical analysis of artifacts from the early metal-using cultures of northwest Argentina shows a somewhat more complicated picture. Metal pieces from the Condorhuasi culture (beginning *c.* 200 BC) show high concentrations of *both* tin and arsenic. Pieces from the Aguada culture (beginning *c.* AD 500–650) also show high arsenic content (Figure 11.4). It is unfortunate that there are so few published analyses of metal objects from this region and that the dating of the various cultures is so very imprecise, since it seems obvious that there was a great deal more going on than simple borrowing of a technology from the highland Bolivians.

The metallurgical tradition of the northern Andes was significantly different from that of Peru and Bolivia, despite the technology apparently having originally been borrowed from the southern cultures. This diffusion seems to have taken a long time, metallurgy passing from culture to culture with concomitant changes along the way, as the techniques and forms were adapted to different materials, social settings, and esthetic ideas. Differences between the two areas are hence not as peculiar as might be initially supposed. In contrast to the central Andean preference for hammered pieces, for large-scale objects with gilded or silvered surfaces, and, in later centuries, for arsenic or tin bronze tools, the northern Andean traditions feature small, intricate ornaments cast by the lost wax method (Figure 11.5). Hammered pieces were featured in some traditions, but everywhere in South America the major forms were pieces intended for personal adornment (or, as among the Muisca, for religious offerings). The favored metals in the northern Andes were gold or tumbaga and depletion gilding was widely practiced. In Ecuador some use was also made of platinum and platinum-gold objects are fairly common in the La Tolita/Tumaco culture of the early centuries AD, more than a thousand years before working of platinum became possible in Europe.

There is little concrete information as yet on the history of metallurgy in the northern Andes. In Ecuador metallurgy appears in the late Formative Chorrera culture and in some slightly later highland sites. Here copper, smelted gold, and gilded copper appear in contexts which show considerable contact with the cultures of northern Peru. Gold sheets, droplets of melted gold, and bits of gold wire (cast) appear at San Agustín in southern Colombia by 500–400 BC. Radiocarbon and thermoluminescence dates from cores of Quimbaya and Muisca objects show those styles to have been fully developed by the early centuries AD; a series of radiocarbon dates for the shaft tomb cemeteries of highland Nariño show the local style there to have been flourishing by AD 800. The picture of northern Andean metallurgy is complicated not only by wholesale looting and widespread fakery of metal objects, but by the fact that certain centers manufactured gold items in a number of styles for trade. This can be documented for the Sinú of the sixteenth century AD, a people who had been practicing their trade for centuries (a

11.4 Bronze plaque of the La Aguada culture of Argentina. This plaque shows a man in an elaborately patterned tunic, wearing long hair and a fez-like cap with a frontal ornament. Feline figures are perched on his shoulders in a pose common in much Andean religious art.

Sinú-style bead was found in a Maya tomb at Altun Ha, Belize, which is firmly dated to AD 300). Pieces in most of the major styles of Colombia were manufactured by the Sinú and it is often very difficult to tell these trade items from the domestic item. Moreover, there were pieces, such as the "eagle" pectorals which from early on were truly international (see Figure 13.14). People both made them and traded for them and, without firm archaeological data, separating out local from imported pieces is well nigh impossible.

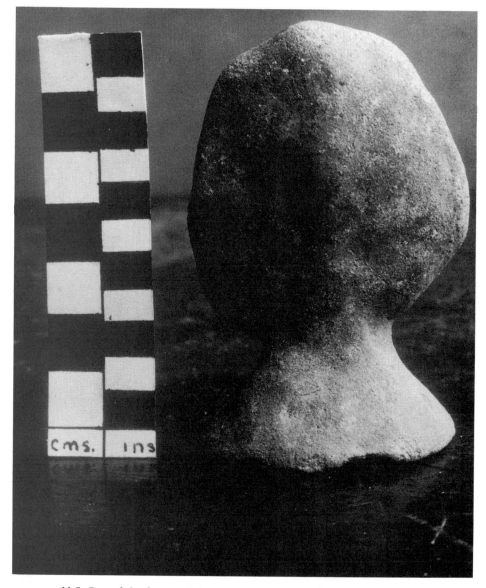

11.5 One of the few surviving prehispanic lost wax casting molds. This mold for casting a little ornament was found in a tomb in central Colombia.

Metallurgy made its way north from Colombia into Panama by perhaps AD 500 and into Costa Rica by the same date. Some metallurgical technology reached Guatemala/Belize by AD 800, perhaps in the form of traveling metallurgists, but complex metallurgy, including smelting and casting, did not really appear among the Mayas and Mexicans until the Postclassic period, several centuries later. The Mexican cultures were not fully metal-using (in the sense of commonly using metal for tools as well as for decorations) when the Spanish invaded their territories and imposed a much different metallurgical technology upon the hapless natives.

Metal was essentially a social artifact in South America and was not much used for tools and weapons until the Inca period. From the very beginning it would appear that the use of metals was associated with high social and political status and with the religious cults which were so important in these early cultures. The most important metals always seem to have been gold and silver, metals which were, by the Inca, identified with the sun and moon respectively. Techniques for gilding and silvering base metals were developed very early to increase the availability of appropriately colored items of display. However, the mere fact of gold being within seems to have been ritually important. We can see this in tumbaga items which were covered with gold rather than depletion gilded and in the golden mummy masks of post AD 1000 Lambayeque (see Figure 16.6). There was no reason to make these of precious metal; many of them were painted or covered with encrustations or cloth and, in any event, they were put away with the mummy where no one would see them. But gold they were.

Metal seems to have had an intrinsic value, even when it was not gold. The Moche commonly put a piece of copper in the mouths of their dead, a custom apparently practiced by some of the other northern Peruvian cultures. From about AD 900 bronze tools which have been identified as agricultural implements were cached or buried with the dead. Many of these are impossibly heavy, decorated, or unfinished, as well as being silvered (by enriching the surface of the high arsenic bronze) and would seem to have been manufactured solely for the display value of the metal. "Axe-money" may have had a similar function as it was buried in carefully graded and wrapped bundles with the dead.

Metal items in both the central and the northern Andes tended to be decorated with religious motifs recalling myths, perhaps their wearers' or users' association with specific supernatural figures or events, and the like. This is clearest in Peru and Bolivia where metal items clearly repeat the religious iconography seen in other media. Thus the metal ornaments from the royal Moche tombs at Sipán show a series of mythic themes apparently associated with the genealogy and politico/religious status of the rulers. Something similar seems to have been true in the northern Andes. Olga Linares's studies of the iconography of the Panamanian Coclé tradition show a concentration on the depiction of animals which are dangerous, poisonous, repellent, or hard. She suggests that this is an iconography associated with warriors and a warlike ideology. Similarly Legast's studies of Sinú iconography show a tendency to depict those animals which we know from historic and ethnographic records were important in myth and religious practices of the northern peoples (see Chapter 13).

Utilitarian items were not common in metal until Inca times and, indeed, most "utilitarian" pieces are clearly rich men's toys: gold tweezers, ear spoons, lime bottles, finials for lime spatulas, etc. The "chisels" and "axes" of Vicús have such elaborate mythic decorations that it is fairly certain that they were not items of daily, mundane use. Similarly the Cañari axes and tupus from southern Ecuador are too fragile or too heavy for any ordinary function. Here and there metal was used for fishhooks, for chisels, adzes, etc. but its main utilitarian use was for mace heads and spear points. Neither of these were all that common and bronze can be seen as an expensive substitute for the equally efficient stone. The major functions of metal then seem to have been as status indicators. There is a definite correlation between wealth, status, and metal in the tomb. The Incas tried to reserve all precious metal to the state to be doled out by the Sapa Inca as gifts to the noble and deserving and for the ritual and display which surrounded the elites and the deities. The Incas, it is true, were spreading the use of metal tools and it is quite possible, had not the Spanish invaded, that the central Andes would have become metal-using in a more western sense, with the utilitarian functions of metal outweighing their display ones, in reality if not in thought.

The Spanish invasions put an end to the metallurgical traditions of the Americas. Although these continued in some areas for a brief time after the conquest – the northern Peruvians, for example, reverted to the use of arsenic bronze during the earliest colonial period – the European metallurgical tradition was imposed, native pieces were destroyed, and under threat of torture or death natives were forbidden to make pieces in their own styles. The vast resources of gold and silver were exploited for the benefit of the invaders, who also began a still-flourishing business in tomb robbery for metal artifacts. Indians died by the thousands in forced labor in the high altitude copper, tin, and silver mines and in the placer mines of the northern Andes. It has been only in this century, with the establishment of museums and the scientific study of the South American past, that the complex technological and artistic developments of this totally independent metallurgical system have come to be once more appreciated.

CHAPTER 12

REGIONAL DIVERSIFICATION AND DEVELOPMENT: 200 BC–AD 600

During the period in which ceramics, ceremonial centers and, later, Chavín influence were being established or spread in much of Peru, the southern highlands and the Titicaca Basin were continuing to develop their own local cultures. A series of quite large sites show that the small Wankarani and Chiripa sites were giving way to towns which had substantial public architecture and a distinctive polychrome ceramic tradition with analogs as far north as Cuzco (Figure 12.1). This region had had its own religious tradition for many centuries and this seems to have fused with some Peruvian ideas to form a hybrid cult which had great appeal throughout the southern Andes.

The best-known site of the region is Pucara, located on the west bank of the Pucara River at an altitude of about 4200 m. Pucara is a one-period site, occupied from about the first century BC to the first century AD. The Pucara site consists of at least three large buildings on a terrace at the base of a huge rock plus a large area of habitation refuse on the flat plain between the terrace and the river (Figure 12.2). Pucara architecture was adobe with stone foundations (which are all that remain). The main temple, named after Alfred Kidder who excavated it, today survives as a series of walls forming a rough horseshoe shape around a sunken court (Figure 12.3). The upper, outer walls enclose a series of small rooms opening into the court, each with a slab altar or two within. The outer wall of the Kidder Temple is of red and the inner one of white sandstone: this decorative use of locally available colored stone was a hallmark of altiplano architecture for centuries to come. In an inner rectangular court reached by a stair on the east were found a number of slab tombs each containing several bodies and very scanty grave goods.

The art style of Pucara is best known from its ceramics and stone sculpture. The sculptures are stylistically very different from Chavín; many represent three-dimensional standing figures, quite blocky, with the head bent and the ribs accentuated (Figure 12.4). These often have prominent square eyes of the same sort that are seen on stone tenon heads and on figures on the ceramics. Pucara ceramics are closely related to the earlier highland styles. Slip painted in red, black, white, yellow, and gray with incision outlining patterns, they feature a wide range of subjects including running angel figures, spotted cats with relief heads, frontal humans, llamas, and a large number of geometric patterns. A study by Sergio Chávez has shown that many of these designs refer to one of two major deity or supernatural figures: a woman who leads an alpaca and carries a staff, and a profile male associated with trophy heads, dead bodies, and felines. The iconography of Pucara pots suggests close ties with the developing site of Tiahuanaco, where the first occupation of the Qalasasaya structure may be contemporary.

12.1 Principal sites and regions mentioned in Chapter 12. 1. Armenia, Filandia, 2. Valle de Calima, 3. Cali, 4. Tierradentro, 5. San Agustín, 6. Mullamica, Cotocallao, 7. Bahía, 8. Manta, 9. Guangala, 10. Sucua, Macas, 11. Loma Negra, 12. Cerro Vicús, 13. Piura Valley, 14. Pacatnamú, Sipán, La Mina, 15. Galindo, 16. Moche, 17. Pañamarca, 18. Recuay, 19. Maranga, 20. Bahia, 21. Quelccaya glacier, 22. Ica Valley, 23. Cahuachi, Pampa de Nazca, 24. Pucara, Taraco, 25. Wankarani, Chiripa, Tiahuanaco, 26. Río de Janeiro, 27. San Pedro de Atacama, 28. Tafi, 29. Condorhuasi.

12.2 The site of Pucara, Department of Puno, Peru, from above, showing the major constructions and terraces.

12.3 The horseshoe shaped foundations of the Kidder Temple at Pucara. The construction on these foundations was of adobe and has disappeared through weathering.

Numbers of contemporary sites are scattered about the altiplano, and it seems that the southern highlands were in the process of developing urban centers, as well as sharing a series of closely related ceramic styles and probably closely related religious beliefs. Pucara may have been the most important site early in this period, but it soon gave way to the growing power of Tiahuanaco on the southeast margin of the lake.

The centuries after the disappearance of Chavín influence were marked by considerable cultural diversification in those parts of Peru which had formerly been linked with that polity. Changes in ceramic technology led to a florescence of oxidized ceramic wares in much of Peru; this is so marked that this time was once referred to as the "red and white horizon." Growing populations and dependence upon irrigation agriculture led to some changes in the coastal subsistence pattern, including a lessened dependence upon shellfish, and, with clearing much of the valley floor for fields, a change from dependence upon deer to one on domestic camelids, perhaps traded down from the highlands in the form of charqui. A tendency towards urbanism is also seen along the north and south coasts although the central coast sites retained the form of vacant ceremonial centers. Finally, throughout much of Peru warfare became a part of the daily lives of people and defensive and/or fortified sites and defensive walls became common architectural features.

The north coast cultures show most clearly the legacy of Chavín, at least in their

12.4 Pucara-style figure now in the Parque Tiahuanaco in La Paz, Bolivia. The large eyes and exaggerated ribs are typical of Pucara anthropomorphic representations.

12.5 Recuay vessel showing an important male wearing a bowl-shaped hat or helmet and a large coca bag around his neck. A little modeled kilt peeps out from beneath his tunic. The sides of this bottle are painted with the important mythological figure known as the Moon Animal.

iconography. In the Callejón de Huaylas region the Recuay culture was dominant. Few Recuay sites have been thoroughly investigated but all show a continuity with Chavín in the popularity of underground chambers and galleries and a taste for massive stone buildings. Recuay relief carving and ceramics, however, show a rather different iconography which can only tenuously be linked with the preceding culture. The ceramics tend to be made out of a white kaolin clay or slipped white over the body. Red slip was then applied in bands and blocks and the vessel fired. Following this, elaborate motifs of supernatural animals and birds and geometric designs were applied in organic resist painting. Recuay ceramics show the most complex development of this technique encountered in the Americas. Recuay vessel forms are extremely varied and include many modeled bottle or jar shapes in the form of birds, animals, composite creatures and humans (Figure 12.5). Outstanding among these are the cacique jars, vessels with a small modeled scene on top of a "muffin-shaped" body. These scenes involve a central male figure and subsidiary warriors, women, or male and female attendants. Other modeled vessels show a "prominent woman," a male with a camelid, or various local

animals or supernatural figures (Figure 12.6). One of these, a crested quadruped known as the Moon Animal from its associations in late Moche art, spread to the coast and appears sporadically in the art of the coastal cultures until the colonial period (Figure 12.5).

On the coast the Salinar and Gallinazo cultures succeeded the earlier chavinoid traditions, continuing the emphasis upon modeled bottle shapes. The repertory of vessel themes was expanded; trophy heads and erotic scenes are noteworthy new subjects. Large nucleated settlements and immense religious structures are associated with both cultures.

In the Moche and Chicama valleys the Gallinazo style was succeeded by that of the Moche. This culture is the most famous of all the ancient Andean cultures owing to its highly realistic art style. Thousands of painted and modeled ceramic vessels, showing details of the flora, fauna, clothing, rituals, and myths of these people, make it the most accessible of ancient South American cultures to western eyes. The major site of this culture is located on the south side of the Moche Valley within shouting distance of the shore. The site consists of two huge pyramids, called the Pyramid of the Sun and the Pyramid of the Moon, separated by a "plaza" some 300 m wide. The Pyramid of the Sun is built on level ground entirely of adobes, more than 50 million of them it has been

12.6 The "Prominent Woman" of Recuay. She wears a head cloth, a dress held with crescent headed tupus, and an elaborately patterned belt. This woman appears alone or with a single male of equal size in modeled vessels.

389-2368

12.7 One of the few surviving Recuay textiles. This woolen kilim tapestry with a design of frontal toothy faces with rays and small "dragons" shows that the iconographic system of Recuay was the same in various media.

estimated (Figure 12.8). Analysis of the makers' marks on the adobes and the locations of differently marked adobes has shown that the pyramid was constructed by erecting many units of roughly the same size, modular units which probably correspond to different villages paying their labor tax. The pyramid was designed as a huge stepped platform with a smaller, higher platform on one end. Much of it is gone today, owing to mining operations in the colonial period, but it still survives, 228 m in length, 136 m in width and about 50 m high even in its ruinous state. Several elaborate burials were encountered in excavations on the pyramid, though not in tombs which were an integral part of the structure. Thus it seems unlikely that this structure was mainly mortuary in function. The Pyramid of the Moon is much different in form and significantly smaller, built on a rock outcrop of the hill against which it backs up. This pyramid is actually a

12.8 The Pyramid of the Sun at Moche, in the Moche Valley, Peru, from the middle of the Great Plaza. Rain, looting, and colonial mining operations have damaged, but not managed to destroy, this immense brick platform.

huge room and platform complex, with many of the rooms once decorated with murals. The area between the two pyramids is generally covered by blowing sand. It is not a vacant plaza, however, but is filled with the remains of structures among which has been identified what may have been a house or temple of the runners shown on so many Moche vases (see Figure 13.2). It seems likely that there was a habitation area associated with the pyramids, but this has not been studied.

The only other major Moche site which has been extensively investigated is Pañamarca in the Nepeña Valley. The site is a true ceremonial center consisting of a group of walled platforms and a large stepped pyramid. Pañamarca is best known for its murals, one of which portrays a polychrome version of the Sacrifice Scene (the others show processions of warriors and a kind of battle in which the protagonists pull each other's hair, probably a mythical scene as well).

There is a seriation of Moche stirrup shapes which has given five sequential phases enabling some relative dating of events in the southern valleys of the north coast (Chimbote to Casma). The northern variant of the Moche style has yet to be dated and evidently does not follow the same stylistic trends as vessels from within the Moche sphere proper. This sphere of influence, almost certainly corresponding to a multi-valley political entity by Moche 3, seems to have been founded in Moche where its major site is located. The polity was not very long lived and by the end of Moche 4 there was some crisis. It has been suggested, on the basis of cores taken from the Quelccaya ice cap in the eastern cordillera, that a series of severe droughts, one seventeen years in length, as well as several Niños between AD 562 and 594 were major factors in the dissolution of the Moche polity. Moche 5 saw the abandonment of the pyramids and other structures at Moche and a mass movement inland to Galindo, a large defensible site with no giant religious architecture. Whatever the nature of Moche control or influence over other areas may have been, at this time there is a very definite regionalization of the Moche tradition and different areas show more or less influence from the site of Huari in the highlands. The location of Galindo inland, on the main route to the highlands, also reflects this new influence and, probably, the actual military threat of Huari and/or its allies. It is very likely that the religious and then military and political events that we associate with Huari were also influenced by the unprecedented onslaught of droughts and Niños and that the chaos of many economic systems, leading to political instability, may have provided both an appetite for a new religion and a relative ease of following proselytizing with a secular takeover.

Investigations of power politics in the Andes are still in their infancy. Most of what we know of Moche comes from their burials and studies of their realistic art style. Moche burials everywhere are laid out on their backs, wrapped in a shroud or a shroud and mat. Fancier burials were made in coffins fabricated of canes sewn together. A piece of copper, crushed and folded, was often placed in the mouth of the corpse, and occasionally in its hands as well. The actual burial was in a rectangular grave or grave chamber with the body surrounded by offerings of ceramics and other artifacts. Royal burials, however, were much different. Although most of these have been looted and are hence known only from a few surviving pieces of consummately elegant and beautiful ceramics or metal pieces, in the late 1980s a series of finds at Sipán in the Lambayeque Valley finally revealed royal Moche burial practices to someone other than looters. Here a number of important males were interred, each in his separate grave within a large adobe brick platform. Each had human sacrifices and, perhaps, the remains of long-dead females of his family buried with him. Royal persons seem to have been buried with all their jewelry, with important goods, and with significant numbers of clay vessels as well as servants and family members. The bodies were enveloped in sets of golden collars, earspools, bracelets, masks, and other precious-metal clothing ornaments. These burials are of a far greater magnificence than any other Moche burials, even very wealthy ones, and give us some insight into the all-encompassing power which the Moche lords must have had over their world.

Moche ceramics are largely oxidized, painted in shades of red-brown and white and often with organic ("fugitive" or carbon) black trim. In the early phases they were hand built, but by Moche 3 ceramic molds had appeared and swiftly became the norm for construction. Even the famous portrait vases, vessels which depict real people, were often made by a general mold which was then touched up to show a specific person. People who were important enough to have many vases made of them, of course, might merit an individualized mold (Figure 12.9). It is from the vessels that we have so much information on Moche architecture, economy, costume, ornaments, and other areas of life for, although it has been convincingly shown that the vessels refer to rituals and

12.9 Moche portrait vessel. The Moche are among the very few peoples in the world to have developed true portraiture. This fellow wears a padded headband decorated with a cat's head and two disk ornaments tied by a scarf over his shoulder-length hair.

12.10 Moche deity in the form of a bunch of manioc tubers. The wrinkled face and fangs are typical of many Moche deities.

myths almost exclusively, the details of these scenes and figures are drawn from the contemporary world of the Moche. Moche religion is only now being seriously studied (See Chapter 13) but it appears that there were several major deities who were associated with rituals and sacrifices on mountains, with the sea and with agriculture (Figure 12.10). Numbers of subsidiary supernatural figures have now been identified, including both agricultural and bellicose deities. Rituals include the "Sacrifice Scene," in which various deities present a rayed supernatural with a goblet (of blood?), while sacrifice of prisoners goes on, ritual deer and sea lion hunts, and a ritual dance (see Figures 13.3 and 13.4). The importance of shamanism and hallucinogens in some aspects of Moche religion can also be documented and, indeed, some of these practices survive until the present.

Evidence from the Piura Valley near Cerro Vicús has modified opinion considering the number of polities involved in the Moche culture and people are now thinking in terms of several Moche states with, perhaps, a multivalley state in the south during Moche 3 times. The Vicús materials, virtually all of which are looted, come from a series of cemeteries of deep shaft and chamber tombs. These contain ceramics in two styles. A local one called Vicús Negative has evident stylistic ties with Salinar and Gallinazo on the one hand and with the contemporary Ecuadorian late chorreroid and early Guangala

12.11 Vicús bottle in the form of a smiling fox (?). The crumbly white slip is well preserved on this piece.

styles on the other. Vicús Negative ceramics are often modeled in animal and human forms, including some of the same themes that are shown in Moche. However, the sloppy black on red and crumbly white painting, and the evident sense of humor of the Vicús potters, set this style clearly apart from the more formal, less spontaneous art of the Moche (Figure 12.11). Other tombs from the Vicús cemeteries were found to contain quantities of ceramics in the Moche style, many with a spout similar to that of the early Moche ceramics of the south. Far more Moche 1 style vessels have come from Vicús than have ever been found in the Moche Valley itself. Many of the Vicús Moche 1 vessels are extraordinary in the fineness of their sculpture and Donnan has hypothesized that most, or all, of them must come from looted royal tombs similar to those of Sipán and La Mina. This is certainly borne out by the Loma Negra finds. From here are reputed to have come hundreds of gold and gilded copper ornaments in purest Moche style, although with a very distinct iconography, including vultures, trophy heads, spiders, and composite monsters of various sorts (see Figure 13.6). Nose ornaments are prominent among the Loma Negra ornaments; this type of jewel is more common to the north in Ecuador and Colombia and their presence here may reflect the geographic (and cultural?) closeness to Ecuador. These metal finds were reputedly associated with Moche-style ceramics. Some Vicús sites have yielded vessels which are in a hybrid Moche-Vicús style. Owing to the utter devastation wrought by looters in Piura, there is no evidence bearing upon the question of Moche origins and relations with the far north save the stylistic ties evident in the artifacts. The existence of royal tombs suggests a northern Moche state, perhaps building upon the remains of the Chavín-influenced cultures in this northern valley. It is possible that the ever-growing interest of the Peruvians in Ecuadorian products, specifically spondylus, led to the foundation and prosperity of these northernmost sites of the central Andean cultures.

Contemporary with Moche on the central coast is a series of closely related cultures of which the most important is called Lima or Interlocking, after the prevailing style of decoration. This was an age of pyramids on the central coast and a great many pyramid groups have been noted. One of the most important is that of Maranga (Huaca Arambaru) within modern Lima. The main pyramid here has a base of some 270 × 100 m and is oriented north–south. It was originally plastered and painted yellow, perhaps with some mural decoration, as has been reported from numbers of other sites along the coast of Peru at this time. It is surrounded with many smaller platforms and, perhaps, residential and storage structures. Many of the pyramid groups seem to have been ceremonial structures and there are numbers of small towns which housed the majority of the population. Burials on the central coast were extended on litters, with offerings of ceramics, pets, and servants.

On the south coast the Nazca culture is the lineal descendant of Paracas; the break between the two is, in fact, entirely arbitrary and Nazca is defined as beginning at that point in which slip painting replaces resin painting on the ceramics, something which probably happened within the space of a few years. The south coast culture at this time was urban; each valley possessed at least one large residential and ceremonial center, although these have not been particularly well studied. One of the largest was Cahuachi in the Nazca Valley proper. Cahuachi is a large complex of pyramids with their attendant compounds and outbuildings, many built on natural outcrops. With the adjacent cemeteries (some of which postdate the main period of use of Cahuachi) the site covers an area some 3 km long and 1 km wide along one side of the valley. Although it has occasionally been described as a city, recent investigations at Cahuachi show that it was actually a vacant ceremonial center. Little habitation debris is present, but there are large enclosures associated with the major building groups which seem to have been meant to provide delimited space for the gathering of large numbers of people for a few days. A similar situation exists today in southern Peru, where numbers of shrines are abandoned between the cyclical ceremonies held at them, ceremonies which are attended for a few days by thousands upon thousands of people. The florescence of Cahuachi and the people who built/used it can be inferred from the sudden appearance of Nazca style ceramics in the other south coast valleys. This florescence may have been due in part to military conquest since, in Acarí, the sites where Nazca ceramics appear all became urban and fortified. The case for conquest of other valleys is not so strong, but there is certainly a cultural dominance. Although there may have been a single polity which was centered on Cahuachi, the preeminence of this group was not long-lived, perhaps 200 years maximum, and a series of small warring polities, one occasionally conquering its neighbors and setting up a bigger realm, seemed to be the rule in this area for centuries to come.

All of these political units were culturally and artistically very close and definitely shared the same religion. This religion was quite different from that of Moche and featured a series of local deities whose provenances concern the productivity of the land and sea, and warfare. These and other figures are shown on the polychrome ceramics which are a hallmark of the Nazca culture. Carefully painted in up to eleven colors on a single vessel, the ceramics of Nazca, like those of Moche, provide us with an unusual view into the life and thought of an ancient people. The major deities of Nazca are the Spotted Cat, a lineal descendant of the Paracas cat deity, apparently associated with fruits and agricultural produce, and the Horrible Bird, a creature which like Killer Whale (not a whale at all, but a shark) is associated with trophy heads and similar bellicose themes as well as fertility. It has been suggested that Killer Whale is the Master of Fishes (Figure 12.12). There is also a host of naturalistic themes including people dressed up as deities in much the manner of the Paracas embroideries, birds, animals, plants, and artifacts (Figure 12.13). Many of these latter may be associated with religious practices, but their rendering is naturalistic and owing to the lack of narrative on Nazca pottery we cannot really associate the various subjects into larger groups. Earlier Nazca pottery is very simple and clear in its rendition, but during Nazca 5 (Nazca pottery has been seriated into a sequence of nine phases, although it has been suggested that some of these may represent regional, rather than temporal, variations) little rays and points start getting added to depictions and there is a process of greater elaboration and abstraction, perhaps a "mythification" of the subjects. Polychrome ceramics seem to have been used for every day as well as for burial. The deceased in Nazca were placed in a seated position and wrapped with textiles and offerings into large mummy bundles. These were placed into plastered subterranean chambers, some of which may have been family tombs, associated with habitation and ceremonial sites.

The other major artifacts of the Nazca are the large rectilinear and zoomorphic patterns in the desert, the so-called "Nazca Desert Lines." Although these geoglyphs have often been credited to supernatural or extraterrestrial intervention, archaeological investigation and ethnographic information support the idea that they were ceremonial pathways to a family or town shrine (shrines or origin places among the Andean peoples were often things like a strangely shaped rock, a crevice, or some other unobtrusive and to the modern eye rather unremarkable natural object). It is also possible that some point to astronomical positions on the horizon although pathway and sacred notations are almost certainly their major function. Recent survey in the Pampa de Nazca has shown that whatever their purpose or purposes, the habit of making these large markings was one which survived the Nazca culture into the late prehistoric period. In Bolivia making and using ceremonial pathways continued until a few years ago among some of the Aymara. Here they were associated with specific shrines and used on days sacred to that shrine. Similar lines have been found in much of Peru, at time periods varying from about the time of Christ to the modern era. None can be shown to have astronomical associations.

In the northern Andes a somewhat different set of cultures developed. The outstanding coastal Ecuadorian traditions of the time are those of Guangala, Bahía, and

Jama-Coaque. Cultures whose wealth was based on fishing, farming and trade, their sites are very poorly known. The Guangala and related cultures are found from the Peru-Ecuador border region north to southern Manabí province; Bahía and Jama-Coaque are to the north. The Guangala peoples produced some distinctive ceramic forms, especially a polypod plate whose long, pointed feet have appliqué human figures on them. Iridescent painting, a legacy from Chorrera, continued in Guangala, which is largely a tradition of darker, reduced wares. Many figurines were produced, hinting perhaps at an active ritual life, as do the characteristic small jars used to hold llipta for chewing coca (Figure 12.14). These had been found along the coast in earlier cultural contexts, but became very common in Guangala sites and burials. Ceramic artifacts include stamps, seals, and musical instruments: whistles and ocarinas. Bone was widely used for tools and for flutes. Copper metallurgy was well established by this time and metal implements are quite commonly found in the primary and secondary burials made within the villages, perhaps within the deceased's dwelling.

To the north of Guangala, the closely related Bahía and Jama-Coaque cultures are found. Sites of these cultures are as poorly known as those of Guangala, although Bahía burials have been found at Salango, including one of a woman with a tumbaga crown. Another site, Los Esteros (now destroyed and under modern Manta), had a large number of high pyramidal earthen mounds, tolas, on top of which had apparently been the dwellings and temples of the inhabitants. These are known from modeled ceramic depictions, which show the structures to have been rectangular, with steeply pitched roofs and elaborate painted, and perhaps carved, decoration. The best-known aspect of these cultures is their modeled vessels and numbers of hollow ceramic sculptures, representing richly dressed and adorned humans, musicians, hunters, dancers, warriors, and lovers (Figure 12.15). The figures are mold-made, with appliqué decorations which were made in smaller molds. Some are attached to vessels, but the majority appear to have been free standing. Like earlier Chorrera figurines, the backs of the figures were made by hand and not elaborately finished, indicating that the figurines were meant to be seen from the front only. The figurines are of light colored clay decorated with brightly colored paint applied after the figurines were fired. The colors include a local version of "Maya Blue," a turquoise color made by mixing indigo with white clay. Many of the figures, especially the seated couples and standing warriors, appear to have adorned mound structures along the beach.

Settlement-oriented investigations in the Jama Valley proper, conducted by Deborah Pearsall and James Zeidler, are adding new information concerning the very long-lived Jama-Coaque culture. Over 150 sites are currently known and they show how population growth is linked to the movement of sites out from the very fertile bottom lands and to the growth of new ceremonial centers, as well as documenting the response of local populations to a series of blanketings with deep volcanic ash.

Farther north, in Colombia, the series of sites which are collectively called San Agustín are found in the mountainous region surrounding the headwaters of the Magdalena River. In this region of fertile land and abundant water arose a culture which has in many ways come to symbolize Colombia's past even more than the legend of El

12.12 Anthropomorphized shark vessel, Nazca 7 phase. This deity, associated with trophy heads and other bellicose activities, may have been the Lord of the Sea or Master of Fishes. Sharks would have been particularly hazardous to Nazca fishermen, who went to sea on inflated seal-skin floats.

12.13 Nazca 4 beaker painted with a design of guanacos and spears. Most of the coastal Peruvians continued to hunt as a supplement to their diet. The flood plains of the river valleys tended to be kept in brush and trees as both a source of fuel and a refugium for deer, guanacos, lizards, and other edible fauna. The lomas also provided a rich seasonal source of animal life for hunters.

12.14 Guangala male figurine from coastal Ecuador. The bulbous head with a close-fitting cap and the low-slung loincloth are characteristic of Guangala fashion. Guangala clothing appears to have been relatively simple, in contrast to the elaborate costumes shown in figurines of other, contemporary, coastal styles.

12.15 Jama-Coaque figurine (Ecuador) of a man playing elaborately decorated double panpipes. The hood-like headdress with whole (stuffed?) birds is typical of musician figures in this style, as are the labret in the lower lip and the huge, hanging ear ornaments.

Dorado. The most outstanding aspect of the San Agustín culture was the carving of large stone sculptures of humans, animals, and supernaturals (Figure 12.16). These statues were usually associated with funerary constructions. Although San Agustín has attracted the attention of treasure hunters, travelers, and more serious investigators since the late eighteenth century, it has only been in the past several decades that archaeological work aimed at cultural reconstruction based upon archaeological data has been accomplished.

The first people in the San Agustín area who made ceramics appeared somewhat prior to the middle of the first millennium BC. The people of this earliest Horqueta phase were farmers who lived in small, scattered villages. They made simple dark ceramics with incised decoration. The succeeding Primavera phase, dated from *c.* 500 BC to the time of Christ is clearly descended from Horqueta and shows a growing population and growing complexity of funerary habits. One of the radiocarbon dates for the Primavera phase comes from a wooden coffin which is closely related to the later stone sarcophaguses. With the following Isnos phase there is greatly increased population density, with people living in all the old villages as well as occupying new sites. Isnos sites seem to have been occupied for long periods since there is considerable midden build up and occasionally the midden has been artificially leveled to provide space for more houses. These people also created large earthworks: ridges, embankments, and perhaps roads. New forms of ceramics appeared including double-spouted bottles, effigy vessels, and red slipped wares decorated with organic resist painting. Metallurgy, in the form of hammered and smelted gold, also appears, although metalworking was apparently never common in the region and many of the statues are depicted wearing metal ornaments of styles indigenous to other regions, especially from the middle reaches of the Cauca Valley (Figure 12.17). Gerardo Reichel-Dolmatoff, whose excavations at the site of Alto de los Idolos form the basis for the ceramic chronology of the area, has postulated that the Isnos people were immigrants who replaced the earlier Primavera folk. It is, however, equally possible that the innovations of the Isnos period represent the natural outcome of increased population, probably increased social stratification, and closer ties with cultures outside of the region, many of whom possessed the technological features typical of the Isnos period. It was probably during the Isnos period that the majority of the statues were carved. Over 300 of these are now known, ranging from about 50 cm to more than 4 m in height. The statues served as sarcophagus covers, as markers on or by burials, and as guardians within or at the entrance of burials. Burials seem to have been made within or just to the side of the village and, just as the statues show a great deal of stylistic variation, so the burials show a great variety of forms. The most outstanding form is the barrow tomb: a chamber or chambers formed of stone slabs and covered with a mound of earth. One of these tombs, at the site of Meseta C, has black and red geometric patterns painted on the interior walls and is dated to the seventh century AD. A lucky find at the site of El Purutal shows that the statues too were originally painted and must have been quite fearsome (at least to western eyes). Some of the tombs contained one or more stone sarcophaguses, covered

12.16 San Agustín caryatid statue from the site of Meseta A, southern Columbia. Although somewhat facetiously dubbed the "Goddess of Maternity," this figure probably represents a supernatural with a human offering.

12.17 Opposite: Front and side view of a feline attack statue from the site of La Candela, San Agustín. The small size of the figure being held and the standing (female?) figure represent relative status. Note the human-like hands on the feline.

with a flat carved statue. These may be an outgrowth of an earlier prototype, since the wooden coffin which dates the Primavera phase must have been preserved in a dry tomb chamber. The barrow tombs sometimes had subsidiary burials made into their sides and around them, perhaps the family or the retainers of the obviously rather special few who were buried in the barrow chambers. Many of these latter graves, and graves where there are no barrows, are stone-lined cists holding one or more flexed or extended bodies. Shaft and chamber tombs are also known. It is possible that these different tomb types are separated in time, but they may just as well be the resting places of people of different statuses. The cists sometimes have a statue within or as a cover and one statue of a squatting woman was buried in a cist tomb in a barrow.

The statuary of San Agustín is varied in style and in detail of execution, but is remarkably consistent in theme throughout the various styles. The most common subject of the sculpture is that of supernatural beings, so distinguished by their fanged mouths (Figure 12.16). It is not known if these represent actual deities, figures of myth and legend, or the deified dead. Two statues showing an attack by a feline on a human suggest the idea that one of the routes to becoming a shaman was to survive a feline attack (shamans are widely believed to be able to turn themselves into felines in order to fight with other shamans and spirits or to attack humans; Figures 12.17 and 12.18). Other statues show ordinary humans, both male and female, dancers, warriors, and a very limited set of animals (batrachians, lizards or alligators, birds). Clothing and decorations worn by the subjects of these statues have their closest analogs in items used by contemporary or historical tropical forest peoples. The distribution of the sculptures and the stylistic differences visible (even at a single site, at some of the larger, longer-occupied sites such as Las Mesetas) suggest that the statues were associated with mortuary rites and were an essential piece of furniture for an important burial (the association of simpler burials with a barrow may show that the statue could extend its function outwards from where it was placed in the passage or chamber of the tomb to the burials without) and that they were carved as needed for the funerary rites of special people, perhaps no more than one or two a generation. Similar practices are found in other areas of Colombia, most notably at Tierradentro, where for a time statues in a related style were erected, and up into Central America. The religion they are associated with would seem to have involved shamanistic rites, perhaps concepts of masters of animals, guardians of the dead, and deified ancestors. Hallucinogenic substances may have been involved, although the only medicinal plant that there is incontrovertible evidence for is coca, as figures with quids in their cheeks and with lime flasks and spatulas are represented.

Other than the statuary and the plethora of theories they have inspired, little more is actually known of San Agustín. The Isnos people disappeared somewhere before about AD 1200 (tombs with trade goods from central Colombia dating to about this time have been found) and were replaced by the Sombrillos phase people who did not erect statues, claimed not to know who had erected the statues, and may be identified with the numbers of linguistically different but culturally rather similar peoples who occupied the region at the time of the Spanish invasions.

During this same time period the Cauca Valley and adjacent cordilleras saw a

12.18 San Agustín figure which may represent a shaman. The man wears a tasseled headdress with a cat skin thrown over his head and a Quimbaya-style metal lime container around his neck. This small figure was found within the tomb chamber.

12.19 Canastero miniature vessel of the Ilama culture, Colombia. The human-like figures appear to be covered with snakes.

considerable development, especially in the ceramic and metallurgical arts. In the region around Cali and in the Valle de Calima the Ilama phase (once called Early Calima) was flourishing. The Ilama people are best known for their modeled and incised pottery. Double-spout and bridge bottles, single-spout whistling bottles, and a curious form called a canastero, a modeled figure with a cylindrical vase attached to its back, are the most notable forms (Figure 12.19). The characteristic stylization includes "coffee bean" eyes and vividly, though stylized, modeled features. Details of clothing, ornaments, and headdresses are finely incised, and animal forms in particular may be covered with incised geometric ornament. Many vessels show a supernatural figure dubbed the Fabulous Beast, a composite creature whose limbs or other features may be formed by serpents. It has been postulated that the Fabulous Beast is an ancestral, transforming figure, rather like those seen in contemporary Arawak Indian myths. Archaeological investigations in Ilama sites have shown that they were maize farmers who buried their dead in shaft and chamber tombs. Ilama-related cultures are common in western Colombia, though their relationships and temporal sequences remain to be worked out.

Some centuries later, just to the north in the central cordillera, a local culture today called Quimbaya, was producing some of the most esthetically pleasing gold work the world has ever known. Massive anthropomorphic bottles, apparently lime flasks for use in coca chewing, are the best-known form, although unmodeled bottles, helmets, pendants, beads, and other ornaments were produced as well. Most figures show standing or seated nude females and males, from their accoutrements presumably rulers, with realistically rendered calm, smiling faces (Figure 12.20). The largest group of these

12.20 Classic Quimbaya (central Colombia) gold lime flask showing a seated female with an elaborate headdress and with danglers from her nose and hands.

gold pieces was found in two tombs near Filandia in northern Quindio in the late 1800s. Although no accurate catalogue of the contents of these tombs has ever been published, the tombs appear to have contained at least a dozen major pieces plus many smaller ones. Other tombs apparently contained much less gold. The tombs were shaft and chamber tombs like those of the Ilama phase people, a form which was widespread throughout the Colombian cordilleras until well after the Spanish invasions (Figure 12.21). Cinerary

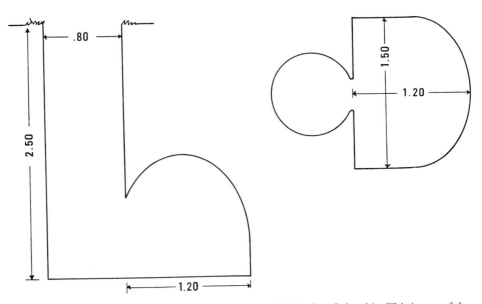

12.21 Shaft and chamber tomb, Department of Quindio, Colombia. This is one of the few such tombs to be investigated by archaeologists. It contained a single extended burial with its head lying on a metate and an offering of some fifteen vessels of the Caldas Complex.

urns and some other ceramic vessels show figures in the same distinctive style and it is assumed that they are contemporary with the gold. The Quimbaya style was influential on local styles as far north as Costa Rica and ornaments with Quimbaya features continued to be made centuries after the Quimbaya themselves had disappeared.

During this same time period northwestern Argentina and the closely connected cultures of northern Chile were undergoing a development which seems to have been closely related to that of the southern altiplano. The northern Chilean peoples had been farmers and herders for centuries, living in smallish villages of agglutinated adobe houses, forming a single architectural complex around patios and passages, such as that of Tulor in the oasis of San Pedro de Atacama (Figure 12.22). Burials at Calama, also in Atacama, show that trade was an important part of the local economy and that contacts were had between northern Chile and the coastal region, the altiplano and, even, the tropical forest, although probably materials like feathers were obtained through their altiplano intermediaries. Because of the extreme dryness of northern Chile, organic materials are preserved and imported materials here give us a much-needed window on the perishable arts of the highland peoples with whom the Atacamaños were trading. One of the most important aspects here is the preservation of evidence concerning the use of hallucinogens. Earlier religious practices in northern Chile had been apparently influenced by the contemporary cultures of northwest Argentina. Clay pipes and lip labrets are common; burial practices such as interment in urns, it has been suggested, were a northwest Argentina trait as well. However, these practices were slowly replaced by materials of evident altiplano origin and both male and female burials at Solcor-3 are

12.22 The site of Tulor, a medium sized village in the oasis of San Pedro de Atacama, Chile, has agglutinated circular houses.

associated with paraphernalia for inhaling snuff, a habit of, by now, considerable longevity in Chile. These snuffs come from a number of plants. The Chilean ones may be local, since an algorrobo tree which grows in the oases of the north is known for its hallucinogenic properties. The snuffing paraphernalia consists of a textile bag containing one or more leather bags of an organic powder, a wooden tablet, and a snuffer. A few bags also contained green pigment, apparently a powdered copper oxide, suggesting that special cosmetics may have been part of the ritual. The tablets and snuffers often are decorated with elaborate depictions of supernaturals of altiplano origin (Figure 12.23). Figures such as the winged human, long-nosed and bird-head angels, supernatural llamas, star animals, and front-facing deities show a clear derivation from Pucara and Tiahuanaco religious iconography. Other, perhaps earlier, tablets have simpler designs with analogs in local or Argentine cultures, mainly human males, singly or in groups, some crowned with "alter-ego" animals, as well as other animals without supernatural attributes.

The role of hallucinogens in Andean religions, especially those of the expansionistic cultures such as Chavín and Pucara/Tiahuanaco, is a vexing one. Certainly there are images in Chavín art which suggest that the use of San Pedro cactus, and perhaps of an hallucinogenic snuff, was an important part of their cults. The relationship between Chavín and the slightly later altiplano cultures is likewise vexing, although, since they share a number of supernatural figures, there apparently was some cross-fertilization,

12.23 Wooden snuff tray from San Pedro de Atacama. The male figure on top holds a cup and is similar to human representations from the altiplano.

perhaps through the south coast Paracas and Nazca cultures. Despite claims that such use of hallucinogens must have had a jungle origin, claims made on the basis of the survival of such practices into the present in the tropical lowlands, the known hallucinogens such as plants of the genus *Datura*, the San Pedro cactus, and trees of the genus *Anadenanthera* grow in the mountain valleys and sheltered quebradas. It is interesting in this regard that Moche vessels often show mountains in conjunction with scenes related to curing through hallucinogens. Thus it is quite possible that the hallucinogenic complex as we see it in San Pedro de Atacama had its origin in the highlands and came to the coastal cultures along with the evidently attractive religions of the highland cultures. Interestingly enough the contemporary northwest Argentine cultures of Condorhuasi, Tafí, Alamito, and Candalaria show little such development of hallucinogenic imagery.

The Tafí culture of the valley of the same name (Tucumán province) produced notable carvings showing feline or feline-human figures, mainly in stone (Figure 12.24). Some of these are mortars and, it could be argued, were associated with the grinding of hallucinogenic substances, but the characteristic bag-tablet-snuffer complex is largely absent and ritual seems to have centered on structures with artificial mounds associated with stone pillars or monoliths, often forming enclosures or placed as the

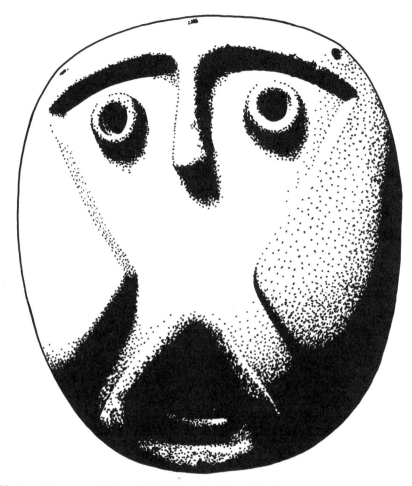

12.24 A small stone mask from Tafí, Argentina, one of the few small pieces from that site. The mask is in the same style as the carved columnar statues and bears also a certain resemblance to contemporary statuary from Puno, Peru.

focal point of a stone enclosure. Both the Tafí people and those of the slightly later Condorhuasi culture in the Hualfín Valley south to San Juan province were notable metallurgists in gold, copper, and copper alloys. Modeled and elaborate polychromed ceramics and small stone sculptures of this culture also commonly depict figures thought to be feline-related (Figure 12.25). Many of these figures, however, seem composite, and may well be part of the widespread appearance of composite "dragon-like" figures in Andean religious art. Certainly correspondences between the Argentine "felines" and the Moon Animal of northern Peru are seen in ceramic, stone, and metal depictions of the various northwestern Argentine cultures. Other Condorhuasi artifacts show females, males, crawling figures which are often part of a double-chambered vessel, and zoomorphic forms. The related Alamito culture also produced elegant small stone sculptures, often showing zoomorphic figures. All of these point to a somewhat

12.25 A Cienaga-style pipe in the form of a feline, northwestern Argentina. The pipe stem is formed by the hollow tail; tobacco was placed in the body and lit through the head opening (there are residues inside). Although tobacco pipes are found throughout the southern Andean/lowland Bolivian region, they are generally not as elaborate as this fantastic feline.

different religious focus than that of the altiplano and the Chilean cultures which had been drawn into their orbit. Although it is moot as to whether this religion encompassed some "felinic complex," as has been suggested, it is certain that true ceremonial centers and a quite different set of supernatural beings characterize the earlier cultures of northwest Argentina. The succeeding Aguada culture also shows these zoomorphic composite creatures as a major part of its iconographic system although slightly later continuing contact with the altiplano is reflected in the appearance of many of the same themes which had made an impact via textiles and hallucinogens on northern Chile. It is quite possible, in fact, that these arrived via San Pedro de Atacama and reflect simply a continuation of centuries-long patterns of exchange between these two regions (Figure 12.26). Certainly the appearance of warrior and trophy head themes in Aguada and Cienaga art suggests that, despite some differences in organization of religion and political life, the widespread warfare of the Early Intermediate and later periods in the central Andes had reached the south.

Contemporary developments in the eastern and northeastern parts of South America seem to have had little direct relationship with those in the Andes. In southeast Argentina the juxtaposition between inland hunters and shoreline gatherers/fishers continued, perhaps with some interchange between the two groups. However, to the north tropical horticulturalists were beginning either to move or to spread their technology and economic adaptation into a region still largely occupied by foragers.

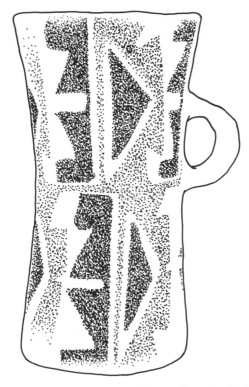

12.26 Río Diablo/Vaquerías-style mug from the Valles Centrales of Argentina. This culture is poorly dated to *c*. AD 300–500. The mug shows Tiahuanaco/altiplano influence in its designs.

Ceramics of various groups, especially along the lower Paraná delta, have plastic decorated vessels with ticked fillets, incision and punctation, and some painted decoration. Along the Pará coast of Brazil the Mina tradition appeared. This very long-lived ceramic tradition is linked to the Periperi tradition of Bahia and to the Alaka phase of Guyana (Figure 12.27).

Slash and burn agriculture had become firmly established on the Amazon and its tributaries, as well as in some interfluvial zones, by the middle of the first millennium AD or slightly earlier. These sites, identified by their terra preta, a dark soil of anthropogenic origin, tend to be shallow (30–50 cm of cultural refuse); they pertain to no single cultural group but rather reflect a widespread agricultural practice of the forested tropics. In the Colombian Amazon on the Caquetá River two successive periods of occupation of the terra preta soils have been identified. The earlier, Camani, is characterized by simple bowls and jars with sponge spicule temper and a bit of reddish slip as decoration. Fire dogs and griddles are present, indicating that bitter manioc was probably being processed. Palm fruits (from the milpeso, *Jessenia polycarpa* Karst) were also found in Camani deposits. Camani dates to between *c*. AD 150 and 830. The following phase, Nofurei, is much later and is clearly a local variant of the widespread and later Amazonian polychrome tradition, widely associated with terra preta in the rest

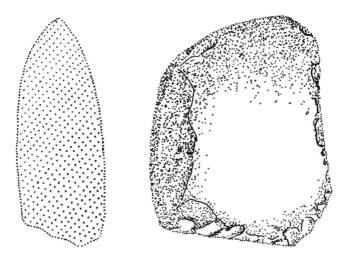

12.27 Alaka Phase (Guyana) polished and chipped stone axe.

of the Amazon. At the mouth of the Amazon on Marajó Island, Formiga phase peoples occupied the same general area as the Mangueiras peoples with whom they are at least partly contemporary. Formiga pottery has brushed decoration and no griddles are present. Formiga sites tend to be located in open country but near both to the forest and to streams. Sites have from one to six mounds, formed of refuse and deliberate fill. These raise habitations and working areas above the swampy ground and protect them from flooding. The houses on top of these platforms appear to have been of wattle and daub, but no indication of their form or size has been found. This was the beginning of the tradition of large mound building elaborated in the succeeding Marajoara phase. Similar developments are seen in Guyana and in the llanos of the Orinoco, where large-scale earthworks may date to this same period. Some intensification of agriculture and population growth is seen in Venezuela as well. On the middle Orinoco the Saladoid tradition was replaced by the Corozal phase and, growing out of Corozal, the Comoruco phases. Corozal is characterized by thin griddles and vessels with a sponge spicule temper. Vessels are colored gray to buff and are decorated with both rectilinear and curvilinear incision with red fill and with appliqué. Comoruco pottery adds new shapes and new figures on the rim tabs, and has some decorative links with the Arauquinoid ceramic series with its characteristic human face decoration. Cylinder "seals," perhaps for body painting, are common in these styles. The Comoruco type site is on an artificial mound on the wet savanna and may have been occupied the year round. The contemporary Matraquero site, upriver from Comoruco, is also reportedly located on a group of artificial mounds. Comoruco sites are also located in the gallery forest. Grinding tools are common in these sites and the thick griddles of Corozal are replaced by thinner griddles of the same general shape. This, and the appearance of both canavalia beans and maize in the midden, suggest that there may have been some changes in staple crops. The Caño del Oso culture of the Orinoco plains is contemporary with the later Comoruco phases, but these had changed to growing a flinty maize with a 12/14 row cob of a type related to Chandelle. This is widely grown today as it has a relatively short maturation period and is adapted to low altitudes. Caño del Oso is likewise associated with earthworks, these of considerable size, supporting habitations and connecting villages during the rainy season. Pottery is smooth, polished, elaborately painted in red, black, and white. All of these sites show that there had been considerable population growth in the north and that this was accompanied by an increased reliance upon agriculture, especially maize agriculture. Very likely the conquest period situation of large villages and dense populations exhibiting distinct social strata and organized into larger groups under paramount chiefs, was developing. De Carvajal in 1648 discusses a Chief Tavacare who ruled at least ten villages with village chiefs and head men under him and, below them, ordinary people and slaves. The latter originated from the frequent skirmishes between these rather bellicose peoples and slaves were important both as household servants and as agricultural laborers. Such details are difficult to get from the archaeological record, but the pattern of largish river-edge villages was well established by the middle of the first millennium AD.

On the tropical eastern slopes of the Andes and the adjacent river valleys a series of ceramic traditions that feature decorated wares embellished with red-painted geometric designs outlined in incision was widespread. These traditions are best known from Ecuador where investigations on the río Napo have delineated the Tivacundo phase, while work to the south along the ríos Upano and Abanico has resulted in the delineation of the Upano Tradition. The few known Tivacundo sites are located on smaller streams and appear to be the remains of villages which were occupied for only a few decades at most, most probably by forest agriculturalists. A few griddle fragments indicate that manioc may have entered the list of cultigens, but was not yet a staple.

Upano Tradition sites as such are unknown; most remains come from fill in the later-constructed mound and terrace complexes which are ubiquitous in the Macas-Sucua area and from excavations in the highland site of Pirincay, as well as from scattered finds at other sites in the Ecuadorian sierra. These finds indicate that exchange between the two regions was common, although products other than the distinctive pottery are as yet unknown. The pottery in question, Red Banded Incised, occurs in a number of shapes of which the most common are a series of bowls and wide mouth jars (Figure 12.28). Analyses of the paste indicate that it was made somewhere on the east edge of Sangay Volcano and, apparently, widely traded both in the lowlands and the highlands. The identity of the somewhat later mound builders, who constructed huge planned complexes such as that of the Sangay site 30 km north of Macas, is unknown, although a number of apparently closely related styles of ceramics have been found both as fill and in (looted) graves in the region. All of these remains are associated with manos and metates, T-shaped stone axes, chipped stone scraping and cutting tools and simple stone sculptures. Clay spindle whorls are also common finds. The historic inhabitants of this region, the Shuar (Jibaro) were forest farmers of manioc, sweet potatoes, corn, and cotton. No archaeological evidence of the Shuar's most famous practice has been found in this region, although a trophy head was found in the late phase of Pirincay, in contexts associated with Red Banded Incised pottery.

As can be seen, during the first half of the first millennium AD patterns which were to

12.28 Red Banded Incised sherds excavated at the highland site of Pirincay, Ecuador. These ceramics were manufactured near Sangay Volcano (see Figure 3.4) and widely traded throughout southern Ecuador. As sherds are non-perishable, these fragments are our only indication of what was once a flourishing trade in organic items.

remain characteristic of much of South America were becoming established. Large states were coming into being throughout the Andes and in much of the rest of South America agriculture had become embedded in local cultures, with concomitant growth and development of more elaborate arts and social structures. Long-distance trade had become well established in western South America, where growing elites needed luxury goods to support their pretensions. The stage was being set for the first conquest states, multinational empires whose interest was in controlling land and resources as much as in obtaining booty or prisoners for sacrifice.

CHAPTER 13

ICONOGRAPHIC STUDIES

Prehistoric archaeology has the disadvantage of dealing with cultures which did not leave written records. In the case of non-western societies, we often have very little in the way of good descriptive material from aboriginal times to flesh out the archaeological record and, when dealing with societies which are so very different from our own, we are at the added disadvantage of not being able to use much beyond the most general analogy with Eurasian ideologies and practices. Thus when we try to infer societal characteristics such as the basic ideologies of social and political relations, even such elementary ones as the relative positions of the sexes (including definition of the sexes, as there are numbers of societies with supernumerary genders), mythology, rituals, and the ideological justifications for those ritual practices which we see reflected in monumental temples, the remains of sacrifices and offerings, and in the art, we are dealing with a closed book. Fortunately, despite the lack of writing *per se*, many cultures were obliging enough to have had realistic, depictive art styles which show aspects of that society which disappeared long ago. Such simple depictions as clothed human figures tell us about technology, style, ideas of modesty, perhaps differential social status and ideas concerning the supernatural. Animal figures, for example, often reflect the mythical as well as the real universe, composite figures show ideas of the relationship of different species within a specific construct, and so on. Until quite recently most studies of the art of ancient South America were either almost purely descriptive, aimed mainly at archaeological problems, such as stylistic studies whose main focus was the construction of finely tuned chronologies, or were derived from traditional western art history, making esthetic evaluations and social interpretations based largely upon the current esthetic values of Euroamericans, coupled with superficial and likewise ethnocentric interpretations. Above all, most of these studies (except the archaeological-chronological ones) were based upon small samples and there was little interest in context.

In recent years this situation has changed radically, owing to a fusion of ideas from classical archaeology, perhaps to the influence of the "new archaeology" of the 1950s and 1960s with its renewed emphasis upon interpretation as well as description, and to the exposure of American archaeologists in particular to descriptive ethnography, ethnology, and ethnohistory (almost all archaeological degrees in North America, except those in classical studies, are through anthropology and would-be archaeologists are exposed to heavy doses of the above-named subjects as well as to anthropological theory). Although some of these studies are flawed by *a priori* ideas regarding shamanism, "feline complexes," or chiefdoms, they still remain our major means of arriving at some knowledge of the non-material culture of the ancient peoples of South America.

13.1 Moche stirrup bottle modeled in an as yet undeciphered scene of a deity (who can be identified as such by his huge fangs) riding backwards on a llama led by an anthropomorphized iguana. The bags on the llama carry strombus shells, imported from coastal Ecuador and used as trumpets throughout the Andean region.

Although people had attempted to use ancient art as a clue to mythology and ritual previously, a really major step forward in this area was in the 1960s, when Christopher Donnan and his students at the University of California at Los Angeles began to compile and then to utilize the first large sample of art from the Moche of northern Peru.

The Moche culture is (or was) an ideal one for iconographic studies and for working out appropriate methodologies for such studies because of the nature of its art which is very realistic, and realistic within canons that the western eye recognizes. Myriads of different depictions of humans, supernaturals, animals, objects, and other aspects of the physical and intellectual universe of the Moche are shown in mural paintings, textiles, wood and shell carvings, metalwork and, above all, ceramics, a large percentage of which are painted or modeled and painted in a highly depictive manner (Figures 13.1 and 13.2). The style is the same in all media and there is a large overlap of subjects between media. Even more important is that some examples of Moche vase painting

13.2 Moche single-spout bottle painted with warriors in the desert about to engage in battle. The desert setting is indicated by the amoeba-shaped, spotted element between the two warriors.

show context. Figures are grouped in scenes and within these scenes there is often indicated the physical setting of the action (desert, strand, rocky shoreline, settlement), architectural features, and artifacts associated with the action (Figure 13.2). Thus the relationship of many different figures is shown within a context which is clearly identifiable. The establishment of context in this manner is almost unique among the ancient art styles of the New World. In South America only the Moche-influenced Nazca 7 style of the south coast of Peru regularly shows any context at all (and then only in rare warrior or camelid-in-landscape scenes or in the extremely rare modeled/painted scenic vessels), aside from a few metal pieces from the north which are within the late Moche tradition (see Figure 15.4).

The use of a large sample made it possible to separate out standard representations from idiosyncratic ones. Almost from the beginning of the assembly of the Moche archive it became evident that the common concept of Moche art as depicting all aspects of the Moche universe was false. Only a select number of people, animals, plants, artifacts, etc. out of the theoretical total ever appeared and these appeared in rather different numbers. For example, figures which are definitely male outnumber females tremendously. The certain identification of males and females also became possible, since numbers of erotic vessels show figures with genitals. By utilizing the associated features of hair styles, ornaments, and clothing one can separate male from female without resorting to unsupported inference such as long hair equals female or short dress equals male, inferences which may well be wrong, especially when dealing with cultures as exotic as those of South America. With the identification of male and female (this work was done by Patricia Lyon in a study of supernaturals in Peruvian art) it became possible to consider gender roles, at least as they appear in an art style which is showing only a few, probably mythological, subjects. Unfortunately, this possibility has largely been ignored in favor of traditional, unsupported, ideas of what males and females *should* have been doing in ancient cultures.

The greatest revelation of the Moche archive, and one which its subsequent enlargement (it now numbers more than 15,000 pieces) has not changed, is that Moche art actually shows a very few basic subjects, most of which can be correlated with specific myths or legends and/or their ceremonial enactment. From an examination of scenes painted upon pottery vessels it has been possible to put together an entire scene with all of its characters and associated artifacts. From these it can be seen that, just as in western religious art, a myth or legend may be recalled by a detailed depiction including all of the elements of the story or by any smaller number of the figures or by a single figure alone. Thus the Nativity may be shown as a complete scene with Mary and her Baby, Joseph, shepherds, angels, wise men, star, sheep, palms, etc., by the Mother and Child alone, by a baby, by some angels, or a sheep or a star. The same is true in Moche art; many of the painted or modeled single figures or small scenes can be shown to be parts of and presumably evocative of a larger narrative. It is thought that there may be no more than fifteen or twenty such themes in Moche art and that, with relatively rare exceptions (perhaps including the famed portrait vessels), Moche art is religious in focus and is associated with a relatively small mythological corpus.

13.3 The Sacrifice Scene. Formerly called the Presentation Scene, this version of a ceremony involving the sacrifice of prisoners and the presentation of cups of their blood to a rayed deity shows (*L–R*): a bat warrior drawing blood from the neck of a prisoner, a female supernatural personage with long braids ending in snakes' heads holding a disk and presenting a goblet of blood to a rayed deity, and a feline warrior.

The major scene identified to date is the "Presentation Scene" or "Sacrifice Scene" in which a bird-headed supernatural presents a goblet of blood to a rayed figure while numbers of other figures, including a feline sacrificing a prisoner, a female supernatural with long braids, bird- and animal-headed warriors and a host of other figures look on (Figures 13.3 and 13.4). Another scene seems to involve the burial of an important figure; incompletely understood scenes involve ritual deer hunts (the deer was somehow associated with prisoners of war, who seem to have been the major source of sacrificial victims), and a kind of line dance. A newly delineated narrative involves the sequential battles and victories of a wrinkle-faced deity over various monsters.

The study of Moche iconography has also indicated how important a close cooperation between ethnographers and archaeologists can be, as from work by Douglas Sharon and his main informant, the curandero Eduardo Calderón, it has become evident that there are depictions in ancient Moche art which can be explained with reference to practices and beliefs surviving to the present in native healing systems. Sea lion hunts shown on ancient Moche vessels show the animals with stones in front of their mouths. These stones are considered to be power objects by contemporary healers. Similarly many of the depictions of objects and of people or supernaturals manipulating these objects refer to the contemporary sacred ground, the mesa, its power objects and their manipulation within ceremonies. The figures often referred to by the unwary as merchants or vendors because they carry numbers of pots and other objects likewise may be depictions of curers holding their ritual paraphernalia, the whistling expression of many relating to the whistling of contemporary curers when they are calling up their guardian spirits (Figure 13.5). The depiction of bat figures with the same paraphernalia supports this identification; bats, creatures of the night when curing ceremonies are held, today are believed to be able to detect the causes of witchcraft.

The historic accounts we have of north coast society in the sixteenth century, although few and incomplete, also help to interpret Moche art, especially since there

13.4 The rayed deity can appear alone, as in this sheet gold ornament from Loma Negra in the Piura Valley. The deity holds a tumi knife in one hand and a trophy head in the other.

appears to have been a considerable continuity of practices from before the Moche into the sixteenth century. Thus accounts of condemning thieves to be staked out alive to be consumed by birds may account for the similar figures in Moche art, and a depiction of a female supernatural figure alternatively with small lice and small human figures crawling over her body can be identified with the historic "witch" Mollope the Lousy, of whom it was said that as her lice multiplied so would the people. Similarly reports of ritual orgies and cannibalism, a preference for sodomy (as a sure means of birth control), and the draconian punishment of doctors who killed their patients through ineptitude by staking them out alive to be eaten by birds are all shown in Moche ceramics as well (see also Figure 15.5).

It has also proved possible to test these interpretations drawn from art against the archaeological record, something which is essential if one is not simply to write new mythologies. Excavations at Moche uncovered several burials which had repoussé copper disks as part of their headdresses. Similar headdresses are commonly shown being worn by runners, perhaps the Moche equivalent of the Inca chasquis. Both supernatural (part bird or feline) and human runners are shown in Moche art and it seems likely that, in the Moche concept of the supernatural, conditions, actions, and occupations on earth were mirrored in the supernatural. Excavations at the late Moche site of Pacatnamú in Lambayeque have revealed evidence that the gory, mutilated,

13.5 Moche stirrup bottle: curandero with his rolled mat for the mesa (ritual "table") under one arm and carrying both a number of vessels and a burden (presumably with the other tools of his trade) on his back. The plain tunic with embroidered or tapestry decorated sleeve bands is worn by musicians as well as curers.

exposed culprits shown in Moche art had their counterpart in people who had had their limbs pulled so far apart that they were disarticulate, and had been exposed for a considerable time to the populace. And the on-going excavations at the "royal" Moche tombs of Sipán and San José de Moro are showing that there were apparently people who dressed like the major figures in these religious scenes, perhaps *were* these people in some sense, and who were buried with the ornaments and costumes which showed their status and identification with the supernatural. At this point the major problems with the iconographic approach to studying the Moche reside in the lack of provenience or dating for most artifacts. Because most known Moche remains come from looting activities, the basic evidence that would permit the delineation of local cults and of changes in mythology and practice through time is not present.

Despite the resounding successes coming from the Moche archive, work in establishing or utilizing other such large samples has lagged, although some other approaches have proved fruitful in specific cases. Anne Paul's studies of burials from the Paracas Peninsula in southern Peru have focussed on the bundle itself as a single unit of contemporaneity, thus avoiding some of the problems of both specific context and specific date. Paul has been able to show that the very different linear and block color styles of embroidery are, in fact, contemporary. The linear embroideries mainly depict the Oculate Being in his several guises, whereas the block color ones show dancing figures in costume, perhaps players in ceremonial reenactments of myths, supernaturals such as the Killer Whale, and naturalistic creatures such as birds (Figures 13.6, 13.7, and

13.6 Linear-style embroidery from Paracas showing the Oculate Being in his human form. The frontal pose, derived from that of the Staff God of Chavín, became a deity signifer in later cultures. The Oculate Being holds equally smiling trophy heads in each hand and his headdress tresses likewise end in Oculate Being heads.

13.8). The study of bundles as units suggests that the inhabitants of those bundles belonged to or were devotees of specific deities, may have taken part in rituals shown in the embroideries, since similar paraphernalia is found within the bundles, and may, when more bundles have been carefully dismantled, permit the distinguishing of family lines. The existence of a very few bundles, all from one tomb, with a broad-line style of embroidery on their textiles suggests to Paul that these people were from a single region or site. Again, it should be possible to test many of the hypotheses of Paul in the field. Her work has already proved a valuable lesson for those who see all variation as being temporal and has provided new insights into Paracas culture.

Iconographic studies of the Chavín style, the cult and style ancestral to both Moche and Paracas, have again indicated new lines of investigation. Ties with warmer climes, perhaps the tropical lowlands to the east, perhaps the warm upper valleys of the farther north coast, are suggested by the close association of supernatural figures with warm-land cultigens such as cotton and ají. Analysis of painted textiles in the Chavín style, coupled with depictions at Chavín-related sites, both shows how this style may have been spread and tells of something which is not evident in either the monumental art of Chavín or the ceramic artifacts in Chavín style: that hallucinogens were an integral part of religious practices. These studies also suffer because of the paucity of archaeological data for the (largely) looted Chavín textiles and coastal ceramic, shell, and metal artifacts, but have provided suggestions concerning the origins and spread of this greatest of America's pristine civilizations.

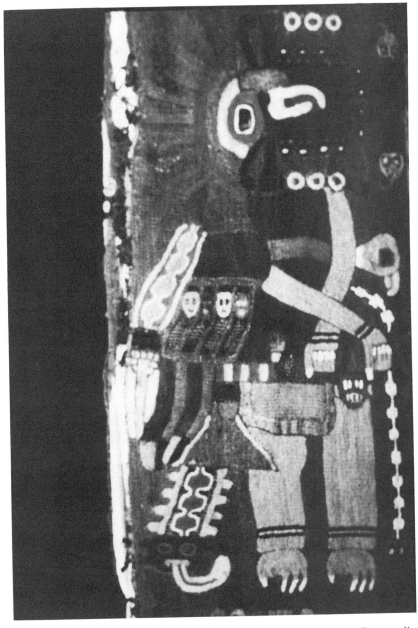

13.7 Block color-style representation of a Condor Man, from Paracas. Reportedly burials which contained bird-man costumes have been found by looters.

13.8 Embroidered dancer (?) with elaborate feather crown, from Paracas. Golden forehead ornaments like the one this figure wears are common in Paracas burials. The figure carries a decorated staff in one hand and a monkey in the other; the monkeys are echoed in the elaborate hanging ornament springing from his headdress.

13.9 Sinú-style feline ornament from northern Colombia. The pelage markings of this small hollow pendant (?) are formed by lost wax cast spirals.

Outside of the central Andean region iconographic studies have been largely small scale because of both a smaller number of representational art styles and of the significantly smaller amount of controlled excavation of artifacts. The most successful iconographic studies in the northern Andes have been concerned with the gold work of the Sinú region of the Magdalena flood plain and of the Tairona, an historic people of the Sierra Nevada de Santa Marta and, perhaps, the ancestors of the present day Kogi. The basic iconographic work has been done by Anne Legast, working with the very large collections of gold pieces in the Museo del Oro in Bogotá. Legast notes that Sinú gold ornaments are dominated thematically by birds and animals which are native to the region. Mammals especially are so clearly portrayed that identification to the level of genus and even species is often possible although birds and fish are less realistically depicted (Figure 13.9). A comparison of the corpus of animals shown to accounts of the Mompos Depression of the río San Jorge in the sixteenth century shows that the very rich fauna that formerly was found in the Sinú is reflected in the gold work. However, there is some skewing as to frequencies of species shown. Nearly 90% of Sinú gold pieces are birds (Figure 13.10). There is also some numeric emphasis on aggressive animals such as the jaguar, cayman, king vulture, eagle, and shark, whereas depictions of people and of frogs, common in the other gold work styles of Colombia, are absent. Legast's Sinú study is mainly a very careful enumeration of the animal themes and their frequencies in Sinú ornaments and is the kind of study which is basic to more interpretative works.

In her later study of Tairona gold work she had the twin advantages of more pieces with provenience to work with and historical and ethnographic accounts of both the Tairona and of the contemporary Kogi. Unlike the Sinú style, in which human figures are largely restricted to pieces made in imitation of other styles, presumably for export,

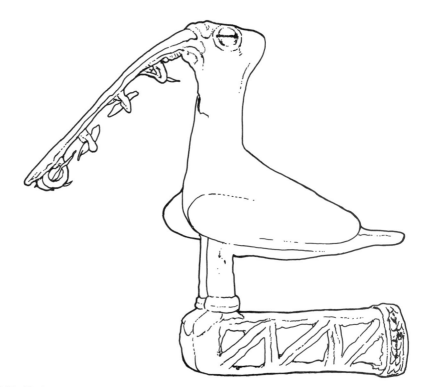

13.10 Sinú ornament with a spoon-billed water bird (perhaps an ibis). Although this type of ornament is commonly called a baton head, they are more likely to have been headdress ornaments. Spangles once hung from the bird's long beak.

Tairona gold features human beings and composite creatures: human and animal mixed or compositions drawn from features of several animal species (Figure 13.11). The Tairona had two major centers, Muica and Bonda; these correspond to two important Indian provinces: Betoma and Bonda. Early chronicles speak of the gold jewelry worn by the people of this area, especially from Bonda and San Pedro de la Sierra (Pasiqüeica), where much known (provenienced) Tairona gold is said to have originated. Some Tairona pieces, however, come from areas that were not historically Tairona, suggesting that they were traded over considerable distances. In Tairona gold mammals, birds, and reptiles are shown in approximately equal numbers. Moreover, most of these subjects are also seen in shell artifacts and in ceramic vessels and artifacts, particularly ocarinas and whistles. Common mammals are felines, kinkajous, raccoons, anteaters, and bats. The bats in particular are often combined with human attributes. Legast notes that among the Kogi there is no sharp division between the animal and human world. Bats are important in Kogi myths, although there is no bat deity. However, the Kogi do make bat masks hauntingly like the faces shown on the bat-man gold figures, which are used in some ceremonies. Likewise jaguars, common in gold work, are a central figure in modern Kogi myths. Other figures show the bat associated also with bird and serpent figures as well as other animals with serpent heads or

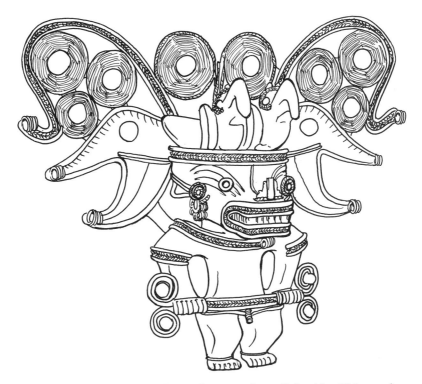

13.11 Tairona anthropomorphic figure from northern Colombia. This pendant combines features of the bat (muzzle, nose) with an otherwise human male body. The figure holds some sort of staff and wears an elaborate headdress with two sets of stylized birds.

mammal-amphibian-reptile and bird-reptile mixes (Figure 13.12). Tairona animals, unlike those found in the Sinú style, are largely non-edible species, often nocturnal raptors, or are combination figures.

Although Legast relates many of the Tairona pieces to Kogi mythology and shamanistic practices, this theme has been taken much farther by Gerardo Reichel-Dolmatoff. Reichel stresses the intrinsically shamanistic nature of most Colombian gold work. He notes that birds, either as main subjects or as attributes on headdresses, staffs, and other paraphernalia of other figures, form an astonishingly large thematic percentage of prehispanic gold pieces in northern and central Colombia. Bird-men are common in Tairona art: bird-man pectorals are found among the Muisca and in the Popayán styles as well as, perhaps, in others such as the Calima and Tolima styles (Figure 13.13). He suggests as well that the heart-shaped pectorals known both in gold and as pendants and back racks on sculptured figures throughout Colombia represent the folded wings of a bird. He then relates this preponderance of birds and bird symbols (including seated figures with their knees drawn up and their arms wrapped around them, a common trance pose among modern peoples) as referring to shamanistic flight. He suggests that this flight was induced by the ingestion of hallucinogenic drugs,

13.12 Tairona snake-bird pendant (?). This piece, now in the Field Museum of Natural
History in Chicago, was reportedly found on La Plata Island, Ecuador.

particularly snuffs. The use of these snuffs is widely attested to in Colombia, as in much
of the rest of South America, and small gold snuff trays are quite common among
Muisca gold offerings. Ancient Colombian gold also includes large quantities of coca-
using paraphernalia: many of the famous Quimbaya gold figures are póporos, and the
majority of the finest miniature sculptures, erroneously identified as pins in many
museums, are the spatulas used to extract the lime from the póporo (which was, and is,
frequently a gourd). Coca quids in the cheek are found in Capulí and Piartal ceramic
figurines and in stone statues from San Agustín and Popayán. Stools, seated figures,

13.13 Double-headed bird ornament from central Colombia (Popayán style?). The bird has human genitals and wears human nose (beak?) and ear ornaments.

representations of musicians (as well as the instruments themselves in metal, both replicas and real instruments), dancers, masked figures and masks, all suggest shamanistic practices. The correspondences with modern Indians' myths and practices are too numerous to explain as coincidence. For example, a large number of the "eagle" pectorals (often misidentified as "Veraguas Eagles," as the first ones with any provenience came from Panama) show swallow-tailed kites, the major shamanistic bird from Costa Rica to the Orinoco (Figure 13.14). Similarly the bird-men, the fantastic animals, and so on suggest that they represent figures of shamans in flight or of mythic ancestors and culture heroes.

Although Reichel's interpretations can be criticized as being reductionist, the coincidence between ancient gold work themes and modern Indian myths and rituals is considerable and his studies, as well as those of Legast, have begun to return these

13.14 Gold "eagle" pendant from northern or central Colombia. Our understanding of both use and style of gold pieces is hampered by the fact that most have been looted and, like this and the previous piece, have no provenience at all.

beautiful pieces to the realm of history and ethnology and have given us new and important insights both into ancient belief systems and into the longevity of native mythic traditions.

It is evident then that cautious studies of the artistic production of a culture can reveal aspects not immediately evident in such mundane things as site plans, architectural histories and reconstructions, and ceramic sequences. It is the combination of archaeological and artistic data, however, that makes such further revelations possible. All of the studies mentioned have come up against the very real lack of control of time or place. Huaquería has been rampant in South America since the first invaders began to loot sites and tombs for their gold. It is an ever-growing problem as foreign collectors and museums seek to fill their coffers at the expense of a continent's history, destroying the context that would enable the integration of iconography with other aspects of the culture and enable us to look at the history and development of these macro-themes, such as shamanistic flight or the Sacrifice Scene, among their constituent cultures.

CHAPTER 14

MILITARISTIC AND RELIGIOUS
MOVEMENTS IN THE ANDES: AD 500–900

The major events on the South American continent beginning *c.* 500 AD were the rise of two related polities which may have been the first true empires in the Andes (Figure 14.1). The first of these, long reputed to be the source of the religion which the second, brandishing it like the sword of Islam, used as an integral element in its formation of a multinational conquest state, was Tiahuanaco, located in a small valley some 25 km from the southern shore of Lake Titicaca at an altitude of 3840 m above sea level. The Bolivian altiplano was one of the early centers of plant domestication and a highly developed agriculture featuring special high-altitude crops such as quinoa (*Chenopodium quinoa*), cañihua (*Chenopodium pallidicaule*), potatoes (*Solanum tuberosum*), oca (*Oxalis tuberosa*), ulluco (*Ullucus tuberosus*), and a host of other, less well-known (to non-Andean peoples) grains, legumes, and tubers, had been present for many centuries. Another feature of the altiplano environment is the abundant grazing land, both on the wet lands close to the lake and the farther away high puna. There is some reason to think that the altiplano was one of the original centers of camelid domestication and the possession of extensive pasture and abundant herds must have been a significant factor in the rise of Tiahuanaco to power in the early centuries after Christ. Quite early too, people began to reclaim low-lying lands along the lake shore by constructing huge systems of raised fields. These came to be essential in provisioning the growing urban center.

The site of Tiahuanaco had been occupied for at least 500 years before it became a large urban center some time in the third century AD (Epoch III, a phase defined on the fill of the Qalasasaya temple enclosure). It reached its greatest size in the next century or so and at that point covered some 7–8 sq km, with the ceremonial core of the city covering perhaps 16 ha. This core contains five major structures with a number of others spread out through the urban area which itself fills much of the small alluvial valley in which Tiahuanaco is situated. The core area, and the zone directly around it, contained both ceremonial structures and the palaces of the ruling elite. Only the fanciest architecture at Tiahuanaco was of cut stone, a trait shared by many earlier and later cultures of the highlands. Residences seem to have been both circular and rectangular (Figure 14.2), presumably arranged in the courtyard fashion which is still common today (a family residence consists of a number of one-room houses used for sleeping and storage, arranged around a central courtyard; walls keep out intruders and, just as important, shield the inhabitants from the wind). More elaborate structures such as the "palaces" may have been multiroomed buildings with numerous courtyards built with foundations, lintels, and other features of cut stone with carved decorations. Walls, even in elaborate buildings, were often of adobe. Much of the adobe has been destroyed over the centuries, so that large stone architectural elements litter the landscape, often with little immediately evident association with a structure. The heart of Tiahuanaco

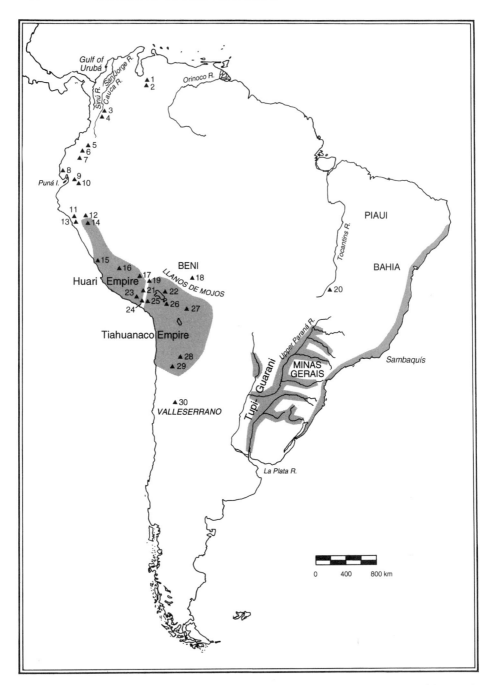

14.1 Principal sites mentioned in Chapter 14. 1. La Betania, 2. Caño del Oso, 3. Quindio, Armenia, 4. Yotoco, 5. Pupiales, 6. Carchi, 7. La Florida, Pinchincha Volcano, Quito, 8. Salango, 9. Cuenca, 10. Chordeleg, Sigsig, 11. Pacatnamú, 12. Cajamarca, 13. Galindo, 14. Viracochapampa, 15. Pachacamac, 16. Ayacucho, Huari, 17. Pikillacta, 18. Mound Velarde, Mound Hernmack, 19. Sicuani, 20. Mossamêdes, 21. Quispisisa, 22. Niño Korin, 23. Maymi, 24. Ariquipa, 25. Moquegua Valley, Cerro Baúl, 26. Tiahuanaco, 27. Cochabamba, 28. Calahoyo, 29. San Pedro de Atacama, 30. Aguada.

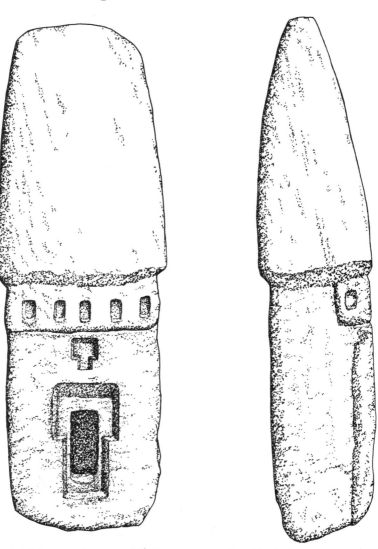

14.2 Early Tiahuanaco house model. This tiny piece, found in the lowest excavations in the Qalasasaya of Tiahuanaco of Bolivia, is a whistle. The high, presumably thatched, roof and the elaborate inset doorway and window or niche above it presage Inca architecture.

today consists of a series of enclosures and a pyramid. The earliest structure is the Semisubterranean Temple, a stone-lined sunken courtyard approximately 28.5 × 26 m in measurements (Figure 14.3). The walls are lined with tenon heads of humans and supernaturals executed in a variety of styles (the temple was renovated some centuries after it was built and replacement tenon heads in the current style were inserted to replace those which had presumably been either lost or damaged). The temple contained four statues of which one, in a version of the Yayamama style, represents a bearded (?) figure. This statue may have been the original cult object of the Semisubterranean Temple (Figure 14.4). A "Classic Tiahuanaco" statue (after AD 350) and two poorly

14.3 The Semisubterranean Temple, Tiahuanaco, from the top of the Akapana. The Qalasasaya is to the left.

14.4 The Yayamama-style statue in the Semisubterranean Temple is probably the original cult object.

14.5 The Qalasasaya from the Akapana. This immense walled platform has been largely reconstructed. It contained numbers of small buildings (shrines?) and large statues of humans with offerings. The huge statue visible in the middle of the Qalasasaya is very similar in subject and style to El Fraile (Figure 14.9). The Panamerican highway cuts through Tiahuanaco and is visible on the far side of the compound.

preserved statues with no diagnostic features were also found in this early temple. The Semisubterranean Temple shows close affinities with ceremonial structures in other parts of the southern highlands, such as the sunken part of the temple at Pucara and the sunken temple of Chiripa, and was probably one of the first major constructions (surviving) undertaken by the growing town of Tiahuanaco. Somewhat later was the construction of the Akapana, an artificial platform so large that even specialists in highland Andean archaeology have referred to it as a natural hill. Originally it seems to have been a seven-stepped rectangular platform with a wide projection on its east side. The sides were faced with stone and there were a number of buildings on its top. The Akapana apparently had some symbolic association with the mountains to the south of Tiahuanaco, perhaps as an artificial sacred mountain. The top and upper terraces were covered with a water-worn green gravel brought from these mountains. Within the platform itself was a cut-stone drain which could be activated to let water rush along the steps of the pyramid. This building is truly unique in South America and the meaning of its elaborate water works and highly unusual form is only now being unraveled. Next to the Akapana is the Qalasasaya, a large enclosure with associated sculptures (Figure 14.5). This has been largely reconstructed, but may have contained a number of shrines or other special purpose religious structures. Numbers of large, finely carved statues representing either deities or their worshipers have been found associated with the Qalasasaya and with the other major buildings of Tiahuanaco. There is unfortunately a certain amount of confusion about exact associations, and even the famous "Gateway of the Sun," a monolithic doorway which depicts the major deity of Tiahuanaco and his attendants, may well have been moved several times before finding its present home next to the Qalasasaya (Figure 14.6).

The major constructions of Tiahuanaco do not show any regular orientation one to the other, although there may have been some astronomical orientations originally intended for individual buildings. The lack of planning which the present eye sees is related to the disappearance of the perishable adobe structures which made up the majority of Tiahuanaco architecture. Temples and other religious and administrative structures were oriented to now-gone buildings and roadways in the ancient town.

The art of Tiahuanaco, in stone and in ceramics as well as in the more rarely preserved wood, textiles and other materials, shows a pantheon whose major deity is clearly ultimately derived, in form if not in associations, from the Staff God of Chavín. This frontal male figure, wearing a rayed headdress and holding a staff in either hand adorns the "Gateway of the Sun" surrounded by attendant angels, human, animal or bird headed winged figures shown in profile (Figure 14.7). This deity can be represented by his rayed head alone, a form more common on ceramics and smaller objects. Other important figures, seen mainly in ceramics, are animals (camelids, felines, snakes, and composite creatures) with supernatural features associated with light colored circles (Figure 14.8). It has been argued repeatedly that these are star animals, representatives of constellations important in the mythology of the Tiahuanacan peoples. Human figures, both male and female, are also common, especially in the monumental sculpture, and the wide staring eyes seen on some of them imply that they too may be representations of supernaturals (the large ovoid-rectangular staring eye is a signifer of supernatural status in earlier altiplano sculptural styles) (Figure 14.9).

Tiahuanaco was a major power in the altiplano for many centuries, superseding the earlier power of Pucara on the north end of the lake, a site which seems to have furnished many religious and artistic ideas to Tiahuanaco. Our understanding of details of Tiahuanaco's rise to power and consolidation of this power is limited, but it seems evident that Tiahuanaco conquered and administrated the altiplano as the core area of its state. Tiahuanaco influence in ceramics and other artifacts is visible in the lowlands around Cochabamba and extended into the modern states of Oruro and Tarija, albeit in a somewhat diluted form. Tiahuanaco's influence is also evident in northern Chile, especially in the Atacama region, where it supersedes earlier Pucara influence on the local cultures. Here excavation has shown imports of ceramics and textiles in both Pucara and Tiahuanaco styles as well as some influence on local manufactures. Tiahuanaco influence, and perhaps a Tiahuanaco presence, is visible in Peru north to around Sicuani and towards the coast into the Moquegua Valley. This valley, rich in mineral resources, seems to have been where Tiahuanaco and Huari finally met, competing for the turquoise, lapis lazuli, and obsidian that were important to both as

14.6 The Gateway of the Sun, front and rear. There are a number of these monolithic doorways at Tiahuanaco, but this is the most elaborately decorated. The front surface has an elaborate frieze with the Staff God at the center; the back has elaborate large and small niches of unknown use.

14.7 The lower register of angels from the Gateway of the Sun. Angels such as these, shown in profile and carrying a staff of some sort, are also common in Huari art. They may have heads of humans (as do these), hawks, or other animals. The rayed heads in the bottom register are another common Andean icon.

well as, perhaps, for the deposits of copper which now form an important part of the modern economy.

In Peru, near the modern city of Ayacucho in the south central highlands, a similar development was taking place. This area in the preceding centuries had developed a series of urban centers and a prosperous economy based upon agriculture, herding, and trade. Control of the puna was important to all the early Andean states and the Ayacucho area was especially favored in having the resources of the nearby Pampa de Junín with its vast areas of grazing land to draw upon. Contact with the Nazca culture of the south coast is evident in the pottery, a style called Huarpa. Sometime in the mid sixth century a new style of ceramics began to appear in the Ayacucho region. This pottery is found only in the form of outsize urns painted with realistic polychrome figures. The urns have been located at several offering deposits in the Ayacucho suburb of Conchopata, where they had been placed in stone-lined pits and broken in place with a blow to the face of the main figure on each urn. The main figure on these urns is clearly very closely related to the main deity of Tiahuanaco, being a frontal male figure with a rayed headdress and a staff in each hand. As at Tiahuanaco he is associated with profile running figures with wings; later (in Peru) the male deity is associated with a female figure who has similar attributes, although the finials on the rays of her headdress and on her staffs are different. The Conchopata offerings are the first appearance in Peru of a

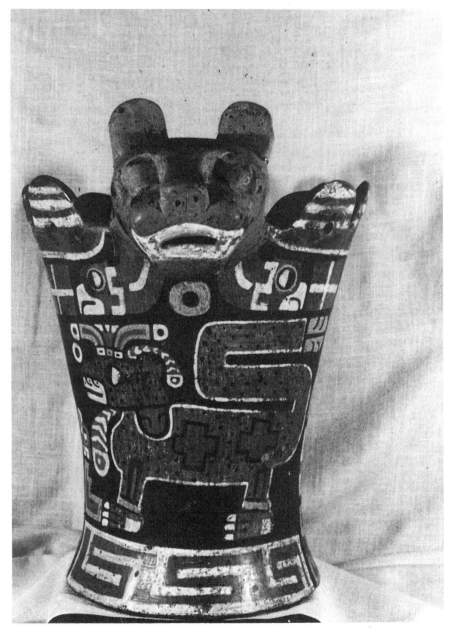

14.8 A puma-headed incensario, Tiahuanaco. The function of this peculiar shape is not known. The design on the front shows a stylized animal, perhaps a feline, who has a headdress and necklace with light circles, indicating that the animal is a star or a constellation.

style which for many years was called "Coastal Tiahuanaco" because of its obviously close affiliations with that style. On the basis of the relationships, both in figures (the Staff God, the angels, star animals, etc.) and in their mode of representation, people hypothesized that Tiahuanaco had somehow intruded into Peru, either as a religious movement or as an outright conquest state. However, this does not appear to have been the case. The style found in Peru, called Huari after the site which appears to have been its central distribution point, is different enough that it may well have been derived somewhat independently from the Pucara religion – that is, the religions and the associated art of both Huari and Tiahuanaco would appear to be major, but different, sects of the same cult, both being adopted by expansionist states and spread over broad regions. No imported objects from Tiahuanaco have been found outside of a circumscribed region in southern Peru and no Huari objects are known to have come from the region occupied by Tiahuanaco. The only area occupied by both cultures was the Moquegua Valley, where a short-lived Huari presence has been detected, perhaps the remains of an attempt to wrest this mineralogically important region from Tiahuanaco.

The manner in which an essentially southern highland religion appears in the

14.9 Statue of a male carrying a keros and some unknown object, from Tiahuanaco. The large, staring eyes may indicate that this figure, commonly called El Fraile ("The Friar"), is a supernatural.

Ayacucho region suggests that it may well have been spread by religious means, perhaps through some sort of missionary movement or revitalizing movement out of the southern sierra. There is reason to think that some vestiges of Chavín religion had survived in the Peruvian highlands, so that the appearance of Pucara-Tiahuanaco elements may have been in the form of the presentation of a more elaborate cult of an existing religion to the prospering central sierra cities. Within a relatively short time the new religion was firmly established in the Ayacucho region which then became the center for an expansion which can be traced along the coast from Acarí to north of Lima and in the highlands to Huarás in the Callejón de Huaylas (Figure 14.1). The influence of this political expansion and the religion which accompanied it can be seen in the strong regional states of the north coast, although there is little reason to think that these were ever under the political control of the Huari. The pattern of the appearance of Huari influence in ceramics, textiles, architecture, and settlement pattern strongly suggests a military expansion similar to that of the Incas some centuries later.

The religious themes first expressed on the giant urns of the Conchopata deposits shortly thereafter began to appear on elaborate pottery, fine textiles, and other objects associated with ceremonial precincts and rich burials, suggesting that the elite of Huari were deliberately associating themselves with this new religion. The religion seems to have featured the male deity shown on the urns. He was shortly joined by a female deity and the pair may have been associated with the sun and moon as the female is shown associated with maize and other crops which in later times were deemed to be under the moon's control. There was also a series of other deities, some of whom were identified with the stars or constellations. Another feature of this religion was oracles, the most important of which was to be found at Pachacamac, just south of Lima. This oracle survived into the historic period and the god spoke through a statue to deliver his messages to supplicants (Figure 14.10). Stone statues (the Pachacamac one was of wood, much to the disgust of the Spanish looters who had hoped that such an important figure would be made of gold and jewels) with a funnel-shaped opening from the front to the back have been found in the highlands at both Pucara and Huari. Oracles thus appear to have been an important part of this religion and, if one can judge from the historic records concerning Pachacamac, a means of integrating political and religious aims and conveying these to the populace.

At the same time that there is evidence of the spread of this religion in Peru there is evidence of increasing wealth at the site of Huari: numbers of stone buildings, both the hallmark multistory residential enclosures and ceremonial structures with cut-stone masonry and slab tombs similar to those of Pucara. Within a short period of time (Epoch 2 A – relative dating is much more precise for this period than absolute dating) there appears to have been some sort of struggle for power in the Ayacucho region, with Huari winning. The other urban sites of the region were abandoned and Huari became much larger, perhaps as the result of government directed resettlement. This is not to say that there were no other Huari sites. The Huari government found it useful to initiate large urban and governmental/military centers in numbers of areas of the state, including the Cuzco Valley (Pikillacta) and the Cajamarca region of the northern sierra

14.10 The Temple of the Oracle of Pachacamac, central coast of Peru. The platform on which the temple stood has eight tiers and an inset wide stair, presumably for easy access to the oracle himself. The building was originally painted with multicolor murals of humans, fish, sea birds, and plants.

(Viracochapampa) as well as smaller centers such as Jargampata, which evidently were regional political centers related to the administrative and economic structure of the Huari state. These centers combine living quarters for administrators and military personnel with immense storage facilities, no doubt for storing the tribute levied on conquered regions.

Investigations at Huari have shown that the city reached an eventual size of some 1000–1500 ha with a core of substantial stone architecture covering some 400 ha. Huari buildings show a distinctive plan. High exterior walls enclose a (usually) rectangular space, which was filled with cellular constructions consisting of long narrow rooms surrounding rectangular patios (Figure 14.11). Buildings were often several stories tall and were apparently laid out at once, although the inner cells were completed as needed. The compounds show considerable social diversity, the larger, finer built ones containing remains of luxury goods such as carved shell, semi-precious stones, bronze implements and elaborate pottery. They also have sacrificial caches (often of human skulls) in the floors, and such architectural niceties as wall niches, plastered and painted walls, and plastered floors. Compounds were laid out in a regular fashion along streets with major thoroughfares cutting the site into four sectors. Very similar construction and layout is seen at the Huari regional centers, especially the very large ones such as Pikillacta, and there seems little doubt that there were government architects and engineers charged with the design and erection of Huari buildings and centers, with administrative quarters, craft quarters, storehouses, and perhaps military garrisons.

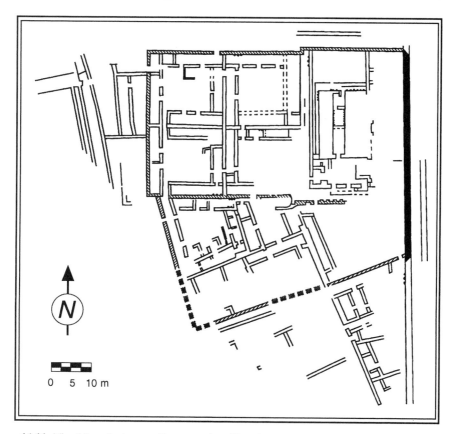

14.11 The Moraduchayuq Compound at Huari, near Ayacucho, Peru. This walled
enclosure originally had at least eight patios and was several stories high. The
excavator, William Isbell, interprets it as the home of an extended family of
middle-level administrators who also used some of the patios and associated
rooms for their administrative duties and for feasting and entertaining their
retainers.

Excavations at Huari have shown a long developmental history to these architectural
and city planning ideas, beginning perhaps as early as 1000 BC. Despite iconographic
similarities in their decorated artifacts the total form of Huari sites is very different from
the sites of Tiahuanaco and its affiliates.

The Huari state expanded very rapidly, establishing new centers both in the
highlands and on the coast. Pachacamac became a large city because of its oracle and,
perhaps, because of its strategic importance. North of Pachacamac, Huari was not as
strong and sites such as Chimu Capac were little more than garrisons on the border of an
expansion which never came. The Pachacamac version of Huari religion was somewhat
different (as is its highly distinctive art style), perhaps because it was the center of
worship of a different deity (Figure 14.12). South of Pachacamac Huari influence was
considerable. The earlier south coast cultures had been in close contact with those of the
Ayacucho basin and Huari religious iconography was quickly integrated into the

14.12 A modeled bottle from Ancón, on the central coast of Peru. The subject is a seated man, wearing a labret in his lower lip, in the act of taking coca. He has a póporo in his right hand. The details of the jewelry are unusual in this piece and we can see that his necklace is made of two strands of tubular and round beads with ties at the back, while his ears have holes for multiple ear ornaments around the edge of the ear itself.

14.13 Huari-style (Robles Moqo-substyle) vase from the offering deposits at Pacheco in the Nazca Valley. The rim patterns are of cotton, maize, and ají plants and the dotted rectangles below the face may refer to a tie-dyed shirt. This vase too was broken in place with a blow to the modeled face.

existing system. There was a branch of the Pachacamac oracle in Ica and offerings of huge jars with mythical figures and feather curtains have been found at Pacheco in Nazca (Figure 14.13). Other offering deposits have been located at Maymi in the Pisco Valley, a site which also contains large potters' workshops. Minor differences in offering practices and in iconography at these various centers indicate that there may well have been several major cults within the Huari religion, each with its own favored deities and their associated symbols, much as one sees in modern Christianity.

The final extent of the Huari state reached from the sierra near Cajamarca (excluding the northern valleys) south to the region of Arequipa, about at the border between Quechua and Aymara speakers today. This state can be traced through its characteristic complexes of administrative, storage, and military (?) buildings which were located at key points for controlling traffic between major population or resource zones. One of the best known of these is Pikillacta, at the southern end of the Cuzco Valley, a strategic

14.14 A panoramic view of Pikillacta, in the southern Cuzco Valley, Peru. This major Huari administrative, storage, and, perhaps, military center is located at a strategic point to control traffic from the Huari Empire's southern frontier.

point between the Huari and Tiahuanaco polities. Pikillacta consists of a series of large rectangular compounds containing multistory gallery structures similar to those at Huari itself, and walled storage structures, regularly laid out with walls, streets, and a large plaza at one side (Figure 14.14). The unfinished Viracochapampa near Cajamarca was a similar installation (Figures 14.15 and 14.16).

Huari administrative/religious/military sites were connected by a road system similar to that of the Incas. Inca and Huari roads are not exactly the same, however. Huari ones go a number of places Inca ones do not and vice versa; the two states were certainly not identical. There was also a planned expansion of irrigation and terrace systems opening up new lands, especially in the maize and coca growing belts. It was at this time that maize agriculture seems finally to have become profitable, and representations of maize and of maize deities become common in a number of art styles. Bronze metallurgy was also introduced and metals began to be used for tools and weapons as well as for adornments. The identification of several Huari quipus suggests that this aid to administration was being used to govern the empire.

The Huari state, however, was short lived. At the end of Middle Horizon 2, roughly AD 800, the Huari state completely collapsed. Huari and the regional centers, including the unfinished Viracochapampa, were abandoned and the Ayacucho region ceased to have any interaction outside the local area. In the rest of Peru variations on themes of

14.15 One of the great niched halls of Viracochapampa, Peru, a Huari administrative center near Cajamarca.

this period continued, but with ever increasing regionalism in the art styles and with increasing input from the cultures of the north coast, which survived the fall of Huari and flourished. The fall of Huari brought to an end the tradition of urban settlements that had existed in southern Peru for nearly 2000 years. There were no more cities in this region until the Spanish reimposed them in the colonial period.

The collapse of Huari led to a general depression in those areas which had been most firmly under its domination: the southern sierra and the south and central coasts. No elaborate goods were manufactured, no wealthy burials made; sites became smaller and poorer. Moreover, there are fewer sites dating from this epoch than there had been previously, indicating some population loss in the former Huari state. On the coast Pachacamac managed to survive, but the urban area around it was abandoned and renewed prosperity had to await the next conquest state. It is notable that this depression did not reach the north coast, where a series of closely related local cultures were becoming increasingly industrialized and prospering through intensive trade and manufacture with the sierra and with Ecuador.

The tendency towards state formation and expansionistic religious and political

14.16 Detail of the inside of one of the multistory buildings at Viracochapampa. Projecting corbels are placed to hold upper floors of wood and plaster or of stone slabs. Similar construction techniques are seen at Huari itself, Pikillacta, and other Huari centers.

movements seems to have been largely confined to Peru and Bolivia, where Tiahuanaco struggled on for some centuries. In northern Peru in the areas not controlled by Huari there was the development of local polities growing out of a Moche substratum, although with considerable input from Huari in terms of technology, iconography, and organizational ideas (Figure 14.17). Urban centers such as Galindo in the Moche Valley and Pacatnamú in Jequetepeque rose to prominence. The existence of large areas for storage in Galindo and the rather different forms of the new ceremonial buildings, with their large walled enclosures, show some new ideas coming in. Along the Peruvian coast it seems that a new maritime orientation in religion was becoming important, perhaps in conjunction with increased trade with southern Ecuador, the closest source of the highly desired spondylus shell. It is possible that this increased contact was partly responsible for the appearance of urbanism and large-scale architecture at sites such as Salango in southern Manabí, a known center of spondylus trade and ritual activity (Figure 14.18). To the south of Tiahuanaco in the Valliserrana region of northwestern Argentina, the Aguada culture succeeded the earlier Cienaga and Condorhuasi cultures

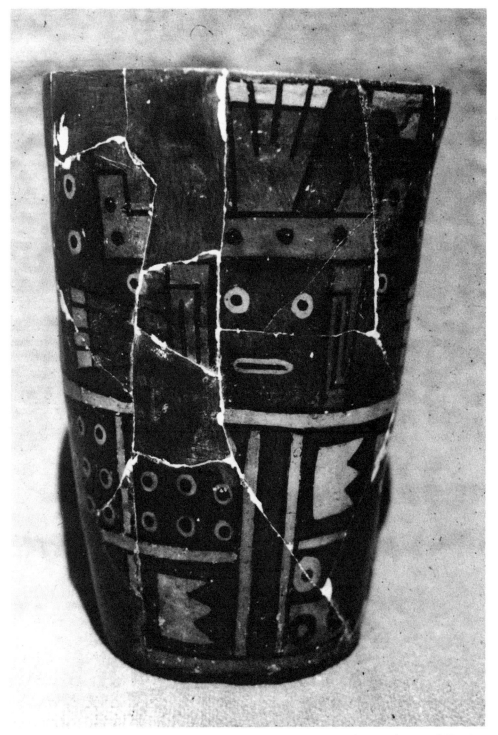

14.17 Large beaker from the site of Moche. This beaker is decorated in good Huari style with the face of a deity and various geometric elements which apparently refer to a specific deity as well as to textile motifs.

14.18 The Sacred Isle of Salango from the northeast. Salango was an important site from Valdivia times onwards, perhaps because of its proximity to the spondylus fisheries of the Ecuadorian coast.

with their developed metallurgy, elaborately decorated pottery, and little villages of farmers and herders. Relatively little is known of the Aguada culture, which is often referred to as "draconian" because of the reptilian and feline composite creatures which decorate the polychrome and gray incised ceramics (Figure 14.19). Many have suggested iconographic ties between various Peruvian cultures and Aguada. Features such as the crest on supernatural animals are clearly derived from Peruvian prototypes (where this motif first appears in Paracas and coastal Chavín ceramics) but there are few clear ties with either Tiahuanaco, with which the Aguada culture must have been at least partly contemporary, or with other cultures. Bronze working was highly developed in the Aguada culture (see Figure 11.4). Despite the strong evidence of social differentiation seen in the multiple flexed burials with offerings of vessels, tools and weapons, there does not seem to have been any single political unit of any size. Houses continued to be arranged around patios; there is apparent population growth and a concomitant increase in terracing and other methods of increasing the land under cultivation. Aguada-related materials have been found associated with the San Pedro culture in Atacama, perhaps as a result of both groups exploiting the same metal-bearing regions and herding lands. Tiahuanaco and Cochabamba ceramics are quite common in San Pedro as well, but apparently as trade goods. There is no Tiahuanaco influence on

14.19 Motifs from Aguada painted and incised ceramics, Argentina. The dragon-like figures are especially typical of this culture and hint at participation in the wider Andean mythological realm.

the local highly polished plain ware ceramic styles nor in architecture and burial/ceremonial patterns.

The existence of snuff trays in altiplano-related styles in northern Chile and in Bolivia suggests that Tiahuanaco and the southern peoples shared some religious practices, perhaps those in the realm of curing. A medicine man's burial from the site of Niño Korin near Tiahuanaco contains *Ilex* leaves, syringes, and snuff trays among other paraphernalia of the type historically associated with Callawaya herbal curers. These "medicine men" traditionally have journeyed throughout the central and south central Andes plying their trade. It has been suggested that a similar group existed as far back as the Middle Horizon and that these people, with their commerce in health and the paraphernalia associated with regaining or maintaining it, were responsible for much of the dissemination of Tiahuanaco goods and ideas throughout the zones peripheral to the Tiahuanaco state. The appearance of foreign elements in the ceramics of Aguada and the preceding cultures in the Valliserrana region may suggest an earlier dissemination via the same routes.

At San Pedro de Atacama there is evidence of a considerable increase in population and of intensified agriculture to support it. Some changes in mortuary practices are seen, and although urn burial continued to be practiced, there are other burials which seem to show that status differentiation had arisen. Some people now had deformed skulls, and were buried with elaborate headdresses, feather ornaments, imported textiles and pottery, suggesting that they were richer and/or more important than the majority. A recent excavation here uncovered one of the few Chilean burials to contain gold, among which is a small head in Tiahuanaco style. Similar gold pieces (a diadem, a plume, and some circular pectorals) have been found in burials in western Bolivia. This corresponds with other evidence that northern Chile had joined the altiplano sphere of influence and was reflecting this in the adoption of strong status differences such as were common in the contemporary central Andean cultures. It is possible that there were Tiahuanaco

14.20 "Island" villages connected by causeways on the Llanos de Mojos, Bolivia. Extensive raised field systems are dimly visible in the surrounding land. Raised field systems in the Orinoco and along the río San Jorge of Colombia are essentially identical to the Mojos ones.

colonies at Calahoyo in the puna some 300 km from Atacama and, perhaps, at some considerably closer sites. It has been suggested that, aside from their strong interest in the high-country copper mines and grazing lands, the Tiahuanaco peoples had a certain interest in the semi-precious stones of the area.

Andean influence is not visible much farther than northwestern Argentina, although it has been suggested that some of the archaeological remains of the Department of Beni are very distantly related to Tiahuanaco. Investigations by Erland von Nordenskiold in the 1940s uncovered one of the few stratified lowland sites yet known, a site called Mound Velarde. The Llanos de Mojos of southeastern Bolivia are given to yearly inundations. To combat the inconvenience of this the aboriginal inhabitants constructed artificial mounds with causeways and walled pathways connecting them to keep their dwelling places dry (Figure 14.20). Away from the river levées these are located in slightly elevated areas which support trees, areas called "islands" in modern terminology. Modern as well as ancient settlements are found on them (Figure 14.21) Mound Velarde is fairly typical in size, being some 5 m in height and approximately 45 × 25 m in overall dimensions. At the time of excavation it was occupied by peasants employed on the modern land holding, although it had been inhabited within living memory by Siriono Indians. The mound was adjacent to an area of refuse deposited in two distinct strata. In the upper stratum were a series of urn burials plus a fair amount of midden containing painted tripod bowls, a large grater bowl, and some bone and shell

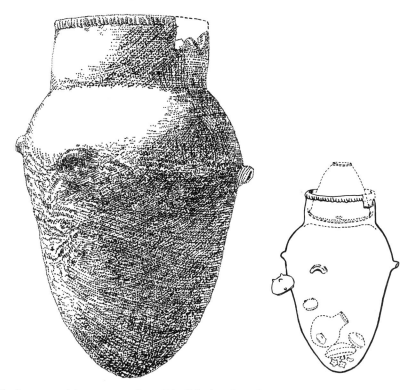

14.21 An urn and its contents from Río Palacios, Sara Province, Bolivia. Urn burial became increasingly common in lowland South America after *c*. AD 500.

remains (Figures 14.22 and 14.23). The lower stratum at Velarde is the one which has attracted the most interest. Rounded bowls with ring bases and shouldered globular bowls look quite Andean while anthropomorphic adornos and handles recall the Amazonian traditions as does a quartz labret. Numerous animal bones were found, apparently of the same local species as in the upper level (deer, paca, opossum, alligator, and dog seem to have been most common). Nordenskiold surmised from the existence in the midden of many small, fragile shells of the genus *Ampullaria* (a mollusk of the local marshes) that the houses had been on stilts. An urn burial in a small globular tripod vessel with a rounded lid was also found.

The excavations at Mound Velarde have no absolute dates associated with them, but are rare evidence of the temporal relationship of cultures in this region of small shallow sites. The dating of Lower Velarde as AD 600–700 is mainly on the basis of fancied Barrancoid traits in the ceramics; Upper Velarde is closely related to materials from Mound Hernmack, also excavated by Nordenskiold, and may be significantly later. The frequent occurrence of grater bowls in Upper Velarde suggests the cultivation of bitter manioc. Recent work in the Llanos de Mojos by Clark Erickson and José Estevez has resulted in some radiocarbon dates for the area. As might be expected, however, these cover a long period of time (roughly last century BC to AD 1100), corresponding to the long use of the earthen features in the llanos.

The cultures of southeastern Brazil began to become agricultural and to make pottery

14.22 A painted urn from Mound Velarde, Bolivia. Elaborate painted burial urns are typical of the later phases of riverine lowland South American cultures.

in about the time span suggested by Donald Lathrap for Lower Velarde. Along the broken, rocky coastline with its numerous broad beaches, and offshore inlets with mangrove and salt marsh, are a series of sites consisting of sambaquís, shell heaps up to 25 m in height (see Figure 5.9). These tend to be located in places where the base line of the site was above high tide and where the off-shore breeze could be caught (for relief from both heat and mosquitoes). Also important in site location seems to have been access to fresh water and to an open waterway. Once established these shoreline villages tended to be occupied for a very long time. The earliest well-dated sambaquí sites are *c*. 2000 BC and there is good evidence of their use until *c*. AD 1400. The sambaquís were periodically abandoned in times of low water (there have been significant oscillations in

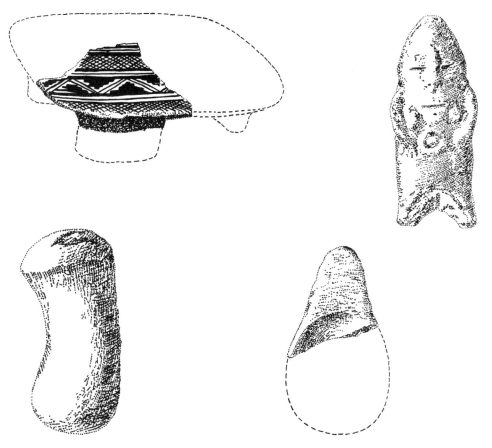

14.23 Ceramic objects from Mound Velarde. Objects of this type are typical finds in many lowland archaeological sites, but those from Mound Velarde have both site and stratigraphic context. The ceramic stool, from Upper Velarde, is found throughout northern and eastern South America and figurines like the example here are likewise common. The clay fire dog and the spoon from Lower Velarde are common utensils. Clay fire dogs were especially important in the huge riverine flood plains, where there are no rocks to form a hearth with.

the sea level here during the Holocene) and many sambaquís have superimposed levels of floors, fireplaces, and burials. The major economic adaptation was to the mollusks of the rocky shore and mangrove, especially members of the genera *Ostrea* and *Mytilis*, although some cockles and other mollusks were also eaten. Only estuary and bay fish were taken; there is no evidence of exploitation of deep sea species, except for the rare whale – almost certainly beached. Hunting was practiced and later levels contain abundant bone projectile points. The early occupations of the sambaquís are preceramic; pottery appeared only at about AD 500 or even somewhat later. Burials, often accompanied by personal adornments and sparse grave goods, show a high incidence of infant mortality. Burials seem to have been made under houses. The few of the latter which have been delineated are large enough to have been multifamily residences. Excavations in the Praia da Tapeira near Florianopolis have revealed houses some 15 m in diameter with pole walls. The villages on the shell mounds may have been seasonally occupied with populations moving inland during the colder seasons of the year.

Inland the earliest horticultural tradition is called Mossamêdes. This first appeared in the upper Tocantins and Araguaia rivers some time in the seventh or eighth century and then spread eastwards into Minas Gerais (where it is called Sapucai), Bahia, Piaui, and neighboring states (where it is called Aratu). Mossamêdes and its relatives represent an agricultural community making spherical and piriform vessels. The earlier ones have a sand temper, although this soon changed into a type of cariapé. There are no griddles in the ceramic inventory, suggesting either that bitter manioc was not present or that it was not being made into flour or cakes. Pedro Schmitz and his colleagues, who have done much of the investigation of this cultural tradition, suggest that Mossamêdes represents a people growing corn, beans, manioc, and other tubers. Mossamêdes and related peoples were numerous throughout central and eastern parts to the Goiâs-Matto Grosso and the upper reaches of the rivers named above. This tradition continued into historic times.

It is also possible that the so-called Tupi-Guaraní tradition began as early as *c.* AD 500–600. This tradition of coiled ceramic vessels decorated with corrugation, red and black on white paint or simple plastic motifs in the historic period is said to pertain to the expansionistic Tupi-Guaraní peoples. Such an affiliation is, of course, impossible to show on the archaeological level, but the term has been so widely applied that all of the very large number of closely related ceramic traditions which show corrugation, red on white or red and black on white painting, simple globular bowls, etc. are identified as belonging to the Tupian peoples. The earliest Tupi-Guaraní sites are on the Atlantic coast and lower rivers where they date to *c.* AD 500–700. They are associated with a people who practiced tropical horticulture in the forests, an adaptation to the low-lying flood plains along major river systems. The Tupi-Guaraní sites spread south and to the interior, where on the southern planalto they encountered and replaced sites of people practicing hunting and gathering. By *c.* AD 1300 sites with Tupi-Guaraní pottery (although this is often mixed with ceramics of other traditions) are found along the Alto Paraná and into Uruguay and Paraguay. In the sixteenth century the Tupi-Guaraní occupied a broad area from north of the Amazon to the Río de la Plata and were found throughout interior Bolivia and Paraguay. Tupi-Guaraní migrations, often following a prophet, are documented well into the historic period.

Artificial mound building was also common in Venezuela where on the western Orinoco plain a series of sites of the Caño del Oso and La Betania phases contain conical mounds and causeways. The mounds and causeways seem to have been a response to seasonal flooding of the area, although it is possible that some of the larger, conical mounds had ceremonial functions as well. This has been suggested by Alberta Zucchi for the site of Hato de la Calzada. Evidence from this site suggests that here the first inhabitants practiced hunting, fishing and maize agriculture, only acquiring manioc sometime after *c.* AD 500. It was at this point that they began seriously to construct artificial earthworks, suggesting that here as well as in lowland Bolivia there was a considerable population which could provide the workforce needed for such large-scale

14.24 A pair of circular hammered gold ornaments from a looted Nariño tomb in southern Colombia. The feline design is a common one both here and in many contemporary Ecuadorian traditions.

undertakings. It is probable that the earthworks are associated with drained field systems, but rapid alluviation in the area has obscured these. Ridged field systems have been reported from farther south in the state of Barinas although many of these may be slightly later.

The eastern half of South America then shows somewhat different responses to growing populations and the movements of peoples and/or ideas. In place of the expansionistic states of Huari and Tiahuanaco, there is very little evidence of any political grouping much larger than, say, a number of villages. Later occupations of the Llanos de Mojos did form large chiefdoms and it is possible that we see such tendencies beginning at sites like Mound Velarde, Marajó, and even perhaps at Caño del Oso and related sites far to the north. Mound and causeway building seems to be related to movement out into seasonally flooded regions, itself probably the result of population growth. Some of this growing population was taken care of by migration, as inland pottery-making agriculturalists were moving into regions still occupied by foragers and part-time horticulturists.

In the northern Andes Huari influence is seen up into the southern highlands of Ecuador, where at Chordeleg and Sigsig a series of deep shaft and chamber tombs looted in the last century yielded both metalwork in a Huari-influenced style and at least one imported vessel, a bottle in the Pachacamac style. The metal pieces are of hammered gold and silver, and represent rayed heads and Huari style angels. Also from these tombs comes a large amount of hammered metal in purely local styles, including circular ornaments with feline faces of a type known from southern Ecuador to Nariño in Colombia, where they are likewise associated with burials in deep shaft and chamber tombs (Figure 14.24). Local ceramics in southern Ecuador have been lumped into a

14.25 Small hilltop pucara near Cumbe in the southern Ecuadorian highlands. Although there is a tendency to call all pucaraes Inca, there is an interesting association between them and trade routes and sites of the Tacalshalpa and related indigenous cultures.

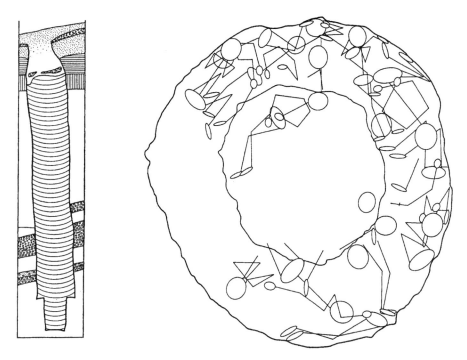

14.26 Section of one of the La Florida tombs (near Quito, Ecuador). These tombs are 15–18 m in depth, the central pit, containing the principal burial, being 1.5–3 m in depth. The schematic drawing shows the disposition of the bodies, with the principal burial in the center and the retainers, seated and bundled in textiles, placed on the bench around the central pit along with ceramic vessels and other offerings. There is also a small pit in the floor which contained other offerings. The whole was originally roofed with wood, but as this rotted the fill of the shaft collapsed downwards moving the bodies and breaking the offerings.

single style called Tacalshalpa. This style is clearly a descendant of the earlier styles of the region, sharing the peculiar reduction and superficial oxidation of these styles. The cheerful faces typical of many Tacalshalpa vessels are reminiscent of Vicús or Gallinazo, but the very sketchy dating available suggests that it dates from *c*. AD 400 to the time of the Inca conquest. Sites seem to be largely located in defensible places and it is possible that some of the many pucaraes that dot southern Ecuador pertain to the Tacalshalpa culture (Figure 14.25).

North, in the region of Quito, a series of shaft and chamber tombs containing elite burials has been excavated by Leon Doyon at La Florida on the slopes of Pinchincha Volcano (Figure 14.26). The La Florida tombs date to around AD 500 and contain multiple seated bundle burials and many offerings, including large quantities of ceramics. The jars are of elongated oval forms and there are numbers of compoteras and annular base cups painted with red slip and organic resist (Figure 14.27). The forms and decoration are reminiscent of the somewhat later Capulí style of Carchi. The La Florida tomb offerings also included bone and stone implements (T-shaped stone axes are

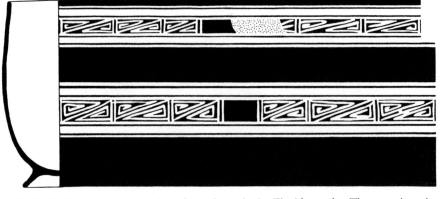

14.27 Rollout drawing of a footed cup from the La Florida tombs. The organic resist designs are very similar to those of the Capulí style of the north.

notable among these), and textiles, a rare find in this damp climate. Most of the textiles are cotton, but a single woolen piece also had copper spangles sewn to it. The La Florida tombs are obviously chiefly or noble burials. It is unfortunate that, to date, the tombs cannot be closely associated with any habitation sites. Some correspondences are seen between the La Florida ceramics and those found associated with the tolas of the adjacent Guallabamba River valley, and it is possible that the tombs reflect an earlier phase of this culture.

The coast of Ecuador shows no particular influence from the south. On the coast the Guangala culture was slowly changing into that of the Manteño, a people who reached their apogee somewhat later. Excavations at the continuously occupied site of Salango, which seems to have been an important port and, perhaps, affiliated with the nearby site of Agua Blanca, an immense urban center on the coastal hills slightly inland from Machalilla, show an important Manteño occupation there as well. Salango was in historic times part of a league of merchants involved in the spondylus trade. Elaborate terrace systems show that intensive agriculture was also important as was ceramics manufacture. Farther north in the Esmeraldas region local cultures, whose contact with the rest of Ecuador was more limited than previously, were found. Inland a riverine orientation is suggested by a series of small sites of the Herradura phase along the río Cayapas and its tributaries. Herradura villages are small and the ceramic component is greatly simplified. Apparently the movement inland which typified the following Tumbavido phase, when sites were defensively located away from rivers and a pattern of forest agriculture is seen, was in process.

The most interesting cultural manifestations of this time seem to be in the highlands where in northern Ecuador and southern Colombia (province of Carchi and department of Nariño, respectively) an extremely interesting culture appeared *c*. AD 800. This culture, previously referred to, from its ceramics, as "Negativo del Carchi" or "Nariño," can be divided into two major phases, with a third phase which seems to have been a short-lived regional variant. The ceramics of this culture are distinguished, as might be supposed, by their organic resist decoration. In the Capulí style proper this decoration is found over plain red slip. Shapes are highly distinctive: figurines of seated women with their legs in front and of males seated on benches, both with coca quids in their cheeks, pedestal cups and bowls, some with anthropomorphic or zoomorphic figures forming the base, and various jar and bottle forms, some of which bear applied decoration forming human figures in a manner reminiscent of contemporary cultures to the north (Figure 14.28). A highly unusual production was anatomically perfect strombus shell trumpets, formed entirely out of clay. These ceramics are found in shaft and chamber tombs, numbers of which have been excavated in the region of Pupiales, Nariño by María Victoria Uribe and her colleagues. The La Propicia site contained single burials, with the flexed bodies laid on mats and surrounded by vessels which contained remains of food stuffs. Textile remains have also been found in these tombs.

Capulí ceramics are more or less contemporary with those of Piartal (in earlier works called Tuncahuan). These are not, apparently, found in the same sites or tombs, although their territories are contiguous to overlapping in the Colombia-Ecuador border region. Piartal ceramics are painted with organic resist on a base of red and white slip and include some unique forms of which the most characteristic is a large amphora with an elongated, egg-shaped body. Both Capulí and Piartal appear to be succeeded by the Tuza or Cuasmal style. Tuza ceramics change from organic resist painting to red on cream slip painting and include a series of lively realistic figures of warriors, dancers, and various animals, especially stylized monkeys, generally painted on the interiors of annular base bowls which, in form, are identical to those of Piartal (Figure 14.29). The Tuza culture can, perhaps, be identified with that of the historic Panche, the people living in the region at the time of the Spanish *entradas*.

A series of tombs looted in the 1960s has given evidence of the high degrees of artistry in metal reached by these northern cultures. The booty includes a vast array of gold and tumbaga ornaments: ear pendants, nose ornaments, and pectorals or pieces meant to be sewn on to fabric. The pieces are cast or hammered, and both gilding and plating overlay are common, as are bimetallic pieces of gold and silver. The most characteristic form is a round plate, a costume element or hung through the ear on a metal ring (see Figure 17.13). They are decorated with repoussé feline faces and embossed dots. These ornaments are identical to those from the Chordeleg tombs and help to place the northern metalwork in time. However, another characteristic piece from this lot is an ornament with monkeys identical to those painted on Tuza-style bowls, suggesting that this style of metalwork was continuous throughout the last 800 or so years of prehistory.

North into the Cauca Valley, this time period saw the development of the "Calima" and "Quimbaya" cultures, now generally referred to as Yotoco and Middle Cauca. These closely related cultures occupied the hills and valleys of the western and central ranges of central Colombia and the northern part of the Cauca Valley. Both are characterized by ceramics decorated with organic resist on red and white slip on a highly characteristic series of forms of which the hemispherical Yotoco bowl is the type form (Figure 14.30). Yotoco bowls are found both in Yotoco proper and in the more northern Middle Cauca style. Other forms include hollow figurines of nude men and women, the men sometimes seated on benches, large amphora-like vessels, and a large variety of annular base bowls and plates (Figures 14.31 and 14.32). Excavations in the Valle de Calima and

14.28 Capulí figurine from southern Colombia, of a man with a coca quid in his cheek. The garment slung across his body is probably a folded up mantle.

14.29 Tuza bowl (southern Colombia and northern Ecuador) with a dance (?) scene of nine men in identical tabards. The tunic appears to have been unknown in Ecuador until the Inca introduced it; the local male garment was open sided and often heavily decorated.

14.30 Yotoco bowl. These red and white slipped bowls have a characteristic decoration of spiral, step fret, and lightning bolt patterns in black organic resist.

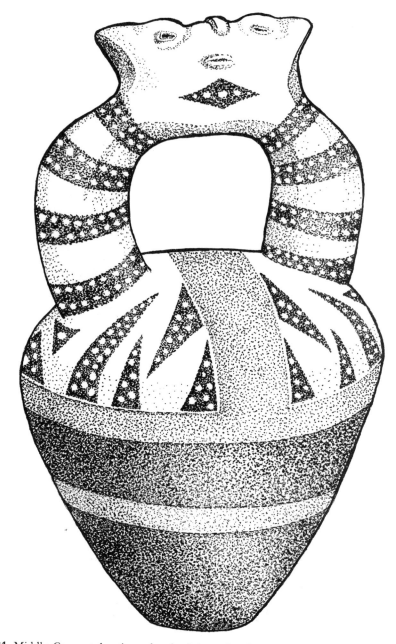

14.31 Middle Cauca-style stirrup bottle. Stirrup bottles are a relatively uncommon form in Colombia, but appear in funerary offerings of the Middle Cauca culture. The spout is always a head like those found on figurine vases and the thick stirrup and body bear geometric organic resist patterns on red and white slip. Like figurine vases, the opening is in the top of the head.

14.32 One of the characteristic slab figurines of central Colombia. These may be related to the Middle Cauca culture, but have a somewhat more northerly distribution.

survey in Quindio have shown that these peoples lived in large villages associated with drained field complexes. Burial was in shaft and chamber tombs either within the village or in cemeteries along ridge tops. The deepest tombs contain multiple burials often associated with metal artifacts. Because many of these tombs contain gold, looting has been intensive and not a single tomb containing metal has been excavated by an archaeologist. The metal associated with the Yotoco and Middle Cauca styles tends to be simple cast figurines and hammered sheets of metal formed into bracelets, diadems, etc. (Figure 14.33). The most complex pieces are cast spatulas for lime flasks. These show figures elaborately dressed, and with artifacts indicating that they are hunters, warriors, or dancers. These and some small hammered figures from the Calima area show figures identical to the masked dancers of San Agustín statuary. Dates from both Yotoco and Middle Cauca sites indicate that these cultures flourished in the ninth to tenth centuries AD. The variety of substyles and variations in tomb types suggest that then, as later, this region was politically organized into a series of closely related chiefdoms, all with their own slightly different ceramic style and burial habits, but all in close contact with each other through both trade and war.

The dense populations of central Colombia are reflected in events to the north and east. At this time the Sabana de Bogotá was inhabited by people ancestral to the historic Muisca, while in the lower Magdalena region immense drainage systems reflect the need to provide for a growing number of people. Here, just as on the Orinoco plains, ridged field systems, perhaps with fisheries between the raised fields, were constructed on a grand scale. Along the margins of these systems, elongated artificial platforms provided dry ground for the construction of houses. Semi-conical mounds were also constructed for funerary uses. These systems began to be constructed in the fourth century, but were beginning to be abandoned by the eighth. At the time of the conquest the lower San Jorge region, where these hydraulic systems have been best studied, was inhabited by a small population of village farmers and fishermen still living on artificial platforms and burying their dead in tumuluses.

By the tenth century AD the central Andes had produced its first conquest states, those of Tiahuanaco and Huari. Closely related in religion, and perhaps in ideas of trade and conquest, these two political entities controlled most of the Andean region. Tiahuanaco, however, was much longer lived than Huari, and its demise did not have such a dramatic effect within its sphere of influence. Away from the Andean regions growing populations resulted in the development of large-scale hydraulic works and the establishment of what seem to have been large political groups in much of the eastern lowlands. The northern Andes, however, began to show cultural patterns visible at the time of the conquest, specifically many small warring polities which occasionally were welded into temporary larger political groupings. Although there are no "imperial" art styles outside of the central Andean cultural sphere, the stratified societies to the north evidently produced considerable demand for elaborate artifacts reflecting mythology and the status of the user. Many of these pieces rank among the finest art works of the ancient Americas, just as the small warring chiefdoms/kingdoms of Italy produced some of the master works of their continent.

14.33 A hammered gold disk from central Colombia. These simple ornaments are very common in the tombs of the region. The figure is one that is also seen in petroglyphs.

CHAPTER 15

TRANSPORT AND TRADE

The exchange of commodities between regional and political groups was of major importance in ancient South America. In the highlands of the Andean chain the vertical nature of the landscape led to the existence of many different ecological zones, each with its own specific resources. In the somewhat less differentiated tropical lowlands exchange between groups, if we can judge from the ethnographic record, served an extremely important social and political role, integrating societies which would otherwise be either isolated or warring. This kind of trade as social/political interaction is seen in South America among groups which do not need to trade basic goods, but do so to have a wider range of contacts outside the village in case of famine or other disaster. Arrangements like these are common throughout South America (and are, or were, in much of the rest of the world) and underscore the importance of exchange to the societies on other than an unencumbered economic level. In the case of the tropical lowlands, where preservation is extremely poor, the existence of widespread trade networks is one explanation for the really rather astounding similarity of ceramic styles on the eastern Andean watershed and along the major rivers at various times in prehistory and the apparent rapidity with which such styles occasionally spread. We can assume that other, more important, items were being traded, including information (social, technical, religious), but have little real evidence owing to the perishability of such items and the lack of written records.

In western South America we have a much more complete archaeological and historical record. The central Andean peoples were alone in the Americas in possessing a draft animal, the llama (Figure 15.1). It has been hypothesized that the domestication of the llama (and the alpaca) was closely related to the development of agriculture, sedentary communities, and the desire for commodities not present in the local region. It seems that the development of herding (mainly confined to the high-altitude grasslands) was in the Americas, as in the Old World, a response to larger settled agricultural communities and their need for animal products – wool, hides, meat, and dried meat (charqui) – as well as other raw materials, which could not be acquired where the land was entirely devoted to agriculture and people had to stay at home and farm. Certainly by the late centuries BC llama caravans are evident in the well-documented trade between the various communities of northern Chile and between them and those of the altiplano. Llamas also appear in highland Ecuador at this time, along with complex metallurgy, maize agriculture, and a central Andean pattern of llama sacrifices and of feasting/beer consumption. The highland Ecuadorians were involved in long-distance trade and it is quite likely that they adopted llama caravans as being suitable to their economic orientation.

15.1 Llama with a burden in an elaborately decorated bag. The frequency of llamas carrying burdens in Moche art reflects the importance of the inter-regional movement of goods to the Moche economy.

The social setting of trade in the central Andes may have been somewhat different from the market-based, middleman trade typical of Eurasia and Mexico. Because this is the major arrangement for exchange in our own culture, and because market-based trade was also well entrenched in Mexico at the time of the Spanish invasions, archaeologists have been somewhat too prone to explain South American trade in terms of traders and markets. This explanation has been bolstered by early colonial accounts from coastal Peru in which numbers of individuals attempt to explain to the Spanish authorities that they are traders and used to traveling about with their merchandise to make a living buying and selling. What is seldom realized is that by the time these accounts were written native exchange systems, with their very different valuables and, apparently, quite different systems of movement of these valuables, had collapsed and been replaced by Spanish systems of exchange, including the use of money. The people identifying themselves as traders were trying to escape paying a tax in labor and also trying to avoid the Spanish attempts to prohibit any movement of peoples from one place to another, prohibitions made (at least in part) because of the serious labor shortages resulting from loss of life in epidemics and through maltreatment on the part of the Europeans. The utter lack of understanding by the Europeans of the structure of Andean economic life, with its exploitation of multiple environments by the same person or people, continues to this day, with equally appalling results. The colonial documents then do not necessarily reflect any, by this time long gone, native systems of exchange and must be used with extreme caution. In much of Peru we have no particular reason to think that there were professional traders *per se* or that market exchange was important. It was not among the Incas, and much of Inca practice was firmly based on earlier systems. Also, trade in basic necessities was not very important in much of the Andean realm. Although the ancient Mexicans (or at least the sixteenth-century ones) had an elaborate system of markets to move materials efficiently to and from groups living in different ecozones, the Andean peoples had another solution to verticality: many communities had lands in a series of different environmental zones, the so-called "archipelago" system. Thus a given community might have lands ascending the cordilleras from lower mountain valleys through high puna and down into the tropical montaña, working these lands seasonally as necessary. Other resources, such as obsidian and metal ores, may have been considered as part of the natural produce of a community, to be worked as the agricultural/herding schedule permitted and exchanged through barter for other rare materials needed and not present in a community's territory. In historic times long-distance trade using llama caravans was organized between male heads of households who, accompanied by a few of the younger males of the family, would go on journeys of some hundreds of kilometers, bartering along the way with specific people/kin groups with whom they had formal bonds of trading partner or kinship. Such llama caravans were (and are) capable of moving large quantities of merchandise for long distances without any formal marketing system being involved. It is, of course, quite possible that the Andean state governments tried to centralize and control such caravans. The distribution of obsidian in Peru and changes in this distribution through time may reflect prehistoric centralization and distribution of this vital, but highly localized, resource. Obsidian sources are located mainly in the high puna of southern Peru; some seven sources have been identified through neutron activation and X-ray fluorescence analysis, although only one, Quispisisa, near the headwaters of the Pisco River, has actually been located on the ground. This source was exploited (and the obsidian distributed about the south coast) from preceramic times onward. Most of the obsidian found at Chavín is from this source too, indicating some fairly widespread trading networks, although probably down-the-line type ones, in the Early Horizon. However, with the spread of the Huari state in the mid first millennium AD obsidian tools (mainly points, knives, and some scrapers plus the odd mirror or decorative item) became much wider spread in use, and throughout the area controlled or heavily under the influence of Huari Quispisisa obsidian is found. With the demise of Huari this source was apparently abandoned and those cultures which continued to use obsidian got it from other sources.

The pattern of appearance of Quispisisa obsidian in the Middle Horizon strongly suggests that it was being distributed through some centrally, or at least governmentally, controlled mechanism in much the same way that the Incas later controlled and spread tin bronze: managing the mining/smelting processes through the labor tax, establishing specialist groups who worked for the government, and controlling the distribution of tools and other items.

Llama caravans may also have been involved in the movement of metal and of spondylus between Ecuador and Peru. After the collapse of the Huari and the rise of a series of complex kingdoms in northern Peru demand for the colored shell increased dramatically as shells became increasingly important in central Andean religious practices. Although balsa rafts are usually considered to have been a main means of transport, there is a strong Peruvian presence in the southern highlands of Ecuador. Llamas had been present in this area since the late centuries BC and must have been used for transport in this mountainous region with no navigable rivers. Llamas would also have been useful in moving large quantities of materials inland and south from the raft landing sites.

It is not the case, however, that all trade was governmentally controlled in the Andean region. It is well known that there were some specialized traders as well as some market trade in late prehistoric times and it is quite possible that market trade dominated in areas beyond the reach of the conquest states with their centralized collection and redistribution of goods and labor as well as in times of political fragmentation. In the Quito area in late prehistory there was a special, semi-hereditary group of traders known as mindalaes who formed a corporate body responsible to the local lord and, later, to the Inca. The latter made them reside in the upper quarter of town, a prestigious neighborhood and one in which they could be closely supervised. Traders have often been used in fifth column activities. Mindalaes did not pay ordinary tribute in labor or local produce, but paid in imported materials: cotton mantles, probably from Manabí, gold from the north and from Colombia, capsicum peppers and coca from the lower, warmer, elevations and salt. They seem to have dealt in high-status raw materials and in luxuries such as salt, coca, and gold, exporting finished goods in return. Although some of their profit went to tribute, it seems that there was a market in Quito where such materials were exchanged with the local people. On the Esmeraldas coast a 1535 report mentions a large market called Ciscala which was patronized by people of different ethnic and political groups. Ciscala was apparently a real port of trade, a neutral zone in an area of many warring tribes. Another early document mentions an important market at Quijos in the montaña which also may have functioned as a port of trade. Professional traders seem to have been well established in late prehistoric Ecuador and it is likely that the famous traders of Tumbes, in northernmost Peru, were actually Ecuadorians. Tumbes in historic times was mainly a Cañari town and the Cañari's main territory was the southern highlands of Ecuador, not within modern Peru. The Tumbes traders were seafarers, however, and may likewise have been related to the traders of Isla Puná in the Gulf of Guayaquil. The existence of trading and manufacturing centers, especially those which controlled access between major resource zones, is known from much earlier in Ecuador and, however it was organized, long-distance trade in luxury goods was established from the later Formative Period onwards. Models of canoes show one means by which these materials were moved along the rivers and estuaries of coastal Ecuador (see Figure 9.20). Very likely rafts were also in use, as historically these were the most important vehicle in riverine and coastal trade.

The most important coastal Ecuadorian contribution to national and international trade was spondylus, the "thorny oyster" (Figure 15.2). Spondylus live at depths of

15.2 *Spondylus princips*, the thorny oyster.

20–40 m in warm waters, ranging from the Gulf of Guayaquil to the Gulf of California. The spondylus was highly valued for its brilliant color; the rim and exterior of the shell were bright orange red to vibrant purple, depending upon the species and age of the specimen. Spondylus shells were used to make ornaments and inlays all over nuclear America and the shell itself was an important constituent of religious insignia and offerings from preceramic times onwards in Peru, and from considerably earlier (Valdivia III is the earliest well-documented example) in Ecuador. From the Early Horizon to the time of the European conquest there was a steadily increasing desire for spondylus in Peru. This could only be satisfied through exchange with the coastal Ecuadorian peoples. It is surmised that spondylus was traded down the coast, perhaps on the famous Guayaquil balsa wood rafts. Overland routes, including ones through the Andes, are also known, as highland people as well as coastal ones, wanted spondylus. For example, some of the huacas of the people of Huarochirí in central Peru "ate" spondylus and no other offering was acceptable (Figure 15.3). Special spondylus fishing and trading groups were present in the sixteenth century and depictions of spondylus fishing are found in Late Intermediate period north coast art (Figure 15.4), suggesting that Peruvians may well have visited the spondylus fishing grounds themselves. Ecuadorians seem also to have visited the northern kingdoms of Peru. A Manteño stamp shows the peculiar north coast punishment of staking the criminal, who had first had his legs ripped from the hip sockets, out for the vultures (Figure 15.5).

15.3 Shells are still used as religious offerings. This shrine on the beach at Machalilla, on the central coast of Ecuador, marks where the bodies from a fishing accident were washed ashore. The shrine is decorated with strombus (another very widely traded shell, even to the present) and other small shells.

15.4 Spondylus fishing scene on a gold ear spool from Lambayeque, Peru. Two men holding stylized spondylus sit on a raft under a thatched(?) shade while below divers attached by ropes hunt the thorny oyster. Birds are above the raft and the border shows more spondylus.

It is not known how the spondylus trade was organized. Spondylus fishing sites such as Isla Puná and Salango became large and wealthy with the escalating market for the thorny oyster. There is some indication of professional traders in this region and in Tumbes in northern Peru, traders doubtless involved in moving the spondylus from its point of origin to Peruvian courts and religious establishments. Existing direct evidence for sea trade is late and comes from historic accounts such as that of Francisco de Xerez, Pizarro's secretary on his second voyage to Peru. They met with a large sailing raft carrying various trade goods along the coast. Other Spaniards similarly encountered such rafts, which remained in use until this century (Figure 18.1). We do not, unfortunately, know the antiquity of such rafts and must depend upon artistic representations (all from AD 1100 or later) and the evidence of non-perishable materials in places other than their point of origin to infer their existence.

Peru itself was poor in seaworthy craft, mainly because of a lack of appropriate construction materials. Peruvian coastal (and lake) craft consisted of reed floats and boats and, to the south, seal-skin floats. With these, fishermen went into deep water and managed to exploit the offshore guano islands for fertilizer, but such small craft were

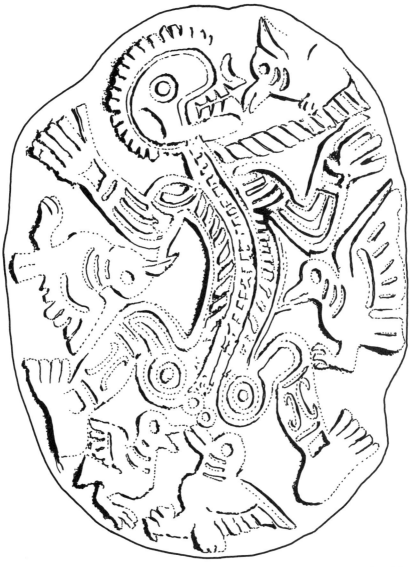

15.5 A Manteño stamp from Cerro de las Hojas, Manabí province, Ecuador. The scene shown is one of a common punishment among the northern Peruvian peoples: staking the malefactor out for the birds to devour. Such macabre scenes apparently impressed the Ecuadorians enough that a stamp was made to demonstrate to the people at home the strange habits of the southerners.

neither safe nor efficient (in terms of the amount of goods possible to move) for long voyages. Larger reed boats are represented in Moche art, but these do not appear to have been more than two to three person craft. Cane and gourd rafts are known from the north coast of Peru from Moche times onwards; but their use in coast-wise commerce is unknown. Elaborately decorated board-like implements which many have identified as steering boards or paddles for rafts or similar water craft have now been unequivocally

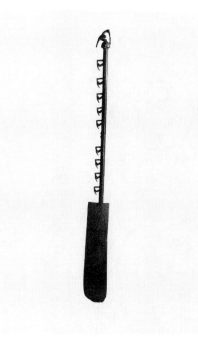

15.6 A wooden "paddle" from southern Peru. This elaborate example has minimal wear from scooping or thrusting on it and was probably used ceremonially.

identified as ceremonial farming implements (Figure 15.6). Yae Koda, through a combination of ethnographic and ethnohistoric data and use wear analysis, has been able to show that the patterns of wear on simpler tools mirror those of tools used for digging, cleaning ditches, etc. The relatively minor wear marks on the elaborately decorated examples, although they are of the type and in the same places as the greater use marks on simple wooden tools, probably reflect the longevity of a custom found among the Incas: that the nobility and other persons who did not normally farm themselves had to participate in the first and last work of the year in order to have claim to the fruits of the field. This is much the same as the ceremonial first spadeful of dirt turned by a politician on a construction project.

Outside of the central and north-central Andean area, exchange was also important, although again we know little of how it was organized. Salt, extracted by boiling down the briny water from the salt springs of Zipaquirá and Nemocón near Bogotá, was widely traded through the Magdalena Valley and the eastern and central cordilleras. The large-scale exploitation of these salt springs had begun by the early centuries before Christ and continues to the present. Some of this may have been distributed through markets, at least in later periods, since historic sources mention that markets were held every four days in the major Muisca (Chibcha) settlements. It may be worth noting that the vessels for boiling the saline water to get the salt are made in a separate, non-salt-boiling village and traded to the salt makers to this day. Other, smaller-scale, salt works have been found in the middle Cauca Valley near modern Caicedonia and may have supplied salt to that area. Spring salt seems to have been more highly valued than sea salt, although the latter was also available. Salt never seems to have been a particularly important item of exchange in the Amazonian tropics where many tribes historically did not use salt at all and professed to dislike it.

In northern Colombia, along the Gulf of Urubá and inland along the río San Jorge, lived the people known in the sixteenth century as the Sinú. Metal smiths of considerable renown, these people produced small cast gold and tumbaga ornaments in virtually all the styles of central Colombia. These ornaments were exported to many Colombian groups and to Central America where much of the gold work found in archaeological contexts can be demonstrated (on the basis of stylistic details) to have been manufactured by the Sinú. However, once again, the mechanics of distribution and exchange are not known and certainly much of the pre-twelfth century gold work in northern Central America and Mexico probably results from gift exchange and down-the-line trading.

Regarding other forms of acquiring imported items, we are equally in the dark. It is quite possible that the intrusive Huari presence in the Moquegua Valley is the result of the Huari trying to establish a colonial enclave to exploit that valley's mineral resources. Ports of trade are not known to have existed, although these would be extremely difficult to identify archaeologically (the Ciscala port of trade is only known from sixteenth-century documents). Luis Lumbreras has suggested that the smaller valleys which connect the highlands to the eastern lowlands were important in early civilizations and that the rise of civilizations such as Chavín from a position of *primus inter pares* to cultural domination was probably linked to control of the inter-areal trade networks. Certainly both Chavín and the later Huari, as well as Tiahuanaco, had ample grazing lands for the necessary beasts of burden as well as key locations for channeling the movement of materials from one environmental zone to the next. There is also evidence now for industrial production of some items. Large-scale ceramics and metal manufactories have been identified for numbers of Andean cultures, as have metal-smelting sites and mother of pearl and rock crystal bead manufacturing sites. However, the organization of trade in these items is even less understood than that of the sea trade.

What is very evident, when one looks at ancient South America, is that methods of exchange were very complex and did not necessarily depend upon market trade. This, in western South America, may not have been all that common and other forms of movement of goods, such as kin organized barter and state organized exploitation, manufacture, and distribution, were definitely very important. None of these trading systems seems to have involved serious movement of foodstuffs, despite the existence of pack animals. A llama can carry about 50 kilos and will eat just about anything; also, it can be eaten. Alpacas can be used as draft animals, although they can manage only a much smaller load (and moan constantly about it). Even the Inca seem to have stored most food collected as tribute locally, reserving movement to lower-bulk, high-status luxury and manufactured goods. The highly developed road systems of the Andes were apparently less important for trade than for the movement of information and people (Figure 15.7). Access to Inca roads was limited to people on official business and to

15.7 Ancient road in Cañar province, Ecuador. This road is still in use by local peoples as many of the rural hamlets have been in the same place since well before the Incas.

government regulated movement of materials. All of the Andean civilizations had road systems (the earliest known roads are from the Early Horizon) and many of the simpler cultures also had road/path networks connecting important centers and regions. Work on tracing these has just begun and there is no particular reason to think that they were all organized or used in the same manner. Some were doubtless important for trade, others, such as the roads of Chincha in southern Peru, can be demonstrated to have been ceremonial, just as many of the Nazca desert lines were pathways to huacas or temples (some of the desert lines go straight to buildings in Cahuachi). Intensified study of the pattern of distribution of non-local goods in ancient South American sites is beginning to sharpen our view of exchange between cultures, but it is unfortunate that "trade," much like "diffusion" and "migration," is all too often used as a "black box" to cover our ignorance of the mechanisms of exchange of goods and information.

KINGDOMS, CHIEFDOMS, AND EMPIRES:
AD 900–1438

The 500 or so years between the collapse of Huari and the beginning of the Inca expansion saw a series of new developments throughout the Andean area and in South America in general. Populations continued to grow and this affected settlement patterns, economies, and political adjustments. Although we have many, many more sites from these later periods, in some ways knowledge of them is proportionally less (Figure 16.1). Archaeological interest has tended to be with the earlier periods, as western thought has continued to have a preoccupation with origins. Moreover, most of the western South American peoples had metal by this time, including precious metals, and so their sites have suffered the depredations of looters more heavily. Many of these sites were still in use at the time of contact and so the earliest Europeans started the looting which has been enthusiastically continued by their successors to the present (Figure 16.2). However, a series of major archaeological projects has begun to add to our understanding of this period and has led to an appreciation of the cultures which have been all too often snubbed as being neither Inca nor early.

The north coast of Peru was less affected by the demise of Huari than the central and southern reaches of the country and a series of important local states continued to flourish. The only one of these which has been seriously investigated to date is that of Bataan Grande in Lambayeque where a large number of elaborate burials (most unfortunately looted) indicate the importance of this site, not simply as a metallurgical center, but also as some sort of elite necropolis (Figure 16.3). These Sicán burials are the continuation of the royal Moche burials of Sipán, La Mina, and other sites, and show the continuity of thought and of wealth in the northern valleys of Peru. Burials were made in deep shaft tombs and were associated with a wealth of valuables, including not only the gold and silver objects which have made this area a target for huaqueros, but spondylus, wooden and textile offerings, and ceramics as well as human sacrifices. In 1992 an only partly looted important burial was excavated by the Sicán Archaeological Project under Izumi Shimada. The tomb, in Huaca Oro, was over 12 m in depth and has some six levels of artifacts and human burials reaching to more than 10 m below the modern surface. Human remains, bundles of cast arsenic bronze metal, gold, tumbaga and silver jewelry, the remains of a litter, piles of spondylus and conus shells, beads of various stones, and other artifacts were layered over the seated burial of a middle-aged (40–50) man whose body was covered with cinnabar and wrapped in a cloth with precious metal foil squares sewn on it and with the remains of elaborate bead jewelry. He wore a golden mask similar to the face of the "tin woodmen" vessels, wore piled up collars of thousands of semi-precious stone beads, and had two tumbaga gloves at his

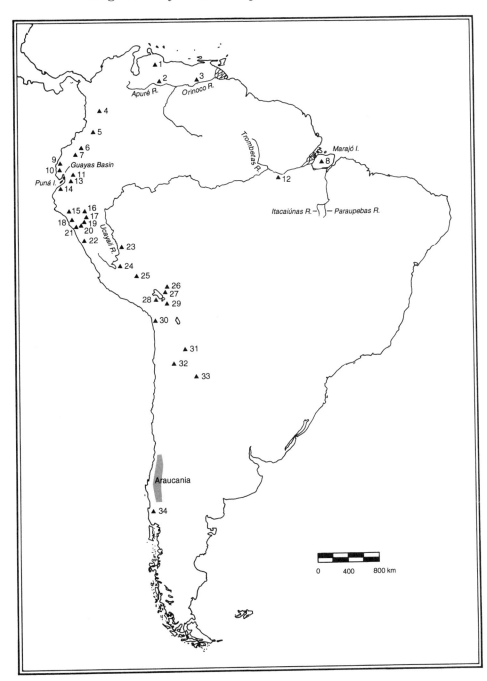

16.1 Locations of principal sites, cultures, and cultural traditions mentioned in Chapter 16. 1. La Mata, 2. Cano Ventosidad, Valencia, 3. Parmana, Corazal, 4. Cali, 5. Popayán, 6. Carchi, 7. Otavalo, Guayallabamba, Cochasquí, 8. Aterro dos Bichos (mid-Marajó), 9. Manta, 10. Salango, 11. Ingapirca, 12. Santarém, 13. Cuenca, 14. Tumbes, 15. Bataan Grande, 16. Chachapoyas, Kuelap, 17. Gran Pajatén, Los Pinchudos, 18. Jequetepeque Valley, 19. Cajamarca, 20. Galindo, 21. Chan Chan, Moche, 22. Manchan, 23. Cumancaya, 24. Sivia, 25. Cuzco, 26. Iskanwaya, 27. Mollo, 28. Chuquito, 29. Tiahuanaco, 30. Arica, 31. Quebrada de Humahuaca, 32. San Pedro de Atacama, 33. Salta, 34. Temuco.

16.2 Cerro Zapamé, a thoroughly looted site in the southwest corner of the Bataan Grande Archaeological Complex, Lambayeque Valley, Peru.

16.3 A looter's pit in Huaca Rodillona in the Sicán Precinct. The deep central shaft with its radial small shafts or minaduras enables the looters to look efficiently for burials and their goods. It is estimated that there are over 100,000 such looter's pits within the Bataan Grande Archaeological Complex.

16.4 Aerial view of Huaca Chotuna, presumably the Chot where Ñamlap and his wife set up their first court. This small site shows many of the characteristics of ceremonial architecture of this late period: a high huaca with a ramp leading up to the room complexes on top and rectangular, walled, architectural groups attached, presumably for storage, retainers, administration, etc.

sides. Female sacrifices and a wealth of other items, currently in conservation and repair, accompanied this Sicán lord to the other world. Like the earlier Moche lords, apparently those of Sicán did take the wealth gained during their lives to the grave with them. This tomb, more than anything excavated before, shows the importance of metal and metalworking in the Sicán culture. Large amounts of sheet metal, including scraps and pieces to be reworked, were buried in the tomb, along with hundreds of axe-monies, at least two dozen masks and head ornaments, and a wealth of other objects in metal.

The metallurgical activities in Lambayeque were not entirely dedicated to furnishing the graves of its rulers, but led to a wider importance of this realm. It now appears that the famous "axe money" was manufactured here. Not only did it find its way into local burials, it seems to have been traded north into the Gulf of Guayaquil and from there into the rest of southern Ecuador. It may be significant that it is at this time that spondylus fishing scenes begin to appear on Lambayeque gold work (and on the clay reliefs at Chan Chan) and that origin myths from the Lambayeque kingdom speak of the first king, Ñamlap, as having arrived on a raft (Figure 16.4).

The Middle Horizon state of Lambayeque was centered on Pampa Grande, an important urban and metallurgical center. In the Late Intermediate Period the center of the Middle Sicán culture moved to the "Sicán Precinct," a T-shaped area with some dozen monumental adobe pyramids (Figure 16.5). A multiyear project headed by Izumi

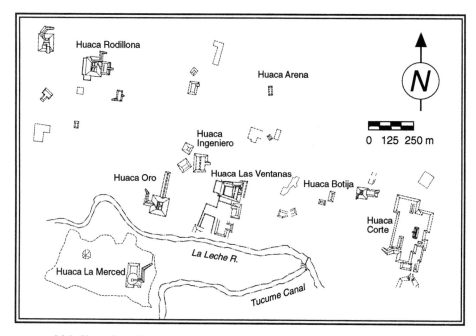

16.5 Plan of the Sicán Precinct, a huge sector of religious buildings, manufacturing workshops, administrative buildings, and living quarters.

Shimada has shown that the Sicán Precinct was inhabited for many centuries previous to its becoming what he thinks may be a sort of Peruvian "Vatican," a polity which promoted its ideology through pilgrimages and a rigid, though sumptuous, art style, wielding considerable political and economic power as a patron of the arts and as a provider of luxury goods. The Sicán Precinct may have been a ceremonial center with only a small resident population, although metallurgical manufacture may have been carried out in adjacent structures. The pyramids seem to have had structures on top whose roofs were supported by columns, direct descendants (apparently) of a structure with gigantic pink columns of the earlier Huaca Lucia and the somewhat later Huaca Soledad, which had been deliberately buried in clean sand in some sort of ritual entombment. Ceremonial burial of entire structures has been reported from earlier sites in other parts of Peru, notably the Chavín-related site of Cardal in the Lurín Valley and from Cahuachi in Nazca. This ceremonial disposal of entire buildings or religious precincts was apparently a common part of the religious practices of the central Andes, although we do not know what sorts of beliefs were involved. These ritual entombments often include offerings placed in the clean fill and sometimes human sacrifices as well. The pyramids of the Sicán Precinct were formed of adobe chambers filled with gravel and sand, and the columns were set in adobe boxes. At the Huaca Rodillona these boxes had dedicatory human burials in them. The burials were seated or semi-reclining and wrapped in reed mats together with spondylus, bundles of cotton fiber, and copper foil wrapped in cotton cloth. Other dedicatory offerings consisted of spondylus and copper foil bundles without the accompanying humans.

16.6 Sicán gold burial mask. Remnants of the textile which once covered the mask are visible on the sides of the face. The long spikes in the eyeballs probably once held stone beads.

The culture of Lambayeque was characterized by a high degree of cultural syncretism. As part of the Moche cultural area (and perhaps once incorporated into a Moche state), ceramics and other materials show a strong Moche derivation in style and in iconography. This is combined with Huari influences and with local ideas and icons, resulting in a very distinctive art style depicting, especially, a winged-eye person with a semi-lunar headdress. Other characteristic artifacts include gold alloy masks showing a similar winged-eye face, apparently used to cover the faces of important cadavers, and the highly distinctive "tin woodman" bottles which, it has been suggested, represent the culture hero and founding father, Ñamlap (Figures 16.6 and 16.7). The Sicán culture seems to have been much involved in exchange with different environmental zones, ranging from the tropical forests of the Zaña Valley and the eastern Andes to the highland valleys of the Cajamarca culture and north to the Gulf of Guayaquil. In addition to ritual paraphernalia and luxury goods the Sicán people probably provided salt, fish, marine shells (it is possible that they were the Peruvian conduit for the highly desired spondylus), cotton, and metal objects. The lavish use of these latter, especially the double-T artifacts called "axe-money" or naipes (playing cards), in burials and offerings must have proved a considerable source of wealth to the Sicán manufacturers.

16.7 A "tin woodman" bottle, Sicán culture. The pointed, slanted eyes, elaborate fringed earrings, and small subsidiary figures, here humans, but in other examples foxes, frogs, or birds, are typical of this highly distinctive vessel form.

16.8 A corroded stack of naipes from the immense Huaca Menor (looted) tomb in the Sicán Precinct. This tomb contained at least 500 stacks of naipes and dates to *c.* AD 900–1050.

Axe-monies are found into Ecuador where they are widely found in late burials both on the coast and in the highlands. A Cañari tomb looted by a group of Spaniards in 1563 contained, among other metal objects, between 600 and 1000 of these non-functional metal axes. Excavated examples of axe-monies in Ecuador show that they were packed into lots in multiples of five, most commonly twenty (Figure 16.8). It is quite possible that they were also used as tokens of exchange, in much the way that chaquira, beads of gold, bone, or spondylus, were used as quasi-money in the northern highlands and coast at this same time. .

In the Moche Valley to the south of Lambayeque the end of Huari influence may have provided the impetus for a similar spectacular development. Here arose the kingdom of Chimor, with its capital at the immense site of Chan Chan, located on the northern edge of the Moche Valley and directly on the sea coast (Figure 16.9). Chan Chan succeeded inland Galindo as the capital of a valley-wide state and then became the chief site of a major conquest state which eventually encompassed the coast from Casma in the south to as far north as modern Tumbes (Figure 16.1). John Rowe has suggested that the abrupt and wholesale movement of people first from Moche inland to Galindo and then from Galindo to Chan Chan is indicative of practices better known among the Incas, those of moving entire villages or regional populations and sending them to populate areas opened up by similar removal of populations or to occupy newly conquered or

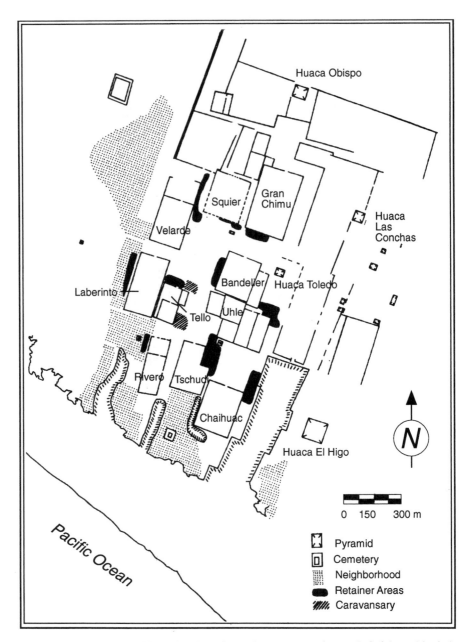

16.9 Plan of Chan Chan showing the major compounds or ciudadelas with their surrounding quarters for retainers, the neighborhoods where the lower-ranking crafts producers worked and lived, and the caravansaries, where goods were brought into the city.

16.10 Irrigated fields at El Milagro de San José in the Moche Valley of northern Peru. These fields were built especially to feed Chimu workmen and were in use for a very short time. The utter dryness (and the lack of people, animals, etc.) have preserved these fields in working order.

unpopulated zones. In any event, these mass population movements during the Middle Horizon and early Late Intermediate Period are mute testimony to the power of the central government of the time as well as to changing concerns both economic and defensive.

The founder of the kingdom of Chimor was a man named Taycanamo, who, like Ñamlap, was supposed to have arrived on a raft and to have brought with him various arts and ceremonies. Whether the northern origin of these lords is historic fact or not, it is evident from the location of Chan Chan that the northern polities and the sea were important in its economy and policies. The only defensive structure at Chan Chan is a huge wall along the northern part of the site; this is probably also significant. Chan Chan is adjacent to a wide flat plain; today this is largely desert, but in the past elaborate irrigation systems were devised to create a productive hinterland at Chan Chan's doorstep, thus increasing the amount of land which could be utilized for food while still keeping a considerable work force at home in the city where their free time could be utilized for other projects (Figure 16.10). The early history of Chan Chan is not too well known; Taycanamo was succeeded by his son who appears to have consolidated the lower valley. His grandson, Ñancen-pinço appears to have got the state really going by conquering the upper valley and some of the neighboring valleys, beginning *c.* AD 1370. We have no names for the next seven rulers, although the last of them was probably responsible for conquering Lambayeque or for consolidating Chimu power throughout that large valley system. The next king, Minchaçaman, was the last

16.11 A view across a major room sector with decorated patio walls inside the Ciudadela Tschudi at Chan Chan.

independent ruler of the kingdom of Chimor and conquered the north coast from Tumbes to Caraballo, apparently in response to danger perceived from another expanding state, that of the Incas.

There are many problems in associating the meager historical sources for Chimor with the archaeological record. A major project at the capital city of Chan Chan, headed by Michael Moseley and Carol Mackey, has done something towards our knowledge of the nature of that city, but has posed almost as many problems as it has solved. Chan Chan was a most peculiar city in western terms, although it has certain continuities with other Andean cities, most particularly with that of Huari (the Chan Chan compounds, however, are single storied and much of them was apparently not roofed, rain not being a problem on the coast except during the rare Niño). The city as preserved consists of some ten extremely large walled areas (the walls survive in some instances to 10 m or more in height) called compounds or ciudadelas. The correspondence of the number of compounds to the number of known kings has led some investigators to suggest that each was a royal palace and that, as the later Inca did, each succeeding king built his own palace in which he lived and was later buried, although there seems no way to prove this allegation and a number of scholars have rejected it. The compounds are extremely imposing and the later ones, in particular, contain storage facilities as well as large and small courtyards suitable for levées and, in some instances, huge burial platforms (Figure 16.11). There is little evidence of living refuse in the larger compounds, although none has been completely excavated. There is no adequate relative chronology for Chimu ceramics nor building techniques and the compounds can only tentatively be

16.12 An audiencia or U-shaped structure at Chan Chan. Although it is unlikely that all audiencias had the same exact function, many of them seem to have been small roofed areas where the person in charge sat for whatever purpose (some audiencias may have been the scenes of rituals or homage to the living or dead, others may simply have been where the accountant sat).

put into a chronological order. What is evident, however, is that the later compounds had more construction within them, especially more storage and administrative structures. This may be related to the enlargement of the kingdom of Chimor and a need for increasing bureaucracy. Aside from the large compounds there are smaller ones; these sometimes mask the entrance to the larger compounds, although others are completely separate. Both compounds (and some other buildings) feature U-shaped structures called audiencias. These are located in courtyards, as if these were where whoever was overseeing or heading an activity was located or guarding access to inner areas or storage areas. Audiencia-like structures are featured in modeled ceramics from a series of north coast cultures, beginning with Salinar, and appear to have been the equivalent of a throne or an executive's pavilion (Figure 16.12). Thus the number of audiencias in a building or area should give some clue to the amount of business being carried out there.

There are some other structures in Chan Chan, some of them platforms of apparent ceremonial or religious use such as the Huaca el Dragón (Figure 16.13); again there are some problems in relating these other structures chronologically to the compounds. We know very little of the uses of these; such platforms are religious structures in earlier cultures, but most evidences of ritual in Chan Chan are within compounds or other walled areas and the platforms outside the compounds are themselves walled.

Burial structures, chambered structures which had the external appearance of a

16.13 Clay reliefs on the Huaca el Dragón in Trujillo, Peru, reflect the increased importance of the sea in later north coast life. These reliefs were made by applying a thick layer of clay over the adobe wall. Then the designs were traced and the background cut out. The double-headed dragon-wave motif is also common on textiles.

16.14 The looted and weathered burial platform in the Ciudadela Tschudi, Chan Chan. This mausoleum had several stories of small cells and was finished to look like a solid platform with a ramp ascending it. It is thought that these platforms contained important burials, although none has been found unlooted enough to test this hypothesis.

platform, were associated with some compounds and there are isolated ones as well (Figure 16.14). The only one of these which has been investigated other than by looters is the Las Avispas platform, an unusual platform in that it is within its own encircling wall and has associated rooms, rather than being part of a larger compound. Las Avispas has been provisionally associated with the nearby Laberinto ciudadela which has no burial platform within its walls. Las Avispas had been looted, but there remained some of the offerings, among them the bodies of at least ninety-three young women, stacked like cord wood in the small cell-like rooms of the platform. Fragments of piles of folded cloths (the bodies were apparently unclothed), spondylus, metal ornaments, pottery, and gourd bowls containing food remains were also recovered from areas disturbed by the looters, along with the remains of hundreds of camelids, apparently also part of the offerings to whoever was the focus of the Huaca Las Avispas tomb. Aside from the burial platforms, Chan Chan has huge areas of (looted) cemetery surrounding it, where the humbler dead found their penultimate resting place.

The monumental and smaller, but still impressive compounds, structures presumably used by the ruling classes of Chan Chan, were surrounded by areas of what the excavators have called SIAR (small, irregular, agglutinated rooms). These seem to have been the dwelling and working places of the working classes. Different neighborhoods dedicated to different activities, including metal-working, wood-working, weaving,

16.15 Modeled Chimu stirrup bottle. Chimu pottery shows a great deal of thematic continuity with the previous cultures of the north coast. This man carrying a deer on his back first appears in Chavín-influenced coastal ceramics of some 1500 years earlier (see Figure 9.7).

and service activities (servants of the dwellers of the compounds, cemetery functionaries) have been identified along with purely residential structures with kitchens and sleeping quarters. Some of the SIAR groups have their own walk-in wells, while others, especially those associated with the major compounds (which are also constructed on platforms) are dependent upon separate wells. Along the shore side of Chan Chan are a series of pukios or mahamaes, garden plots excavated to the level of the water table to provide continually damp areas for agriculture.

Craft specialization was highly developed among the Chimu. Most of our evidence comes from ceramics, which were mold made in industrial quantities, especially the simpler vessels intended for domestic uses. Chimu pottery is largely smoked black ware, with smaller amounts of red ware and some multicolor painting, especially in the early ceramics (which are influenced by the classic Lambayeque and the Cajamarca styles to the extent of having small cursive designs painted over the surfaces) and again after the Inca conquest, and is clearly derivative from and archaizing from the earlier Moche and coastal Chavín (Cupisnique) traditions. Vessels are simpler in that they are most commonly made in two-part molds, but many of the subjects are the same as those seen in earlier cultures. Additions to the iconographic repertory include a derivative of the Staff God/Principal Deity of Huari, deities of maize, and the use of spondylus shells as second chambers on the newly popular double-chambered, often whistling, vessels (Figures 16.15, 16.16, and 16.17). There are more continuities than changes in the iconography of vessels and this, coupled with the historical information we have on the Chimu, has made it possible to infer something of both later and earlier religion. For example, a figure held by two other figures, often birds, probably refers to the constellation Orion, conceived of as a thief between two policing emissaries of the Moon, the principal deity, ready to be thrown to the vultures: the four stars below Orion's belt. The punishment for thievery in the kingdom of Chimor was being staked out for the birds, scenes which are shown in Moche ceramic art as well (see Figure 15.5). Sea birds and mammals are common, as are fish and depictions of people in reed boats, reflecting the continuing importance of the sea economically as well as in mythology. Historical materials indicate that the sea was a major deity and sacrifices of ocher, corn flour, and other objects were made to it along with prayers for abundance. Interestingly, no fish seem to have been sacred to the Chimu. Specific minor supernaturals, such as the peanut man/flute player and the Moon Animal, also continue in the Chimu ceramic tradition. Although much Chimu pottery is rather crude and definitely mass-produced, it was highly valued by people of the surrounding cultures, who either imitated it themselves or traded for it. Chimu ceramics are common along the coast of Peru and into the Ecuadorian highlands. The Inca imported Chimu potters to Cuzco and a Chimu vessel, probably colonial but perhaps Chimu-Inca in date, has been found as far afield as Panama. Moreover, the Chimu pottery style survived into the colonial period, adding some new motifs to its modeled depictions (Figure 16.18). In a sense it survived into the present century, although only in its utilitarian aspects, while the modeled style has revived again to provide souvenirs for tourists and replicas for art galleries.

The administration of the kingdom of Chimor is currently being investigated, largely through a project centered in Casma, the southern frontier of the north coast. Apparently there were regional administrative centers in some of the annexed territories. These are not as fancy as the later Inca tambos, nor are they particularly Chimu in form. The best known is at Manchan in the Casma Valley, where investigations by Carol Mackey (formerly co-director of the Chan Chan Project) and A. Ulana Klymyshen have revealed three rather Chimu-looking compounds associated with storage facilities. At Farfan in Jequetepeque there are two compounds, but Manchan has no audiencias and the one at Farfan is in an unusual place. Since audiencias are intimately associated with the bureaucracy and with administrative functions, their lack in these two centers is puzzling. Other claimed administrative centers, such as El

16.16 Huari influence on the cultures of northern Peru was extensive, even though there was no political takeover. This Chimu jar shows the frontal deity holding felines in the place of staves and surrounded by birds, anthropomorphized birds, and other, smaller, felines or dogs. This theme is an amalgamation of Huari symbols mixed with local ones.

16.17 Although the theme of a man holding a sea bird existed in the earlier Moche culture, the double-chamber bottle with the rear chamber in the form of a spondylus shell reflects new ideas and concerns in the later Chimu culture.

Milagro de San José, up-valley from Chan Chan, appear to have been built to administer specific projects, in the case of El Milagro a large canal, and were then abandoned.

One fortress associated with the Chimu expansion is known, Cerro Paclo in Jequetepeque, overlooking Farfan. This fort was probably built to protect Farfan and consists of a long oval walled area with short spur walls coming off to control access to the hillside. Piles of sling stones were found in various parts of the fort. This fort was occupied for only a short time and it seems that after consolidation of an area the Chimu administrators felt no need of defensive structures.

The Incas conquered the kingdom of Chimor between 1462 and 1470. Chimor was the largest state they had encountered and they seem to have adopted many of the Chimu administrative practices to their own needs. The Incas looted Chan Chan, taking the gold and silver back to Cuzco to adorn their own temples. Their policy for breaking up Chimor involved taking the ex-king off to Cuzco to live in luxurious exile while a son ruled as a puppet in his place. The succeeding grandson had been raised in Cuzco and

16.18 The Chimu ceramic tradition remained vigorous after the European invasions. This European mermaid with her guitar fits right into the sea-oriented iconography of traditional belief systems.

was acculturated to the Inca way of life; meanwhile the former territory was divided up and administered by descendants of the former dynasties directly under Inca supervision. It is tempting to think that the Incas took this means of defusing a new and giant territory from the policies of those that they conquered. In any event, with no ruling elite resident in Chan Chan (or at least a somewhat decimated one), the craftsmen moved or were moved on to where there was employment. Chan Chan itself dwindled. It was still occupied at the time of the Spanish conquest, but was pretty much of a ghost town. The importance of the site of Chan Chan in controlling the north coast is shown by the fact that when the Spanish decided to build a town, they built it right by Chan Chan. Today, with increasing population, Trujillo is gradually spilling over into the old capital and will probably finally obliterate it. Peruvian cultures on the south and central coast had been devastated by the collapse of Huari and only slowly recovered. The most notable central coast culture is that of Chancay, just to the north of Lima. The Chancay culture is best known for its matte black and white ceramics, many of which are modeled, and for its elaborate tapestries (Figure 16.19). These latter are said to have inspired the modern Dutch artist M. C. Escher (Figure 16.20). On the south coast local kingdoms had made a slower recovery, but by about 1400 had recouped and were organized into a number of kingdoms of the Ica culture.

In the southern highlands the demise of Tiahuanaco may not have been as abrupt as that of Huari, but by Tiahuanaco V (perhaps as late as AD 900–1000) its influence was over and a plethora of local styles, derivative of the later Tiahuanaco ones, are seen in the

16.19 Chancay "doll," Ancón. Hollow, mold-made figurines of nude humans, often with elaborate body paint, were common funerary offerings. The hands-up pose is typical of these figures from the central coast of Peru.

16.20 Tapestry fragment with stylized birds in lines of alternating direction and colors from southern Peru. The late prehispanic period in Peru (and perhaps in southern Ecuador) saw the development of a true international style, especially in textiles.

ceramics of the altiplano and wherever Tiahuanaco had had control or substantial contact. This demise was probably influenced by a very long drought, which crippled the intensive agricultural systems which had supported the city of Tiahuanaco. The most widespread of the local ceramic styles is called Mollo. Owing to problems of lack of detailed presentation of archaeological materials it is difficult to separate out the various subdivisions and local variants of Mollo, but it is probably safe to say that local versions of this ceramic style and the culture it accompanied were found over much of the altiplano and down into the warmer valleys of the north east and into northwestern Argentina. The ceramic inventory consists of both plain and decorated vessels; the decorated ones having designs of dull black and thin, yellowish-white paint on the natural red-clay surface of the vessel. These designs consist of cross-hatches, diamonds, rectangles, etc., arranged in somewhat linear patterns. Characteristic of Mollo pottery are shapes such as bowls of various forms, shoe pots, cylindrical vases, and a peculiar type of vessel which consists of attaching a small vessel to the handle of a larger one, a sort of Andean "chip and dip" vessel. The Mollo culture was centered in fairly arid regions; both the warmer scrub-filled lower valleys and the cold upper valleys were occupied and agriculture involved considerable terracing and irrigation. One of the most spectacular sites related to this culture is Iskanwaya, located to the northeast of Lake Titicaca in the thorn forest of the mid-Llika River valley. Iskanwaya is quite similar to some of the Marañon sites: it is located on a precipitous slope with very steep paths down to the river (Figure 16.21). It was a planned town whose center covers some $6\frac{1}{2}$ ha and with suburbs across the quebrada and trailing to the west to Naranjani (where the vehicle road stops) adding another $6\frac{1}{2}$ ha to the total. The structures of Iskanwaya are built of the local shale, split into natural slabs and cut for lintels, door jambs, etc. Rectangular houses with windows and interior niches are grouped around patios (Figure 16.22). Some show signs of having been plastered and painted with red ocher. A number of houses have circular pit or cist tombs located in the floor. These contained the skeletons of infants associated with various offerings and may have been religious caches rather than burials *per se*. The entire site has east–west streets crossing it and was designed to have running water available to the agglutinated house groups. Houses at Iskanwaya are on platforms and terraces, a characteristic of other sites of the Mollo culture such as Piniqo. Mollo burials were of single adults placed in chullpas. Burials at Khargi, where the Lokomayu and Llika Rivers join, contain Iskanwaya plain and painted pottery associated with very typical Mollo pottery as grave offerings.

Similar cultures are found through the arid valleys of southern Bolivia and northwestern Argentina and into Chile. All feature ceramics very loosely derived from late Tiahuanaco prototypes. Agriculture, maize in the warmer regions, potatoes and herding in the colder ones, was well established and there is ample evidence of fairly elaborate terrace and irrigation systems associated with such cultures as those of La Isla and El Alfarcito, and the succeeding Hornillos and Tilcara, as well as the Bolivian/Chilean Allita Amaya, Collao, Chiribaya, and Arica. In the Quebrada de Humahuaca a new series of cultures arose throughout its 150 km length. As with earlier cultures in this region, those of the upper Quebrada specialized in cold weather agriculture and exploiting the nearby puna. The cultures of the Middle and Later Periods here are

16.21 The precipitous landscape around Iskanwaya, Bolivia, has led to this site being much less known than it deserves.

16.22 A group of houses around a patio at Iskanwaya. The site is regularly laid out and must have been a planned community.

characterized by small villages of rectangular stone houses, gradually growing by Tilcara times into small urban or semi-urban sites. A fair number of these, such as Pucara de la Cueva, are fortified and all the later towns are in defensive sites; many are walled. La Isla and El Alfarcito cemeteries are surrounded by low walls. Adults are buried in graves, babies in urns, and there is ample indication of the taking of trophy heads. Metallurgy was fully developed in this area and bodies wear pectorals, bracelets, masks, and bells, and have tumis in gold, silver, and copper alloys. Bone tools are also common and obsidian projectile points were a major weapon. Later sites have the bodies of adults placed face down in burials inside houses or in stone-lined tombs. There is evidence of trade with the Bolivian cultures in the form of imported ceramics, especially with the Huruquilla culture, and a small amount of Pacific shell has been found in tombs. Ceramics are largely black on red, with geometric decoration. The later cultures show considerable interchange, perhaps even population intrusion from Salta. Wooden objects become even more common, and one sees the full development of snuff using, with elaborate tablets and snuffing tubes as well as wooden boxes, digging sticks, and bows and arrows. Cast metal is commoner in the later cultures. Among these later cultures there is considerable cultural uniformity, which is, indeed, seen into Bolivia and northern Chile. In Bolivia the Allita Amaya style is known only from burials and seems to be restricted to the territory which, slightly later, is known to have been inhabited by the historic Lupaca kingdom. The type site itself is only 3 km from Chuquito, the Lupaca capital. The tombs this style has been found in are collective ones with some nineteen to twenty people in each (Figure 16.23). Collao pottery, a two-color (black on red) style is found in many habitation sites within the Collao area and is not associated either with burials or with Allita Amaya pottery. All of the sites known to have Collao pottery appear to have been fortified, as indeed are perhaps the majority of southern Andean sites of this period. Although slightly later we have (historic) evidence of fairly large kingdoms in this region, as yet there is little evidence bearing upon the late prehistoric cultures' political organization.

To the far south, in the Araucania of Chile, an area with a long tradition of foraging cultures, horticulture finally appeared sometime after AD 500. Excavations in the Padre Las Casas site near Temuco show an unusual pattern of burial in urns placed within funerary canoes. Grave goods clearly show status differences with richer burials having not only ceramic offerings, but stone beads and copper rings as well. There are a number of similar sites throughout the Araucania, showing this to have been a widespread, although late, florescence.

The northern Andes saw a similar florescence, although the earlier cultures had also been quite elaborate. In the highlands of Ecuador the Cañari kingdoms of the south were rich, powerful, and controlled enough desired resources to make them an immediate target for the Inca expansion. Few Cañari sites have been investigated aside from the early occupations of such sites as Tomebamba (within modern Cuenca) and Ingapirca (Hatun Cañar) in Cañar proper. Both have yielded elaborate burials containing pottery of the latest Tacalshalpa/Cashaloma tradition and copper ornaments such as tumi knives, heavy dress or headdress pins, and hammered headbands, plumes, and so on. One of the Ingapirca burials was of a woman, buried with her attendants, both male and female. The grave was marked with a stone pavement and a stele (Figure 16.24). Much of the Cañari metal tradition is an outgrowth of earlier Huari-influenced metallurgy seen in the proto-Cañari tombs of Chordeleg and Sigsig, where both hammered and cast objects were present. Cañari pottery is likewise an outgrowth of earlier local traditions, although the later pieces shown Inca influence in forms and placement of decoration (Figure 16.25).

North of the Cañari were a series of local kingdoms of which those of the so-called Cara Phase of Imbabura and Pinchincha provinces are best-known, although related peoples are found as far north as Popayán in southern Colombia, where the northernmost tola, the "Morro de Tulcán," is located. The sites of these peoples are typified by large rectangular tolas, many with long earthen ramps leading to the top. The tolas are found in clusters which apparently were the residences of chiefly families and their retainers. Of these the most investigated is Cochasquí, midway between Quito and Otavalo. Here some fifteen rectangular "pyramids," most with ramps, and an unknown number of circular funerary platforms covering shaft and chamber tombs,

16.23 Burial tower or chullpa from Sillustani, Peru. These towers became the common tomb type over much of the altiplano in the last centuries of the precolumbian era.

16.24 This stele and pavement mark the tomb of a Cañari noblewoman 20–30 years old, who was buried in all her jewelry and accompanied by ten other attendants of varying ages. The tomb is in the patio of a building constructed for the purpose and which may have served for funerary and remembrance rituals. Ingapirca, Ecuador.

have been found (Figures 16.26 and 16.27). The rectangular pyramids had one or more circular structures made of wood and thatch on their tops and apparently functioned as elite residences. The tombs contain both positive and negative resist painted ceramics, although metal objects are extremely scarce. A similar site underlies the modern town of Otavalo and numbers of others have been documented for this northern region. Each was apparently the capital of a small chiefdom; all were quite closely related culturally speaking, although burial practices in particular vary in such features as chambers in the tombs, retainer burials, and details of the ceramic and other offerings.

On the coast the Manteño-Huancavilca peoples, who formed several distinct political units reaching from the Gulf of Guayaquil and Puná Island to Manta, grew rich from control of the long-distance sea trading routes and, especially, from the ever-growing desire of the Peruvians for spondylus. Their urban centers were located both on the coast and inland with smaller coastal ports, perhaps because of piracy. Manteño ceremonial centers are best known for their stone-fenced "corrals," which had relief stelae showing "heraldic women" and stone thrones: U-shaped chairs with an animal or human supporting the seat. Inland, in the Guayas Basin, the closely related Milagro-Quevedo peoples seem to have been less urban and to have practiced a different mode of disposal of the dead. In place of cemeteries of shaft and chamber tombs containing single and multiple burials, the Milagro-Quevedo peoples tended to bury their dead in artificial platforms, often as "chimney burials," long strings of pots with their bottoms

16.25 A Cañari drinking vessel in the form of an anthropomorphized deer.

broken out, perhaps to form access to the dead for post-mortem offerings. A secondary interment was placed in the bottom-most vessel. Such chimney burials are also seen in the far north, both along the coast and in the Carchi region, at this time. Distinct differences are seen in the wealth of burials throughout Ecuador. The Manteño and the Milagro-Quevedo peoples were accomplished metal-workers and elaborate ornaments are known from both cultures, as are cast copper axes and axe-monies. Fish hooks, bells, tweezers, and similar small tools are also common among both cultures. Stylistic continuities are quite strong between Milagro and Cañari cast metalwork and it seems that coastal–highland exchange continued to be extensive. Manteño pottery is mainly smoked black ware, relying on sculptural qualities for effect. The most famous shape is

16.26 A view of the tolas at Cochasquí, in northern Ecuador. These huge platforms served both residential and religious purposes. It is thought that Cochasquí was the capital of a large kingdom centered just to the northwest of the Guayallabamba Valley.

that of the urns or urn lids, with standing human figures on top, although many open forms such as high pedestal plates (compoteras) and modeled anthropomorphic and zoomorphic jars are common (Figure 16.28). The large numbers of pornographic vessels which have flooded the foreign antiquities market in past years are modern fabrications. Milagro-Quevedo ceramics are somewhat different from those of the Manteño, featuring fair numbers of painted jar forms, many with organic resist decoration, and relief decorated tripod or annular base bowls. Both cultures continued the tradition of carved seals and stamps, often with designs of animals or people engaged in various activities. The Manteño also produced small, dark spindle whorls with similar carved designs (Figure 16.29). Although these have sometimes been identified as beads, their size and weight is identical with spindle whorls (found on spindles) from coastal Peru, where they were used to spin fine cotton thread.

The eastern slope of the Central Andes from the high puna at the top of the cordilleras down into the precipitous slopes and heavy rainforest of the montaña proper saw a curious, exuberant cultural development in the last 500 or so years before the European invasions. It is quite possible that these areas had earlier occupations, but the difficulties of travel, the hot, wet climate, and the extreme difficulty of finding sites which are small or which had perishable constructions in most of this area have led to earlier time periods being almost completely unknown. The late cultures, however, built in stone and their populations were evidently quite large. Indeed, large ruined towns are so prevalent in parts of the Peruvian montaña that various explorers have claimed that there are huge cities hidden in the jungle, an idea pounced upon by the popular press as

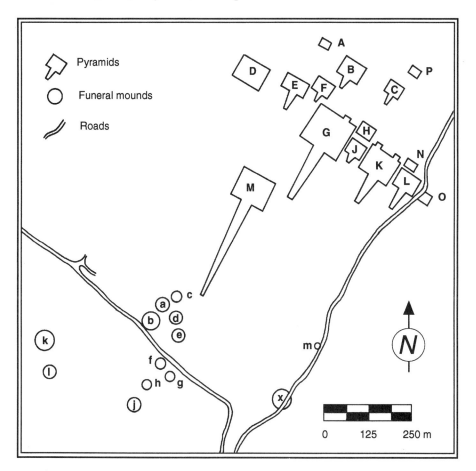

16.27 Plan of central Cochasquí.

much of this area is close enough and forested enough to fit comfortably into the mythic "green hell of the Amazon," so beloved in western adventure stories.

Although there were numerous different cultural groups represented in this region, much of which is coterminous with Antisuyo, the fourth quarter of the Inca empire, archaeologically they share a fair amount in common. To the north in the puna and higher reaches of the montaña, especially in the upper Utcubamba and along the middle reaches of the Marañon, settlements are characterized by multistory stone buildings, often with slab roofs and corbel or beehive vaulting (Figure 16.30). Most of these sites are located on high places easy to defend. Sites such as Kuelap, which was a large town divided into two halves by a wall, also sport a defensive wall surviving to 8–10 m in height. Kuelap is famous for its circular towers, probably also related to defense. The layout of such sites seems to be closely related to the (vertical) topography. Sites like Kakta, with its neat rows of beehive vaulted houses, are arranged in rows on terraces on the upper part of the hill, while Kuelap is on a broader flatter area and has agglutinated houses. Some other villages show a combination of such ideas (Figures 16.31 and 16.32).

16.28 A Manteño figurine from coastal Ecuador, showing a woman in the typical short wrap skirt of the region. Her simple jewelry consists of a necklace, ear spools, and a labret; her long hair is parted in the middle and combed back over her artificially shaped head.

16.29 Motif from a Manteño spindle whorl showing a man carrying two large fish. Manteño spindle whorls are often decorated with everyday scenes such as these.

More forbidding are sites like Tinyash, in the puna proper, whose large masonry structures in this bleak landscape immediately raise the question as to why such an impressive site was built in an area where it seems unlikely that a large population could be supported. Tinyash may have been an administrative center supported by other agricultural and herding sites around it.

To the south and lower in the montaña are a plethora of sites with agglutinated round houses built in multistructure groups around courtyards (although little other urban planning is visible in many of these sites). Many of the towns were then walled. Towns such as these come in all sizes, from the romantic and impressive Abiseo (also, although inaccurately, called Gran Pajatén) with its stone mosaics of hawks, splayed humans and meanders on the large platforms and circular buildings, to small villages of several house groups strung out along a ridge top. Abiseo has been "discovered" any number of times, publicity which has helped in the formation of the Abiseo National Park. As known it is not a large site, containing some eighteen structures in the characteristic split shale dry-stone construction of the Chachapoyas sites. Although most of the structures are large circular buildings, there are two rectangular pirca enclosures at one end of the precipitous ridge on which the site is constructed. Although many of the sites of this region have stone mosaic decoration, Pajatén is famous because, in addition to simple zigzag and meander patterns, two of the largest buildings (called Structures 1 and 2 by Duccio Bonavia, the only person to have done substantial controlled excavations at the site) also show human figures made with tenon heads and mosaic bodies and birds, apparently hawks (Figure 16.33). The nearby Los Pinchudos is similar, its three main buildings topping an impressive crag. Los Pinchudos is unusual in that there are wooden statues hanging from the surviving beams (Figure 16.34). The towns of this area are distinctive in their large structures built upon high terrace-platforms as well as in their construction. Towns outside of this limited area of Chachapoyas tend to be built of fieldstone and/or pirca and, although often on terraces or platforms, not to have the impressive high platforms and stairs of sites like Abiseo and Los Pinchudos.

The eastern Andean peoples tended to bury their dead in chullpas, small, square, rectangular or round buildings. Some of these are very large, suggesting family vaults (such as the somewhat earlier Wilkawain, in the Callejón de Huaylas). A curious

16.30 One of the multistory structures at Tantamayo, in the highlands of the middle Marañon River, Peru. Over fifty sites of this sort are currently known.

16.31 Chihiarurín, a town on the upper Marañon River. The multistory tower is typical of both burial (chullpa) and living structures in this region.

16.32 Garu (or Garo) in Huánuco, near the headwaters of the middle Marañon River of Peru. This immense site has round and oval houses arranged in clusters around patios, the typical layout of sites in this region. The houses originally would have had tall thatched roofs.

16.33 Structure 1 at Abiseo (Gran Pajatén), Chachapoyas, Peru. This large circular building is decorated with reliefs of humans.

exception to this practice has been noted on the upper Utcubamba River near the site of Chipurik where the dead were encased in anthropomorphic clay cases placed in rows on ledges high up the cliffs along the rivers. In the same general region (near Revash) a variant of this idea was to place the dead in small clay houses, often with two stories and decorated, but similarly located along ledges on steep cliff faces.

Ceramics from this area are largely undistinguished, although some of the northern sites have pottery decorated with cursive motifs said to be vaguely similar to the decoration of the late Cajamarca style. In general, however, these sites seem to have been founded quite late, and a great many of them were inhabited at the time of the conquest and indeed some were not abandoned until well into the colonial period.

The problems of lack of investigation and of settlement oriented survey (which alone can reveal how many sites there are, their relative sizes and locations, and other bits of information one needs to tease out social and political structure), as has been mentioned before, plague much of the tropical lowlands (and, indeed, the highlands as well). Later developments in the Amazon-Orinoco region seem to have involved steady population growth along the major river courses and large-scale projects to extend agriculture and human occupation into the seasonally flooded savannas. Earthworks are notoriously hard to date, especially since they often do not directly connect with habitation sites. In the Orinoco the first settlements on artificial mounds seem to date to the Corozal 1 phase

16.34 A chullpa, of similar construction to that in Figure 16.33, at Los Pinchudos, Peru.

16.35 Tripod bowl in the Tierra de los Indios style of Venezuela with elaborate geometric designs in red and black on white, from Venezuela.

of the Parmana area, dated at either the late centuries BC or the mid-centuries AD. Upriver in the Apuré region and on the Llanos de Barinas, investigation has shown large areas of drained field systems dating to about AD 600 and later. These were formed by digging canals back from the water source in the gallery forest into the flood plain, throwing the topsoil up on either side to form ridges. When in use such systems require at least yearly cleaning, with the water weed and sediments that have grown/collected in the drainage ditches being thrown up on the ridges for fertilizer. At Cano Ventosidad Erika Wagner located a system some 15.5 sq km and other large systems have been found in the same region. Study of these systems has shown that they are especially good for growing tuber crops. Ceramics associated with these drained field systems and with earth and stone mounds used as platforms for settlements and causeways connecting these settlements can be associated with the Tierroid tradition. This pottery has a sand temper and is extremely elaborate, with high legs and annular bases and elaborate polychrome painting (Figure 16.35). In the Andes a simpler version of this style is associated with shaft tombs and rock piles. Here shrines seem to have been in caves associated with the local Mirinday style of the Tierroid tradition. The sites of the Venezuelan Andes, however, were, as might be expected, more closely allied with cultures of the Colombian Andes and the northern littoral and the late cultures are somewhat provincial versions of these more complex cultures.

In the Valencia Basin a local tradition shows a mixed manioc and maize agricultural base. The Valencia culture is best known for its figurines of women and animals, a peculiar development of this style which also featured modeled human heads on jar necks and lugs (Figure 16.36). The La Mata site shows people living in houses on artificial mounds succeeding houses on piles. A fairly elaborate development of polished stone includes not only celts and hammers but the bat-wing pendants more typical of the highlands.

16.36 Valencia-style female figurine from Venezuela. The incisions across the top of the forehead may refer to an ornamented head band.

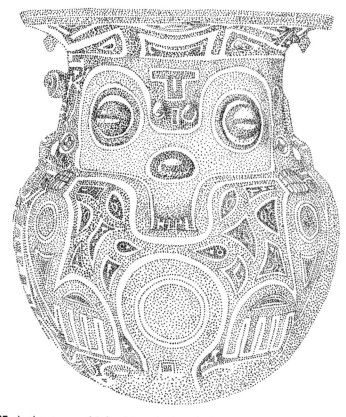

16.37 Anthropomorphic burial urn in the polychrome Marajoara Phase, Joanes Painted style from Marajó Island at the mouth of the Amazon River in Brazil. In addition to the main face, the neck has small modeled human figures and head adornos and the body, painted in front to be the body of the large neck face, is painted with an anthropomorphized frog.

In the Amazon proper a series of polychrome painted styles has been dated, often on the somewhat flimsy grounds of polychrome painting alone, to the late prehistoric period. On Marajó Island the Marajoara style shows an extremely decorative version of the polychrome style, not just on vessels, but also on stools, spoons, spindle whorls, and other artifacts (Figure 16.37). Here villages were also built on artificial mounds, with some differential use of these identified (some of the mounds may have been for burial alone). The Aterro dos Bichos site, in the central part of the island overlooking the Arari River, is *c*. 2 ha in area and survives to some 4 m in height. At least twenty large houses were located in this site, along with a series of hearths arranged in clusters as if for communal cooking. Middens between the houses contained most of the ceramic types reported from earlier excavations in cemeteries on Marajó Island. Large earthworks, perhaps for defensive purposes, were also associated with this site. Burial was in urns placed in regular patterns in cemeteries and both primary and secondary burial seem to have been practiced (Figure 16.38). The polychrome traditions of the Amazon are all

16.38 Cemetery of urn burials in the Magno Mound of the Camutins site, Marajó Island.

quite similar and it has been hypothesized that they are the result of migrations or diffusion along the riverine pathways. The direction of this diffusion varies with the investigator. Meggers and Evans have wanted to see movements of peoples and ideas going upriver, whereas Lathrap and his followers have pushed for a central Amazonian origin of polychrome painted ceramics and their subsequent diffusion both up and down stream.

Numbers of terra preta sites have been identified for this late time period. In the Trombetas River region a large number of sites, all close to either the main river or its tributaries, have been located. Some of these terra preta sites have yielded no artifacts and the excavators suggest that these represent either fields or sites of some unknown ceremonial. Ceramics are of the Kondurí style, a relative of the flamboyant Santarém style of the historic Tapajós kingdom. They are tempered with sponge spicule and decorated with bimorphic and anthropomorphic incision. Tripod vessels are characteristic of this ceramic style as well. Similar sites between the Itacaiúnas and Paraupebas Rivers are somewhat deeper, averaging 60 cm instead of the more common 30–50 cm. Vessels here are tempered with crushed rock and have extremely varied forms and decoration, including red and white slip, incision, and rocker stamping. Vessels are also frequently polished. Scarce stone artifacts include grinding stones, nutcrackers, scrapers, and T-shaped stone axes. These sites, which date from *c.* AD 400–1500 are said to be similar to those of the Tupi-Guaraní of southern Brazil. The Pacoval site, on the Amazon River northeast of Macapá, shows the common late practice of secondary burial in urns. The Pacoval urns are anthropomorphic and often show signs of interior burning. The urns are arranged in cemeteries, in straight rows or semicircles. Other ceramics include plates with sherd temper. Pacoval dates to *c*. AD 1000; its ceramics are quite similar to those of the Mazagao culture of the mouth of the Amazon, a culture which continued into the historic period, to judge from the glass beads found in some Mazagao burial urns. The Marajoara phase was succeeded by the Aruá phase, whose cemeteries have been identified on Mexiana and Cauiana Islands as well as on the north and east coasts of Marajó proper. These cemeteries are on high ground and the large burial urns contain a lot of European trade goods such as glass beads, scissors, steel knives, etc. This is also a polychrome tradition, although there are a lot of jars with simple ticked/stamped fillet decoration and some adornos. Aruá phase ceramics are quite similar to contemporary styles upriver, all representing the ill-fated contact period cultures, so soon to become extinct.

In the upper Amazon region, along the lower Apurimac and central Ucayali, the Cumancaya tradition flourished from the ninth to the fifteenth century. This tradition, which features pedestal bowls, and organic resist and incision outline red geometric patterns, is thought to have had its proximate origin in the earlier Sivia tradition, although its broad connections with ceramic styles all along the eastern slopes of the Andes cannot be denied. Urn burial was practiced by both cultural groups, who likewise were both flood plain agriculturalists. The type site stretches for more than 500 m along the lake shore and is thought to have had at least 2000 inhabitants. This tradition slowly expanded, with some intrusions, perhaps, by peoples producing other polychrome styles, but all practicing flood plain agriculture. Although attempts have been made to identify these peoples ethnically, it is not until the period of European contact that we can give a name to the ceramic styles. At that time there were numbers of different ethnic groups resident in the region, linguistically distinct, but with similar material cultures, including similar ceramic styles. The upper Amazon situation mirrors many of the problems of tropical lowland prehistory: known ethnic diversity in historic times with close correspondence of style in the only artifacts likely to survive, ceramics and stone axes. In such a situation it is difficult indeed to pick up solid evidence of migration or of ethnic dispersal. However, it is evident that by the end of the fifteenth century, the eastern Andean slopes and the Amazonian lowlands supported very large populations who lived in large settlements, made elaborate ceramics, and were probably organized into varying forms of chiefdoms. The exact relationships of these polities remain to be worked out and, given the nature of preservation in the Amazon and the close resemblances between styles, will probably have to be defined on the basis of paste analysis first and style only second. It is, however, evident that there were no "lost civilizations" of the degree of complexity of those seen in the western Andes, however large the settlements and grandiose the ideas of their inhabitants.

CHAPTER 17

THE SIXTEENTH CENTURY

By the beginning of the fifteenth century Andean South America had seen considerable change. Recovery from the collapse of Huari was general and a series of large coastal states extended from near the border with Chile in the south to north of Manta in Ecuador. The highlands were more divided politically, with a series of small kingdoms such as the Lupaca, the Cañari, the Cara, and the multiplicity of small, warring entities found throughout central and northern Colombia (Figure 17.1). Events of the early fifteenth century were to change the face of the central Andes considerably, leaving this region especially vulnerable to the European invasions of little more than a century later.

These events were triggered when a small farming group called the Inca, under what tradition claimed was their eighth ruler, Wiracocha, began meddling in local politics, first conquering down the Urubamba Valley (the Ayarmarcas) and then interfering in the affairs of the Aymara kingdoms in the Lake Titicaca basin. At the same time, a neighboring group to the west, the Chancas, were also trying to form a larger political unit, moving into what is now modern Andahuaylas, not too far from Cuzco. In 1438 they attacked Cuzco, the Inca capital, in a bid to form a yet larger kingdom by annexing their neighbors and their neighbors' territory. This kind of pushing and shoving was typical of Andean politics, and had previously led to the formation of fairly large states, including, perhaps, that of Huari. However, the Chancas had reckoned without three factors: Wiracocha's two very able generals, Apu Mayta and Wika Kiraw, and a secondary Inca prince, Kusi Yupanki. Wiracocha Inca decided that it would be difficult to defend Cuzco and so he withdrew to the fortified site of Calca in the Urubamba Valley, taking his chosen heir, Inca Urqon, with him, leaving his generals and Kusi to organize whatever defense they might. At this point official Inca reports say that Kusi had a vision promising him supernatural powers. Whether this was an *ex post facto* invention or not, Kusi in later life was renowned for his interest in religion and founded a large number of religious establishments along with a state religion of his own. Kusi and the generals inflicted an unexpected defeat on the Chancas and pursued them, defeating them again and chasing them back to Andahuaylas. The upshot of this defeat was a change in the succession as Kusi put himself forward as the new heir, causing the priests to read the omens and then crowning himself as the new emperor under the name of Pachacuti, "earthquake." This was to set an unfortunate precedent among the Inca royalty, as Pachacuti was, in essence, an usurper. Pachacuti's later history was one of continued military activity as he set about conquering as much of the known world as he could. Beginning with the highland areas to the north and east of Cuzco, the Incas proceeded to challenge every political power they could and to absorb these polities into their own empire. Within fairly short order the south coast was visited and the central

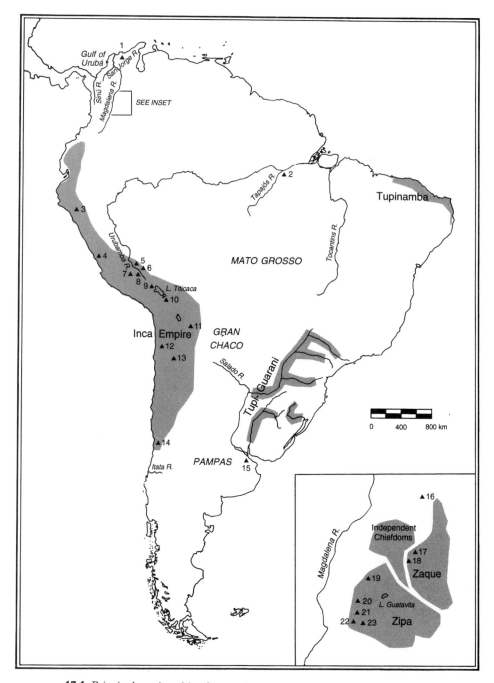

17.1 Principal empires, kingdoms, ethnic groups and sites of the sixteenth century. 1. Pueblito, 2. Santarém, 3. Cajamarca, 4. Pachacamac, 5. Machu Picchu, 6. Ollantaytambo, 7. Andahuaylas, 8. Cuzco, 9. Hatuncolla, 10. Tiahuanaco, 11. Potosí, 12. Loa Valley, 13. San Pedro de Atacama, Quitor, Catarpe, 14. Aconagua Valley, 15. Buenos Aires, 16. Bucaramanga, 17. Sorocatá, 18. Tunja, 19. Nemocón, 20. Chia, 21. Zipaquirá, 22. Funza, 23. Bogotá.

highlands were added to the nascent empire. Subsequent campaigns involved the invasion of the Junín/Huancavelica area, the mythic homeland of the Chancas (the Inca origin spot was at Maulkallacta near Paucauritampu, outside of early Inca territory), the conquest of Cajamarca (in the course of which campaign Pachacuti had his brother and able general assassinated, ostensibly for insubordination, but probably because he was getting too popular), the Titicaca basin, and the Chancas themselves. Pachacuti's armies, under his son and designated heir Topa Inca, also marched into Ecuador as far north as Manta, where Topa made a brief foray into the ocean on a sea-going balsa raft. The Inca armies had to avoid the Gulf of Guayaquil, however, as the Manteño-Huancavelica kingdom was not welcoming. On the homeward journey the kingdom of Chimor was attacked from the north and, although the Chimu put up a stiff resistance, the Incas prevailed and sacked the city, looting the shrines and burial platforms and taking an immense treasure in metal, textiles, and artifacts back to Cuzco. It is very likely that the lion's share of the gold that Pizarro stole from Cuzco had originally been taken from Chan Chan some ninety years before.

The rapid expansion of the Inca state, which had been a simple village society ruled by a non-hereditary headman (a zinchi or "strong man") not long before, made reorganization essential. Hereditary rulers (qhapac or capac) had been established for several reigns, but there was little structure available for administering what was already the largest empire the Andean region had ever seen. Moreover, several inherent weaknesses in the Inca system of rulership existed and never were resolved. One of these was inheritance. The Incas had a type of double descent and did not practice primogeniture; the Sapa Inca was supposed to choose the most capable from among his various sons. Since the Inca rulers were polygynous and had numbers of secondary wives – later chosen from the local ruling families of conquered states – besides their main wife, the coya, who was supposed to be a full sister of the ruler, there were generally a fair number of contestants for the throne. Pachacuti himself was a secondary prince and, when his father refused to name him as heir in place of Inca Urqon, had simply taken the throne, sending Wiracocha into forced retirement and seeing to it that the ex-heir did not have a long and prosperous life. The other weakness may have been partly responsible for the continuing expansion of the empire. When a ruler died, he was mummified, and his descendants formed a corporation (called a paqana) which inherited and administered all lands, goods, etc., using these for the maintenance of the royal mummy and its cults. Thus each new ruler had to start over again from the beginning and amass enough property both to maintain his own cult and descendants and to have land to give as gifts to nobles, religious institutions, and other worthies, as rewards and to bind them to him through obligation. This system may have been set up by Pachacuti himself, who incorporated the existing royal descendants into ayllus (corporate kin groups), acquiring mummies or sacred objects standing for the mummies – the first, legendary, ruler, Manco Capac, was represented by a stone – and putting together ayllus for them, to expand the nobility to meet the new needs for administrators and professional military personnel. Additional ideas for the administration of the empire appear to have come from the conquered kingdom of Chimor: perhaps the idea of maintaining royal estates for the cult of the dead rulers, some of the ideas concerning storage and disbursement of goods and labor collected as taxes, the forced resettlement programs (mitamaes), moving populations around for both economic and political ends, the chosen women, women removed from childbearing who wove and made beer for the government, and so on came from this source. Many of these administrative ideas appear to have originated with Huari and were preserved in the large states of the north coast from where they passed to the new Inca empire. Pachacuti also put together a series of new ideas and institutions, including a state religion in which the traditional nature gods were organized under a new deity, a creator god, Viracocha, who was personified by the sun. This cult was embedded into the royal administration and supported by taxes levied on the population. Pachacuti validated many of his new rituals, prayers, and ceremonies as well as more secular institutions by revelations. The Incas talked to their gods and Pachacuti ... re vocal than most. Pachacuti began major reconstruct... d city, and created a number of royal estates of which ... ith its numerous shrines and sacred constructions.

The two rulers who fol... ayna Capac, continued the policy of continuous co... e south coast of Peru, and much of Ecuador t... famous system of roads reached its peak. ... ces was essential. In 1525 Huayna Capa... ... came of a terrible epidemic in the southern r... pean disease, probably measles or smallpox, comin... ires had entered the empire. In short order the ... re infected. Although he quickly chose a succ... ... e before he could be named. This left two sons, Huasca... est claim to the throne and, after much double dealing, as ... e, there was a civil war which Atahuallpa won, only to fall into the ... ly arrived Europeans within the year. The Europeans, aided by pestilen... ing a complicated political and military game with the many disaffected ethnic g...s and members of the various Inca administrations, were able to take the empire in a relatively short time.

The Inca expansion can be documented historically through the histories and administrative paperwork of the early colonial era. Many of their sites have been studied archaeologically and a good idea of Inca material culture, especially as it relates to the art of empire, has resulted. Inca architecture is highly distinctive in its standardization of both style and construction. Ceramics are similarly standardized and distinctive as are textiles, in both weave and designs. The modern textile arts of the Andes, with their emphasis upon warp patterned weaves can be traced back to the Inca prohibition on the use of weft face tapestry by ordinary people. After the conquest indigenous weavers simply elaborated on the warp weaves they were now used to, having forgotten the tapestry techniques of earlier traditions. Sumptuary laws were rife among the Incas and details of costume were designated by statute by the ethnicity and status of the wearer. Such standardization tends to make Inca remains easy to recognize, wherever they might be. Local imitations and Inca influence on local ceramics and textiles are common and make dating the latest indigenous cultures of the Andes more precise.

17.2 "El Castillo" at Ingapirca in southern Ecuador. The Incas took over an important Cañari site. Although often referred to in romantic tones as a great temple, this was more probably a major administrative center and garrison.

Inca sites have been identified from north of Quito southeast into Argentina, where a series of fortresses were built by the Incas to stave off attack by the nomadic tribes of the Chaco (in the north it appears that the Incas simply took over fortresses already constructed by the not particularly peaceable inhabitants of Ecuador, especially in the frontier region north of Quito). Elsewhere, because of the speed of the Inca expansion, most identifiably Inca sites are administrative or cult centers. The Incas had the policy of co-opting existing shrines and cults to their own use. Thus the great oracle Pachacamac was incorporated into the Inca state by Topa Inca, who built a new temple to the sun at the shrine and established branch oracles (described as sons and wives, although Pachacamac also had possessions, such as a house at Chan Chan) in areas where the Incas had not yet consolidated their power. The alliance with Pachacamac was useful in that the priesthoods and branch oracles served as an intelligence force in areas the Inca planned to take over, as well as providing the ruling Topa Inca with supernatural backing which was not affiliated with his father's family. Since Pachacamac had appeared as an important religious cult at the time of the Huari, this provided another tie with past practices and suggests that similar mechanisms may have been in place with the earlier empire.

Inca architecture is best known for the tightly fitted "cyclopean" walls that typify the main terraces of sites such as Sacsahuamán – the "fortress" of Cuzco – and Ollantaytambo, the fortress/palace that served as the last major site of Manco Inca, as well as other imperial establishments, such as the administrative center of Ingapirca in southern Ecuador (Figures 17.2 and 17.3). Other buildings, however, were made of

17.3 Trapezoidal door and niche in the "Governor's House" at Ingapirca. Although decorative doors and niches were known in earlier Andean architectural traditions (see Figure 12.2), the trapezoidal form is characteristic of Inca architecture. The fine masonry of this building and the adjacent "Castillo" indicates that they were the most important structures of the site.

17.4 "House of the Virgins" at Pachacamac. The Incas took over the oracle of Pachacamac and converted him to an important ally. They also built a number of new structures at the site, including a temple to the sun and an acllahuasi, where the chosen women who made beer and textiles for the deities and their human servitors lived. An important building, it is done in plastered adobe with long lines of large double niches in the lower interior courtyard walls and smaller double and single niches in other rooms and corridors.

masonry whose degree of workmanship was proportional to the importance of the structure and/or adobe (Figure 17.4). Adobe structures were characteristic of both highland and coastal sites and were often plastered and painted with solid colors (usually red or yellow) or with murals whose designs were identical to those found on textiles (Figure 17.5). Such features as double-jamb doorways and niches, and trapezoidal niches, windows and doors, show some affinities with earlier highland styles, but the lack of continuity in surviving architecture between Huari, Tiahuanaco, and the Incas has not permitted the identification of any direct antecedents for the monumental state architecture of the Incas. The Inca government had state architects who designed new administrative and religious sites, roads and their way houses, and the vastly enlarged systems of terraces found over much of Peru (Figure 17.6, see also Figures 6.4 and 15.7). These terrace systems brought more land under cultivation, specifically maize and coca cultivation, for the support of the Inca administration.

Inca ceramics were likewise very standardized, or at least the imperial Inca style from Cuzco was. These vessels were given to local administrators and others who had helped the state and may have formed the basis for the plethora of provincial Inca or Inca-influenced styles which appeared across the empire. Forms such as the aryballos, a tall-

17.5 A decorative double niche at Tambo Colorado in the Ica Valley, Peru. The site gets its name from the still surviving red paint. This niche is painted yellow with a red center.

17.6 Catarpe Tambo at San Pedro de Atacama, an important administration, storage and, perhaps, manufacturing site on the Inca road to the southernmost reaches of the empire. There is enough water at the San Pedro oasis for both agriculture and keeping animals and so it has been an important way station since the first trading civilizations in Peru and Bolivia appeared.

necked jar with a pointed base, are found all through the Inca-occupied area, often with designs borrowed from local styles but applied to this foreign shape (Figure 17.7). The Chimu also produced Inca shapes in their internationally favored black ware and in the north Inca ceramics even influenced Cañari Cashaloma-style pottery in proportions and rim forms. The keros, a wooden drinking vessel which had ancient antecedents in the highlands, again was spread throughout the empire both in its original wooden form and in ceramic imitations (Figure 17.8).

Inca sculpture was fairly simple and restricted largely to the occasional relief on a building stone, the elaborate carved rocks such as Kenko, and the small carved camelids used to hold offerings (Figure 17.9).

Most of the clearly identifiable Inca textiles that survive are uniforms, woven by the chosen women and distributed as part of administrative/military pay. The most characteristic piece is an uncu, a tunic which is roughly rectangular, reaching below the knees of the average male. These are woven in fine double-sided tapestry or kompi, a weave which was restricted to official textiles. Other high-status textiles of the sixteenth century seem to have been locally manufactured; the tradition of fine weaving of sumptuous garments and hangings was not co-opted by the Inca, although the history

17.7 Inca aryballos. This lavishly decorated miniature vessel (22 cm in height) bears designs taken from both Inca ceramics and Inca textiles. It is exactly the same shape, handles, adorno, and all, as the large storage vessels of up to a meter or so in height.

and distribution of late textile types has been badly compromised by extensive looting of coastal sites (see Figure 10.5).

Inca metallurgy, aside from tin bronze weapons and tools such as plumb bobs and chisels, did not have much of an effect on local traditions. Partly this seems to have been because of Inca sumptuary laws, which restricted all gold and silver to the Inca or to those to whom the Inca had given such objects. This edict does not seem to have had much effect on the coast, where precious metal ornaments and vessels continued to be manufactured for the upper classes, nor did it affect the north, where Ecuadorian metallurgical traditions continued relatively unaffected by the Inca edicts.

Most surviving Inca metalwork is from burials, especially sacrifices made to the various deities. Among a large number of female sacrifices and burials at the palace of Tomebamba in Cuenca is that of a dwarf buried with offerings of miniature vessels and gold and silver figurines of humans and llamas. Similar figures, still wearing their textile and featherwork clothing, were found with the mummy of a boy in Cerro el Plomo in 1954. This child had apparently been made drunk and left to freeze to death, a sacrifice to the apu of the mountain. Numerous sacrifices of this type have been found in the southern Andes, where isolation and extreme high altitudes have preserved them from plunder. Inca figurines, like those of earlier Peruvian traditions, are hammered and

17.8 Inca keros. This colonial piece from Ecuador has designs identical to those seen on textiles.

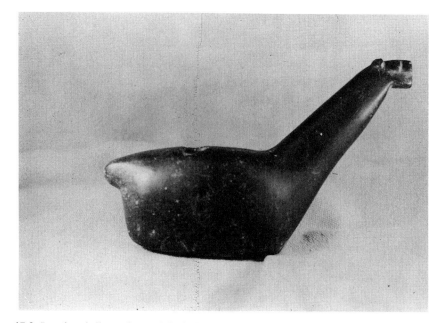

17.9 Inca basalt llama figure. The hole in the back is for placing fat and coca leaves. These llamas were buried in the fields and pastures as part of rituals to assure fertility among the animals, a practice which continued into the twentieth century.

soldered, not cast. Bronze tools were cast in open molds, but this technology was not applied to sumptuary items in the central Andes.

Inca burials which were not sacrifices tended to be made above ground in caves or grottoes. The mummies of important people, especially the dead rulers, were kept dressed and in their houses, treated much as if they were living, according to the Spanish who saw these grisly relics. In 1533 a major showing of the royal mummies was made as part of a celebration held by Manco Inca to celebrate his victory over the forces of Atahuallpa's general Kiskis. The conquistador Miguel de Estete described this celebration, saying that every day a large number of members of the royal paqanas came into the plaza where the music and dances of the fiesta were held and that they brought their dead ancestors with them on litters, all dressed up and with their diadems on their heads, their fans in their hands, and surrounded by their women and servants as if they were alive. Less important ancestors did not, perhaps, merit such treatment, but the mummy bundles of ancestors were consulted and had their offerings renewed in much of Peru until well into the eighteenth century.

Although the Incas managed to conquer most of the "civilized" world within the three short generations of their hegemony, there remained much of South America untouched by this empire. The Incas clearly had designs on the large Manteño-Huancavilca kingdoms on the southern and central coast of Ecuador, but had not even really had time to consolidate their control of the highlands before the European invaders arrived. These kingdoms, such as Puná and Salangone, controlled the spondylus trade, and perhaps other sumptuary trade, between Ecuador and Peru. Since spondylus was a religious necessity, it is obvious that the Incas were not going to be content to leave the source of supply in foreign hands. The merchants of these kingdoms seem to have dominated sea trade in Ecuador south as far as Lambayeque. Their towns were wealthy and populous, engaging in both trade and manufacturing on a large scale. The Inca did manage to put a shrine on La Plata Island, where local shrines had been located since Valdivia times, perhaps as another attempt to co-opt local cults into the empire.

To the north in Colombia, an area the Incas had only briefly entered (Inca armies had advanced a short distance over the modern border between Colombia and Ecuador), there were a series of small chiefdoms, continually at war with each other, throughout much of the central highlands. Groups such as the Quimbaya, the Panche, the Pijao, and the Calima are now known mainly as misapplied ethnic labels for much older metallurgical styles. Larger political entities had formed along the lower Magdalena flood plain, where extensive ridged field systems and large burial and village platforms pertain to the Sinú kingdoms and their predecessors. This was an area in which mining and the manufacture of gold and tumbaga ornaments for long-distance trade had been established for some centuries and it was probably from here that metallurgical technologies spread north, first into lower Central America, and finally, in the twelfth century, into Mexico. Conquest period accounts speak of large mining centers such as Buriticá, where the actual mining was done by large slave forces; evidently these were major commercial establishments, trading their metal north and east to areas without much of the precious metal. Padre Simón, writing in the seventeenth century, speaks of three major chiefdoms here, one of them ruled by a woman, their temples with wooden idols covered with gold to which golden offerings were made, and their widespread trade systems within and without the Sinú area. He also speaks of how much of this gold ended up in the chiefly burial tumuluses, something which has not gone unnoticed by the army of huaqueros which have spread across the Sinú like locusts.

In the Sierra Nevada de Santa Marta the Tairona kingdoms flourished, the dense population living in large towns built of stone (Figure 17.10). The Tairona were known for their lapidary and metal work and were active traders across northern South America. Although not much is known of their religion, aside from the Spanish comment that they had special houses where they kept statues of their "devils," their little cast metal ornaments give us a look into the world of the Tairona supernatural (see Chapter 13).

One of the most complex of the northern Andean cultures was that of the Chibcha or Muisca, a people who had occupied the Sabana de Bogotá and adjacent highlands perhaps since the early centuries AD when this area was repopulated by ceramics-making farming peoples. By the eighth century these early Herrera Phase people are clearly identifiable as the predecessors of the historic Muisca, people who spoke one of the macro-Chibchan languages which are so widely found in northern South America and lower Central America. The Muisca, at the time of the Spanish invasions, were organized into two paramount chiefdoms, those of the Zipa, whose sphere of influence

17.10 Stone road at the large Tairona town of El Pueblito in the department of Magdalena, Colombia. Tairona towns are generally on hill tops and slopes and the houses were placed on terraces or circular platforms which were connected by stone slab roadways and stairs.

was the Sabana proper, and of the Zaque, whose power was centered around the modern town of Tunja (Figure 17.1, inset). There were some other independent chiefs, one of whom, Ramiriquí of Samancá, was beginning to absorb the communities around him into what promised to become yet a third paramount chiefdom.

The Muisca were not urban. Reckoning inheritance matrilineally, they lived in small avunculocal clusters of round, thatched houses called uta. These had lineage head men who owed fealty to the next-highest-ranking chief, the one of a group of these uta. Above this were the higher-ranking chiefs of the dispersed community, called by the name of the community, hence "The Guatavita," "The Bogotá." Above these chiefs were the paramount chiefs, the Zipa and the Zaque, and, apparently, those who aspired to a similar position. The political situation was quite fluid and the Zipa was energetically attempting to extend his allies and control of territory at the expense of the Zaque. The chiefs lived in large households which were often palisaded and had special-purpose structures such as temples or store houses as well as living quarters. Some of their relatives and close allies might live with them, so that chiefly household clusters could be quite large, perhaps the size of a small town in western terms.

Excavations at the capital of the Zipa, near Funza on the Sabana de Bogotá, have revealed a site that stretched for nearly 3 km along the Pantano de Gualí, one of the long, nearly stagnant, lagoons which dot the Sabana de Bogotá, slowly draining into the rivers. There are no visible constructions at all at Old Bogotá (modern Santafé de Bogotá was constructed on the edge of the Sabana near a native settlement called Tensacá or Tensaquillo) and investigations suggest a fairly dispersed settlement (history tells of thirteen such settlements close together), with perhaps a bigger cluster right around the residence of the Zipa.

Muisca religion centered on nature and astral deities such as the sun and the moon. Ceremonial buildings and shrines were thus also dispersed, although there were important shrines, such as the one to the moon at Chia, which were of more than local importance. Chiefs were the major players in important ceremonials and priests were chosen from chiefly families. The priesthood was an inherited, full-time occupation, involving some twelve years of preparation (the Muisca thought in multiples of six) and then a life of fasting and ritual activities. Communities had many temples, small huts for worship and sacrifice as well as storage of sacred articles. Offerings were also made at sacred places in streams, lakes, woods, and roads. The most famous of these ritual spots is Lake Guatavita, where the ritual of "El Dorado" that so impressed the Spanish was enacted. This was basically a reaffirmation of the right to rule by the chief who, with his priests and helpers, made offerings of gold objects and emeralds from a raft. Everyone wore gold and feather ornaments, music played, and large incense burners poured smoke into the air. The difference was that the chief himself was powdered with gold dust which he washed off himself in the lake waters; the use of gold as some sort of high-class soap, albeit ritual soap, inflamed the imagination of the Spanish and continues to excite imaginative schemes among treasure hunters to this day.

Muisca gold objects, especially the tunjos, small figures of human beings, are highly distinctive (Figures 17.11, 17.12, 17.13). The Muisca had to trade for the raw gold. Trade was an integral part of Muisca economy and regular markets were held at a number of sites within Muisca territory, especially at Sorocatá, where people from both the Zipa and the Zaque's realms, unaffiliated Muisca groups, and people from the surrounding tribes traded gold, cotton, tobacco and other drug plants, emeralds, marine shells, and pottery. The main center of gold-working seems to have been the Guatavita region. The gold was intended for ornaments and, above all, for offerings. Figures of humans, animals, and small artifacts were fabricated in great numbers. Among the most spectacular pieces are the small scenes, especially ones representing the raft of El Dorado. These were stored in ceramic figurine vases or in painted jars and were kept in the houses as well as in the shrines. Offerings were made by tying the figures in trees, by casting them into the waters, and by burying them. Although most Muisca gold comes from huaquería, some of these offerings have even been found by archaeologists. A small pot found buried at a shallow depth in an open field near Funza was filled with little gold figures including some twenty-five tunjos, pins, snakes, little cups, and similar pieces of gold. Gold was also used as burial offerings: both the tunjos and ornaments such as nose hangers and pectorals are found in burials.

Muisca burials were varied: flexed mummies have been found in dry caves: both extended and flexed burials in the ground were also common. Some of these were in

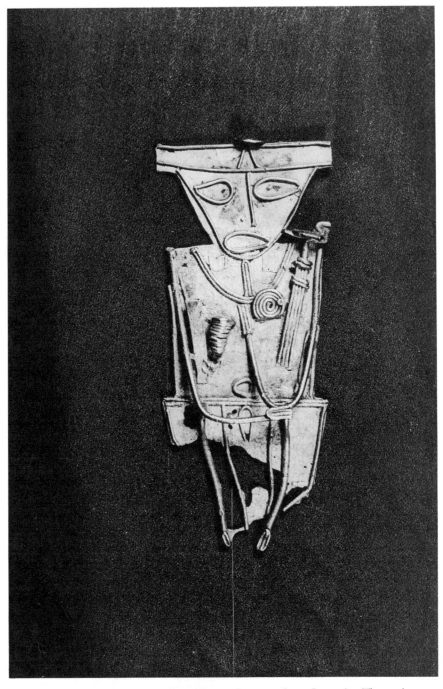

17.11 Tunjo of a woman with a necklace and scepter, from Guatavita. The casting was incomplete in the lower half.

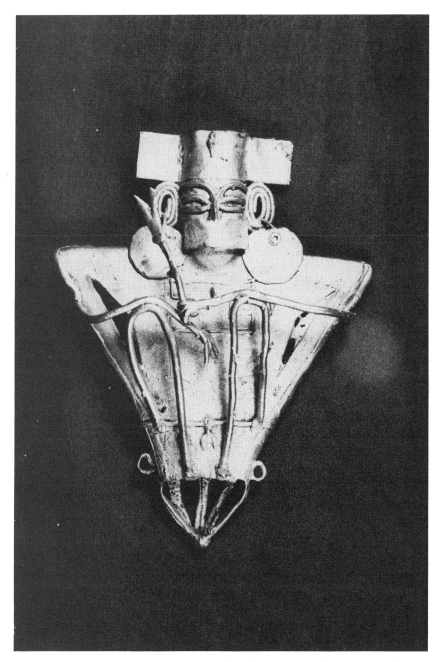

17.12 Tunjo of a man wearing large earspools and earrings as well as a rectangular nose ornament, from Sogamoso. He is nude, save for a penis string, and carries a scepter or spear thrower.

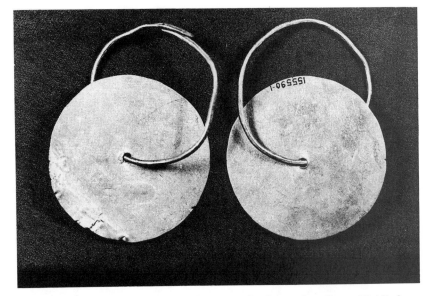

17.13 A pair of gold ear ornaments like those worn by the previous figure (17.12), from Colombia. Earrings like these, often suspended from ear spools, are common throughout Ecuador and Colombia.

urns, but excavations at the Marin site near Samancá have shown some other patterns, including enveloping the body either in cloth and matting or in cloth and then in clay and ash to make a solid mass in the shaft or boot-shaped tomb. Historical sources mention that chiefs were buried in special tombs. Some stone-roofed chambers near Guatavita may be the remains of these tombs. Although the Muisca did not build in stone in general, these are chambers which are either excavated out under large rocks or, in several cases, were deliberately roofed and lined with stones. They correspond to descriptions of the chiefly tombs which were looted and destroyed by the Spanish early in the colonial period.

Numbers of megaliths, especially pillar-shaped stones, have been found in Muisca territory, but it is not known if they were constructed by the Muisca and some have suggested that most of these belong to the Herrera Phase peoples. Growing populations, especially in the Sabana de Bogotá, not only predicated expansionist political policies on the part of the Zipa, but led to extension of farming lands. Hillsides were terraced, perhaps to provide drained land to grow potatoes, and extensive drained field systems were constructed out on the Sabana. Muisca communities generally were built where they had access to a number of different environmental zones: woodlands for fuel, construction materials and for hunting, swamp areas for gathering, and drained land for agriculture. Numbers of communities also controlled lower lands in warmer zones where they could grow crops which were too cold-intolerant for the highlands. This use of multiple environmental zones was not understood by the Spaniards, either here or in the rest of the Andes, and some of the collapse of native economic systems can be traced to the Spanish determination to make people stay in one place, where they could be more closely controlled. The Muisca themselves strongly resisted Spanish attempts to force them into nucleated settlements and to interrupt their agricultural systems. Peasants even today tend to live in a dispersed manner with the towns being the homes of the mestizos, whose culture is derived from that of the Spanish.

Aside from gold-working, the Muisca produced distinctive pottery and textiles. The ceramics are largely plain wares, with decorated vessels being painted in small geometric designs in red on cream or buff. A characteristic form is the múcara, a jar with an elongated neck which is decorated with an appliqué and painted face or human figure. Múcaras were commonly used to hold sacred objects and are often found in burial and other offerings. Figurines and figurine vases are unpainted and decorated with incision and appliqué. Many show priests or warriors with bandoleer belts and a high cap (Figure 17.14). These too were used to store gold and other offerings.

Muisca textiles were all of cotton. Aside from descriptions, numbers have survived in dry caves. The plain weave fabrics were painted in elaborate designs, often of religious significance. Apparently some of these textiles served as sacred objects or, like Catholic vestments, were decorated with the symbols of the deities and rites. There are references to idols made of cotton (as well as of wood), and the invaders soon prohibited the painting of textiles as it was associated with idolatry.

Although there have been unwary references to a Muisca state, there is no evidence that there was any such tendency among the sixteenth-century occupants of the modern departments of Boyacá and Cundinamarca. A system of ranked chiefs and strong tendencies towards inheritance of rank had led to a situation of paramount chiefs whose influence, however, was largely linked to personal attributes. The priesthood and the chiefly class were essentially the same and there was no apparent social division save for nobles/chiefs, commoners, and slaves. Slaves were mainly destined for sacrifice in one of the important ceremonies to the Sun or Moon or to the construction of a chiefly residence. In this latter case, slave children (bought or captured) were placed alive in the corner post holes and killed by stamping the house posts on them. Cannibalism was not present among the Muisca; but they were in contact with peoples who practiced it, such as the gold miners of Buriticá in northern Antioquia, among whom slaves were killed for food and for their fat – used for illumination – when they got too old or infirm to be miners. The Muisca were active traders, industrious farmers, craftsmen, and warriors. Expansionist tendencies among the paramount chiefs and their rivals seem to have been related to the need for more land to support growing populations, and to a desire to control resource areas and trade routes. It is possible that the Zipa, who was currently the most successful of the paramount chiefs, might have succeeded in bringing the Muisca territory under a single government, but the Spanish intervened, and, at the time of the foreign invasions, Muisca culture and politics were still very similar to those of other cultures in the northern Andes.

Large chiefdoms were not restricted to the Andean region. Both archaeological investigations along the Amazon and a number of historical sources indicate that this region too had developed dense populations and hereditary rulers. Of these groups one of the best known is the Tupinamba, who occupied the coast from the Amazon to the southern part of the state of São Paulo as well as parts of the sertao. Related peoples were found along the interior river systems where Tupian-speaking groups had been moving

17.14 Figure of a warrior (?) broken from the top of a Muisca vessel, Sabana de Bogotá. The patterned headband and elaborate bib-like necklace refer to actual articles of adornment; similar headbands have been found on Muisca mummies and the bib necklace was common throughout Colombia. The figure carries two trophy heads with fancy headdresses and necklace-like decorations. The size of the heads suggests that the art of shrinking heads, which survived until this century among the Ecuadorian Shuar (Jibaro), originally was known far to the north.

in for some centuries, practicing gallery forest agriculture and making distinctive corrugated and painted pottery. Although the Tupi-Guaraní expansion can be more or less documented archaeologically (to the extent that one can assume any connection between ceramic style and linguistic affiliation), conditions of preservation in eastern South America, combined with the fact that the majority of the material culture of these peoples was in organic materials such as wood and feathers, have meant a very vague picture of these cultures. However we have a number of detailed descriptions of the Tupinamba, especially the memoirs of a German mercenary, Hans Staden, who was captured by them and who lived among them for several years in the 1550s. Staden was in Brazil before the full effects of European pressure were felt; the Tupinamba were still practicing a traditional way of life which had not been interrupted by European warfare and slaving. Also, the Tupinamba were the only reasonably well-described group of South Americans known to the sixteenth century Europeans in Europe; thus their influence on ideas concerning what South Americans were really like – erroneous or not – was considerable. Various Tupinamba were taken to Europe, including some fifty who participated in a great recreation of Tupinamba life (aided by many local folks) in Rouen in 1550, to fête the visiting king.

The Tupinamba proper lived on the coast between the Paranaiba and Pará rivers. They were organized in 100–150 independent villages, all of which, although culturally and linguistically closely related, were constantly at war with one another. Because of this villages were palisaded. They consisted of four to eight rectangular, thatched houses, each one the residence of a patrilineage of up to thirty families. Inside the houses each nuclear family has its own compartment, including its own fireplace. The houses were arranged around a large rectangular plaza. The villages, which were moved every five years or so, tended also to be located on low rises to catch the breeze.

Villages had house heads, the heads of the lineages which occupied them. Among social customs were found bride service, which involved living with and working for the bride's family for two or three years, a task perhaps made less onerous by the fact that cross-cousin marriage and mother's brother–sister's daughter marriage were the preferred forms of union. The Tupinamba also placed a high value on good manners and, like many other Brazilian tribes, practiced the wailing greeting for visitors. Puberty rituals were well developed as was the couvade. We are told that death was greatly feared and that often the dying person was prepared for burial before he had drawn his last breath. The body was wrapped in a hammock and squeezed into a large beer jar, the typical "urn burial" of the Amazon peoples. Food offerings were placed with the corpse and the urn closed with a bowl on top. The head of a lineage was buried in the house; other people within the village. Often a small hut was erected over the grave and a fire lit nearby to ward off evil spirits. According to Staden, some direct interment was also practiced. The Tupinamba had both male and female shamans who cured by cleansing the sick person with tobacco smoke and by sucking out the illness. Beer, tobacco, and probably datura and other hallucinogens were used by shamans and by others on specific occasions. Beer was also drunk in quantity at feasts and various ceremonials (Figure 17.15).

The Tupinamba were tropical forest farmers who grew bitter manioc, sweet

17.15 Tupinamba women making manioc beer, from Hans Staden's sixteenth-century
memoir of his captivity among the Tupinamba. According to Staden, the women
would gather the manioc, peel and boil it until it was soft, and when it was cooled
off a little, young girls would chew the cooked manioc. The chewed paste was
then mixed with water and put in special jars, covered, and left to ferment. This
manner of making fermented beverages is still practiced in the Amazon.

potatoes, *Xanthosoma* (a rhizome known to West Africans and people of the West Indies
as dasheen or coco yam), and similar crops. They also grew cotton, gourds, and tobacco
and may have had other drug plants as well. Protein was provided from fishing with nets
and drives, and with poison and by hunting, as the only domestic animals the
Tupinamba possessed were the dog and the duck. Water craft were quite developed:
rafts, bark canoes, and dugout canoes were used.

Like most South American agriculturalists, the Tupinamba made pottery, much of
which was admired by the European interlopers. Cooking vessels were unpainted and
decorated with corrugation. Other vessels were painted in red, black, and white and
many were rubbed with resin when warm, to give them a shiny finish. Gourds,

17.16 Two Tupinamba men: one with a bow and arrows, the other with a decorated wooden spear. The drawings show clearly the elaborate feather ornaments and the body painting which form the majority of costume for many tropical forest peoples. The right-hand figure also wears a large labret in his lower lip.

however, provided the main eating and drinking vessels; ceramics were serving vessels or for cooking and brewing.

Staden's drawings of the Tupinamba are extremely important in what they show us of clothing and ornaments. The Tupinamba commonly went naked, although young men wore a penis string and old men a sheath of leaves around the genitals (Figure 17.16). Tattooing and body painting were universal and there were specialists in body decoration. Ornaments were common: shell and seed necklaces and stone labrets were commonly worn as were elaborate feather headdresses and ornaments, especially for ceremonial occasions.

It is, however, one aspect of Tupinamba life which has captured the greatest interest

17.17 The classic western icon of cannibalism – from *Playboy* to Bugs Bunny cartoons – is a person in a large pot. The origin of this icon is this picture, where the Tupinamba are cooking parts of their sacrifice in a large pot similar to the ones used to ferment beer. Staden shows himself at the side, praying for the soul of the sacrificed man.

in the west: this is cannibalism (Figure 17.17). Cannibalistic practices were quite sensational to Europeans among whom cannibalism tended to be confined to famine situations or to small, clandestine religious sects (where it was charged, although not proven), so that Europeans wrote about it (Columbus himself noted the practice on Hispaniola). However it is basically because we have Staden's account, plus those of a number of Portuguese and other adventurers, that we know so much about Tupinamba practices in this regard. Although claims of cannibalism among Native American peoples may have been exaggerated in individual cases, largely for personal gain by a specific group of Spaniards as cannibalism was one of the few grounds upon which enslavement of Indians was legally permitted, it is evident that cannibalism was widely practiced and had been part of many cultures for some thousands of years. Evidence of cannibalism has been found at Chavín de Huántar in Peru and at many other Andean sites, although it became less common after the rise of Huari. Although organic preservation is poor and much less excavation has been carried out, there is reliable archaeological and historical evidence of cannibalism in Ecuador and Colombia as well as north through the Central American isthmus and up into Mexico, where cannibalism was practiced by both Mayan and Mexican peoples. Tupinamba cannibalism perhaps has acquired more fame because Hans Staden was in daily expectation of being on the menu and his descriptions of cannibalistic feasts have a certain personal urgency that communicates itself across the centuries and the old-fashioned prose.

Tupinamba cannibalism was highly ritualized. The victims were captured in war and had often been kept as slaves for a long period before being dispatched and consumed. Slaves were treated well; it was said that if a man had not enough food for two, he would feed his slave first, since decency and status demanded that slaves be happy and well fed. Slaves were often married to the daughter or sister of their owner and had children by them, while female slaves became concubines or secondary wives. All, however, slaves and their children alike, were destined to be eaten eventually.

Sacrifice of a slave was carried out in a ritual that lasted several days. The victim was decorated and painted, the long cord with which he would be confined during the sacrifice was plaited, and much dancing and singing was carried out. The slave sang as well, and was expected to denounce his captors and praise those who would avenge his death. The slave was then tied in the plaza, although often permitted to throw stones and fruits at his tormentors, and finally killed with a club by a designated killer. The killer had to retire immediately to a hut and stay quiet, avoiding the rest of the ritual. The victim was singed, dismembered, and cooked, specific parts going to people who had been designated during the early part of the ritual. The only exception to this ritualized killing, which was accompanied by singing and various rituals to prepare the killing weapon, etc., is that the corpses of people killed in battle were roasted right there; the heads and sexual organs were then brought home for display. The heads of sacrificial victims were displayed on the stockade and, later, when warfare had stopped, the Tupinamba would dig up the heads of previous victims and display those.

The reasons for cannibalism are much debated. It has been claimed, with considerable supporting evidence, that cannibalism was perhaps most common among those peoples who had large populations, few domestic animals, and pressure on the hunted protein resources. This does not, however, describe the Tupinamba, who had abundant river and sea resources, as well as domesticated dogs and ducks to eat. The Tupinamba themselves said that they liked human flesh, that it was lovely and fat. Still, cannibalism was highly ritualized and was not at all the same sort of thing as eating hunted meat. The sole exception was that the killer of a jaguar had to observe the same rituals as the killer of a slave.

The accounts of early invaders, missionaries, administrators, and so on, although admittedly incomplete and biased, give us a much enlarged picture of what these native South American societies were like. Even though organic preservation conditions in the central Andes are exceptionally good and we have materials which are seldom to never found in the rest of the continent's archaeological sites, archaeology cannot give us the details of the spread of an empire. We could, perhaps, pick up the rapid growth of the Inca empire, much as by using a combination of Inca history and field archaeology we can pick up the equally rapid spread of the Huari empire some thousand years earlier. But the distribution of sites and artifacts would not give us much indication of the importance of Ecuador or of Chile to the empire, nor would it tell us such things as the existence of acllahuasi or problems with inheritance, or even the existence of sumptuary laws. Armed with information on Inca history, material culture, and religion from the colonial accounts, we can flesh out the archaeology, arriving at a blend of history and archaeology such as is found in parts of the eastern Mediterranean.

When we move out of the central Andes the historical accounts make us even more keenly aware of the limitations of the earlier record. Virtually nothing of the Muisca culture would survive in the chill damp of the Colombian highlands. Their architecture was wood and left no trace save the occasional post mold. No distribution study would tell of the emergence of paramount chiefs and of the problems they had with those who aspired to the same situation; no excavation of Lake Guatavita would reveal the ritual bathing habits of the local chiefs, since although many golden offerings have been recovered from the lake, they don't tell us how they got there.

When we turn to the eastern lowlands the situation is yet more dismal. Archaeologically, the Tupinamba have left only some pottery, some badly decayed burials in urns, and a few post holes here and there on their village sites. Were it not for Staden and a series of other European accounts we probably would not know of their anthropophagous habits and would certainly have none of the ritual surrounding this custom. The facts of archaeological recovery and its extreme limitations are made very evident by the early colonial accounts. Even with ever better means of recovery of economic information and of dating, we cannot but be aware of the small fraction of these impressive human societies we are missing. When the first Spaniards descended the Amazon in 1540–1, they reported dense populations along its length. The great river served as a superhighway for the peoples along it but also facilitated the invaders. In response to the slaving expeditions of the Portuguese, which alone through removal of population, outright murder of many peoples and the introduction of disease, decimated the large Amazonian towns and their populations, the survivors moved up the smaller rivers to escape the Europeans. Very shortly the Amazon proper was totally depopulated, leaving Europeans free in later centuries to make grandiose theories about how the "green hell" could not support any but simple farming societies. Partly this sort of theorizing was based on the paucity of the archaeological record. Even historically known sites have left very little, although recent site-oriented projects utilizing modern subsurface prospection technologies are at last yielding some ideas concerning the sizes of these sites. This work is, incidentally, confirming the first reports of good-sized sites and dense populations along the major waterways. It is also becoming evident that numbers of traditions, although modified by first the Tupi-Guaraní expansion and then the depredations of the early explorers/slavers, continued into the historic period. In the

Evidence
Mitamaes *(handwritten annotation)*

Matto Grosso and basin of the Tocant[...] [...]otably the Urû
Phase of the Urû Tradition and the Jau[...] [...] through to the
seventeenth century. The Urû Phase p[...] [...]y with either a
sand or a cariapé temper. Vessels with a [...] [...]l base are very
similar to vessels used in historic times [...] [...]pindle whorls indicate
the use of cotton and cylinder seals are probably associated with body painting. The
Jaupaci Phase people were tropical gardeners growing manioc as were the contemporary Urû Phase peoples, although their pottery was simpler and undecorated. These
peoples and several other less well-defined archaeological groups correspond to later
historic ethnic and linguistic territories and it is upon the basis of these later accounts
that their life ways can be somewhat fleshed out. The same is true of peoples in south
central Brazil where the Una Phase peoples were still practicing a basically foraging way
of life. Una Phase rock shelters have been dated from *c.* AD 1000–1800. Una Phase
artifacts are very distinctive and consist of large stone artifacts made on big flakes. These
may have served either as wood-working or soil-working implements, as the Una Phase
peoples are known to have been agricultural, growing maize, squash, and peanuts in
gardens which were probably associated with villages in the open. The rock shelters are
clearly seasonal hunting camps. An economic pattern of living in villages and practicing
agriculture for part of the year, but leaving the villages for several months while the
crops were growing and hunting and gathering for a living was seen until this century
among some Brazilian groups, notably the Apinayé (Western Timbira). Hunting was
practiced with both bone and wooden points. The Una Phase people do not seem to
have made pottery, although their coiled and twined baskets have been found in dry
rock shelters along with the flexed, ocher-covered burials. Paintings in the rock shelters
indicate a continuation into the modern period of the thousands of years old tradition of
rock painting. The Una Phase people seem to have been yielding to the Tupi-Guaraní
expansion at the time of the conquest, an expansion that continued well into the historic
period as their messianic religion led them to search for the "land without sin."

Elsewhere in southern South America it is again the early accounts of explorers/
conquerors and their followers that flesh out the meager archaeological remains and
give us a better basis from which to begin to interpret earlier sites. The hunting and
foraging traditions of the pampas region and Patagonia remained much the same as they
had been for many centuries where, especially in Patagonia, the division between inland
hunters and coastal foragers continued. Northwestern Argentina was being drawn into
the Inca empire. A series of fortresses – which have been identified by Vince Lee on the
basis of both historic accounts and site survey – along this southeastern frontier testify
to both the unsettled nature and slowness of the imperialist expansion. Investigation of
sites in the department of Salta, especially Guitián, an Inca tambo, has revealed ceramics
that suggest that mitamaes from the puna and from elsewhere in the region
(Jujuy) were present as part of the Incas' pacification plan. Likewise a number of sites in
the Quebrada de Humahuaca seem to show various mitamakuna ethnic groups living
side by side and testify to the effort the Inca were putting into the expansion of their
power.

An Inca presence is likewise noticeable in Chile where in Atacama the pressures put on local ethnic groups by expansionistic Aymara groups such as the soon to be historic Lupaca, Colla, and others led to the building of a series of fortresses. The highland groups were, in the vacuum left by the final demise of Tiahuanaco, trying to establish colonies in different ecological niches from the altiplano to the sea. The Solor Phase people, dated to *c.* 1000–1470 (the date of the Inca invasion), built the impressive fortress village of Quitor (in front of which the Inca later built Catarpe Tambo) as well as building numbers of other villages of agglutinated houses, such as Solor-4, with its large rectangular clay structures. The tradition of monochrome pottery continued in Atacama, although the later vessels with their thick red slip are not as finely made as earlier ones. Burial was in large urns, which seem to have been recycled beer or water jars. Peoples closer to the altiplano, in the río Salado and río San Pedro subregions and in northern Loa were also building large sites, with chullpas located in the higher parts of the habitation areas. Some of these sites appear to have been walled. These large villages testify to the fairly dense population as well as to strong cultural ties with the highlands as seen both in burials and in their ceramics.

To the south in the region of the "Green North," in the valleys which connected the high puna with the sea, the Diaguita culture flourished. The Classic Diaguita or Diaguita II culture buried their dead in elaborate stone cists which may have had small mounds of earth on top. The burials show considerable variation, from single extended burials under mounds such as those discovered at Punta Sant Ana de Teatino to simple flexed burials, probably those of the ordinary folk. Simple, though elegant, copper ornaments were produced, including some pendants which are remarkably like the axe-monies of the north. Metal was, however, still relatively scarce – in contrast with the rest of the Andean region where a true metal age was being achieved. Ceramics were often very elaborate and include modeled vessels painted with geometric (textile?) designs. More representational patterns show details of hair arrangement and face decoration. When Topa Inca Yupanqui and his armies began to conquer Chile, reaching at least as far as the valley of Aconagua in 1470, the Diaguita began to produce provincial Inca-style ceramics with characteristic Diaguita designs. At this point the Diaguita too pass into history, from which we know details of their society not visible in the archaeological record, including that the encounter between them and the Incas was violent and ended in the imposition of an Inca administration.

It is, however, from history more than from archaeology that we know of the Mapuche (Araucanians). The Mapuche had the dubious honor of being the last (major) indigenous group to be vanquished by the Europeans, holding out until the late nineteenth century when machine guns and barbed wire brought their independence from the now-mestizo government to a close. The Mapuche are also interesting archaeologically because they provide a contrary case to the common interpretation of various Chilean groups as being either inland farmers/pastoralists or coastal fishers/foragers, with material culture held in common being the result of trade between inland and littoral groups.

The Mapuche, during the later prehispanic period, occupied Chile from the sea to the cordillera south of the río Itata in what is today the province of Arauco. Their most important (and longest held) regions were in the central valley south and east of the Cordillera de Nahuelbuta. They also lived around various lakes in the cordilleras. The Mapuche were agricultural, growing corn, potatoes, squashes, and some local domesticated or near-domesticated grasses. Hunting was important as were fishing and collecting, both inland and along the sea and lake shores. Although the Mapuche had llamas and alpacas (although some have claimed that their camelids were a distinct species, the chilweke), these were scarce and seem not to have been used as draft animals but only as gifts in ritual exchanges and as meat for banquets.

Mapuche cemeteries have been much better explored archaeologically than other sites, although Tom Dillehay's ethnoarchaeological studies of Mapuche ceremonial and shamanism have done much to clarify the nature of vacant ceremonial centers throughout the Andes. These cemeteries tend to be large and show a considerable diversity of burial patterns: in canoes, stone cists, or simple earthen graves. There was no urn burial among the Mapuche, in contrast to the very widespread occurrence of this custom among contemporary and even neighboring peoples. Differences in burial type may be temporally related, but more probably have something to do with the specific subgroup. Offerings include abundant pottery, both utilitarian and elaborately decorated jugs, shoe pots, plates and so on, spindle whorls of wood, stone or ceramic, copper needles and pins, and so on. Post-conquest burials also include glass beads, iron tools, iron stirrups, bridles and, not infrequently, the horse itself.

The Inca expansion had not had any effect on the Mapuche, but the Spanish one did. The Spanish began their conquest in 1550, and their rapid development of mines and encomiendas made the Mapuche restless under what amounted to slavery. This restlessness formed the basis for an unprecedented resistance of the Spanish. Robert Padden's documentation of the first 200 years of this resistance details the development of an effective spy system, of military training, and of psychological warfare against the Spanish, including adopting cannibalism when they discovered the horror with which the Spanish regarded this practice. But maintaining a state of guerrilla warfare at all times cost the Mapuche tremendously in terms of having to refashion many of their cultural values and much of their way of life. They may have been the most successful, in terms of length of resistance, but, like the other native South Americans, eventually they lost everything: language, religion, civil and human rights, to the Europeans who set out to get rich and to remodel the continent to this end.

CHAPTER 18

INTERCONTINENTAL MOVEMENTS
BEFORE COLUMBUS

The question of the influence or lack of influence by Old World cultures upon those of the American continents has been hotly debated since the discovery of America by the Europeans. Interestingly enough, this problem did not emerge among those most closely connected with the precolumbian cultures; most of the conquistadors and those who followed them assumed that the monuments of antiquity they saw had been put up by the ancestors of the local natives (when they thought about such things at all; most European interest in native cultures was strictly monetary). Diffusionist theories concerning native Americans really came to the fore in the latter eighteenth and in the nineteenth centuries as part of stage theory and cultural evolutionism, socio-historical theories used to bolster ideas of the inferiority of peoples whose lands were being seized for colonies. These theories remain popular to the present, especially in non-technical literature, although they periodically reemerge among archaeologists and art historians as well. The basic premise of theories of transcontinental contact and diffusion is simple and racist: native Americans were incapable of developing even simple technologies or art forms and so must have had help from culturally more "advanced" peoples; these latter are usually defined as having been Europeans or Asians. The possibility of diffusion in the other direction has generally not been considered either reasonable or possible (except for Alice Kehoe's masterly presentation of the Aztec origin of the Sacred Heart cult's popularity and iconography).

Transoceanic diffusion models take as a given the superiority of Old World cultures, although in many cases this is far from being established. The European conquest of the Americas was effected mainly by disease, coupled with some military astuteness, political manipulation, and chicanery, not by any real "superiority." Even the possession of firearms was not as important in the conquest as many have assumed. European firearms in the sixteenth century were unreliable and mainly for shock effect. Horses and mastiffs, the latter trained on captives to kill Indians, were the real advantages the Spanish had in South America. Superiority in other technological realms, in social organization, or in religion has never been proven. And in the one documented, by both historical documents and archaeology, case that we do have, which is that of the Vikings, it is very evident that the technological and social *inferiority* of the Europeans were important factors in the failure of the Norsemen to colonize North America.

A major problem of the transoceanic contact scenarios is that the supporting evidence tends to be simplistic, vague, and/or conveniently displaced. A list by John H. Rowe of features held in common by Andean and ancient European societies includes some sixty items including divinatory practices, boat bridges, metal finger rings, false heads on mummies, the use of animal dung for manure, and so on. None of these items can be shown to have been imported from, say, Rome or Egypt to the Andes; most can be shown in both the Old and the New Worlds to have long, local, developmental histories and to be embedded in a web of local beliefs and practices. More direct evidences of a postulated contact are often not available for intensive, non-partisan scrutiny, somewhat like the famed "lost" photographs of a modern African dinosaur. For example, a favorite piece of "evidence" is what has been said to be a tablet with a Phoenician inscription, discovered at the mouth of the Amazon in the nineteenth century. Claims abound that the inscription contains details of the Phoenician language unknown to students of that culture in the 1800s. Unfortunately, the tablet itself cannot be produced; it disappeared at some unknown time and only a poor copy is available to scholars.

Statements such as those that depictions of humans with large noses or with facial hair must be pictures of Israelites or northern Europeans, that red colored pottery is proof of Roman colonization, that spiral designs are Chinese in inspiration, that architectural columns must have come from either Greece or India, that realistic depictions of water lilies show an Indian presence, etc. are likewise weak. Stated baldly many of these supposed evidences of contact reveal their intrinsic silliness. Less evidently silly, and so more widely accepted, are such theories as one concerning the introduction of pottery from Japan to Ecuador via drifting fishermen. Although this theory has been rather soundly trounced in scientific circles, owing to the simplicity of the supposedly shared traits, the fact that Pacific Ocean currents would not bring drifting fishermen to rest in Ecuador, and to the utter unlikelihood of some fishermen (who also conveniently were potters) surviving a many months' long transpacific voyage without any preparation or adequate sea craft, the Japanese hypothesis has not been relegated to the obscurity it so richly deserves and continues to be brought up in popular publications. Further research in coastal Ecuador has shown that there were ceramics in that region prior to the ones supposedly brought by the Jomon fishermen to Valdivia and that some of these ceramics were predecessors of the ones claimed to have been Japanese inspired. Thus, all theory aside, one has to deal with the introduction of something to an area in which the identical something was already known.

Most claims of foreign contact rest upon similar bases, but they gain wide acceptance, especially if published first in some supposedly reputable place or by someone who claims to be an archaeologist. This ease of acceptance is largely because such ideas reinforce Euro-Afro-Asian ideas of cultural superiority. This is not to deny that there may have been shipwrecked sailors, drifting fishermen, or other human flotsam washed up on American shores from time to time in the past. There undoubtedly were. The question is: what sort of influence did they have upon native cultural development? But, alas for long-distance diffusion theorists, to date no one has found any evidence whatsoever of significant cultural contact, that is to say evidence of the introduction of technological, social, political, or religious ideas, actual artifacts, or plants and animals from the Old World to the Americas between *c.* 10,000 BC and AD 1492. When in 1929 the famous Americanist scholar Erland Nordenskiold wrote on the "American Indian as Inventor" he carefully delineated those items of economic or cultural practice which could definitely, even taking a diffusionist stance, be shown to have been independently invented in the Americas. Unfortunately, Nordenskiold has been much ignored, especially in popular presentations, which consider that if there exist similar artifacts or practices in two different places, however isolated geographically or temporally they may be, why then such artifacts or practices *must* have originated in Eurasia or Africa and spread to the Americas. Even the most cursory look at reality dispels such fantasies.

Leaving aside problems of sea currents and traveling fishermen and looking at core elements in native life, well, New World domestic animals can be shown to have been all of native origin. The supposed spread of the chicken in precolumbian times was postulated on incomplete and poorly understood evidence. Numbers of plants and animals spread throughout native cultures with no help from the Whites. Among these were bananas, coconuts, onions, chickens, pigs, and horses. Similarly native American plants spread throughout the world with little help from the conquerors. The influence of New World horticulture on Eurasia has been tremendous, and tremendously undervalued by European and Euroamerican historians. This is probably because the greatest number of native American cultigens are tropical plants and we have typically undervalued tropical agricultural systems and the cultures which used them. Sweet potatoes, for example, became a staple in much of China within a very few years of their first appearance in a Chinese port in the mid-1500s. This spread was due not to any official policy, but rather to the widespread adoption of them by local farmers looking for an acceptable tasting, highly productive plant. Similarly it is impossible to imagine Indian and Southeast Asian cuisines before capsicum peppers and tomatoes (or Italian, North American, British, or African cuisines, for that matter). Manioc, sweet potatoes, and yams are staple tropical crops around the world; chocolate, peanuts, and tobacco (along with pineapples) are among the most important cash crops of many tropical countries. Yet all of these crops can be shown to have been introduced to non-American countries in the terminal fifteenth century or later. None is a precolumbian traveler. Since one would expect a situation of significant contact to result in influences both ways the lack of any evidence of precolumbian exchange anywhere is telling.

Intercontinental diffusion and migration is another matter entirely. It has always seemed reasonable that there should have been some contact between North and South America, linked as they are by a wide, inhabited subcontinent. There is also no reason to doubt that the waves of humans who, in the very terminal Ice Ages, populated the South American continent moved from north to south. Economic adaptations and technologies of the earliest cultures are quite similar throughout the Americas, although cultural diversification in response to new habitats and a changing resource base soon wiped out these similarities.

One problem in discussing possible trade or diffusion between South and Central America (including Mexico) is the problem of definition of where one ends and the other begins. The hypothesis of an "Intermediate Area" encompassing Ecuador, Colombia, and Central America north to mid-Honduras and El Salvador states quite simply that the cultures within this region were more similar to each other than to the areas of more complex civilizations to the north and south. This concept is a useful one for some purposes, since there are considerable similarities, especially on the level of what the cultures of these areas did not have (monumental permanent architecture, multi-tier political-social units, state religions used to unify conquered peoples, "great" art styles, etc.), but it ignores the fact that frontiers, by their very nature, fluctuate. The frontier between the regions of Mexican/Mayan cultures and the simpler Central American groups can be shown to have moved erratically between southeastern Guatemala and central Nicaragua. Ecuador, which is where one would expect to find the southern frontier between the central Andean cultures and those of the Intermediate Area, is only now beginning to be seriously studied archaeologically and Colombia is similarly poorly known. Archaeological field work in Costa Rica indicates that for parts of the prehispanic past that country might as well be considered culturally part of Colombia. The lack of concrete information on the Intermediate Area is unfortunate since it dichotomizes thoughts about cultural contact, so that people consider only the central Andes and central Mexico/Guatemala, and because the Central American isthmus is the region through which any diffusing ideas not spread by direct sea routes would have had to pass.

A methodological error in the consideration of meaningful contact between the developed civilizations of Mexico/Guatemala and the central Andes is the emphasis on looking at isolated elements, usually artistic or technological ones, rather than at these elements in their cultural context. History and ethnology tell us that cultural influence is seldom manifested in a single item or motif, but rather that groups of traits, artifacts, practices, etc. tend to travel together. The Chinese influence on Europe (especially in the seventeenth and eighteenth centuries) is one example. Manifestations which would have been unhesitatingly identified by Europeans as Chinese (whether they actually were or not; "Chinese" tended to mean simply "eastern exotic" to a people with a very sketchy idea of geography and cultural differences) can be seen in ceramics and ceramic technology, in textiles (both basic fabrics and decoration), interior decoration, furniture, decorative techniques and motifs as well as in landscape architecture and, perhaps, epidemiology. On a more modest scale is the traveling trio of Christianity, monogamy, and trousers, an inseparable, but not logically associated, set which has made its way around the world. Bearing this in mind, isolated motifs or artifacts which bear a close resemblance to similar motifs or artifacts in the other region are probably best explained away on the basis of copying a foreign oddity, but an oddity which, unlike Chinese artifacts to Europe, was not reinforced with a flood of other oddities from the same general place – whether this be "China," "Mexico," or "Peru." Thus the appearance of a central Andean figure, the Moon Animal, in Colombian San Agustín sculpture is very likely due to some artifact, probably a textile, making its way hand to hand to the north where a sculptor or his patron saw it and incorporated it into the local sculptural style for two monuments. The oft-cited Mixteca-Puebla Polychrome vase (from southern Mexico), with a double-headed snake design typical of South American textiles from Chile to Colombia, may well be due to the same situation, as may a claimed

Peruvian motif painted on the bottom of a West Mexican bowl. People travel, souvenirs are acquired, and exotic goods are often considered appropriate presents and even models for a brief time. Elements such as these, occurring in isolation with no further evidence of contact, may most parsimoniously be explained in this manner.

There are, however, situations which are more complex. One of these is the origin and diffusion of domesticated plants and animals and the influence of each so-called nuclear area on the basic economic system of the other. In this context maize has been most often cited as evidence of spread of a domesticated plant (from Mexico to South America) as it has seemed unlikely to many that such a peculiar, human modified plant, could have been developed twice. Current evidence, however, could support a multiple centers of domestication hypothesis for maize and, as mentioned previously, the purposive spread of a plant which was not viable in the wild through thousands of kilometers of peoples who did not practice agriculture or over the sea by people for whom we have no evidence of sea-going craft is not logical. On the basis of what we know about *modern* occurrences of wild species there are other plants which may well have been spread from the south to the north, although most likely overland through Central America and not by any direct contact between South American and Central American cultures. Manioc, a native of the southern tropics (probably Amazonia), was an important part of prehispanic agricultural systems in both Mexico/Guatemala and western South America from the earliest Formative. The sweet potato (*Ipomoea batatas*) and the yam (*Dioscorea* spp.) seem to have moved north and south by at least 2000 BC from a center hypothesized to have been in Panama or northern Colombia. These were significant parts of the agricultural systems of many of the earliest farming peoples and remain as such, although their importance is not often acknowledged by grain plant centered Euro-American agronomists. The pineapple (*Ananas comosus*) was a late arrival in Mexico and likewise must have (eventually) come from Colombia or Brazil, but there is no special reason to see its appearance in late prehispanic contexts in Mexico as being due to direct trade with either of these areas, especially since we know so little about the contemporary cultures in the intervening area. One might note also that the cultigens which traveled were all tropical ones, adapted to conditions met in the environments in between their point of origin and where they eventually ended up. All also traveled after the development of complex local agricultural systems.

The question of contact and diffusion is made infinitely more complex by widespread Spanish slaving in Central America in the early colonial period and by the lack of scientific investigation of contact period sites. The pineapple in Mexico may well be an early, unrecorded, Spanish introduction. The duck certainly was, but had completely integrated itself into local economies in the Maya area by the time of Diego de Landa (who wrote his account of the Maya between 1562 and 1573). The introduction of the guinea pig as far north as El Salvador, where it is still called by its Quechua name *cui*, was probably also a result of this mixture of populations as the Spanish tried to keep work forces up in the face of demographic disasters in the Andes and Mexico. There must be other introductions, on both continents, that we are as yet unaware of.

Other theories of contact, usually in the form of a postulated direct contact by sea

18.1 An Ecuadorian balsa raft in the mid-1500s. This raft was illustrated by Giralomo Benzoni, who has also left us our best early description of one of these trading rafts. This illustration has been reinterpreted many times through the centuries, but is the basis for most later illustrations. In the background are fishermen on smaller rafts.

rather than indirect spreading of a trait or technology from group to group, rest upon supposed identities of form, material, or technology employed in the two separate regions, combined with speculation based upon historical descriptions of sea-going craft at the time of the conquest. These have been discussed previously, but it is worth mentioning that in the sixteenth century both the Maya and the people of the southern coast of Ecuador (and northernmost Peru) possessed craft capable of long coastal voyages. On his fifth voyage Columbus met, and robbed, a large sea-going trader's canoe and described its contents and its presumed destination. The Guayaquil rafts with their cotton sails were apparently capable of traveling coast-wise for considerable distances before waterlogging (Figures 18.1 and 18.2). However, we have little information concerning the time depth of these craft and very little evidence that local peoples were really interested in long voyages of what can only be termed exploration. Coastal sailing is possible up and down the South/Central American land mass and some seems to have been done in very late precolumbian times, although we do not know the

18.2 A modern balsa raft belonging to a fisherman from Río Chico, Ecuador, identical to those shown in the background of Figure 18.1. This one-man raft is used for fishing, the nets, etc. being put in the little box. The fisherman has a number of rafts, as they have to dry out between uses.

extent of individual voyages. Early sightings of sea-going rafts are all from southern Colombia to far northern Peru. Canoe travel from Mesoamerica to South America seems to have been restricted to the eastern side of the Central American isthmus, probably because of the long stretches of unprotected coastline and the unpredictable, but tremendous, storms that hit parts of the western coastline. There may have been a colony of Nahua (Aztec-related) traders resident in eastern Panama in the sixteenth century, a reflection of the late cultures' magnified interest in foreign trade and the expansionist tendencies of some of the Mesoamerican polities (most notably the Aztec), but there is no actual evidence of any Mesoamerican peoples actually reaching even Colombia.

The Guayaquil rafts might have been capable of deep-sea travel but, although it is quite simple to sail north to Central America or even farther on the ocean currents, to return home one must sail southwest to the Galapagos. Only then is it possible to move eastwards to the continental coast. The Spanish early discovered this route, but there is no evidence of any aboriginal use or occupation of the Galapagos Islands. Also, we know little to nothing about ancient navigation methods. It would appear that navigation was by land fall, just as it was in pre-instrument navigation Europe. It does not appear that the ancient Ecuadorians had a tradition of deep-sea navigation, since the farthest from land that precolumbian materials have been found is La Plata Island, some 20 km off shore. La Plata is visible from the shore in good weather.

Another problem in looking at current ideas about intercontinental travel and trade is that the materials involved in these postulated long sea voyages are rather strange. An often-cited case is that of the appearance of iridescent painting on pottery of the Ocós style in southeastern Guatemala. This is a fairly complex procedure and the alleged appearance of it on both Chorrera ceramics from Ecuador (*c*. 1000–200 BC) and Ocós, Guatemala (1200 BC?) has been considered significant. The mechanisms by which a very complex Ecuadorian ceramic tradition would have been spread have not been considered. There are no other signs of a foreign presence either at Ocós or at related sites. This area is now quite well known archaeologically and no foreign presence has been detected elsewhere, even in nearby and contemporary sites. The important question of why there should have been direct contact resulting in the transfer of only one trait, a somewhat strange and complex slipping technique, between some Ecuadorian Chorrera-related cultures and several insignificant Guatemalan fishing villages (the major centers of this culture were inland) has never been answered.

A somewhat similar problem exists for the claimed connection between west Mexican metallurgy and that of the coast of Peru. Shortly after *c*. AD 600 a curious metallurgical tradition, featuring tin, tin bronze, lead, gold, and silver made into tools as well as into ornaments, appeared in western Mexico (mainly in the states of Nayarit and Colima). This metallurgical tradition has been said to represent a direct introduction from coastal South America. The only problem is that coastal South American metallurgical traditions at this time did not feature tin, tin bronze, or lead, and were not concerned with making tools. In later contexts, however, both southern Ecuador and western Mexico seem to have had axe-monies, a peculiar enough trait that would make it definitely worth the effort of actually excavating some of the few known late prehispanic port sites along the way (Figure 16.8). The real problem is that as yet there is no evidence from those coastal sites which have been investigated (and there is an ever growing number of them) of any Ecuadorian or other South American presence, although this would be expected in a situation of enough contact that a complex technology could be transferred.

The problem of spondylus trade between Ecuador and Mesoamerica is another one of these very interesting situations. Several people, especially Jorge Marcos, have postulated that spondylus shell was traded from southern Mexico to the Ecuadorians around the Gulf of Guayaquil, largely on the basis that in early contact times there were balsa rafts sailing from Guayaquil north to Esmeraldas. Esmeraldas is not anywhere near Mexico, of course. The Mesoamericans were interested in spondylus, which they used for offerings and as raw material for colored shell ornaments from the late first millennium BC onwards. Spondylus occurs naturally in the warm waters off western Mexico north to the Sea of Cortez. The thesis is essentially that, with the growing desire for spondylus by the Peruvians, spondylus beds were depleted and the Ecuadorians were forced to get on their rafts and sail into the unknown on the off chance that there might be some more trade goods somewhere else. However, because of the total lack of evidence of contact (in terms of Ecuadorian artifacts present in Central American or Mexican sites or vice versa) and given the fact that the extent and productivity of the

Ecuadorian spondylus fisheries are utterly unknown, the supposed "thorny oyster cartel" sailing north and south seems a bit premature.

Another trait which has been touted as proving direct contact between Mexico and South America is the shaft tomb: a method of disposal of the dead in which the corpse and offerings are deposited in a subterranean structure consisting of a vertical shaft with a lateral chamber of some sort (the same term is also applied to simple shafts with the burial at the bottom in the western manner). Shaft tombs occur in west Mexico in the last centuries before Christ, in Colombia *c.* AD 500–1500, in Ecuador *c.* AD 500/700–1500 and in northern Peru *c.* AD 200–300 (and probably before and after). There may also be one or two in Inca Cuzco, *c.* AD 1500. The existence of vaguely similar tombs (all vary greatly in details of shaft and chamber or chambers, in contents, and in placement *vís-à-vís* one another – that is to say, in cemeteries, under house floors in occupied villages, in temple complexes, or in some other place) has frequently been claimed to be evidence of a shaft tomb complex or cult, a cult which was spread from place to place by direct contact. The direction of derivation varies with the theorist. This sort of contact again seems to be mainly in the (muddled) eye of the synthesizer. On the face of it there is no such thing as a "shaft tomb cult," and the claimed congruity of such features bears as little relation to reality as the claimed diffusion of architectural columns from India to South America (or Mexico) because such a complex item could really only have been invented once, according to diffusionist thought.

When one looks for tactile evidence of South American/Mesoamerican contact, there is very little. The gold pieces found in the Sacred Cenote of Chichén Itzá (Mexico, state of Yucatán) were probably imported from Costa Rica, or maybe ultimately from the Sinú region of Colombia. Ceramic forms such as shoe pots and stirrup vessels and ceramic decorative techniques such as organic resist (negative) painting have such a wide and temporally various distribution that it is difficult to escape the conclusion that these were ideas that occurred to everyone once in a while. The early ceramic traditions of South America and Mesoamerica are so unalike as to impress upon one the likelihood of multiple independent inventions and the claimed similarities between decorative motifs later on are similarly unconvincing.

The real problem is not the lack of evidence for multiple inventions or parallel historical/cultural trajectories, but the popularity of diffusionist thought in western art history and archaeology (as well as in popular culture). For example, few seem to be comfortable with the rise of complex civilizations at approximately the same time in Mesoamerica and Peru. Because of this discomfort (based upon an unproven assumption that most things could not have been invented more than once and that coincidence is so unlikely as not to be a possibility) people have turned themselves inside out to prove that the Chavín and Olmec civilizations were somehow connected. Most arguments, aside from their unspoken conviction that there *had* to be significant contact, rest upon the mistaken idea that the major icon in each culture is a jaguar. No one has ever demonstrated that the images in Olmec art are jaguars. They may, perhaps, be felines, but they seldom have pelage markings; moreover there are numerous species of felines in the Americas with spotted pelts. And now there are some revisionist theories that claim that the Olmec "felines" are caymans or toads! The secondary importance of felines in Chavín art *has* been demonstrated. Felines are companions to the deities, not the deities themselves. Moreover there is a considerable body of work which has clearly shown that fangs are a mark of supernatural status; they do not indicate that a figure is necessarily a feline. There is even some reason to believe that the ultimate inspiration for these fangs was with some other species, perhaps one of the monkeys or bats, and hence no felinity whatsoever is implied. Caymans and toads do exist in northern Peruvian art, but careful species delineation has shown them to be local (forest) species not present in Mesoamerica. Other evidence is mainly superficial comparisons of images, especially highly simplified, geometric images, and should be viewed with skepticism. Dotted circles, cross motifs, and meanders are highly unlikely to be proof of trade or diffusion between widely separated cultures. When one looks at the Olmec and at Chavín without believing that they must have been related, simply because they are more or less contemporary, one can see that their settlement patterns, architecture, economy, ceramics, religious practices, and so on were very different. In both cases there is evidence of the appearance of these cultures out of local ones and that they were, in their turn, ancestral to later cultures in the area.

This is not to say that there was not contact between Mesoamerican and South American cultures. There doubtless was. But its nature, whether direct or indirect, whether superficial or meaningful, has yet to be demonstrated. Most arguments for or against contact have been based upon emotion and upon an incomplete understanding of the archaeology of both areas. This, given the lack of information concerning the prehistory of the regions in the way – the northern Andean countries and lower Central America – makes most current statements of contact exceedingly tenuous.

CHAPTER 19

THE FUTURE OF A CONTINENT

By 1492 the cultures found on the South American continent ran the gamut from the humblest of hunting and foraging tribelets with minimal material goods and social institutions to a giant, expanding, conquest state. This in itself was the current representative of several thousands of years of advanced civilizations in the central Andes. Then, as every school child knows, Columbus made his first landfall somewhere in the northeastern Caribbean, moving quickly to the island of Hispaniola (modern Santo Domingo and Haiti). In 1493 Pope Alexander VI, acting under a (European) medieval tradition which gave the Pope dominion over the islands of the sea and the right to cede this dominion to a third party, issued a bull claiming the – as he thought – islands. In 1494 the Treaty of Tordesillas was promulgated, dividing these new found, unknown lands between the Spanish and the Portuguese, who had not, as yet, got that far. The Portuguese reached Brazil in April of 1500, when Pero Alvares Cabral and his thirteen ship expedition were blown off course as they attempted to get to India via the newly discovered Cape of Good Hope. Fortunately Cabral had a literary gentleman with him, one Pero Vaz de Camuha, who wrote a letter (delivered to King Manoel I by a ship they met *en route* to regain their original trajectory). In this Brazil was described as a "land of parrots," inhabited by beautiful naked people of good will. Balboa made it to the Río de la Plata (named variously, according to folklore, after a silver Inca knife he found there or because there was an immense bloom of silver-colored zephyr lilies) in 1513 and it was from the early colony at Buenos Aires that the first plagues to hit western South America came. Although the European invasion and conquest of Mexico preceded major attempts on South America, and greatly influenced the course of the southern invasions, particularly the planning of the conquest of Peru by Pizarro, the impact of the conquest of South America on the rest of the world was immense.

The most immediate and, perhaps, the most widespread effects, were upon western Europe, which felt the full brunt of the new discoveries. The economic effect of the European invasions has been well documented, especially the enormous inflation that the treasures from the first conquests of the two American empires caused. Gold and silver from the pillage of Tenochtitlán, the Aztec capital, and from Inca Cuzco flooded Spain. It is estimated that in Andalucia, for example, prices during the first fifty years after the conquest quintupled. Inflation was relatively less (although always significant) in other parts of Europe, but the development of the huge mines of Potosí and other Colonial-period mining operations had an astronomical effect on the economies of all the European states and the treasure from America is directly implicated in the rise of capitalism.

Economic changes arising from the introduction of American plants and animals were relatively slower (see Appendices A and B). However, plants such as maize and, especially, the cold-temperate-adapted potato eventually became very important in Europe, as did crops such as tomatoes, beans, squashes, the capsicum peppers, and tobacco. Potatoes, in particular, had a tremendous demographic effect on Europe after the natives had, at first unwillingly, taken them up. Moreover, who can imagine the Mediterranean cuisines without tomatoes, courgettes, and chiles? As well have no olive oil! The effects of native American cultigens (and other plants) were much greater in the tropics where crops such as manioc, maize, sweet potatoes, yams, peanuts, and chocolate have become staples of both subsistence and commercial economies. The colonial frame of mind, that the tropical world is inherently inferior, has led to a widespread ignorance of the very real importance of New World cultivars in the modern world. Most people are not, in fact, even aware of how many of our commonest garden and house plants are natives of the Americas and of South America in particular (Appendices C, D, and E). Those few items which are important in Europe are linguistically denied their South American origin: the "Irish" potato, the "Muscovy" duck, "Egyptian" cotton, even "turkey" for that most American of domestic fowl.

South American drug plants were also relatively slow to be taken up in Europe. This was largely because of the opposition of the European medical establishment, with its theories based upon the classical works of Galen, Pliny, and Dioscorides, works in which new remedies had no real place. The only native drug – and an ineffective one at that – to be in widespread use early was guaiac wood; this was because of a medical dictum that where a disease had originated there too the deity had arranged for its cure to be found. Venereal syphilis was an instant import from the New World, rapidly achieving epidemic proportions in the Old. However much the ultimate origin of venereal syphilis has been argued by those who desired another origin, it seems the sixteenth century Europeans had the correct perception: it was an American disease. Syphilitic lesions have been found in precolumbian mummies and skeletons over a wide area of the Americas; it was an old disease in the Americas and, typically, an epidemic one when it hit a susceptible population. Thus the cure had to be from the Americas as well. Tobacco also came into wide use speedily, preceding the arrival of the Europeans into much of Africa and Asia, although probably because tobacco use had come into the European ken from one of the few groups to smoke it as a recreation: the Aztec. In South America tobacco use was largely medicinal, something which could not have failed to impress the newcomers. Tobacco smoke also wards off insects: a major use in the tropics. Malaria, which had been a scourge in much of Europe and which became even more widespread as more and more people ventured into the newly opened up malarial regions of the New World, is effectively treated with the bark of the cinchona (*Cinchona* sp.). However, it was not until 1658, when the wife of a viceroy of Peru had been treated with it and thus made it fashionable, that cinchona was widely prescribed for fevers by European physicians. The search of native pharmacopoeia and the hunt for native plants with medicinal properties is an artifact of a paradigm revolution in medicine and of nineteenth- and twentieth-century botanical and medical research. Currently, of course, there is a polarized attitude to the drugs of South America: the environmental movement is, quite correctly, promulgating the argument that saving tropical environments, especially the rainforests, is essential because of their potential in providing humanity with new pharmaceuticals. On the other hand, tobacco and an extract of the coca plant, cocaine, are just as widely proclaimed as being near-demonic in their harmful effects on both individual and social health and are the focuses of major efforts to stamp out their use. Unfortunately, the attempts to stamp out coca growing have led to increased genocidal and ethnocidal policies against many of the Andean peoples, whether or not they are providing coca for the international narcotics cartels which feed the First World markets.

Perhaps the most important effects of the discovery of the Americas on Europe were ideological. The European viewpoint of the unknown world, that there were wonders, was first upheld. The first accounts of the Indians described them in idyllic terms, terms affected by the widespread ideas of "wild men" in the European folkloric and literary tradition. The wild man lived in the forest, naked, hairy, solitary, with no religion and no society, hunting and gathering wild foods. But the wild man was capable of redemption, that is, he could be taught proper religion and behavior. Since the American Indians were visibly *not* hairy, and even though they were growing strange crops, were definitely agricultural, they didn't exactly fit into the wild man category and different theories of whether they were innocents, pure and untainted by the fall of Adam, or whether they were animal-like brutes, fit only for slavery and/or extermination raged. This latter was settled, at least officially, by Pope Paul III, who on June 9, 1537 issued the bull *Sublimis Deus* in which he proclaimed the Indians true men and worthy of being redeemed. This had little practical effect, either on the secular treatment of the Indians or on their status as religious prey. Missionary activities have been going on since 1502 and continue until the present. Only the sects have changed.

Whatever the individual's viewpoint on the nature of the aboriginal inhabitants of the Americas, one thing was certain: they fit none of the traditional models of what humans were supposed to be like, whether these were the official biblical models or those derived from fabulous travel tales such as those of Prester John. Moreover, the environment that these peoples lived in was very different from those known to the Europeans and contained vast numbers of totally exotic plant and animal species along with its exotic cultural species. Columbus, on his return from his first voyage, described the flora and fauna as being closely related to Old World types; but then he still thought he had found the East Indies. By his second voyage it was evident that he was wrong. Not only was there a whole new world full of plants and animals no one had ever seen before, there were also species which were evidently related, but were not exactly the same, as their Eurasian counterparts. The discovery and conquest of the Americas in general led to wide changes in botany, zoology, and geography (especially once it was evident that it was not just islands, but an entire set of continents in between Europe and Asia) as well as to the development of anthropology and the comparative social sciences. The sciences in Europe, where the Renaissance saw attempts at throwing off the intellectual shackles of medieval theology, were enormously expanded by the discoveries in the Americas. These discoveries both intimated the inadequacy of the biblical paradigm concerning the origin and nature of the universe and provided new data to challenge this paradigm.

The discovery and conquest of the Americas had considerable effects on the world outside of Europe as well. North Africa was part of the European sphere and had been since time immemorial. Here the effects were much the same as on the rest of Mediterranean Europe, especially in terms of the spread of a few culinary and drug plants. Egypt, an important agricultural nation, got a major new cultigen or, better put, a valuable improvement over one which they already had. This was long-staple Peruvian cotton, now called Egyptian cotton, a cotton which spins a strong thread and from which very fine cloth can be woven. The growing desire for cotton in Europe, where it was used largely for domestic cloth and undergarments along with linen, coupled with price-fixing strategies of the Ottoman Empire, made the price of raw cotton very high. This led to a new competitor for the Egyptian (and the Asian) cotton industry: the plantation growing of cotton in the Americas. Cotton plantations only really got going in the eighteenth century and were a later factor in one of the major effects which the discovery of the Americas in general, and of South and Central America in particular, had on subsaharan Africa: the African Diaspora. Although this term has been commonly used for the scattering of the Jews after the Babylonian exile, in the Americas it has come to be applied to the forced immigration as slaves of hundreds upon hundreds of thousands of West African peoples.

The slave trade in Africa was old as time. Africans from the Sudan and perhaps from other areas had been brought into Egypt and the early Eurasian civilizations as slaves, although mainly as house and body servants, not as field workers. This practice continued through Classical antiquity, and representations of black Africans and references to them are not infrequent in art and literature. Islam continued Roman (and Asian) practices, and slaving seems to have increased somewhat, with both East and West African peoples being moved by caravan to the slave markets of North Africa or to where they could be transshipped to the eastern markets. The few African slaves (and freedmen) in fifteenth century Europe probably came from adjacent Islamic countries. The discovery of Hispaniola changed both the volume and the organization of the slave trade. The Europeans had a taste for sugar, and sugar was very, very expensive. So expensive in fact that it was sold by apothecaries, not by grocers. Columbus brought sugar cane to Hispaniola on his second voyage on the order of Ferdinand of Spain. The first sugar mill was in operation by 1509 and within fifty years there were twenty large mills and four or more small ones on Hispaniola alone. In the beginning the workers in the sugar fields and mills were enslaved Indians. However, the native Hispaniolans were extinct within about two decades of Columbus's first visit and Indian slaves captured on other islands or even on the mainland succumbed to the same diseases and ill treatment. So African slaves were brought in increasing numbers to man first the sugar industry and then other industries, such as mining, coffee, and cotton. At the same time American crops were introduced into Africa, many, such as manioc, yams, tomatoes, chiles, and sweet potatoes, becoming subsistence staples while a few, especially peanuts and chocolate, have become key elements in commercial production in much of tropical Africa. The effects of the African Diaspora on both continents, both socially and economically, were immense and are only now beginning to be fully documented.

The conquest of South America had fewer direct effects on east Asia, except as this region too was drawn into the colonial schemes of the Europeans. As in Europe and Africa, tomatoes and chiles became incorporated into local culinary traditions and tobacco spread widely. However, two South American crops became extremely important in China: peanuts and sweet potatoes. Peanuts were so well established by the 1530s that they were considered to be a local product. It seems likely that peanuts came into south China either via the Portuguese or via Chinese traders who had contact with the Portuguese elsewhere. Sweet potatoes may have arrived almost as early; whether overland from India and Burma into Yunnan or again via the Portuguese has not been settled. They were grown quite commonly but came to official notice only in 1594, a year of widespread crop failure. The governor of Fukien issued information concerning the cultivation of sweet potatoes, encouraging people to cultivate this fast-growing and very productive plant to stave off famine.

Maize is known to have arrived in China overland, probably around 1530. Maize, although grown as an interesting plant and used as a tribute payment by western tribesmen, was never as important as the other cultigens, probably because it had well-entrenched competing grains in rice and millet.

As influential as the discovery and conquest of South America was on the economy, history, and various ideologies of the Old World, from the point of view of the native South Americans the European invasions were an unmitigated disaster. Although the first impressions of Columbus, Vespucci, and others were favorable to the Americans, the desire to extract instant wealth, accompanied by popular ideas of the basic bestiality of these unfamiliar peoples and their fulfillment of the prophecies of the Apocalypse, led instantly to their mistreatment on an immense scale. Even the Bull of 1537, which gave the native Americans status as human beings and limited the legal overt enslavement which could be exacted on them, did little to stop the unending tragedy. Where claims of cannibalism did not suffice to enslave a group, debt peonage and tenant farming on lands taken from them, as well as their "debt" to the Church for being Christianized, could enslave a population just as firmly.

Along with the wars and devastation of the European-led armies came an even greater destroyer: disease. The Americans had been cut off from the Eurasian plagues for some 14,000 years. Native populations had no resistance to the diseases of the foreigners; even diseases which were generally not fatal to the invaders were so to the native peoples, peoples who, moreover, were genetically similar enough that it was as if the introduced diseases had hit but a single population. Measles, the common cold, smallpox, pulmonary tuberculosis, typhus, malaria, and a host of other diseases endemic in Eurasian populations came to the Americas all at once and with devastating effect: within a very few decades wherever the Europeans went there was demographic collapse. The diseases of the invaders often preceded them. Western South America was ravaged by measles or smallpox some years before Pizarro made even his first trip to Peru. In many places 80–90% of the population was dead within a few years and the survivors, in shock over the demise of their families and culture in one blow, simply gave up. Cieza de Leon, perhaps the most important chronicler of the invasion of western South America, mentions that in Colombia people would just sit by the side of the road and die, having totally lost the will to live. The loss of population was so great that many Andean countries did not recover demographically until the middle of this century.

Apart from the outright death and destruction of the actual conquests, natives and native cultures became instantly something to be denigrated, demeaned, and destroyed, whether for profit or for the sake of their immortal souls. To this day indigenous Americans are overtly denied contact with their past, the great monuments being ascribed to other, better, people. Their languages are denied validity in legal or educational contexts and they have little access to or hope for equal treatment from any of the dominant European-derived institutions, including the Church and foreign development projects. Debt peonage and serfdom were outlawed in most countries only late in this century and still covertly exist. Slavery is still quite open; Indian children are openly sold as servants both by their impoverished families and by their religious guardians. Licenses to hunt Indians as game were canceled somewhat earlier this century (in Brazil), but Indians remain fair game in practically every sense, whether the hunter is the local landowner, official, missionary, development official, or guerrilla. The annals of Amnesty International and other groups which record and protest violations of human rights are overburdened with reports from South (and Central) America, something which is a reflection of the near-universal contempt in which native peoples are held on that continent.

Aside from the pathetic situation of so many native Americans today there is an ever-increasing danger to their past. Growing populations, along with the development of roads, dams, mining, petroleum exploitation, and housing projects, have destroyed many vestiges of the past and are threatening most. The ignorance of local populations contributes. Petroglyphs are widely thought to mark where gold is buried and the rocks are blown up with dynamite; buildings are knocked apart to see if there is gold hidden in the walls and monuments are used for target practice. Even in educated circles, if it is Indian it is unimportant. Sacred shrines, origin spots, even major monuments are destroyed for the ephemeral gain of a few of the ruling class. Vandalism, carried out by both the educated and the ignorant, is another problem. The Pampa de Nazca geoglyphs are fenced to protect them from dirt bikers; many more sites are being torn apart by people in search of thrills. Religious practitioners devastate sites because of their associations with paganism or "devils." Tourism, including "eco-tourism," is playing its part in the extinction of the past. The Inca trail to Machu Picchu is in a sad state with trash strewn its length and damage from camping and fires caused by trekkers. Other sites, like those around the globe, are being beaten into nothingness by the feet of the touring multitudes, many of whom have no idea of the relationship between the ruins they are carving their initials into and the ragged child trying to sell them some chewing gum. And finally, the ultimate insult: looters. Precolumbian art brings a high price on the illicit art market. Although all South American countries have protective legislation and are signatories to the UNESCO accord (as is the United States, Canada, and a number of other First World countries) there is shamefully little support or compliance from officials in the countries which form the major markets for stolen artifacts. Stolen artifacts are freely advertised and traded in North America, Europe, and Japan and are exhibited openly in galleries and public and private institutions. In those few cases in which Latin American countries, central or south, have managed to pursue complaints through the thicket of the foreign legal systems they have often been defeated through a combination of corruption of the judiciary (whose allegiance after all is to those monied and influential people who support political campaigns and who also often collect precolumbian art) and inexcusable ignorance. In a recent decision in the United States, regarding the looting of the royal tombs of Sipán, which are supposedly protected by a special treaty with Peru, a judge claimed that because the Inca empire had covered a much wider area than the modern country of Peru and because the (very brunette) expert witness the Peruvian government had sent was not competent, despite his twenty plus years as a professional archaeologist in Peru and his having held numerous positions of national responsibility with regards to the archaeological monuments of that country, that no one could prove that the smuggled goods were from Peru. This is, of course, analogous to a situation in which an English judge might claim that no one, especially a (brunette) Egyptian, could correctly identify Old Kingdom Egyptian artifacts, since the Roman Empire had covered a much wider area than Egypt. On a happier note, fakery has got much better over the past several decades. It is the practice of art historians and collectors to claim that the only fakes are hideous and obvious. To some extent they are right; the non-hideous, non-obvious pieces grace the museums and private collections of the world. All major, and many exceedingly minor styles (including some fairly ugly pots supposedly from a culture along Río de La Plata), have been and are even now being enthusiastically faked. Valdivia figurines, Chavín clay and soapstone vessels, Nazca polychrome pots, Tiahuanaco keros, Quimbaya figurines, Sinú gold work, even Paracas and Chancay textiles – in this case using ancient plain cloths as a background and ancient threads from looted tombs for the embroidery – have hit the antiquities market and are gracing major museum collections. One might view this as the ultimate exploitation of the ancient South Americans but, perhaps, like the growing concern about and increasing political power of many native American groups, this may actually save the past for the present and the future, if only by reducing pressure upon known archaeological sites. But this is only one aspect of the modern situation.

As of this writing, the condition of almost all indigenous South Americans is poor and getting poorer. They are cut off from whatever economic progress the modern country they might be in is making and, indeed, cut off from any benefits that an economic or political betterment might bring. They are subject to armed pressure to stop being Indian from both the right and the left, from the Catholic and the Evangelical churches, from USAID and every other possible "aid the natives" program. However, native resistance is growing. In Peru, officially, if not in practice, Quechua has become a legal language. Atrocities even sometimes find their way into First World news. Rock stars espouse the cause of the forest and with it its inhabitants. As a fence in Otavalo, Ecuador, said in 1992 (in Quechua and Spanish) "500 Years of Resistance." Perhaps the next 500 years of contact with Eurasia will prove more favorable to the people who first inhabited this Brave New World.

ECONOMIC PLANTS ORIGINATING IN SOUTH AMERICA

corn, maize (*Zea mays*): some varieties, especially those used for parched corn snacks in the US

beans (*Phaseolus* spp.): "green beans," "string beans," Lima beans, kidney beans, etc. (*Canavalia sp.*) jack beans

summer squashes (*Cucurbita* spp.): zucchini, courgettes, patty pan, crook neck, etc.

tomatoes (*Lycopersicon esculentum*)

capsicum peppers (*C. pubescens, C. chinense*): "cayenne," *ají*, not the Mexican chiles

potatoes (*Solanum tuberosum*): "Irish potato," "Finnish potato"

manioc (*Manihot escuelenta* Kranz): manioc, yuca

peanuts (*Arachis hypogaea*)

pineapples (*Ananas comosus*)

tree tomatoes (*Cyphomandra betacea*): tamarillo, grown commercially for North American and European markets in New Zealand

pepino (*Solanum variegatum*): a small yellow melon-like fruit with purple stripes, likewise beginning to be commercially grown for foreign markets

Brazil nuts: seeds of the Brazilnut tree *Bertholletia excelsa*

cashews: kernels of the fruit "marañon" from the tree *Anacardium occidentale*

black walnut: "tocte," "togte," "nogal," seeds of *Juglans honorei* Dode or *J. neotropica* Diels

quinoa (*Chenopodium quinoa*): a grain now very popular as a health food

long-staple ("Egyptian") cotton (*Gossypium barbadense*)

tobacco (*Nicotiana* spp.): native of the southeastern slopes of the Andes, cultivated throughout the Americas at the time of the European invasions

cocaine: extracted from the leaves of *Erythroxylon coca*, also *E. novogranatense*

quinine: extracted from the bark of several trees of the genus *Cinchona*

ipecac, ipecacuanha: a tincture made from the dried rhizome of a tropical creeping plant *Cephaëlis ipecacuanha*

sarsaparilla: from the dried roots of a number of smilax plants

sweet balsam: from several trees of the genus *Myroxylon*

yerba maté (*Ilex paraguayensis*)

jaborandi (*Pilocarpus*): a source of pilocarpine, widely used in the treatment of glaucoma

strychnine: from various plants of the genus *Strychnos*, both woody trees and vines, used in northern South America for arrow/lance poisons

curare: used in anesthesia, dried extract from the vine *Strychnos toxifera*, used indigenously as an arrow or blow dart poison for hunting birds and small arboreal animals such as monkeys

rotenone (insecticide): from several tropical forest bushes, used indigenously as fish
   poison

rubber: from the milky juice or latex of several tropical trees, *Ficus elastica* being the one
   most commonly cultivated

A large number of indigenous plants are under serious consideration for commercial
adaptation by world development organizations. Examples include naranjilla (*Solanum
quitoense* Lam.), a fruit used as juice or in ice cream, tarwi (*Lupinus mutabilis*), a seed plant,
ulluco (melluco, *Ullucus tuberosus*), a small tuber much like a potato, and mashua
(*Tropaeolum tuberosum*), another tuber plant.

ECONOMIC PLANTS ORIGINATING IN THE NEW WORLD TROPICS

maize (*Zea mays*, "corn," "Indian corn")

yams (*Dioscorea* spp.)

sweet potatoes (*Ipomoea batatas*)

avocadoes (*Persea americana*)

papayas (*Carica papaya*): used both for fruit and for papain, a meat tenderizer and ingredient in medicinal digestives

guavas (*Psidium guajava*)

zapote (sapote, marmalade tree, *Calocarpum zapota*)

chirimoya/annona (*Annona chirimola*)

various cactus fruits ("prickly pear," "tuna," "star fruit," "pitahaya," etc.)

achiote (annatto, *Bixa orellana*)

indigo (*Indigoferia suffruticosa*)

cochineal (actually an insect of the genus *Cochinilla* which lives on the *Opuntia* cactuses native to the American dry tropics and subtropics)

henequen (*Fourcroya* spp.): although the Mexican *Agave americana* is now mainly used for ropes and bags, the Andean Furcraeas were widely used for bast fibers prior to the colonial period and are still grown for this use

calabash (*Crescentia cujete*): a tree which bears a fruit with a durable shell much used for containers of all sorts

SOUTH AMERICAN FLOWERS COMMONLY GROWN AS GARDEN ORNAMENTALS

Browalia (Peru)
Bougainvillea (Brazil)
Poinsettia (tropical America)
Fuschias (West Indies, tropical America)
Zephyr lilies (Argentina, Uruguay)
Plumeria (frangipani)
Oxalis (shamrock)
Orchids (especially the Cattleyas, Masdevallias, Sabralias, Epidendrums, Miltonias, Lycastes, Odontoglossums, and Oncidiums)
Petunias
Nasturtiums
Violas (pansies)
"Jerusalem" cherry
Verbena
Mimulus (*Diplacus*)
Geraniums and pelargoniums
Canna lilies
Pampas grass
Lantana/pink lantana (*Brunsfelsia* spp.)
Heliconias
Anthericum

SOUTH AMERICAN BUSHES AND TREES COMMONLY GROWN AS GARDEN ORNAMENTALS*

Araucaria imbricata ("Monkey Puzzle Tree")

Caesalpina spp. ("Bird-of-Paradise Bush")

Cassia spp. (shower trees)

Datura candida (Angel's Trumpet)

Dodonia (Hopseed Bush)

Escalonia and *Encelia* spp. (evergreen flowering bushes)

Feijoa sellowirana (Pineapple guava), along with several other *Psidiums*, guavas, grown for foliage, not for fruit, outside of the tropics

Jacaranda spp. (Jacaranda tree)

Schinus spp. ("Mexican Pepper Tree" or "Pink Pepper Tree")

Solanum macranthum hort. ("Potato Tree")

Thevelia peruvania (yellow oleander)

Tibouchina ("Princess Bush," "Princess Flower")

*Many of these are commonly grown in warm and/or arid regions such as California and the North American Southwest.

SOUTH AMERICAN PLANTS COMMONLY GROWN AS HOUSEPLANTS

Philodendron
Dieffenbachia
Tradescantia ("Wandering Jew," "Chain Plant")
Calathea zebrina ("Zebrina," "Red Wandering Jew")
Begonia
Gloxinia
Fittonia spp. ("Marble Plant")
Iresine spp. ("Beefsteak Plant," "Blood Leaf Plant," "Chicken Gizzard Plant")
Maranta ("Prayer Plant")
some of the Ficuses
Kohleria spp. ("Tree Gloxinia")
Beloperone guttata, *B. tomentosa* ("Shrimp Plant")
many ferns, both indoor and outdoor varieties
Tillandsia ("air grass")

MISCELLANEOUS CONTRIBUTIONS OF SOUTH AMERICA TO THE WORLD

barbeque (actually from the Caribbean islands, which is where the Spanish first encountered this kind of grilled meat)

hammocks

jerky (dried meat, from the Quechua charqui)

freeze drying (invented by ancient dwellers in the Andean highlands who preserved potatoes and other tubers as chuño)

M. C. Escher's art (inspired by Late Intermediate Period Peruvian textiles)

some New Age religion "power spots": Machu Picchu, Sacsahuamán (for Inti Raymi, the solstice celebration), the Galapagos Islands, the Nazca desert lines, Tiahuanaco (more a focus of fantasies than a pilgrimage spot)

some shamanistic ideas widely dispersed in the New Age press, mainly via Eduardo "Chino" Calderón, the famous Peruvian folk curer and world traveler on the New Age shaman instruction circuit, and Dr. Michael Harner, whose work on Jibaro shamanism has excited New Agers and scholars alike

llamas for backpacking (a North American fad)

alpaca and vicuña wool for luxury fabrics

summer ski resorts (Chile)

and, of course, a great many hallucinogenic drugs, without which the 1960s would have been far less interesting

GLOSSARY OF TECHNICAL AND SPECIALIST TERMS USED IN SOUTH AMERICAN ARCHAEOLOGY

Absolute Chronology: A chronology expressed in calendar years, generally using the Gregorian calendar.

Acllahuasi: The houses in which the Inca "chosen women" lived. These women, who were removed from childbearing and other female domestic tasks, wove cloth and prepared beer for the state.

Achira (*Canna edulis*): A species of canna lily grown for its bulb, which is boiled and eaten.

Adobe: Bricks made of a mixture of mud and straw and sun dried. A cheap, sturdy building material, adobe buildings will last for centuries if they have a foundation (usually stone) which prevents damp from entering the wall from below and a roof which protects them from damp from above. Adobe continues to be a major material of domestic construction in much of South America. In prehispanic times adobe bricks were of different shapes and there is a rough correlation of shape with time (in Peru). Thus conical adobes are typical of the Early Horizon, while later periods saw globular, lump-shaped, tooth-shaped, and rectangular adobes in use.

Adorno: Small modeled decoration on pottery. Adornos are usually made separately and then attached to the vessel with slip before firing.

Agglutinated houses: Settlements formed by houses (and other-purpose structures) which shared common walls. The pueblos of the North American Southwest are a contemporary example of a building style which was once widely found throughout the Americas.

Agouti (*Dasyprocta* spp.): A small rodent native to lowland South and Central America. Both the agouti and the related paca were (and are) valued for their meat.

Ají: *Capsicum pubescens* and *C. chinense*, the South American species of "chile" peppers. Cayenne and Scotch Bonnet peppers are perhaps the best known ajíes to northerners, along with the chile habanero of Yucatán.

Alcarraza: Literally a water jar; in Colombian archaeology a bottle with two spouts joined by a bridge.

Alter ego: The "Other I," a concept widely established among Native American peoples, was the idea that people possessed multiple souls. One of these souls was usually animal. Among shamans and other religious practitioners this animal soul was very important and took on the role of another personality, especially when called up ritually. Alter egos are often shown in representational art as an animal peering over the head of the main (human) figure.

Altiplano: The high (4000–4500 m above sea level) basin which contains Lake Titicaca. This region, although it appears rather desolate and airless to outsiders, was always densely occupied and was one of the main centers of plant and animal domestication in South America. Several major civilizations, among them those of Pucara and Tiahuanaco, also originated in the altiplano.

Angel: Winged figure with human, animal, or bird head. Such figures are associated with the major deities of Chavín, Tiahuanaco, and Huari.

Apu (also wamani): Spirits of the mountains who are very powerful and control fertility of plants and animals, weather, landslides, earthquakes, etc.

Avunculocal: When a newly married couple make their primary residence with either the mother's brother or the father's brother.

Axe-money: Small lightweight bronze artifacts which are found buried in tombs in lots of various, but regular, sizes. They appear to have been manufactured in northern Peru, beginning in the Late Intermediate Period, and were traded to Ecuador, perhaps as a special sort of ingot, for spondylus. Axe-monies are also found in northwestern Argentina and a related form was in use in late prehispanic Mexico.

Ayahuasca (yaagi, yaje, *Banisteriopsis* spp.): A large tropical forest vine whose stems and leaves are boiled to make a highly hallucinogenic liquid. Ayahuasca use is widely spread in tropical forest regions, where the vine is cultivated as well as collected.

Ayllu: An Andean kin group, usually (today) based upon loose patrilineal principles. Ayllus were the principal land and other real property holding bodies and still function that way in traditional Indian communities.

Backstrap loom: A common type of loom in native America. One end bar is attached to a tree, beam, post, etc. while the other is held in place by a belt around the weaver's hips. The movement of the weaver back and forth provides the necessary changes in tension of the warp threads while weaving.

Balsa: A wood log raft, often made of the extremely lightweight wood of *Ochroma piscatoria*, a tree which is indigenous to the humid forests of coastal Ecuador and northern Peru. These rafts, apparently first developed for river transportation, by late prehistory were very large and were used for coastal trading.

Bast: Strong, woody fibers from a number of different plants, including members of the genus *Fourcroya* and the genus *Agave*. These were widely used for cordage, baskets, and textiles throughout South America and remain important sources of fibers for ropes, saddlebags, and similar utilitarian objects.

Bataan and chunga: See rocker mill

Bolas: A weapon formed of two or three weights connected by cords or thongs. The weights are generally made of rounded stones and may be attached to the cord by simply tying the cord to the weight (in which case the weights often have a medial groove) or are contained in small bags attached to the cords. Bolas are very effective hunting weapons in open country: they are thrown at the legs of the fleeing prey and wind about the limbs, felling the animal until it can be dispatched.

Broad-spectrum foraging: In essence, collecting and eating just about anything available. A common economic adaptation in marginal environments, such as deserts or swamps.

Brocade: A weaving technique in which supplemental wefts are introduced and "floated" over the plain weave base to form a pattern. More technically called "supplementary weft" fabric.

Camelids: The extant American members of the camel family are the llama (*Lama glama*), the alpaca (*Lama pacos*), the guanaco (*Lama guanacoe*), and the vicuña (*Lama vicugna* or *Vicugna vicugna*). A number of other species were present during the Pleistocene, but are now extinct. The llama and alpaca are domestic species, raised for wool and meat. The larger llama is also used as a draft animal. Vicuña wool was (and is) harvested from wild herds; guanacos, with their wide range over much of the western and southern continent, were an important game animal.

Cariapé: A type of silicacious ash temper characteristic of many Amazon pottery traditions.

Cauxí: Fresh water sponge spicule temper, likewise found in many lowland South American ceramic traditions.

Charqui: Dried meat (in the Andes usually camelid). The word is the origin of the English term jerky.

Chasqui: Relay messengers in the Inca realm. These runners, who went a prescribed distance and were relieved by runners at the various tambos and smaller way stations, were responsible for carrying government messages and for a certain amount of extra-fast luxury transport, such as fresh fish from the sea for the Sapa Inca or glacier ice to cool his drink. This institution is almost certainly much earlier than the Incas. Runners are common in Moche art from nearly a thousand years earlier.

Chicha: Beer, a fermented beverage commonly made of corn or of manioc. Today it is also made with barley, bananas, and other imported plants as well.

Chiefdom: A political unit in which leadership is hereditary and generally vested in the heir to the highest ranked of a series of lineages. This person generally manages to control considerable amounts of the surplus production through gifts or tribute, using this surplus to support craft specialists, religious specialists and ceremonial, and, often, ambitious building programs.

Chonta: Any of a number of palms of the genera *Guilielma* and *Astrocaryum* which have very hard wood which was aboriginally used for weapons. The word comes from the Inca chunta "palm."

Chullpa: Stone or adobe towers or house-like structures used for burial by many highland peoples. The most famous are those of the altiplano, used by Aymara-speaking peoples up until the time of the Spanish invasions.

Chuño: Freeze-dried potatoes; freeze-drying was invented by early peoples of the puna. Chuño remains a staple foodstuff as it can be stored indefinitely.

Colonial enclave: An intrusive settlement established by a foreign group to exploit some needed resource in an area outside their main region of political/social control.

Compotera: In Ecuadorian and Colombian archaeology a bowl or plate with a high annular base.

Cordillera: A mountain range.

Couvade: A ritual found among many lowland South American groups in which the father observes many taboos during his wife's pregnancy, the birth of the child, and its first days or weeks of life. In its most extreme form, the father not only observes dietary restrictions, but goes to bed and mocks birth pangs, remaining in bed for some weeks after the baby is born in order to draw supernatural danger to himself and away from the mother and infant.

Cross-dating: Dating events, artifacts, or sites of an unknown time period by reference to materials of known date found within them or by reference to features of artifacts which are thought to bear stylistic similarity to artifacts of known date.

Culture history: The synthesis of archaeological data within a historical framework without the use of an *a priori* interpretational scheme such as cultural evolution, Marxism, etc.

Curandero: An indigenous curer who through ritual acts and/or various medicines attempts to cure physical or mental illnesses.

Depletion gilding: A method of gilding metal by forming an object of a low gold content alloy and then treating the surface of the finished artifact with an acidic solution to eat away the base metal and leave a thin layer of pure gold on top giving the illusion of high-karat gold. Also called *mise en couleur* and "pickle gilding."

Diffusion: The spread of artifacts, styles, or technologies from one group to another; generally the exact mechanisms of this spread are unspecified. See also Stimulus diffusion.

Double spout and bridge bottle: A type of closed vessel, typical of south and central coastal Peru, in which two spouts on top of the vessel are connected by a horizontal handle. In Colombia called an alcarraza, the generic name for water bottle.

Down-the-line trade: Movement of goods from one person/center to the next and then to the next and so on without middlemen or markets. Although every individual movement of objects tends to be small, vast distances can be covered over time. Down-the-line trade probably explains the presence of South American and Costa Rican gold objects in southern Mexico and similar rare appearances of exotic artifacts far from their place of manufacture.

Early Horizon: In the Peruvian Master Sequence this is defined as the beginning of influence from Chavín de Huántar in the Ica Valley of the south coast. Often (inaccurately) used to mean the time of Chavín influence over much of Peru, roughly 1000–200 BC.

Early Intermediate Period: In the Peruvian Master Sequence the period of time between the cessation of Chavín influence in Ica and the beginning of Huari influence in the same valley. A time of the rise of regional states such as those of the Moche and the Nazca. Roughly 200 BC–AD 600.

El Dorado: The "gilded man." A ritual in which a Muisca paramount chief made offerings of gold to the sacred lake of Guatavita.

El Niño: The reversal of the Humboldt (Peru) current off western South America. The change in the direction of the off-shore winds causes the upwelling of cold water from the depths to cease, with disastrous effects upon the food chain. Rain also occurs, contributing to the ecological and cultural disaster.

Fish tail point: A type of point found widely over South America (and even further north) in the 6000–5000 BC time frame. It has a wide tang with a convex end which looks vaguely like a fish tail. See Figure 4.4.

Formative Period: In Ecuadorian and Colombian archaeology the period from the end of the Pleistocene until approximately 200 BC; a span of time which witnessed the end of the Paleoindian traditions, the establishment of first foraging and then agricultural societies, the domestication of plants and animals, the invention of ceramic, textile, and metallurgical technologies, and the development of specialist manufacturing of luxury goods and elaborate trade networks throughout the northern Andes and into lower Central America. Among some Bolivian archaeologists the term Formative is used to refer to any cultural manifestation prior to the rise of Tiahuanaco.

Gallery forest: Forest which borders waterways. Typical of much of lowland South America.

Geoglyph: Ground markings such as the Nazca desert lines and other patterns. Found widely throughout the Americas.

Gran Chaco: A region of south-central South America, encompassing parts of Bolivia, Paraguay, and Argentina. Characterized by extremes of temperature and a largely scrub forest cover, the Gran Chaco was the home of foraging groups from the end of the Paleoindian period onwards; agriculture was quite late in appearance in this relatively inhospitable environment.

Guano: The dung of sea birds, which is deposited on rocky offshore islets. This was harvested from ancient times onwards to be used as fertilizer.

Heddle: A device on a loom which makes it possible to change sheds, thus obviating the need to move the weft thread over and under the warps by hand.

Holocene: The modern climatic era which began *c.* 8000–6000 BC in the Americas.

Horizon style: A style which appears over a large area in a short period of time. Because such styles move speedily and are taken up by people to whom they are foreign, one can cross-date all levels, structures, or artifacts manifesting such a style and thus achieve a broad horizon of contemporaneity. The Chavín, Huari, and Inca styles are all Horizon styles as is the Chorrera style of Ecuador.

Huaca: From the Inca word for a sacred place. Used in much of the Andes as a term for an ancient building or site.

Huaco: An ancient artifact, usually a ceramic vessel or similar portable object.

Huaira: Clay smelters used by late prehispanic metallurgists. They were placed on windy hillsides to use the natural breezes as a draft for achieving the temperatures necessary to melt the ores.

Huaquero (guaquero): A person who works in huacas, specifically a looter of ancient sites. Hence huaquería (guaquería): looting of ancient sites.

Initial Period: In the Peruvian Master Sequence the period from the initial introduction of ceramics making to the Ica Valley until the beginning of the Early Horizon, roughly 2300–1300 BC. Generally used to refer to the time of the first appearance of ceramics in any area of Peru.

Integration Period: In Ecuadorian archaeology the ultimate prehispanic epoch, *c.* AD 500–1500.

Kenning: A form of symbolic expression in which the object is verbally ("her snaky hair," "her nest of snakes," speaking of the Gorgon) or visually (as the representation of long narrow parts of a figure as snakes and thicker protrusions as tongues coming from mouths in Chavín supernatural depictions) compared.

Keros: "Wood," the wooden beakers used for drinking beer among the Inca. Generally used as a term for beaker or tumbler of any material much as English-speakers use "glass" for the same form, regardless of what it is made of.

Kompi (cumbi): The fine tapestry of the Incas, woven by the chosen women, and used mainly for clothing for nobles and other government functionaries.

Kotosh Religious Tradition: A set of religious practices which involved burning offerings in sunken circular rooms or plazas, replastering the burning pit after each use. Found widely in highland and coastal Peru in the late Preceramic and Initial periods. Also called the Mito Religious Tradition.

Labret: A ceramic, stone, shell, or metal ornament placed in a hole pierced below the lower lip or, rarely, in the cheeks.

Late Horizon: In the Peruvian Master Sequence the period from the appearance of Inca culture in the Ica Valley until the Spanish conquest. AD 1476–1534 (the dates are fixed through references in early colonial documents).

Late Intermediate Period: In the Peruvian Master Sequence the period between the demise of Huari and the Inca conquest of the Ica Valley, roughly AD 1000–1476.

Llanos: Strictly speaking plains; used especially to refer to flat, seasonally inundated
regions such as the llanos of the Orinoco or the Llanos de Mojos.

Llipta: Lime which is folded with the coca leaf to make a quid for placing in the cheek
and masticating.

Lomas: Xerophytic forests watered by seasonal heavy fogs along the coast of Peru and
northern Chile.

Lost wax casting: A method of casting metal objects which involves making a wax
model of the object, covering the model with clay to form a mold, firing
the clay to remove the wax and to leave a hollow shaped like the desired
metal artifact, then pouring molten metal into the mold. Once the metal
has hardened, the mold is broken to reveal the artifact. This was the main
casting method used in ancient America and survives today among fine
jewelers around the world. Also called *cire perdue* casting.

Mahamaes: See Pukio.

Manglar: Coastal and estuary mangrove swamp.

Mano and metate: Grinding implements characteristic of many New World peoples.
The metate is a relatively flat or dish-shaped piece of stone; the mano a
hand stone used to rub whatever is being ground or crushed upon the
metate.

Master/Mistress of Animals/Fishes/Birds: A widespread concept concerning the
organization of the animal kingdom. Animals are conceived of as having
a ruler who must be placated in various ways to allow members of his/her
kingdom to be utilized by humans.

Master Sequence: A means of relative dating used for Peruvian prehistory in which
events are located chronologically with reference to the detailed relative
chronology worked out on ancient pottery from the Ica Valley. See Table
2.1 and individual entries in the Glossary.

Maté: *Ilex paraguayensis*, a shrub whose leaves are used to make a tea-like infusion.
Generally, any herb tea.

Megafauna: Literally "large animals." The general term used for the now extinct very
large species of mammals which were characteristic of many terminal Ice
Age ecosystems in the Americas. Examples are the glyptodon, a giant
armadillo, and the mammoth and mastodon, large cool-weather
elephants.

Middle Horizon: In the Peruvian Master Sequence the period of Huari influence in the
Ica Valley; often used to refer to the period of Huari influence over much
of Peru. Approximately AD 550–1000.

Mindalá: A corporate, mainly hereditary, group of professional traders of late
prehispanic Ecuador. The mindalaes were apparently in charge of long-
distance trade in desired raw materials such as gold, salt, cotton, and
finished goods, especially luxury items.

Mit'a: Among the Inca a tax in labor owed by all taxpayers. This tax was what built and
repaired roads, cared for the government and religious fields, worked the

mines, etc. In modern times mit'a labor is more informal and is organized within the community for those tasks for which more labor than the nuclear family can provide is necessary (such as harvesting) or, in some communities, for construction and repair of communal amenities such as roads, footbridges, etc.

Mitamakuna (mitamaes, mitima): Settlers brought into an area newly conquered by the Inca. Generally these people took the place of the more recalcitrant villages, which were moved to the settlers' original home. The Inca shuffled populations on a very large scale and many of the mitamakuna villages are still known, although over time and with the vicissitudes of the colonial period they have blended in with the surrounding indigenous populations.

Moon Animal: A hump-backed animal with a crest on its head and large fangs and claws originating in the Recuay culture but found in other northern Peruvian art styles until the eighteenth century AD. The name comes from some Moche representations of this creature, which show it within the crescent moon.

Mordant: A substance used to fix the color when dyeing fibers or textiles.

Mummy bundle: A common method of preparing the dead in ancient Peru. The corpse was tied in a seated or flexed position. Layers of textiles, including clothing, household, and ritual cloths, were wrapped and draped around the body, often with offerings of botanical material and various personal belongings inserted between the cloths. The resultant bundle was then corded up in a net or sewn up in a coarse shroud. Some cultures placed a false head on the bundle at the end of this process. The bundle was placed in a tomb, grave, chullpa, or cave, depending upon local cultural practice. The bodies were preserved through natural dryness or cold, not through artificial embalming.

Neutron activation analysis: A method of trace element analysis in which a sample is irradiated to transform certain isotopes of the elements in the sample to radioactive isotopes so that they may be identified as to type and absolute quantity in the sample. Since different clay and obsidian (the commonest materials analyzed) sources contain different trace elements in differing amounts, by comparison it is possible to identify the source of the clay or obsidian and thus find out about trade or the distribution of the various materials.

Nudo: A knot, term used for the east–west ranges which connect the major cordilleras in Ecuador.

Oculate Being: A major deity of the Paracas and Ocucaje cultures of the south coast of Peru. This figure, which commonly appears as a feline, human, or anthropomorphic feline, has very large round eyes and a wide grin. It is associated with weapons and trophy heads.

Olla: Term commonly used for a clay cooking pot with a semi-closed body and a low neck.

Organic resist painting ("negative painting"): A method of achieving black on red decoration without double firing. Generally the slipped vessel is oxidation fired, then dipped in or painted with an organic solution (plant saps and gums were probably used). The parts of the vessel which the potter wishes to remain the base color are blocked out with slip and then the vessel is heated, charring the exposed organic material. When cooled the vessel is brushed or wiped to remove the now dry protective slip, revealing a black design on the fired base color. Organic resist painting seems to have been invented many times and was widely used throughout Mexico, Central America, and South America. It continues to be used, but only in the faking of ancient ceramics, mainly those of Colombia and coastal Ecuador.

Oxidation firing: Firing ceramics in such a manner that there is a free flow of oxygen around the vessels as they are being fired. With clays that contain iron oxides this results in an orange to red vessel.

Oxidation smelting: A method of smelting sulfide ores involving a number of steps of which the most important is roasting the ores in an oxygen-containing atmosphere to remove the sulfides before proceeding with the reduction smelting.

Paca (*Cuniculus* spp.): A large rodent native to South and Central America.

Paleoindian: The late Pleistocene inhabitants of the Americas.

Palynology: The identification of fossil pollen from archaeological contexts in order to reconstruct the climate, economy, and diet.

Páramo: The wet high-altitude grasslands of Ecuador and Colombia; lower in altitude and better watered than the puna, they support cloud and scrub forest in their lower ranges.

Patrilineage: A corporate group formed by people who are related through male relatives.

Penis string: An item of male clothing found among a number of lowland groups. A string is wound tightly around the foreskin, covering the glans. This string is then usually tied around the waist or to a belt, holding the penis erect.

Phase: A term with two very different usages in South American studies. The most common meaning, shared with archaeology in general, is a unit of contemporaneity, that is a period of time (usually named or numbered for the convenience of the archaeologist) in which all artifacts, etc. are so similar that it is reasonable to treat all materials and events within this span of time as being contemporary. Phases vary immensely in length because of differences in the amounts and types of investigation done on any given area, site, or culture. In practice, even with the most sophisticated types of stylistic analysis, it has not proven possible to delineate phases of less than about twenty-five years in length. If absolute dating methods alone are relied upon to establish limits the shortest length of time a phase can possibly be is about 150 years, owing to the nature of the methodologies available. The term phase is also used by many archaeologists working in the tropical lowlands of South America (and following them, a few elsewhere) to mean what is more commonly called a culture or a cultural tradition. Within these "phases" ceramic traditions may be distinguished, but differences between the different traditions are considered less important than shared features.

Phytolith or Opal Phytolith: A method of climatic and economic reconstruction based on a peculiar property of plants. Ground waters contain dissolved silica. Some plants, when they take up water, deposit this silica around the cells of their leaves, stems, bark, etc. When the plant decays the silica skeletons are often preserved so that analysis of the archaeological soils in which they lay can reveal which genera of plants were present.

Pirca: Fieldstone and mud mortar construction.

Planalto: The highlands of east-central Brazil, roughly located between the Paranapanema River on the south and the Araguaia River on the west and bordered by the North Atlantic Ocean on the east. Varying between 200 and 1200 m in altitude, it is characterized by irregular rainfall, and by savannas and open parkland in the drier areas and by scrub forest and deciduous forests in the damper ones. The planalto was an early focus of human occupation.

Poncho: A rectangular, usually two web, outer garment worn by many native American peoples. The poncho has a central slit for the head and open side seams. It is not a precolumbian garment, but rather is an adaptation of the native South American shirt or tunic (whose side seams were sewn up and which often had set-on sleeves) by the Pampas Indians in the sixteenth century. The native outer garment, a mantle which was tied in front or over one shoulder, was not suitable for riding horses in cold weather and so the traditional shirt was reworked into a heavy outer garment. This garment proved so useful that it was adapted by both native peoples and mestizos as far north as Mexico.

Póporo: The container used to hold lime for coca chewing, often a gourd or an imitation gourd in ceramic or metal.

Preceramic: In Peruvian archaeology the long span of time between the last Paleoindians and the invention and diffusion of ceramics making between *c.* 2300–1900 BC.

Prill: A smelting technique characteristic of the Late Intermediate Period in northern Peru. The arsenic-bearing sulfide ore was reduction smelted in furnaces, the end result being a thick slag with small droplets of the arsenic-copper alloy trapped within it, as the local technology could not sustain a high enough heat to turn the slag liquid enough to allow the metal to flow together and form an ingot at the bottom of the furnace. These droplets of metal, the prills, were extracted by crushing the slag with a rocker mill and picking them out. In family-organized work units probably it was the elderly and the children who actually picked out the prills.

Pristine civilization: A civilization which developed *sui generis*. The conditions which led to the development of these few earliest complex societies are thought to have been different from those which led to the spread of civilizations from their points of pristine development.

Pukio: A type of sunken garden found mainly along the north and central coasts of Peru where the water table is very close to the surface. Here fields are dug down to the water table, providing a constantly damp area for the cultivation of crops. Pukios (also called mahamaes) are very productive as they are well watered and protected from the wind.

Puna: The high-altitude frigid and semi-desertic grasslands of Peru, Bolivia, Chile, and western Argentina. Well above the tree line, agriculture is possible only in sheltered border zones and the puna is mainly given over to herd animals (llamas, alpacas, and now sheep).

Quebrada: A gorge or small canyon.

Quipu: An elaborate knotted string device used by the Incas and some other, earlier, peoples in Peru for record keeping. Inca quipus used a decimal system with the farthest out knot on the string representing the ones, the next one the tens and so on. Numbers were indicated by overhand knots, a single knot being one, two turns for a two, etc. Sets of strings recording the same thing were attached to a long string, often with a totals string hanging on the other side. There was also a coding by color and texture, but this has been lost, as the quipus were an aid to remembering, not a system of writing.

Radiocarbon dating: Dating organic objects by measuring the amount of radioactive breakdown that is occurring within them. The ratio of radiocarbon (whose half-life is known) to non-radioactive carbon gives the date of death of the organism (grass from a basket, wood from a beam, bone or hair of a human or an animal, etc.). A new method, using an accelerator and a tandem mass spectrometer, can measure the actual amount of radioactive carbon present and so requires much smaller samples. Only the remains of something once living can be dated by this method; it does not work on stone, metal, or pottery.

Reduction firing: Firing ceramics in such a manner that there is no free flow of oxygen around the vessels during the firing process. This results, if the clays contain iron oxides, in a gray paste. If smoky fuel is added to the fire, the vessels will turn black.

Reduction smelting: Smelting ores in an atmosphere in which there is no free flow of oxygen. This is the commonest method of smelting the simple ores.

Regional Developmental Period: In Ecuadorian and Colombian archaeology the period of time between *c*. 200 BC and AD 500.

Relative dating: Dating objects and events relative to one another, e.g. B is older than A but younger than C.

Retainer burial: The sacrifice and burial of servants or other people with a person. This practice is found among most of the early civilizations of the world, including the Egyptians, the Chinese, and a number of ancient South American groups.

Rocker mill: The Andean rocker mill is a crushing and grinding device which was (and is) used for grinding foodstuffs, mashing vegetable foods, and crushing clays and ores for further processing. It consists of a large flat bottom stone, the bataan, and a heavy, somewhat rounded (on the bottom) upper stone, the chunga. Materials are placed on the bataan and the chunga is rocked across them until the desired degree of pulverization is reached.

Rocker stamping: A means of decorating ceramics by rocking a shell or some small thin implement across the damp surface of the clay, leaving a characteristic zigzag pattern. Dentate rocker stamping involves using a shell with a serrated edge to make dotted lines.

Sacrifice Scene: Formerly called the "Presentation Scene" this major theme in painted and modeled Moche pottery shows the sacrifice of prisoners by various supernaturals and the presentation of goblets of their blood to a rayed deity. Recent excavations at Sipán and at San José de Moro indicate that the individuals in this scene existed and that it was played out.

Salar: Salt lakes or pans, specifically the high, dry, salt lakes and pans of the southern Andes.

Sambaquí: The immense shell mounds of the southern Brazilian coast. Some of these are natural, but many show signs of human occupations dating from perhaps 4000–5000 years ago to relatively recent preconquest eras.

Secondary burial: Reburial of the bones of an individual after the flesh has been removed through natural or other means.

Series: In Venezuelan and Caribbean archaeology a cultural tradition characterized by specific types of ceramics and ceramic decoration. Phases (smaller units of time) are then distinguished within a series.

Shaft and chamber tomb: A type of tomb common in the northern Andes, but found throughout much of precolumbian America. It consists of a circular, oval, or rectangular shaft which descends 0.5–60 m (the known range of depths) in a vertical, sloping, or stepped manner to one or more chambers of varying sizes, shapes, etc. The number and kinds of burials and offerings within these chambers likewise vary immensely with the time, place, and cultural affiliation of the people so disposing of their dead.

Shaman: A non-institutionalized religious practitioner who personally contacts the supernatural through trance for divination, curing or other purposes. This term is often used in a slovenly manner to refer to *all* non-institutionalized religious or medical personnel in non-western societies.

Signifer: An element in a representation which helps the viewer to identify who or what is being represented. Common signifers in South American iconographic systems are large fangs to indicate that a figure is a supernatural (*not* that it is a feline or related to a feline), or the use of specific colors to delineate specific supernatural figures. Common signifers in western art are the halo, used to indicate that a human figure is a supernatural, or a blue cape or dress to show that a woman is the Virgin Mary, not some other female saint.

Slip casting: A means of forming very thin ceramic vessels or objects by making a heavy fired clay mold and then pouring in slip, leaving it until a layer of clay of the desired thickness is deposited on the interior surface of the mold, then pouring out the unneeded slip and leaving the mold until the clay is dry enough that the mold can be safely removed. Slip casting is found along the south coast of Peru at the end of the Early Horizon where it was used to form panpipes and bottle spouts.

Snuff tray: A small flat tray used to hold one of the hallucinogenic snuffs for inhaling (by means of a bone or ceramic tube or snuffer). These trays are usually made of wood, although some metal ones are known.

Spindle whorl: A small counter weight used on a hand spindle. Most are circular and made of ceramic, stone, or wood.

Spondylus: The "thorny oyster." A bivalve which has long spines on the exterior and, often, a bright orange shell or shell rim. The most commonly used species were *Spondylus princeps* and *S. calcifer*, both of which occur in deep coastal waters from the Gulf of Guayaquil north to the Sea of Cortez. Spondylus was a key element in exchange between coastal Ecuador and Peru. It was used through the central Andes in the manufacture of ornaments and as religious offerings.

Staff God and Goddess: The most important deities of the later Chavín culture, they get their names from their mode of representation, standing in a full frontal position with a staff in each hand. They may be the earliest representatives of the later solar/sky/weather and lunar/earth/agriculture deities.

Stimulus diffusion: Diffusion of the *idea* of an artifact, practice, or technology as opposed to the thing itself.

Stirrup bottle: A ceramic form consisting of a closed body and a tubular handle in the form (more or less) of an up-ended U and with a spout in the middle. This form is found all over the Americas at various times, but is especially typical of the cultures of the north coast of Peru, who often formed the body of the vessel into a small sculpture.

Strombus: A univalve mollusk which inhabits shallow tropical waters from lower California to southern Ecuador as well as the Caribbean coast. The largest and most commonly used species was *Strombus galeatus* Swain. Strombus is called conch in English and the meat is edible. More important to the ancient South Americans, the shell can be made into a trumpet or into shell ornaments and inlays. The Moche also had a supernatural being who was a monster with a Strombus shell body. Today strombus trumpets are still used in native Andean rituals.

Tabard: The central Andean tunic (uncu) was not worn in Ecuador until the Inca introduced it. In its place, apparently for formal or ritual occasions, men wore an open-sided garment, usually narrow and heavily decorated with tassels, shells, or beads. The tabard may have been the ancestor of today's kushma, which is similarly open-sided. Tabards and kushmas are made of a single web, unlike the tunic, which may be made of two or more webs.

Tambo: Among the Inca, groups of storehouses and shelters located at intervals along the roads. Generally smaller tambos were strung at a convenient day's journey, whereas larger tambos, called royal tambos by the early historians, were located in towns through which the roads passed.

Tapestry: A plain-weave technique for creating patterned textiles. The wefts completely cover the warps (weft face) and the colors of the wefts are changed every time a color change is desired in the pattern. In interlocking tapestry the wefts dovetail around a single warp whereas in kilim or slit tapestry the wefts turn back at adjacent warps, leaving slits in the fabric where the colors meet.

Tapia: A construction technique in which clay and gravel are molded into large blocks, often using cane or wooden molds. Similar to the Eurasian *terre pisé* or rammed earth technique.

Tecomate: A term adopted from the Aztec for a neckless olla, a ceramic version of the round gourd used to hold seeds or tortillas. Now used for any globular vessel with no neck and a relatively small top opening.

Temper (aplastic): Material such as sand, ground up potsherds, vegetable matter, etc. added to ceramic clays to give them the necessary body to be formed into artifacts.

Terra preta: Literally "black earth." Dark, fertile soils of anthropic origin found along the Amazon and its tributaries.

Thermoluminescence dating: A dating method used on fired clays, especially ceramic vessels. Most clays contain some radioactive trace elements. As these break down they emit electrons which, in unfired clays, simply escape. When the clay is fired, however, microscopic hollows in the fabric are formed and these trap the electrons. When a piece of the fired clay is ground up and heated, the electrons escape from their traps and a photon of light is emitted. Roughly, the more light emitted, the longer it has been since the ceramic was fired, hence the ceramic can be dated. This method is often used to date looted artifacts, since most other methods of dating depend upon the archaeological contact of the artifacts. Thermoluminescence (often abbreviated TL) can also be falsified, either by irradiating the (new) vessel or by inserting a genuinely ancient sherd in a place from which the dating sample is certain to be taken during "restoration" procedures.

Tola: The term used in Ecuador for earthen mounds used as platforms for houses or temples.

Totora: Any of a number of species of reeds or cattails which grow in still or brackish water. By extension the floats or reed boats made from these reeds.

Tournette: A base which can be slowly revolved while forming the ceramic vessel which is placed upon (or within) it.

Tumbaga: An alloy of gold and copper or gold, copper, and silver (often with trace amounts of other metals). This alloy melts at a lower temperature than either gold or copper and is considerably harder, being a kind of gold bronze. Tumbaga was widely used by northern Andean and Central American metal smiths and was often depletion gilded.

Tumi: The crescent-shaped knife used by many Andean peoples.

Tunjo: Small cast metal figurines made by the Muisca and used as offerings. They represent males, females, animals, and artifacts.

Tupu: The pins used by many Andean women to hold their dresses together at the shoulder or their shoulder cloth closed at the front. Usually tupus are a long straight pin with a flattened circular or a fancy figurative head.

Twining: A textile and basketry technique utilizing a pair of wefts which are twisted about the warps.

Ulluchu: An as yet unidentified fruit, in shape somewhat like a gourd or squash, which is commonly depicted in Moche art.

Uncu: The central Andean tunic, a rectangular garment with a central head slit and sewn side seams.

Viracocha: The creator god of the Incas, created by Inca Pachacuti as the nexus of his new state religion.

Wamani: See Apu.

Warp: The vertical threads of a textile.

Wattle and daub: a method of construction in which the walls of a building are formed by daubing mud onto a base of branches, grass, and twigs loosely woven onto a wooden frame. A common construction technique to the present, wattle and daub is also common in Eurasian vernacular architecture.

Weft: The horizontal elements in a textile.

X-ray fluorescence: A means of trace element analysis, generally of obsidian, in which the sample is irradiated with energetic X-rays so that the trace elements emit a spectrum of X-rays which can be passed through a crystal and sorted electronically. The relative intensities of each element are recorded graphically as peaks of different heights. This method is not as precise or detailed as neutron activation analysis and the two are often used together with the more expensive neutron activation analysis being used to pinpoint the important elements that distinguish between different sources so that the faster, cheaper X-ray fluorescence can then be used.

Yaya-Mama Religious Tradition: An early religious tradition of the altiplano which
featured rectangular sunken courts and a dual female-male supernatural.

Yungas/selva/montaña/oriente: The mountainous, heavily forested, eastern slopes of
the Andes.

SELECT BIBLIOGRAPHY

General works

Gonzalez, Alberto Rex, *Arte Precolombina de la Argentina: Introducción a su Historia Cultural.* Imprenta Coni, Buenos Aires, 1977.

Haberland, Wolfgang, *Amerikanische Archäologie: Geschichte, Theorie, Kulturentwicklung.* Wissenschaftlichte Buchgesellschaft, Darmstadt, 1991.

Hidalgo L., Jorge, Virgilio Schiappacasse, Hans Niemeyer F., Carlos Aldunate del S., and Ivan Solimano R., editors, *Culturas de Chile. Prehistoria: Desde sus Orígenes hasta los Albores de la Conquista.* Editorial Andrés Bello, Santiago de Chile, 1989.

Hilbert, Peter Paul, *Archäologische Untersuchungen am Mitteleren Amazonas: Beiträge zur Vorgeschichte des Südamerikanischen Tiesslandes.* Dietrich Reimer Verlag, Berlin, 1968.

Keatinge, Richard W., *Peruvian Prehistory: An Overview of Pre-Inca and Inca Society.* Cambridge University Press, 1988.

Kern, Arno A. (organizer/editor), *Arqueología Pré-Historica do Río Grande do Sul.* Mercado Abierto, Ltda, Porto Alegre, Brazil, 1991.

Lathrap, Donald W., *The Upper Amazon.* Praeger, New York, 1970.

Lumbreras, Luis G., *Las Origines de la Civilización en el Peru.* 6th edition, Editorial Milla Batres, Lima, 1983.

Masuda, Yoshio and Izumi Shimada, *Kodai Andesu Bijutsu.* Iwanamishoten, Tokyo, 1991.

Meggers, Betty J., editor, *Prehistoria Sudamericana: Nuevas Perspectivas.* Taraxcum, Washington, DC, 1992.

Moseley, Michael Edward, *The Incas and Their Ancestors: The Archaeology of Peru.* Thames and Hudson, New York, 1992.

Ponce Sangines, Carlos, *Panorama de la Arqueología Boliviana.* Imprenta y Editorial "Juventud," La Paz, 1980.

Porras Garcés, Pedro I., *Nuestro Ayer: Manual de la Arqueología Ecuatoriana.* Centro de Investigaciones Arqueológicas, Pontificia Universidad Católica, Quito, 1987.

Reichel-Dolmatoff, Gerardo, *Arqueología de Colombia: Un Texto Introductorio.* Fundación Segunda Expedición Botánica, Bogotá, 1986.

Rouse, Irving and José M. Cruxent, *Venezuelan Archaeology.* Yale University Press, New Haven and London, 1963.

Schmitz, Pedro Ignacio, editor, *Contribución a la Prehistoria de Brasil. Pesquisas Antropología* No. 32, Río Grande do Sul, 1981.

Willey, Gordon R. *Introduction to American Archaeology,* Vol. 2, *South America.* Prentice-Hall Inc., Englewood Cliffs, New Jersey, 1971.

Journals and serials

The following list is of those journals which publish a fair amount of South American archaeology and prehistory and which can often be obtained outside of their country of publication. A more comprehensive list of publications can be obtained from the *Handbook of*

Latin American Studies, published yearly by the University of Florida, Gainesville since 1936. Every second year is devoted to publications in the social sciences, listed by subtopic and country.

American Antiquity, Society for American Archaeology, 1–, 1935–

Archaeology, American Institute of Archaeology, New York, 1–, 1948–

Baessler-Archiv, Museum für Volkerkunde, Berlin, 1–, 1910–

Boletín de Lima, Lima, 1–, 1979–

Boletín del Museo del Oro, Banco de la República, Bogotá, 1–, 1977–

Chungara-Arica, Universidad del Norte, Tarapaca, 1–, 1971–

Les Dossiers d'Archéologie, Dijon, 1–, 1974–

Gaceta Arqueológica Andina, Lima, 1–, 1982–

Journal de la Société des Américanistes de Paris, 1–, 1898–

Journal of Field Archaeology, Boston University, 1–, 1974–

Latin American Antiquity, Society for American Archaeology, 1–, 1990–

Ñawpa Pacha, Institute of Andean Studies, Berkeley, California, 1–, 1975–

There is also an English-language (largely) newsletter devoted to Andean archaeology: *Willay*, Newsletter of the Andean Anthropological Research Group, Izumi and Melody Shimada, editors, Department of Anthropology, Peabody Museum, Harvard University, Cambridge, MA 02138 USA. Bi-annually since 1981.

Chapter 2   A matter of time

Menzel, Dorothy, *The Archaeology of Ancient Peru and the Work of Max Uhle*. R. H. Lowie Museum of Anthropology, University of California, Berkeley, 1977.

Rowe, John Howland, "Stratigraphy and Seriation." *American Antiquity* 26, 3 (1961), 324–30.

   "Stages and Periods in Archaeological Interpretation." *Southwestern Journal of Anthropology* 18, 1 (1962), 40–54. Albuquerque, New Mexico.

   "Worsaae's Law and the Use of Grave Lots for Archaeological Dating." *American Antiquity* 28, 2 (1962), 127–37.

Taylor, R. E. and Clement W. Meighan, editors, *Chronologies in New World Archaeology*. Academic Press, New York, San Francisco and London, 1978.

Radiocarbon, *Archaeomaterials*, *Archaeometry*, and *The Journal of Archaeological Sciences* are where the majority of physical dates are published.

Chapter 3   The physical setting

Deneven, William M., "Aboriginal Drained Field Cultivation in the Americas." *Science* 169, 3946 (1970), 647–54.

   "The Pristine Myth: The Landscape of the Americas in 1492." *Annals of the American Association of Geographers* 82, 3 (1992), 369–85.

Fittkau, E. J., J. Illies, H. Klinge, G. H. Schwabe, and A. Alvarado, editors, *Biogeography and Ecology in South America*. Monographiae Biologicae Vol. 18. Dr. W. Junk, Publishers, The Hague. 1969.

Idyll, C. P., "The Anchovy Crisis." *Scientific American* 228, 6 (1973), 22–9.

Moseley, Michael Edward, *The Maritime Foundations of Andean Civilization*. Cummings Publishing Company, Menlo Park, CA, 1975.

   "Punctuated Equilibrium: Searching for the Ancient Record for El Niño." *Quarterly Review of Archaeology* (now *The Review of Archaeology*) 8, 3 (1987), 7–10.

Patzelt, Erwin, *Fauna del Ecuador*. Banco Central del Ecuador, Quito y Guayaquil, 1989.

Quinn, W., V. Neal, and S. Antuñez de Mayolo, *Preliminary Report on El Niño Occurrences Over the Past Four and a Half Centuries.* College of Oceanography, Oregon State University, Pullman, OR, 1986.

Salati, Eneas and Peter B. Vose, "Amazon Basin: A System in Equilibrium." *Science* 225, 4658 (1984), 129–38.

Sauer, Carl O., "Geography of South America." *Handbook of South American Indians*, Vol. 6, pp. 319–44. Bulletin 143, Bureau of American Ethnology, Smithsonian Institution, Washington DC, 1950.

Shimada, Izumi, Crystal Barker-Schaaf, Lonnie G. Thompson, and Ellen Moseley-Thompson, "Cultural Impacts of Severe Droughts in the Prehistoric Andes: Application of a 1,500-year Ice Core Precipitation Record." *World Archaeology* 22, 3 (1991), 247–70.

Walker, Ernest P., *Mammals of the World.* Johns Hopkins University Press, Baltimore, 1975.

Chapter 4   The first peoples: 12,000–6000 BC

Abel Orguera, Luis, "Advances in the Archaeology of the Pampa and Patagonia." *Journal of World Prehistory* 1, 1 (1987), 333–413.

Bird, Junius Bouton, with Margaret Bird, edited by John Hyslop, *Travels and Archaeology in South Chile.* University of Iowa Press, Iowa City, 1988.

Bryan, Alan Lyle, "Paleoenvironments and Cultural Diversity in Late Pleistocene South America." *Quaternary Research* 3, 3 (1973), 237–56.

editor, *Early Man in America From a Circum-Pacific Perspective.* Occasional Papers of the Department of Anthropology, University of Alberta, No. 1. Archaeological Researches International, Edmonton, 1978.

Chauchat, Claude, "L'Approche technologique dans une étude régionale: le Paijanien de la Côte du Pérou," in *25 äns d'études technologiques en préhistoire*, pp. 263–73. XI Rencontres Internationales d'Archéologie et d'Histoire d'Antibes. Editions APDCA, Juan-les-Pins, 1991.

Chauchat, Claude and Jean Paul Lacomb, "El Hombre de Paiján: ¿El Más Antiguo Peruano?" *Gaceta Arqueológica Andina* 11 (1984), 4–7, Lima.

Correal Urrego, Gonzalo and Thomas van der Hammen, *Investigaciones Arqueológicas en los Abrigos Rocosos del Tequendama: 12,000 Años de Historia del Hombre y su Medioambiente en la Altiplanicie de Bogotá.* Biblioteca Banco Popular, Bogotá, 1977.

Dillehay, Tom D., *Monte Verde: A Late Pleistocene Settlement in Chile*, Vol. 1, *Paleoenvironment and Site Context.* Smithsonian Institution Press, Washington DC, 1989.

Dillehay, Tom D. and David J. Meltzer, *The First Americans: Search and Research.* CRC Press, Boca Raton, 1991.

Gibbons, Ann, "Geneticists Track the DNA Trail of the First Americans." *Science* 259, 5093 (1993), 312–13.

Guidon, Neide and B. Arnaud, "The Chronology of the New World: Two Faces of Reality." *World Archaeology* 23, 2 (1992), 167–78.

Lynch, Thomas F., editor, *Guitarrero Cave: Early Man in the Andes.* Academic Press, Orlando, New York and London, 1980.

"Quaternary Climate, Environment, and the Human Occupation of the South-Central Andes." *Geoarchaeology* 5, 3 (1990), 199–228.

"Glacial-Age Man in South America?" *American Antiquity* 55, 1 (1990), 12–36.

Martin, Paul S., "The Discovery of America." *Science* 179, 4077 (1973), 969–74.

Núñez Atencio, Lautero and Betty Meggers, *Investigaciones Paleoindias al Sur de la Línea Ecuatorial.* Taraxcum, Washington DC, 1987 (*Estudios Atacameños* No. 8).

Ortiz-Troncoso, Omar R., "Punta Santa Ana et Bahia Buena: deux gisements sur une ancienne

Ligne de Rivage dans le Dêtroit de Magellan. *Journal de la Société des Américanistes de Paris* 66 (1979), 133–204.

Prous, André, "Fouilles du Grande Abri de Santana de Riacho (Minas Gerais) Brésil." *Journal de la Société des Américanistes de Paris* 67 (1980/1), 163–83.

Rick, John W., *Prehistoric Hunters of the High Andes*. Academic Press, Orlando, New York and London, 1980.

Salazar, Ernesto, *Talleres Prehistóricos en los Altos Andes del Ecuador*. Departmento de Difusión Cultural, Universidad de Cuenca, 1980.

Schmitz, Pedro Ignacio, "Pleistocene Hunters and Gatherers of Brazil." *Journal of World Prehistory* 1, 1 (1987), 53–126.

Vuilleumier, Beryl Simpson, "Pleistocene Changes in the Fauna and Flora of South America." *Science* 173, 3999 (1971), 771–80.

Chapter 5   Settling down: 6000–3500 BC

Bird, Junius Bouton, "Pre-Ceramic Art From Huaca Prieta, Chicama Valley." *Ñawpa Pacha* 1 (1963), 29–34.

Bird, Junius Bouton and John Hyslop, *The Preceramic Excavations at Huaca Prieta, Chicama Valley, Peru*. American Museum of Natural History Anthropological Papers Vol. 62, Part 1, 1985.

Donnan, Christopher B., "An Early House From Chilca, Peru." *American Antiquity* 30, 2 (1964), 137–44.

Estrella, Eduardo, *El Pan de América: Etnohistoria de los Alimentos Aborigines en el Ecuador*. Ediciones Abya-Yala, Quito, 1988.

Guffroy, Jean, "Les Débuts de la sédentarisation et de l'agriculture dans les Andes méridionales de l'Equateur." *L'Anthropologie* 91, 4 (1987), 873–88, Paris.

Heiser, Charles B., *The Gourd Book*. University of Oklahoma Press, Norman, 1979.

LaVallée, Daniele, "L'Occupation préhistorique des hautes terres andines." *L'Anthropologie* 89 (1985), 409–30.

Llagostera Martinez, Agustín, "9,700 Years of Maritime Subsistence on the Pacific: An Analysis by Means of Bioindicators in the North of Chile." *American Antiquity* 44, 2 (1979), 309–23.

Núñez Atencio, Lautero, *La Agricultura Prehistorica en los Andes Meridionales*. Universidad del Norte, Antofagasta, 1974.

Núñez H., Patricio and Vjera Zistai, "Tiviliche 1b y Aragón 1z (Estrato V): Dos Comunidades Precerámicas en Pampa de Tamarugal, Pisagua, Norte de Chile," in Ramiro Matos Mendieta, editor, *III Congreso Peruano, El Hombre y la Cultura Andina*, Vol. 2, pp. 734–57, Lima, 1978.

Pearsall, Deborah Marie, *La Producción de Alimentos en Real Alto*. Biblioteca Ecuatoriana de Arqueología, Corporación Editora Nacional, Guayaquil, 1988.

Rivera, Mario A., "The Prehistory of Northern Chile: A Summary." *Journal of World Prehistory* 5, 1 (1991), 1–47.

Stothert, Karen E., *La Prehistoria Temprana de la Península de Santa Elena, Ecuador: Cultura Las Vegas*. Miscelánea Antropológica Ecuatoriana, Serie Monográfica 10. Museos del Banco Central del Ecuador, Quito y Guayaquil, 1988.

Torres, Constantino Manuel, David B. Repke, Kelvin Chan, Dennis McKenna, Agustín Llagostera, and Richard Evans Schultes, "Snuff Powders From Pre-Hispanic San Pedro de Atacama: Chemical and Contextual Analysis." *Current Anthropology* 32, 5 (1991), 640–9.

Towle, Margaret A. *The Ethnobotany of Pre-Columbian Peru*. Aldine, Chicago, 1961.

Wassén, S. Henry, "Anthropological Survey of the Use of South American Snuffs," in Daniel F. Efron, editor in chief, *The Ethnopharmacological Search for Psychoactive Drugs*, pp. 233–89. United States Government Printing Office, 1967.

"Convergent Approaches to the Analysis of Hallucinogenic Snuff Trays." *Annals; Göteborgs Etnografiska Museum Årstryck* (1983/4), 26–37.

West, Michael and Thomas W. Whitaker, "Prehistoric Cultivated Cucurbits from the Viru Valley, Peru." *Economic Botany* 3, 2 (1979), 275–9.

Wheeler Pires-Ferreira, Jane, Edgardo Pires-Ferreira, and Peter Kaulicke, "Preceramic Animal Utilization in the Central Peruvian Andes." *Science* 194, 4264 (1976), 483–90.

Chapter 6   The problem of maize

Beadle, George, "The Ancestry of Corn." *Scientific American* 242 (1990), 112–19.

Bird, Robert McK., "South American Maize in Central America?" in Doris Z. Stone, editor, *Pre-Columbian Plant Migration*, pp. 39–65. Papers of the Peabody Museum of Archaeology and Enthnology, Vol. 76. Harvard University, Cambridge, MA, 1984.

Bonavia, Duccio, *Precerámico Peruano: Los Gavilanes: Mar, Desierto y Oásis en la Historia del Hombre*. Corporación Financiera de Desarrolo S.A. COFIDE & Instituto Arqueológico Alemán, Lima, 1982.

Bonavia, Duccio and Alexander Grobman, "Andean Maize: Its Origins and Domestication," in David R. Harris and Gordon C. Hillman, editors, *Foraging and Farming: The Evolution of Plant Exploitation*, pp.456–70. *One World Archaeology*, Vol. 13, Unwin Hyman, London, 1989.

Bruhns, Karen Olsen, "Sexual Activities: Some Thoughts on the Sexual Division of Labor and Archaeological Interpretation," in Dale Walde and Noreen D. Willows, editors, *The Archaeology of Gender: Proceedings of the Twenty-Second Annual Conference of the Archaeological Association of Calgary*, pp. 420–8. The University of Calgary, Archaeological Association, 1991.

Bush, Mark B., Dolores R. Piperno, and Paul A. Colinvaux, "A 6000 Year History of Amazonian Maize Cultivation." *Nature* 340 (1989), 303–5.

Ford, Richard I., "The Evolution of Corn Revisited." *The Quarterly Review of Archaeology* 4, 4 (1983), 12–13 and 16.

Iltis, Hugh H., "From Teocinte to Maize: The Catastrophic Sexual Transmutation." *Science* 222, 4626 (1983), 886–94.

Mangelsdorf, Paul C., "The Mystery of Maize: New Perspectives." *Proceedings of the American Philosophical Society* 127, 4 (1983), 215–47.

Pearsall, Deborah M. and Dolores R. Piperno, "Antiquity of Maize Cultivation in Ecuador: Summary and Reevaluation of the Evidence." *American Antiquity* 55, 2 (1990), 324–36.

Piperno, Dolores R., Karen H. Clary, Richard G. Cooke, Anthony J. Ranere, and David Weiland, "Preceramic Maize in Central Panama: Phytolith and Pollen Evidence." *American Anthropologist* 87, 5 (1985), 871–8.

Prous, André, "Fouilles du Grand Abri de Santana de Riacho (Minas Gerais), Brésil." *Journal de la Société des Américanistes* 67 (1980/1), 163–83.

Chapter 7   Cultural intensification in the Andes: 3500–2000 BC

Benfer, Robert A., "The Preceramic Period Site of Paloma, Peru: Bioindications of Improving Adaptation to Sedentism." *Latin American Antiquity* 1, 4 (1990), 284–318.

Bitteman, Bente, "Revisión del Problema Chinchorro." *Chungara-Arica* 9 (1982), 46–79.

Bonavia, Duccio and Alexander Grobman, "Sistema de Depositos y Almacenamiento Durante el Periodo Preceramico en la Costa del Peru." *Journal de la Société des Américanistes de Paris* 66 (1979), 21–45.

Bonnier, Elisabeth, "Les Architectures précéramiques dans la cordillère des Andes. Piruru face à la diversité des donées." *L'Anthropologie* 91, 4 (1987), 889–904.

"Del Sanctuario al Caserío: Acerca de la Neolitización en la Cordillera de los Andes Centrales." *Bulletin de l'Institut Français des Etudes Andines* 17, 2 (1988), 23–40.

Burger, Richard L. and Lucy Salazar Burger, "Ritual and Religion at Huarikoto." *Archaeology* 33, 6 (1980), 26–32.

Damp, Jonathan, *La Primera Ocupación Valdivia de Real Alto: Patrones Económicos, Arquitectónicos e Ideológicos*. Biblioteca Ecuatoriana de Arqueología, Corporación Editora Nacional, Guayaquil, 1988.

Engel, Frederic, *A Pre-ceramic Settlement on the Central Coast of Peru: Asia, Unit 1. Transactions of the American Philosophical Society*, new series, 53, 3 (1963).

Greider, Terence, *La Galgada: A Preceramic Culture in Transition*. University of Texas Press, Austin, 1988.

Matsuzawa, Tgusio, "The Formative Site of Las Haldas, Peru: Architecture, Chronology, and Economy" (translated by Izumi Shimada). *American Antiquity* 43, 4 (1978), 652–72.

Moseley, Michael Edward and Gordon R. Willey, "Aspero, Peru: A Reexamination of the Site and Its Implications." *American Antiquity* 38, 4 (1978), 452–67.

Pozorsky, Sheila and Thomas Pozorsky, *Early Settlement and Subsistence in the Casma Valley, Peru*. University of Iowa Press, Iowa City, 1987

Quilter, Jeffrey, "Architecture and Chronology at El Paraíso, Peru." *Journal of Field Archaeology* 12, 3 (1985), 279–97.

Life and Death at Paloma: Society and Mortuary Practices in a Preceramic Peruvian Village. University of Iowa Press, Iowa City, 1989.

"Late Preceramic Peru." *Journal of World Prehistory* 5, 4 (1991), 387–438.

Quilter, Jeffrey, *et al.*, "Subsistence Economy of El Paraíso, an Early Peruvian Site." *Science* 251 (1991), 277–83.

Raymond, J. Scott, "The Maritime Foundations of Andean Civilization: A Reconsideration of the Evidence." *American Antiquity* 46, 4 (1981), 806–21.

Chapter 8   Ceramics: their origins and technology

Arnold, Dean E., *Ceramic Theory and Cultural Process*. Cambridge University Press, New York and Cambridge, 1985.

Bischof, Henning, "Canapote: An Early Ceramic Site in Northern Colombia. Preliminary Report," in *Actas y Memorias del XXXVI Congreso Internacional de Americanistas, España, 1964*, Vol. 1, pp. 483–91. Seville, 1966.

Bischof, Henning and J. Viterio Gamboa, "Pre-Valdivia Occupation on the Southwest Coast of Ecuador." *American Antiquity* 37, 4 (1972), 548–51.

Bruhns, Karen Olsen and Norman Hammond, "A Visit to Valdivia." *Journal of Field Archaeology* 10, 4 (1983), 485–7.

"A Reply to J. Damp." *Journal of Field Archaeology* 11, 4 (1984), 428–9.

Buys, Jozef, Juan Chacón, Jaime Idrovo, Alexandra Kennedy, Diego Mora, and Martha Orellana, *Ceramica Colonial y Vida Cotidiana*. Fundación Paul Rivet, Cuenca, 1990.

Carmichael, Patrick H., "Nasca Pottery Construction." *Ñawpa Pacha* 24 (1986), 31–48.

Collier, Donald, "Pottery Stamping and Molding on the North Coast of Peru," in John H. Rowe and Dorothy Menzel, editors, *Peruvian Prehistory: Selected Readings*, pp. 264–74. Peek Publications, Palo Alto, CA, 1967.

Dawson, Lawrence E., "Slip Casting: A Ceramic Technique Invented in Ancient Peru." *Ñawpa Pacha* 2 (1964), 107–12.

Donnan, Christopher B., "Moche Ceramic Technology." *Ñawpa Pacha* 3 (1965), 115–34.

Hill, Betsy D., "A New Chronology of the Valdivia Ceramic Complex from the Coastal Zone of Guayas Province, Ecuador." *Ñawpa Pacha* 10–12 (1972–4), 1–32.

Litto, Gertrude, *South American Folk Pottery*. Watson-Guptill Publications, New York, 1976.

Reichel-Dolmatoff, Gerardo, "Early Pottery from Colombia." *Archaeology* 24, 4 (1971), 338–45. *Monsú: Un Sitio Arqueológico*. Biblioteca Banco Popular, Bogotá, 1985.

Roosevelt, A. C., R. A. Housley, M. Imazio da Silveira, S. Maranca, and R. Johnson, "Eighth Millennium Pottery From a Prehistoric Shell Midden in the Brazilian Amazon." *Science* 284 (1991), 1621.

Rye, Owen S., *Pottery Technology: Principles and Reconstructions*. Taraxcum, Washington DC, 1981.

Salazar, Ernesto, "Los Pescadores de Valdivia," in *Mitos de Nuestro Pasado*, pp. 25–39. Museo del Banco Central del Ecuador, Quito, 1988.

Sjöman, Lena, *Las Alfareras de Jatumpamba*. Fundación Paul Rivet, Cuenca, 1989.

Chapter 9   The first civilizations: 2000–200 BC

Benson, Elizabeth P., editor, *Dumbarton Oaks Conference on Chavín, October 26th and 27th, 1968*. Dumbarton Oaks, Washington DC 1971.

Burger, Richard L. *The Prehistoric Occupation of Chavín de Huántar, Peru*. University of California Publications in Anthropology, Vol. 14. University of California Press, Berkeley, CA, 1984. *Chavín and the Origins of Andean Civilization*. Thames and Hudson, New York, 1992.

Conklin, William J. "The Revolutionary Weaving Inventions of the Early Horizon." *Ñawpa Pacha* 16 (1978), 1–12.

Donnan, Christopher B., editor, *Early Ceremonial Architecture in the Andes*. Dumbarton Oaks, Washington DC, 1985.

Guffroy, Jean, "Le Développement des premières grandes civilisations andines dans l'extrème nord du Pérou: le cas de Cerro Ñañañique (Haut-Piura)." *Cahiers des Sciences Humaines* 26, 4 (1990), 623–45.

Lathrap, Donald W. "Gifts of the Cayman: Some Thoughts on the Subsistence Basis of Chavín," in Donald W. Lathrap and Jody Stuart, editors, *Variation in Anthropology: Essays in Honor of John C. McGregor*, pp. 91–106. Illinois Archaeological Survey, Inc., 1973 (reprinted in Alana Cordy-Collins and Jean Stern, editors, *Pre-Columbian Art History*, pp. 333–52. Peek Publications, Palo Alto, CA, 1977).

Lathrap, Donald W., Donald Collier, and Helen Chandra, *Ancient Ecuador: Culture, Clay and Creativity 3000–300 BC*. Field Museum of Natural History, Chicago, 1976.

Lumbreras, Luis G., *Chavín de Huántar en el Nacimiento de la Civilización Andina*. Instituto Andino de Estudios Arqueológicos, Lima, 1980.

Lyon, Patricia J., "Female Supernaturals in Ancient Peru." *Ñawpa Pacha* 16 (1978), 95–140.

Marcos, Jorge G. and Presley Norton, "Interpretación sobre la Arqueología de la Isla de la Plata." *Miscelanea Antropológica Ecuatoriana*, Boletín de los Museos del Banco Central del Ecuador 1 (1981), 136–54.

Menzel, Dorothy, John H. Rowe, and Lawrence Dawson, *The Paracas Pottery of Ica: A Study in Style and Time*. University of California Publications in American Archaeology and Ethnology, Vol. 50, 1964.

Moseley, Michael Edward and Luis Watanabe, "The Adobe Sculptures of Huaca de los Reyes." *Archaeology* 27, 3 (1974), 154–61.

Paul, Anne, *Paracas Ritual Attire: Symbols of Authority in Ancient Peru*. University of Oklahoma Press, Norman, 1990.

editor, *Paracas Art and Architecture: Object and Context in South Coastal Peru*. University of Iowa Press, Iowa City, 1991.

Proulx, Donald A., "Headhunting in Ancient Peru." *Archaeology* 24, 1 (1971), 16–21.

Rowe, John H., *Chavín Art: An Enquiry Into Its Form and Meaning*. The Museum of Primitive Art, New York, 1962 (reprinted in Alana Cordy-Collins and Jean Stern, editors, *Pre-Colombian Art History*, pp. 307–31. Peek Publications, Palo Alto, CA, 1977).

Tello, Julio C. and Toribio Mejía Xesspe, *Paracas, II Parte, Cavernas y Necropolis*. Universidad Nacional Mayor de San Marcos, Dirección Universitaria de Biblioteca y Publicaciones, Lima, 1979.

Chapter 10   Textiles: the high art of South America

Bird, Junius B. and Louisa Bellinger, *Paracas Fabrics and Nazca Needlework, 3rd Century B.C.–3rd Century A.D.: A Catalogue Raisonné*. The Textile Museum, Washington DC, 1954.

Bruhns, Karen Olsen, "Prehispanic Spinning and Weaving Implements from Southern Ecuador." *The Textile Museum Journal* 27–8 (1988–9), 70–7.

Conklin, William J., "Chavín Textiles and the Origins of Peruvian Weaving." *The Textile Museum Journal* 3, 2 (1971), 13–19.

Cortes Moreno, Emma, "Mantas Muiscas." *Boletín del Museo del Oro* 27 (1990), 61–76. Banco de la República, Bogotá.

Doyon-Bernard, Suzette, "From Twining to Triple Cloth: Experimentation and Innovation in Ancient Peruvian Weaving (ca. 5000–400 B.C.)." *American Antiquity* 55, 1 (1990), 68–87.

Emery, Irene, *The Primary Structures of Fabrics: An Illustrated Classification*. The Textile Museum, Washington, DC, 1966.

Feltham, Jane, *Peruvian Textiles*. Shire Ethnography Series, Shire Publications, Aylesbury, 1989.

Garavanta, Donna M., "Peruvian Textiles." *Pacific Discovery* 31, 4 (1978), 21–7. California Academy of Sciences, San Francisco, CA.

Haffenreffer Museum, *Costume as Communication: Ethnographic Costumes and Textiles from Middle America and the Central Andes of South America in the Collections of the Haffenreffer Museum of Anthropology*. Brown University, Bristol, Rhode Island, 1988.

d'Harcourt, Raoul, *Textiles of Ancient Peru and Their Techniques*. University of Washington Press, Seattle, 1962.

Murra, John V., "Cloth and Its Function in the Inca State." *American Anthropologist* 64, 4 (1962), 710–28. (Another version is published in Annette B. Weiner and Jane Schneider, editors, *Cloth and the Human Experience*, pp. 275–303. Smithsonian Institution Press, Washington, DC, 1989.)

Paul, Anne and Susan Niles, "Identifying Hands At Work on a Paracas Mantle." *The Textile Museum Journal* 25 (1985), 5–15.

Rowe, Ann Pollard, Elizabeth P. Benson, and Anne-Louise Schaffer, editors, *The Junius B. Bird Pre-Columbian Textile Conference*. The Textile Museum and Dumbarton Oaks, Washington, DC, 1979.

Chapter 11   Metallurgy

Benson, Elizabeth P., editor, *Pre-Columbian Metallurgy of South America*. Dumbarton Oaks, Washington DC, 1979.

Bray, Warwick, *The Gold of El Dorado*. Times Newspapers Ltd, London, 1979.

Bruhns, Karen Olsen, "A Quimbaya Gold Furnace?" *American Antiquity* 35, 2 (1970), 202–3.

"Two Pre-Hispanic Cire Perdue Casting Moulds from Columbia [sic]." *Man* 7, 2 (1974), 308–11.

"The Crucible: Sociological and Technological Factors in the Delayed Diffusion of Metallurgy to Mesoamerica," in Frederick Bové and Lynette Heller, editors, *New Frontiers in the Archaeology of the Pacific Slope of Southern Mesoamerica*, pp. 221–8. Arizona State University Anthropological Research Papers No. 39, Tucson, 1989.

Donnan, Christopher B., "A Precolumbian Smelter from Northern Peru." *Archaeology* 26, 4 (1973), 289–97.

Grossman, Joel W., "An Ancient Gold Worker's Tool Kit." *Archaeology* 25, 4 (1972), 270–5.

Helms, Mary W., "Precious Metals and Politics: Style and Ideology in the Intermediate Area and Peru." *Journal of Latin American Lore* 7, 2 (1981), 215–38.

Lechtman, Heather, "The Central Andes: Metallurgy without Iron," in Theodore A. Wertime and James D. Muhly, editors, *The Coming of the Age of Iron*, pp. 267–334. Yale University Press, New Haven, 1980.

"The Production of Copper-Arsenic Alloys in the Central Andes: Highland Ores and Coastal Smelters?" *Journal of Field Archaeology* 18, 1 (1991), 43–76.

Lechtman, Heather, Antonieta Erlij, and Edward J. Barry Jr., "New Perspectives on Moche Metallurgy: Techniques of Gilding Copper at Loma Negra, Northern Peru." *American Antiquity* 4, 1 (1982), 3–30.

Scott, David A. and Warwick Bray, "Ancient Platinum Technology in South America, Its Use by the Indians in Pre-Hispanic Times." *Platinum Metals Review* 24, 4 (1980), 147–57.

Shimada, Izumi, "Perception, Procurement and Management of Resources: Archaeological Perspective," in Shozo Masudo, Izumi Shimada, and Craig Morris, editors, *Andean Civilization and Ecology*, pp. 357–99. University of Tokyo Press, Tokyo, 1985.

Shimada, Izumi, Stephen Epstein, and Alan K. Craig, "The Metallurgical Process in Ancient North Peru." *Archaeology* 36, 5 (1983), 38–46.

Whitehead, Neil Lancelot, "The Mazaruni Pectoral: A Golden Artefact Discovered in Guyana and the Historical Sources Concerning Native Metallurgy in the Caribbean, Orinoco, and Northern Amazonia." *Archaeology and Anthropology: Journal of the Walter Roth Museum of Anthropology* 7 (1990), 19–38. Georgetown, Guyana.

Chapter 12   Regional diversification and development: 200 BC–AD 600

Alcina Franch, José, *La Arqueología de Esmeraldas (Ecuador): Introducción General*. Ministerio de Asuntos Exteriores, Direccion General de Relaciones Culturales, Madrid, 1979.

Alva, Walter, "The Moche of Ancient Peru. New Tomb of Royal Splendor." *National Geographic Magazine* 177, 6 (1990), 2–15.

Bonavia, Duccio, *Mural Painting in Ancient Peru*. Translated by Patricia J. Lyon. Indiana University Press, Bloomington, IN, 1985.

Bouchard, Jean-François, *Recherches archéologiques dans la région de Tumaco, Colombie*. Institut Français d'Etudes Andines, Editions Recherche sur les Civilisations, Memoire 34. Paris, 1984.

Bruhns, Karen Olsen, "Monumental Sculpture as Evidence for Hierarchical Societies," in Frederick W. Lange, editor, *Wealth and Hierarchy in the Intermediate Area*, pp. 331–56. Dumbarton Oaks, Washington DC, 1992.

Deneven, William M., "The Aboriginal Population of Western Amazonia in Relation to Habitat and Subsistence." *Revista Geográfica* 72 (1970), 61–86. Río de Janeiro.

Donnan, Christopher B., *Moche Art of Peru*. Museum of Culture History, University of California at Los Angeles, 1978.

Donnan, Christopher B. and Guillermo A. Cock, editors, *The Pacatnamú Papers*, Vol. 1. Museum of Culture History, University of California at Los Angeles, 1986.

Doyon, Leon G., "Tumbas de la Nobleza en La Florida," in Ivan Cruz Cevallos, editor, *Quito*

Antes de Benalcazar, pp. 51–66, 86–100 (plates). Centro Cultural Artes, Serie Monográfica No. 1. Año 1, Quito, 1988.

Eden, Michael J., Warwick Bray, Leonor Herrera, and Colin MacEwan, "*Terra Preta* Soils and Their Archaeological Context in the Caquetá Basin of Southeast Colombia." *American Antiquity* 49, 1 (1984), 125–40.

Evans, Clifford and Betty J. Meggers, *Archaeological Investigations on the Río Napo, Eastern Ecuador*. Smithsonian Contributions to Anthropology Vol. 6. Smithsonian Institution Press, Washington DC, 1968.

Furst, Peter T., *Flesh of the Gods: The Ritual Use of Hallucinogens*. Praeger Publishers, New York, 1972.

Grieder, Terence, *The Art and Archaeology of Pashash*. University of Texas Press, Austin, 1978.

Hadingham, Evan, *Lines to the Mountain Gods: Nazca and the Mysteries of Peru*. Random House, New York, 1987.

Herrera, Leonor, editor, *San Agustín 200 Años 1790–1990. Seminario: La Arqueología del Macizo y el Suroccidente Colombiano. San Agustín, Huila*. Fundación de Investigaciones Arqueológicas Nacionales, Banco de la República/Instituto Colombiano de Antropología-Colcultura, Bogotá, 1991.

Isbell, William H., *The Rural Foundation for Urbanism*. Illinois Studies in Anthropology No. 10, University of Illinois Press, Urbana, 1977.

Kauffman Doig, Federico, *Sexual Behavior in Ancient Peru*. Kompactos, Lima, 1978 (available in Spanish as *Comportamiento Sexual en el Antiguo Perú*).

Mohr Chávez, Karen L., "The Significance of Chiripa in Lake Titicaca Basin Developments." *Expedition* 30, 3 (1988), 17–26. Philadelphia.

Ponce Sangines, Carlos, *Wankarani y Chiripa y Sus Relaciones con Tiwanaku*. Academia Nacional de Ciencias de Bolivia, La Paz, 1970.

Proulx, Donald A., *Local Differences and Time Differences in Nasca Pottery*. University of California Publications in Anthropology Vol. 5, University of California Press, Berkeley and Los Angeles, 1968.

Reichel-Dolmatoff, Gerardo, *San Agustín: A Culture of Colombia*. Thames and Hudson, London, 1972.

Roosevelt, Anna C., *Parmana: Prehistoric Maize and Manioc Subsistence Along the Amazon and Orinoco*. Academic Press, Orlando, 1980.

Schuster, Angela, "Inside the Royal Tombs of the Moche." *Archaeology* 45, 6 (1992), 30–7.

Silverman, Helaine, "The Early Nasca Pilgrimage Center of Cahuachi and the Nazca Lines: Anthropological and Archaeological Perspectives," in Anthony Aveni, editor, *The Lines of Nazca*, pp. 208–44. The American Philosophical Society, Philadelphia, 1990.

Spenser, Charles S. and Elsa M. Redmond, "Prehispanic Chiefdoms of the Western Venezuelan Llanos." *World Archaeology* 24, 1 (1992), 134–57.

Stumer, Louis M., "Playa Grande: Primitive Elegance in Pre-Tiahuanaco Peru." *Archaeology* 6, 1 (1953), 42–8.

Wolfe, Elizabeth Farkass, "The Spotted Cat and the Horrible Bird: Stylistic Change in Nasca 1–5 Ceramic Decoration." *Ñawpa Pacha* 19 (1981), 1–62.

Chapter 13   Iconographic studies

Donnan, Christopher B., "The Thematic Approach to Moche Iconography." *Journal of Latin American Lore* 1, 2 (1975), 147–62. Latin American Center, University of California, Los Angeles (reprinted in Alana Cordy-Collins and Jean Stern, editors, *Pre-Columbian Art History*, pp. 407–20. Peek Publications, Palo Alto, CA, 1977).
     "Dance in Moche Art." *Ñawpa Pacha* 20 (1982), 97–120.

Donnan, Christopher B. and Luis Jaime Castillo, "Finding the Tomb of a Moche Priestess." *Archaeology* 45, 6 (1992), 38–42.

Donnan, Christopher B. and Donna McClelland, *The Burial Theme in Moche Iconography.* Studies in Pre-Columbian Art and Archaeology No. 21, Dumbarton Oaks, Trustees for Harvard University, Washington DC, 1979.

Legast, Anne, *La Fauna en la Orfebrería Sinú.* Fundación de Investigaciones Arqueológicas Nacionales, Banco de la República, Bogotá, 1980.

 El Animal en el Mundo Mítico Tairona. Fundación de Investigaciones Arqueológicas Nacionales, Bogotá, 1987.

Paul, Anne, *Paracas Ritual Attire: Symbols of Authority in Ancient Peru.* University of Oklahoma Press, Norman, 1990.

Reichel-Dolmatoff, Gerardo, *Goldwork and Shamanism.* Editorial Colina, Bogotá, n.d. (*c.* 1986).

Sharon, Douglas and Christopher B. Donnan, "Shamanism in Moche Iconography," in Christopher B. Donnan and C. William Clewlow Jr., editors, *Ethnoarchaeology,* pp. 49–77. Archaeological Survey Monograph IV, Institute of Archaeology, University of California, Los Angeles, 1974.

Chapter 14   Militaristic and religious movements in the Andes: AD 500–900

Bastien, Joseph W., *Healers of the Andes: Kallawaya Herbalists and Their Medicinal Plants.* University of Utah Press, Salt Lake City, 1987.

Browman, David L., "New Light on Andean Tiwanaku." *American Scientist* 69, 4 (1981), 408–19.

Bruhns, Karen Olsen, "Stylistic Affinities Between the Quimbaya Gold Style and a Little Known Ceramic Style of the Middle Cauca Valley, Colombia." *Ñawpa Pacha* 7/8 (1969–70), 65–84. (Reprinted in Alana Cordy-Collins and Jean Stern, editors *Pre-Columbian Art History*, pp. 257–76, Peek Publications, Palo Alto, CA, 1977.)

 "Ancient Pottery of the Middle Cauca Valley, Colombia." *Cespedesia* 5, 7–8 (1976), 101–96. Cali, Colombia.

Cardale de Schrimpff, Marianne, Warwick Bray, Theres Gäwiler-Walder, and Leonor Herrera, *Calima: trois cultures précolombiennes dans le sud-ouest de la Colombie.* Editions Payot, Lausanne, 1992.

Conklin, William J., "Pucara and Tiahuanaco Tapestry: Time and Style in a Sierra Weaving Tradition." *Ñawpa Pacha* 21 (1983), 1–44.

Cook, Anita, "Aspects of State Identity in Huari and Tiwanaku Iconography: The Central Deity and the Sacrificer," in Daniel H. Sandweiss, editor, *Investigations of the Andean Past: Papers from the First Annual Northeast Conference on Andean Archaeology and Ethnohistory*, pp. 161–85. Cornell University, Ithaca, NY, 1983.

 "The Middle Horizon Ceramic Offerings From Conchopata." *Ñawpa Pacha* 22–3 (1984–5), 49–90.

Duque Gómez, Luis, *Los Quimbayas: Reseña Etno-Histórica y Arqueológica.* Instituto Colombiano de Antropología, Bogotá, 1970.

Isbell, William H. and Gordon F. McEwan, editors, *Huari Administrative Structure: Prehistoric Monumental Architecture and State Government.* Dumbarton Oaks Research Library and Collection, Washington DC, 1991.

Isbell, William and Katherina Schreiber, "Was Huari a State?" *American Antiquity* 43, 3 (1978), 372–89.

Manzanilla, Linda and Eric Woodard, "Restos Humanos Asociados a la Pirámide de Akapana (Tiwanaku, Bolivia)." *Latin American Antiquity* 1, 2 (1990), 133–49.

Menzel, Dorothy, "Style and Time in the Middle Horizon." *Ñawpa Pacha* 2 (1964), 65–106 plus plates.

Nordenskiold, Erland von, "Urnengräber und Mounds im Bolivienischen Flachlande." *Baessler-Archiv* 3, 1, pp. 201–56, plus 2 unpaged color plates. Berlin, 1912.

Patiño C., Diogenes, "Pobladores Prehispánicos en el Cauca, Colombia." *Informes Antropológicos* 4 (1990), 35–52. Colcultura, Bogotá.

Ponce Sangines, Carlos, *Tiwanaku: Espacio, Tiempo y Cultura*. 4th edition. Los Amigos del Libro, La Paz, Bolivia, 1981.

Posnansky, Arthur, *Tihuanacu; la Cuna del Hombre Americano. Tihuanacu: The Cradle of Western Man* (Spanish and English text), 2 vols. J. J. Augustin, New York, 1945.

Saville, Marshall H., *The Gold Treasure of Sig Sig, Ecuador*. Leaflets of the Museum of the American Indian, Heye Foundation No. 3, New York, 1924.

Schreiber, Katherina A., *Wari Imperialism in Middle Horizon Peru*. Anthropology Papers of the Museum of Anthropology, University of Michigan No. 87, Ann Arbor, 1992.

Shimada, Izumi, "The Batan Grande-La Leche Archaeological Project: The First Two Seasons." *Journal of Field Archaeology* 8, 4 (1981), 405–46.

Stanish, Charles, *Ancient Andean Political Economy*. University of Texas Press, Austin, 1992.

Uhle, Max, *Pachacamac: A Reprint of the 1903 Edition and Pachacamac Archaeology: Retrospect and Prospects: An Introduction*, by Izumi Shimada. University Museum of Archaeology and Anthropology Monograph 62, University of Pennsylvania, Philadelphia, 1991.

Uribe Alarcón, María Victoria, "Asentamientos Prehispánicos en el Altiplano de Ipiales, Colombia." *Revista Colombiana de Antropología* 21 (1977–8), 57–195. Bogotá.

Zucchi, Alberta and William M. Deneven, *Campos Elevados e Historia Cultural Prehispánica en los Llanos Occidentales de Venezuela*. Universidad Católica Andres Bello, Caracas, 1979.

Chapter 15   Transport and trade

Burger, Richard L. and Frank Asaro, "Obsidian Distribution and Provenience in the Central Highlands and Coast of Peru." *Contributions of the University of California Archaeological Research Facility* 36 (1978), 61–83. University of California, Berkeley.

Cardale de Schrimpff, Marianne, *Las Salinas de Zipaquirá: Su Explotación Indígena*. Fundación de Investigaciones Arqueológicas Nacionales, Banco de la República, Bogotá, Colombia, 1981.

Edwards, Clinton R., "Aboriginal Watercraft on the Pacific Coast of South America." *Iberoamericana*, Vol. 47. University of California Press, Berkeley and Los Angeles, 1965.

Estrada, Jenny, *La Balsa en la Historia de la Navegación Ecuatoriana*. Instituto de Historia Maritima Armada del Ecuador, Guayaquil, 1990.

Hartman, Roswith, "Mercados y Ferias Prehispánicas en el Area Andina." *Boletín del Academia Nacional de Historia* 54, 187 (1971), 214–36. Quito.

Hyslop, John, *The Inka Road System*. Academic Press, Orlando, 1984.

Paulsen, Alison, "The Thorny Oyster and the Voice of God: *Spondylus* and *Strombus* in Andean Prehistory." *American Antiquity* 39, 4, Pt 1 (1974), 597–607.

Rostworoski de Diez Canseco, Maria, "Coastal Fishermen, Merchants and Artisans in Prehispanic Peru," in Elizabeth P. Benson, editor, *The Sea in the Pre-Columbian World*, pp. 167–86. Dumbarton Oaks, Washington DC, 1977.

Salomon, Frank, "Pochteca and Mindalá: A Comparison of Long-Distance Traders in Mesoamerica and Ecuador." *Journal of the Steward Anthropological Society* 9, 1/2 (1977/8), 231–46. University of Illinois, Urbana.

Shimada, Melody and Izumi Shimada, "Prehistoric Llama Breeding and Herding on the North Coast of Peru." *American Antiquity* 50, 1 (1985), 3–26.

Topic, John R. and Theresa Lange Topic, "Coast–Highlands Relations in Northern Peru: Some Observations on Routes, Networks, and Scales of Interaction," in Richard M. Leventhal and Alan R. Kolata, editors, *Civilization in the Ancient Americas: Essays in Honor of Gordon R. Willey*, pp. 211–36. University of New Mexico Press and Peabody Museum of Archaeology and Ethnology, Harvard University, Cambridge, MA, 1983.

Verano, John W., "A Mass Burial of Mutilated Individuals at Pacatanamú," in Christopher B. Donnan and Guillermo A. Cock, editors, *The Pacatnamú Papers*, Vol. 1, pp. 117–38. Fowler Museum of Culture History, University of California at Los Angeles, 1986.

Wassén, S. Henry, "Algunos Datos del Comercio Precolombino en Colombia." *Revista Colombiana de Antropología* 4 (1955), 87–110. Bogotá.

Chapter 16   Kingdoms, chiefdoms, and empires: AD 900–1438

Arellano López, Jorge, *Mollo: Investigaciones Arqueológicas*. Imprental Nacional, La Paz, 1985.

Boero Rojo, Hugo, *La Increible Ciudadela Prehispanica de Iskanwaya: Aucapata y Maukallajta (La Ciudad de Oro)*. Editorial Los Amigos del Libro, Colección "Bolivia Mágica," La Paz, 1977.

Carceda Muro, Paloma and Izumi Shimada, "Behind the Golden Mask: The Sicán Gold Artifacts from Batán Grande, Peru," in Julie Jones, editor, *Art of Precolumbian Gold: The Jan Mitchell Collection*, pp. 60–75. New York Graphic Society, Little, Brown and Company, New York, 1985.

Fresco, Antonio, *La Arqueología de Ingapirca (Ecuador): Costumbres Funerarias, Cerámica, y Otros Materiales*. Comisión del Castillo de Ingapirca, Cuenca, 1984.

McEwan, Gordon F., "Some Formal Correspondences Between the Imperial Architecture of the Wari and Chimu Cultures of Ancient Peru." *Latin American Antiquity* 1, 2 (1990), 97–116.

Meggers, Betty J., "Amazonia: Real or Counterfeit Paradise?" *The Review of Archaeology* 13, 2 (1992), 25–40.

Meggers, Betty J. and Clifford Evans, *Archaeological Investigations at the Mouth of the Amazon*. Bureau of American Ethnology, Smithsonian Institution, Bulletin 167, Washington, DC, 1957.

Moseley, Michael E. and Alana Cordy-Collins, editors, *The Northern Dynasties: Kingship and Statecraft in Chimor*. Dumbarton Oaks Research Library and Collection, Washington DC, 1990.

Moseley, Michael E. and Kent C. Day, editors, *Chan Chan: Andean Desert City*. University of New Mexico Press, Albuquerque, NM, 1982.

Moseley, Michael E. and Carol J. Mackey, *Twenty-Four Architectural Plans of Chan Chan, Peru*. Peabody Museum Press, Harvard University, 1974.

Pozorsky, Thomas G., "The Las Avispas Burial Platform at Chan Chan, Peru." *Annals of the Carnegie Museum* 48, 8 (1979), 119–37. Pittsburgh.

Reichlen, Henry and Paul Reichlen, "Recherches Archéologiques dans les Andes du Haut Utcubamba." *Journal de la Société des Américanistes de Paris* 39 (1950), 219–46.

Roosevelt, Anna Curtenius, *Moundbuilders of the Amazon: Geophysical Archaeology on Marajó Island, Brazil*. Academic Press, Orlando, New York and London, 1991.

Rowe, Ann P., *Costumes and Featherwork of the Lords of Chimor: Textiles From Peru's North Coast*. The Textile Museum, Washington DC, 1984.

Rowe, John H., "The Kingdom of Chimor." *Acta Americana* 6 (1948), 26–50.

Savoy, Gene, *Antisuyo: The Search for the Lost Cities of the Amazon*. Simon and Schuster, New York, 1970.

Shimada, Izumi, "Temples of Time: The Ancient Burial and Religious Center of Bataan Grande, Peru." *Archaeology* 34, 5 (1981), 37–45.

Shimada, Izumi and John Merkel, "A Sicán Tomb in Peru." *Minerva* 4, 1 (1993), 18–25.

Thompson, Donald E., "The Precolumbian and Colonial Heritage of Rapayán." *Archaeology* 33, 2 (1980), 44–51.

Thompson, Donald E. and Rogger Ravines, "Tinyash: A Prehispanic Village in the Andean Puna." *Archaeology* 26, 2 (1973), 94–100.

Chapter 17   The sixteenth century

Arriaga, Pablo José de, *The Extirpation of Idolatry*, translated and edited by L. Clark Keating. University of Kentucky Press, Lexington, 1968.

Ascher, Marcia and Robert Ascher, *The Code of the Quipu: A Study in Meaia, Mathematics, and Culture*. University of Michigan Press, Ann Arbor, 1981.

Banco Popular, *Arte de Tierra: Muiscas y Guanes*. Colección Tesoros Precolombinos. Fondo de la Promoción de la Cultura, Banco Popular, Bogotá, 1989.

Bingham, Hiram, *Machu Picchu: A Citadel of the Incas*. Memoirs of the National Geographic Society, Yale University Press, 1930. Reprinted by Hacker Art Books, 1979.

Boada Rivas, Ana María, *Asentamientos Indígenas en el Valle de la Laguna (Samancá-Boyacá)*. Fundación de Investigaciones Arqueológicas Nacionales, Banco de la República, Bogotá, 1987.

Broadbent, Silvia M., "The Site of Chibcha Bogotá." *Ñawpa Pacha* 4 (1966), 1–14.

   Los Chibchas: Organización Socio-Política. Universidad Nacional de Colombia, Facultad de Sociología, Serie Latinoamericana No. 5. Bogotá, 1964.

Cardale de Schrimpff, Marianne, "Painted Textiles From Caves in the Eastern Cordillera," in Ann P. Rowe, editor, *The Junius B. Bird Conference on Andean Textiles*, pp. 205–17. The Textile Museum, Washington DC, 1986.

Carvajal, Gaspar de, *The Discovery of the Amazon According to the Account of Gaspar de Carvajal and Other Documents, as Published with an Introduction by José Toribio Medina*, translated by Bertram T. Lee and edited by H. C. Heaton. American Geographic Society, New York, 1934.

Cieza de León, Pedro de, *The Travels of Pedro de Cieza de León, A.D. 1532–50*. The Hakluyt Society, First Series, 33. Reprinted by Burr Hamilton, New York, 1864.

   Crónica del Perú. Primera Parte. Introducción de Franklin Pease. Pontificia Universidad Católica del Perú y Academia Nacional de la Historia, Lima, 1984.

Cobo, Father Bernabé, *History of the Inca Empire: An Account of the Indians' Customs and Their Origin Together with a Treatise on Inca Legends, History and Social Institutions (1653)*, translated by Roland Hamilton; foreword by John H. Rowe. University of Texas Press, Austin, 1990.

Cortes Moreno, Emilia, "Mantas Muiscas." *Boletín del Museo del Oro* 27 (1990), 61–75. Bogotá.

Dillehay, Tom D., "Mapuche Ceremonial Landscape, Social Recruitment and Resource Rights." *World Archaeology* 22, 2 (1990), 223–41.

Faron, Louis C., *The Mapuche Indians of Chile*. Holt, Rinehart and Winston, New York, 1968.

Gasparini, Graziano and Luise Margolis, *Inca Architecture*, translated by Patricia J. Lyon. Indiana University Press, Bloomington, 1980.

Guillén Guillén, Edmundo, "El Enigma de las Momias Incas." *Boletín de Lima* 5, 28 (1983), 29–42.

Hyslop, John, *Inka Settlement Planning*. University of Texas Press, Austin, 1990.

Londoño L., Eduardo, "Santuarios, Santillos, Tunjos: Objectos Votivos de los Muiscas en el Siglo XVI." *Museo del Oro Boletín* 25 (1989), 93–120.

Mason, John Alden, *Archaeology of Santa Marta, Colombia: The Tairona Culture*. Field Museum of Natural History Publication 304, Anthropological Series Vol. 20, Nos. 1–3. Chicago, 1931–9.

Morris, Craig and Donald E. Thompson, *Huanaco Pampa: An Inca City and Its Hinterland*. Thames and Hudson, London, 1985.

Museo de Arqueología e Etnologia, *Arqueología Amazônica (Santarém)*. Museo de Arqueología e Etnología, Universidade de São Paulo, 1972.

Padden, Charles Robert, "Cultural Change and Military Resistance in Araucanian Chile, 1550–1730." *Southwestern Journal of Anthropology* 13 (1958), 103–21. Albuquerque.

Plazas, Clemencia and Ana María Falchetti de Saenz, *Asentamientos Prehispanicos en el Bajo Río San Jorge*. Fundación de Investigaciones Arqueológicas Nacionales, Banco de la República, Bogotá, 1981.

Protzen, Jean-Pierre, "Inca Stonemasonry." *Scientific American* 254, 2 (1986), 94–105.

Ramos Pérez, Demetrio, *El Mito del Dorado: Su Genesis y Proceso: Con el Discovery [sic] de Walter Raleigh (Traducción de Betty Moore) y Otras Papeles Doradistas*. Biblioteca de la Academia Nacional de Historia No. 116, Caracas, 1973.

Rex Gonzalez, Alberto and José A. Perez, *Argentina Indígena: Visperas de la Conquista. Historia Argentina* Vol. 1. Editorial Paidos, Buenos Aires, 1972.

Rowe, John Howland, "Inca Culture at the Time of the Spanish Conquest," in Julian Steward, editor, *Handbook of South American Indians*, Vol. 2, *The Andean Civilizations*, pp. 183–330. Bureau of American Ethnology, Bulletin No. 143, Washington DC, 1946.

"The Origins of Creator Worship Among the Inca," in Stanley Diamond, editor, *Culture in History: Essays in Honor of Paul Radin*, pp. 408–29. Columbia University Press, New York, 1960.

Salomon, Frank and George L. Urioste, *The Huarochirí Manuscript: A Testament of Ancient and Colonial Andean Religion*. University of Texas Press, Austin, 1991.

Spalding, Karen, *Huarochirí: An Andean Society under Inca and Spanish Rule*. Stanford University Press, Stanford, CA, 1984.

Staden, Hans, *The Captivity of Hans Staden of Hesse, in A.D. 1547–1555, Among the Wild Tribes of Eastern Brazil*, translated by Albert Tootal, annotated by Richard F. Burton. The Hakluyt Society, n.d.

Vega, Garcilaso de la, *The Incas*, translated by Maria Jolas; edited and introduced by Alain Gheerbrant. Avon Books, New York, 1961.

Chapter 18   Intercontinental movements before Columbus

Benzoni, Girolamo, *La Historia del Mondo Nvovo, di Giolamo Benzoni. Laqval Tratta delle Isole, & Mari Nuouamente Ritrouati, et delle Nuoue Citta da Lui Proprio Vedute, per Acqua, 7 per Terra in Quattordeci Anni. Nuouamente . . . Appresso gli heredi di G. M. Bonelli, ad instantia di P. & F. Tini*. Venice, 1572.

La Historia del Mondo Nuovo: Relatos de su Viaje por el Ecuador 1547/1550. Translated by Carlos Radicati di Primeglio. Museo Antropológica y Pinacoteca, Banco Central del Ecuador, Guayaquil, 1965.

History of the New World by Girolamo Benzoni, Shewing His Travels in America, From A.D. 1541 to 1556, with Some Particulars of the Island of Canary. Now First Translated and Edited by W. H. Smyth. Hakluyt Society, First Series, 21, B. Franklin, New York, 1970.

Bray, Warwick, "Maya Metalwork and Its External Connections," in Norman Hammond, editor, *Social Process in Maya Prehistory*, pp. 365–403. Academic Press, Orlando, 1977.

Bruhns, Karen O., "Dating the Culture of San Agustín: A Correlation with Northern Peru," in Alana Cordy-Collins, editor, *Pre-Columbian Art History*, Vol. 2, pp. 193–204. Peek Publications, Menlo Park, CA, 1982.

"A View from the Bridge: Intermediate Area Sculpture in Thematic Perspective." *Baessler-Archiv* n.s. 30 (1982), 147–79. Berlin.

Bruhns, Karen O., James H. Burton, and George R. Miller, "Excavations at Pirincay in the Paute Valley 1985–1988." *Antiquity* 64, 243 (1990), 221–32.

Cross, Frank Moore Jr., "The Phoenician Inscription from Brazil: A 19th Century Forgery." *Orientalia* 37, 4 (1968), 437–60.

Edwards, Clinton R., "The Possibilities of Maritime Contacts Among New World Civilizations." *Mesoamerican Studies* 4 (1969), 3–10.

Estrada, Emilio and Betty J. Meggers, "A Complex of Traits of Probable Transpacific Origin on the Coast of Ecuador." *American Anthropologist* 63, 5 (1961), 913–39.

Feder, Kenneth L., *Frauds, Myths and Mysteries: Science and Pseudoscience in Archaeology.* Mayfield Publishers, Menlo Park, CA, 1990.

Kehoe, Alice B., "The Sacred Heart: A Case for Stimulus Diffusion." *American Ethnologist* 6, 4 (1979), 763–71.

McEwan, Gordon F. and D. Bruce Dickson, "Valdivia, Jomon Fishermen and the Nature of the North Pacific: Some Nautical Problems with Meggers, Evans, and Estrada's (1965) Transoceanic Contact Hypothesis." *American Antiquity* 43, 3 (1978), 362–71.

McGhee, Robert, "Contact Between Native North Americans and the Medieval Norse: A Review of the Evidence." *American Antiquity* 49, 1 (1984), 4–26.

Marcos, Jorge G. and Presley Norton, editors, *Primer Simposio de Correlaciones Antropológicas Andino-Americana.* Escuela Superior Politecnica del Litoral (ESPOL), Guayaquil, 1982.

Nordenskiold, Erland von, "The American Indian as Inventor." *Journal of the Royal Anthropological Institute of Great Britain and Ireland* 59 (1929), 273–309.

Riley, Carroll J., J. Charles Kelley, Campbell W. Pennington, and Robert L. Rands, editors, *Man Across the Sea: Problems of Pre-Columbian Contacts.* University of Texas Press, Austin and London, 1971.

Rowe, John Howland, "Diffusionism and Archaeology." *American Antiquity* 31, 3 (1966), 334–7.

Siegel, Peter E., "Demographic and Architectural Retrodiction: An Ethnoarchaeological Case Study in the South American Tropical Lowlands." *Latin American Antiquity* 1, 4 (1990), 319–46.

Chapter 19   The future of a continent

Anderson, A.W., *How We Got Our Flowers.* Ernest Benn, London, 1951; Dover Publications, New York, 1966.

Boone, Elizabeth H., editor, *Falsifications and Misreconstructions of Pre-Columbian Art.* Dumbarton Oaks, Washington DC, 1982.

Chiapelli, Fredi, Michael J. B. Allen and Robert L. Benson, editors, *First Images of America: The Impact of the New World on the Old.* University of California Press, Berkeley, 1976.

Cock, James H., "Cassava: A Basic Energy Source in the Tropics." *Science* 218 (1982), 755–62.

Cook, Noble David and W. George Lovell, editors, *Secret Judgements of God: Old World Disease in Colonial Spanish America.* University of Oklahoma Press, Norman, 1992.

Crosby, Alfred, *The Columbian Exchange: Biological and Cultural Consequences of 1492.* Contributions in American Studies No. 2, Greenwood Press, Westport, CT, 1972.

  Ecological Imperialism and the Biological Expansion of Europe, 900–1900. Cambridge University Press, 1986.

Goodman, Edward J., *The Explorers of South America.* University of Oklahoma Press, Norman, 1992.

Hemming, John, *The Conquest of the Incas.* Revised edition. Penguin Books, Harmondsworth, England and New York, 1983.

  Red Gold: The Conquest of the Brazilian Indians, 1500–1760. Harvard University Press, Cambridge, MA, 1978.

  Amazon Frontier: The Defeat of the Brazilian Indians. Harvard University Press, Cambridge, MA, 1987.

Ho, Ping-Ti, "The Introduction of American Food Plants into China." *American Anthropologist* 57, 2 (1955), 191–201.

Honour, Hugh, *The New Golden Land: European Images of America from the Discovery to the Present Time*. Pantheon, New York, 1975.

Kirkpatrick, Sidney D., *Lords of Sipán: A True Story of Pre-Inca Tombs, Archaeology, and Crime*. William Morrow and Co., New York, 1992.

Las Casas, Bartolomé de, *The Devastation of the Indies: A Brief Account*, translated by Herma Briffault and with an Introduction by Bill M. Donovan. The Johns Hopkins University Press, Baltimore, 1992.

Meyer, Karl E., *The Plundered Past: The Story of the Illegal International Traffic in Works of Art*. Atheneum, New York, 1977.

Nagin, Carl, "The Peruvian Gold Rush." *Art and Antiques* 7, 5 (1990), 98–106, 134–45.

National Research Council, *Lost Crops of the Incas: Little Known Plants of the Andes with Promise for Worldwide Cultivation*. National Academy Press, Washington DC, 1989.

Salaman, Redcliffe N., *The History and Social Influence of the Potato*. Cambridge University Press, 1949.

Sokolov, Raymond, *Why We Eat What We Eat: How the Encounter Between the New World and the Old Changed the Way Everyone on the Planet Eats*. Summit Books, New York, 1991.

Wagner, Erika, "¿Que Debe el Mundo Moderno a los Aborigines Americanos?" *Líneas* 215 (1975), 6–9. Caracas.

INDEX